D0160911

DUTCH:
A COMPREHENSIVE GRAMMAR

Dutch: A Comprehensive Grammar is a complete reference guide to modern Dutch grammar.

It presents a fresh and accessible description of the language, concentrating on the real patterns of use in modern Dutch. The book will remain the standard reference work for years to come.

The *Grammar* is an essential reference source for the learner and user of Dutch, irrespective of level. It is ideal for use in schools, colleges, universities and adult classes of all types.

The volume is organized to promote a thorough understanding of Dutch grammar. It offers a stimulating analysis of the complexities of the language, and provides full and clear explanations. Throughout, the emphasis is on Dutch as used by present-day native speakers.

An extensive index and numbered paragraphs provide readers with easy access to the information they require.

Features include:
- detailed treatment of the common grammatical structures and parts of speech
- extensive exemplification
- particular attention to areas of confusion and difficulty
- Dutch–English parallels highlighted throughout the book

Bruce Donaldson lectures in Dutch and German in the Department of Germanic Studies and Russian, University of Melbourne, Australia.

DUTCH:
A COMPREHENSIVE
GRAMMAR

Bruce Donaldson

London and New York

This edition first published 1997
by Routledge
11 New Fetter Lane, London EC4P 4EE

Simultaneously published in the USA and Canada
by Routledge
29 West 35th Street, New York, NY 10001

Previous edition entitled *Dutch Reference Grammar* 3rd edn,
published by Martinus Nijhott, Leiden, in 1987

Reprinted 1998, 2000, 2002

Routledge is an imprint of the Taylor & Francis Group

© 1997 Bruce Donaldson

Typeset in Times by
The Florence Group, Stoodleigh, Devon

Printed and bound in Great Britain by
TJ International Ltd, Padstow, Cornwall

The author has asserted his moral right in accordance with Section 77 of the
Copyright, Designs and Patents Act 1988

British Library Cataloguing in Publication Data
A catalogue record for this book is available from the British Library

Library of Congress Cataloguing in Publication Data
A catalogue record for this book has been requested

ISBN   0–415–15418–9 (hbk)
          0–415–15419–7 (pbk)

CONTENTS

PREFACE

When I started to write the first edition of this book in 1977, there were no textbooks suitable to the needs of the advanced English-speaking student of Dutch. The descriptions of Dutch written by Dutch grammarians were of very little practical use to the foreign learner, and the few contrastive grammars pitched at English-speaking people were either antiquated or only suitable for the raw beginner, or most usually both. The best book on the market was W. Z. Shetter's *Introduction to Dutch*, Martinus Nijhoff, a book which is now also published, in totally revised form, by Routledge (*Dutch: An Essential Grammar,* 1995). The lack of any comparable predecessor, combined with the limited utility to the foreign learner of the descriptions of Dutch in Dutch, meant that quite a lot of pioneer work went into the creation of this book, particularly with regard to comparing and contrasting Dutch structures with English structures to aid the learning process. The usefulness of this book has proved itself by going through three editions in 14 years and maintaining a constant annual turnover to this day; it is used throughout the world, even in non-English-speaking countries through lack of anything comparable in the languages of those countries.

But since the first edition appeared in 1981 under the title *Dutch reference grammar,* two important changes have occurred in the field, both of which in themselves necessitated a thorough revision of this book, quite apart from my desire to remove the many imperfections that had lingered on through three editions. First, the *Nederlandse Taalunie,* a joint Dutch-Flemish body charged, among other things, with overseeing all projects concerned with the standardization of the language, was founded in 1980. The *Taalunie* was ultimately responsible for ensuring that the *Algemene Nederlandse Spraakkunst* (Wolters-Noordhoff, Groningen/ Wolters, Leuven, 1984) saw the light of day. The *ANS,* as it is now affectionately known, has since established itself as the standard reference work on all issues of Dutch grammar. A thoroughly revised edition of it too is to appear in 1997. The *ANS,* although written in Dutch and from a Dutch point of view (thus no contrast with structures in any other language being made) is of use to the advanced foreign learner of the language. Given that *Dutch: A Comprehensive Grammar* contains 300 odd pages, whereas the *ANS* consists of 1,309 pages, clearly it deals with issues in much greater detail than this book, but its existence by no means renders this grammar superfluous – it simply means that there is now a suitable grammar one can proceed to after having mastered the contents of this book. The *ANS* is also useful, in fact indispensable, if you require more information on a given point than I offer here, but be warned that using the *ANS* is not for the faint-hearted, certainly if one is not well-schooled in grammatical terminology.

The second important development in the standardization and description of Dutch that has appeared since 1981, is the long awaited revision of the *Woordenlijst der Nederlandse Taal* (Martinus Nijhoff, The Hague 1954), the final word on issues of spelling. The new spelling according to the prescriptions of the 1995 edition of the *Woordenlijst* have been incorporated into this book, not only in the chapter on spelling but also in the spelling used throughout the book. The changes have in fact been minimal so the learner should not be intimidated by the fact that there are for the time being two spellings in use.

This reference grammar is aimed at the tertiary and upper secondary student as well as at the private student who has a reasonable knowledge of grammatical terminology and whose knowledge has already gone beyond what the more basic grammars offer. It is not intended to replace the existing beginners' grammars, except perhaps in the case of a student with some prior knowledge who simply wishes to consolidate that knowledge, but it is intended to complement those grammars.

By necessity this grammar is quite strongly prescriptive. In a book of this size it was not possible, nor indeed desirable, to describe every detail of the spoken and written language. I have endeavoured to prescribe forms which I know to be generally acceptable in both the spoken and written languages of The Netherlands. If at any stage I have mentioned spoken forms which are not acceptable in writing, or written forms which are not usual in the spoken language, this has been either clearly stated in each instance or the abbreviations 'coll.' for colloquial, 'arch.' for archaic or 'lit.' for literary/formal have been used. On occasions I use the Dutch word 'plat' in the English text to describe phenomena, as it is commonly used in Holland and has no direct equivalent in English: if a structure is described as 'plat' it is considered substandard or stigmatised and is thus better avoided by the learner – spoken Dutch, like spoken British English in particular, is a language that commonly betrays one's regional and social origins!

The reader who reaches for this book to consult a chapter on syntax will be disappointed. This is a notoriously difficult aspect of grammar to discuss in a limited number of words, given that this book is not intended to be an *ANS* in English, but more importantly I am yet to see an exposé of the syntax of Dutch presented in such a way that it could be of any practical use to the foreign learner of the language. The main syntactical issues are dealt with throughout the book in the context of the particular point of grammar under discussion at the time. There is one other important matter that is not covered separately in this book, namely modal particles. This too is an extremely complicated issue and the descriptions of modal particles I have seen to date are more inclined to confuse than inform the foreign learner about the correct way to use them. Modal particles such as **eens**, **even**, **maar**, **toch** and **wel** are dealt with under various grammatical headings, but I fear that a chapter devoted to them alone would have been unwieldy and of limited practical use. With some regret I decided not to attempt to do more in this respect in the current edition.

If past experience is any guide, it is highly likely that this book will be reprinted at some future date. All constructive criticism and suggestions will be gratefully received and acknowledged by the author and heeded in any future edition. Please send your comments to the following address:

Department of Germanic Studies and Russian
University of Melbourne
Parkville
Victoria
Australia 3052.
b.donaldson@language.unimelb.edu.au

Bruce Donaldson
Melbourne, August 1996

ACKNOWLEDGEMENTS

Professor W.Z. Shetter of Bloomington Indiana, Dr H.C. Wekker of Nijmegen, Dr J. Bennett of Melbourne, Mrs V. Denman, Mrs A. Heineke-Sieuwerts and Ms C. McLiesh, all of Melbourne, were all thanked in the preface of the *Dutch Reference Grammar* for the role they played in the preparation of that book. Their contributions have each in their way left their mark on this edition too. I am grateful also to Marguerite Boland of Melbourne for her work in compiling the index. I would like to offer a special word of thanks to Paulien Zuidema-Slikker of Doorn, from whom I learnt some of my very first Dutch over twenty-five years ago, for her very critical reading of *Dutch Reference Grammar*. Thanks to her, many of the errors that occurred in that book have now been rectified and factual information brought up to date. Dr W. Hüsken of Nijmegen is also to be thanked for the many questions he answered on the Internet during the period that the manuscript was being prepared for publication.

ABBREVIATIONS

ABN	Algemeen Beschaafd Nederlands (i.e. Standard Dutch)
arch.	archaic
c.	common gender
coll.	colloquial
def.	definite
fig.	figurative
i.v.	irregular verb
inh.	inhabitant
lit.	literary, formal
m.o.	modal verb
m.v.	mixed verb
n.	neuter
o.s.	oneself
pej.	pejorative
pron.	pronounced
s.o.	someone
s.t.	something
<	derived from
=	is/means the same as
*	not grammatically correct/not possible

1 PRONUNCIATION (uitspraak)

It is assumed that anyone using this book is acquainted with the basics of Dutch pronunciation and thus they are not dealt with here, but there are certain idiosyncrasies and variants of pronunciation that may be new even to the more advanced student and they are dealt with here. In addition, a few tips of things to look out for are offered.

It is true that the pronunciation of Dutch is not particularly easy for many English-speaking beginners in the language to master. It is commonly believed by the Dutch that it is the consonants that constitute the difficulty, and in particular **ch/g**. Some students do have trouble with this sound for a while, as well as with the **r**, but the real traps lie in the vowels, and in particular in the diphthongs.

1.1 VOWELS

Possibly the one sound that virtually all English-speaking people have trouble in coming to grips with is **ui** [œy]. Pay careful attention to how this diphthong is articulated.

The distinction between **ij/ei** on the one hand and **ee** on the other is also difficult for many. It is very important to clearly distinguish between these two sounds as they are of course phonemic[1] and failure to do so can lead to a breakdown in communication, e.g. **geil** 'randy' and **geel** 'yellow', **krijg** 'get' and **kreeg** 'got'.

After some contact with the living language you may notice that quite a lot of Dutch people pronounce the short **a** in words like **hand**, **land** and **man** in a way that resembles an **o** to an English-speaking ear. You do not need to copy it, but you may become aware of it.

The short **e** in Dutch is usually pronounced [æ] not [ɛ], although the latter sound does occur; in other words like the vowel in 'fat', not that in 'bed'. Failure to distinguish between the vowel in Dutch **bed** and English 'bed' in this way is of only minor importance. This reasonably subtle difference between the languages accounts, for example, for why the Dutch often write the English loanword **tram** as **trem**, as [æ] and [ɛ] are allo-

---

[1] This means that the distinction is significant to meaning. Two sounds that differ in their articulation but which difference is irrelevant to meaning, are said to be allophones of the one phoneme. Examples of this are the two pronunciations of 'th' in English (e.g. 'that' and 'thick') and the voiceless and voiced pronunciations of g in Dutch (e.g. northern **gaan** versus southern **gaan**).

phones in Dutch; the clear difference to an English ear in the vowels of 'Henk' and 'Hank' is hardly audible to a Dutch ear.

Some Dutch people still make a distinction in the way they pronounce the short *o* in certain words, e.g. as in **hok** and **bok**; the vowel in the former is more or less the same as in the English word 'hock' (i.e. more open), but that in the latter is closer to the vowel in English 'born' (i.e. more closed). In the west of the country, where standard Dutch has evolved, it is no longer usual to make this distinction and one can apply the vowel of **hok** across the board. So if you hear people using the vowel of **bok** (the distinction is a historical one), do not feel obliged to follow suit.

The vowel sound in the adjectival endings **-ig** and **-lijk** is identical; it is a *schwa* [ə], i.e. it is pronounced the same as the weak, colourless vowel at the end of **grote**, e.g. **gelukkig**, **vriendelijk**.

If one keeps in mind that one of the basic tenets of Dutch spelling is that long vowels in closed syllables are written double, but not in open syllables[2] (e.g. **eet** > **eten**, **boom** > **bomen**), the e's and o's in loanwords like those given below must be pronounced long, although there is a strong tendency for English speakers to equate them with the same words in English and pronounce these vowels too short (the vowels in question are given in italic type):

> **p*o*litie, pr*o*v*o*catie, p*o*sitief**
> **d*e*finitief, *e*valueren, *e*ventueel, n*e*gatief**

1.2   CONSONANTS

One of the most stubborn traces of an English accent in Dutch is the presence of aspiration after stops, particularly after **p, t** and **k**. If you listen closely to the difference in the consonants between Dutch **pot, top** and **kat** on the one hand and English 'pot', 'top' and 'cat' on the other, you should become aware that the 'breathiness' which follows these consonants in English is lacking in Dutch. Continuing to aspirate in Dutch does not impede understanding at all, but it will continue to mark you as English-speaking, but Germans too have a tendency to do this in Dutch. The tendency for English speakers to aspirate the voiced stops **b, d** and **g** is much less and does not usually pose a problem.

Remember that in Dutch, as in German, voiced obstruents (i.e. **b, d, g, v, z**) do not occur in word final position, thus the final sounds in **bed** and **heb** are pronounced **t** and **p** respectively, and this also explains why the stems of **leven** and **reizen** are **leef** and **reis**, where the change in pronun-

---

[2] Related to this are the principles of syllabic division in Dutch (see 2.6) which are important when it comes to hyphenating a word at the end of a line: **po-li-tie, pro-vo-ca-tie**; **e-ven-tu-eel, de-fi-ni-tief**.

ciation is indicated in the spelling, which is not the case with the verbal stems **wed** (< **wedden** 'to bet') and **heb** (< hebben 'to have').

Intervocalic **d**'s are commonly vocalized in Dutch, i.e. they are pronounced either as **i** or **j**. The advanced learner will already be acquainted with this phenomenon in words like **goede** (pron. **goeie**) and **rode** (pron. **rooie**), but may be unaware of other subtleties in this respect. In many words with an intervocalic **d** one has the option of vocalising it or not, e.g. **raden/raaie** 'to guess', **beneden/beneje** 'downstairs', **rijden/rije** 'to drive', but in **Goede Vrijdag**, **goede** remains **goede** because it is an elevated concept, as it is in **Kaap de Goede Hoop** 'the Cape of Good Hope' and **vergoeden** 'to reimburse'; the **d** in **ouders** is never vocalized either. But in **Leiden** sociological connotations are attached to whether one does or does not vocalize the **d** – to do so is either very low class or very high class, while the masses in between do not vocalize it. In **laden** 'to load', similar as the word might be to **raden**, it is considered **'plat'** to vocalize the **d**.

One should be aware of the substantial difference between a Dutch and an English 'l'; a Dutch **l** is said to be thicker. The difference is all the more obvious when a back vowel (i.e. **a**, **o** or **u**) follows or precedes the **l**. Listen closely to how the Dutch pronounce **land**, **lof**, **vol**, **kul** etc.

Possibly the most difficult of all consonants is **r**. First one needs to decide whether one is going to adopt a dental **r** (**een tong-r**) or a velar **r** (**een keel-r**). Both commonly occur in Dutch, but the latter is on the increase. Remember that **r** in all positions must be audible in Dutch, even in final position where it can be particularly difficult for English-speaking people to pronounce, e.g. **kar**, **puur**, **moeder**.

It often escapes the notice of foreign learners of Dutch that a Dutch **s** is different from an English 's'. As there is not really a 'sh'[3] sound in Dutch for **s** to contrast with, **s** tends to be pronounced with a slight sh-like quality. Listen closely to how the Dutch pronounce **sok**, **centrum**, **los**, **mus**.

Many Dutch speakers break up the cluster formed by an **l** or **r** followed by another consonant by inserting a *schwa* between them (compare substandard English 'filem' for 'film'). Generally speaking the practice is not quite as stigmatized in Dutch as in English as far as **l** plus another consonant is concerned, but between **r** and another consonant it is necessary to facilitate pronunciation: **elf**, **film**, **melk**, **twaalfde**; **lantaarn**, **kerk**, **zwerm**.

---

[3] This sound, written **sj** in Dutch, only occurs perchance in diminutives (e.g. **huisje**) and otherwise only in a few loanwords (e.g. **sjouwen** 'to lug', **sjaal** 'scarf').

1.3   REGIONAL DIFFERENCES

For a linguistic area as small as it is, the Dutch-speaking territories harbour a surprising number of dialects. In The Netherlands monolingual dialect speakers are virtually non-existent these days and in Belgium they are fast becoming a rarity too. Non-native-speakers do not therefore have to fear being confronted with dialect as they will always be addressed in something approximating ABN, as indeed even native-speakers of Dutch from other regions are. Nevertheless, certain characteristics of the dialects are frequently heard in the ABN of people from other regions. Only the most common of these are dealt with below. These differences are no greater to the Dutch than those between British and American English are to native-speakers of English and thus mutual comprehension is not impeded in any way at all.

1.3.1   THE DROPPING OF FINAL **n**

It is usual for most speakers of Dutch, regardless of their regional origins, to drop their n's, in other words to drop the **n** from the ending **-en** which so commonly occurs in infinitives and strong past participles as well as in the plural of nouns. Other than in the slowest, most deliberate of speech, one is advised as a foreigner to follow suit here and drop one's n's; to do otherwise sounds very unnatural. Note that **n**'s that occur in the middle of words as a result of compounding are also dropped, e.g. **boekenkast, zeventien**.

The most distinctive shibboleth of easterners (i.e. from Groningen south to the Achterhoek), however, is that they pronounce their n's. In fact, the **e** of the ending tends to be swallowed, with assimilation of the **n** to the preceding consonant commonly occurring, e.g. **praten > praatn, lopen > loopm**. Because the east of the country is predominantly rural and far from the economic hub in the west, eastern Dutch is commonly stereotyped as yokel-talk.

1.3.2   CHARACTERISTICS OF **plat hollands**

In the west of the country, where everyone fancies they speak standard Dutch, a couple of characteristics of the pronunciation of the underlying dialects are heard in the ABN of the working class which are regarded as stigmatized by the upper echelons. First and foremost this applies to the tendency of many Hollanders to slightly diphthongize – more than is otherwise considered acceptable in ABN – the long vowels **ee** and **oo** as in **weten** and **brood**. Compared with the quite pure long 'eh' and 'oh' sounds of German, even pure ABN-speakers diphthongize these sounds to a degree, but the tendency to diphthongize them needs to be kept in check if one is to avoid sounding **plat**.

The other feature of the pronunciation of **Hollands** that attracts the label **plat**, is the tendency to pronounce initial **z** as **s** (see 1.3.3), but this is not quite as stigmatized as the above.

1.3.3 THE PRONUNCIATION OF DUTCH SOUTH OF THE RIVERS

The great cultural, religious and above all linguistic divide in The Netherlands is between those provinces lying north of the great rivers (**de Lek/Rijn**, **Waal** and **Maas**) and those lying south of them (**ten zuiden van de grote rivieren = beneden de Moerdijk**), i.e. North Brabant and Limburg, as well as part of Gelderland. The primary shibboleth of a southerner is his **zachte gee**, i.e. both **ch** and **g** are pronounced like 'ch' in German **ich**, whereas northerners pronounce **ch/g** with the 'ch' of German **ach**, but usually with even more rasping than in German. But what is more, it is very common for southerners to distinguish between **ch** and **g**, which a northerner never does, by pronouncing **g** as a voiced fricative [ɣ], which is what the distinction in spelling between **ch** and **g** was originally based on, but only in the south is the distinction still made.

The distinction between **f** and **v** (i.e. voiceless versus voiced fricatives) at the beginning of a word is seldom made by northerners; in other words, in their Dutch the two have fallen together in favour of the voiceless sound, which is exactly what has happened with **ch** and **g**. Just as southerners are more inclined to distinguish in pronunciation between the latter two sounds, so too do they distinguish between **f** and **v** – they start off pronouncing **v** as in English but end the sound by saying **f**. This distinction is sometimes made by northerners too in very formal sounding speech. The distinction is a difficult one for foreigners to make and not one worth trying to make: by pronouncing all **v**'s as **f**'s you will sound perfectly (northern) Dutch, whereas by trying to make the distinction there is a good chance your **v** will sound like an English 'v', and this must be avoided at all costs.

It should be pointed out that failing to make a distinction between **ch/g** and **f/v** has also been applied to **s/z** in the colloquial Dutch of the north, e.g. **zeven zakken** is pronounced **seve sakke**. Although most northerners commit this sin from time to time, to do so consistently sounds **plat** and is thus to be avoided for sociological reasons. It is also a characteristic of Surinam Dutch, in which case the sociological connotations are somewhat different.

The tendency of Hollanders to diphthongize **ee** and **oo** (see 1.3.2) is totally absent in the south. Here, if anything, the reverse occurs and the diphthongs **ui** and **ij/ei** tend to be monophthongized. For historical reasons these southern traits are not stigmatized but should not be copied unless one otherwise speaks a consistently southern Dutch.

Of the two **r**'s discussed in 1.3.2, only the velar one occurs in the south, but with a difference from the velar **r** of the north. Here it has a particularly 'throaty' quality, not unlike a French 'r' and it is referred to as a **gebrouwde r**. **Brouwen**, which means 'to pronounce one's r's in a throaty way as southerners do', is the other great shibboleth of a southerner after the **zachte gee**.

1.3.4 DIFFERENCES IN PRONUNCIATION BETWEEN THE NETHERLANDS AND FLANDERS

First, let it be said that in many cases it is difficult to draw a distinction between the pronunciation of the language in the Dutch-speaking provinces of Belgium and the Dutch provinces south of the great rivers but the national border does form a linguistic border to a certain degree. Flemish intonation is commonly rather French sounding to a Dutch ear and Flemings do not have a velar **r**. Many Flemings drop their h's, in which case their g's tend to sound like h. This means that **een gele hoed** can sound like **een hele oed**. In general, the differences between Flemish Dutch and that of The Netherlands are to be found more in the lexicon and word order, and thus go beyond the scope of this chapter.

Students requiring detailed information on assimilation, stress and other aspects of pronunciation are advised to consult R. H. B. De Coninck *Groot uitspraakwoordenboek van de Nederlandse Taal*, Uitgeverij De Nederlandsche Boekhandel, Antwerpen, 1974 (second edition) and E. Blancquaert *Praktische uitspraakleer van de Nederlandse Taal*, De Sikkel, Antwerp, 1969. Pages 141–9 in the latter book contain a very good description of Dutch stress patterns. The most recent authoritative publication on pronunciation, produced under the auspices of the Nederlandse Taalunie, is W. Zonneveld *Uitspraakwoordenboek*, Spectrum, Utrecht, 1997.

2 SPELLING (spelling)

As with the pronunciation, it is assumed that the reader has grasped the essentials of the highly regular spelling of Dutch and that there is no need to repeat them here, but even the more advanced student may need to be made aware of certain archaisms that will be encountered in books printed prior to World War II, as well as of certain recent changes to Dutch spelling. Some comments on the use of accents, apostrophes, capital letters, hyphens and medial letters in compound words are also dealt with here.

2.1 ARCHAISMS IN PRINTED MATTER FROM PRE-1947

There are two main differences between modern spelling and that encountered in works printed prior to 1947:

(a) Many words that now end in -s previously ended in -sch although they were not pronounced any differently from the way they are now:

mensch 'person', **bosch** 'forest', **Duitsch** 'German', **Nederlandsch** 'Dutch'

Derivatives of such words were also written with **sch**:

menschen 'people', **menschelijk** 'human', **boschen** 'forests', **Duitschland** 'Germany'

(b) **Ee** and **oo** were not only doubled in closed syllables, as they are now (e.g. **been** 'leg', **boom** 'tree'), but also in open syllables in certain words; it depended on the etymology of the word whether a double vowel was required or not, e.g. **beenen** 'legs', but **beter** 'better', **boomen** 'trees' but **boter** 'butter'. Needless to say, the Dutch found this distinction confusing, and thus it was abolished.

These archaic spellings are still sometimes found in place and people's names as the spelling changes were not deemed to necessarily apply to proper nouns:

's-Hertogenbosch, de Nederlandsche Bank, Heerenveen, Hoogeveen

(c) In Belgium an archaic spelling of long **a** (now written **aa** or **a**), namely **ae**, continued to be used in place names until 1946, but was then abolished, e.g. **Schaerbeek, Laeken**. The French spelling of Flemish towns containing **ae** took no notice of this reform, thus the French write **Schaerbeek** and **Waterloo** where the Flemings now write **Schaarbeek** and **Waterlo**. The combination **ae** can still be found in personal names, even in The Netherlands, e.g. **Van Haeringen**.[1]

(d) In some proper nouns the archaic combination **gh** is found, but it does not differ in pronunciation from **g**, e.g. **Breughel, Van Gogh, Veghel**.

2.2   RECENT CHANGES TO DUTCH SPELLING

Modern Dutch spelling is based on a spelling reform that was introduced in 1947 (1946 in Belgium). The recommendations appeared in 1954 in the *Woordenlijst van de Nederlandse Taal – samengesteld in opdracht van de Nederlandse en de Belgische regering*, 's-Gravenhage, 1954. This reform abolished the now archaic spelling conventions mentioned above. *Het Groene Boekje*, as this publication is known colloquially because of its compact format and green cover, attracted a great deal of criticism over the subsequent forty years, particularly with respect to the spelling of loanwords, called **bastaardwoorden** in Dutch. The most controversial aspect of the new spelling was that it allowed many loanwords to be written in one of two ways (e.g. **cultuur** or **kultuur, succes** or **sukses, organisatie** or **organizatie**), while making clear that one was 'preferred'; this was known as **de voorkeurspelling**. The most recent spelling reform, which was introduced into schools from August 1996, dictates that the 'preferred spelling' become the only permissible spelling.[2] There is most likely to be confusion for quite some time to come as meanwhile many people are no longer aware what variant of a given spelling is regarded as 'preferred', compounded by the fact that in 39 instances the spelling committee scrapped the preferred spelling for the sake of consistency, e.g. now **product**, previously **produkt**. Above all one should note that where there were previously two possible spellings of such loanwords, only one is now permitted. The guidelines of this most recent official spelling, and a spelling list containing 110,000 words, are contained in *Woordenlijst Nederlandse Taal*, Sdu Uitgevers, Den Haag/Standaard Uitgeverij, Antwerpen, 1995. The following issues are all discussed in detail in the preface of the *Woordenlijst*. The spelling reform, and indeed all official issues concerning the Dutch language since 1980, have been conducted under the auspices

---

[1] In similar vein the spelling **uy** or **uij** is archaic for **ui** and **eij** is archaic for **ei**; they are commonly found in personal names, e.g. **Kruyskamp, Meijer**.

[2] The consequences of this change of policy are likely to be greater in Flanders than in The Netherlands. In the latter the government always advocated use of the **voorkeurspelling**, but in Flanders the alternative had the advantage of making loanwords look less French and thus attracted many followers, especially the Flemish press. In fact permitting two spelling variants was from the beginning an attempt to arrive at a compromise between what the two Dutch-speaking nations desired.

of the *Nederlandse Taalunie*, a joint Dutch-Flemish body founded in 1980 and based in The Hague.

2.3 USE OF ACCENTS

2.3.1 ACUTE AND GRAVE ACCENTS (**accenttekens**)

The numerous French loanwords written with é (acute) and è (grave) in that language usually retain those accents in Dutch where they are still regarded as loanwords:

attaché 'attaché', **café** 'cafe', **coupé** 'coupé', **volière** 'aviary'

Note that diminutives of words ending in -**é** do not require the accent:

café – **cafeetje** 'cafe', **logé** – **logeetje** '(overnight) guest'

Words of French origin ending in -**ée** drop the accent in Dutch:

attachee '(female) attaché', **logee** 'female (overnight) guest', **orchidee** 'orchid', **marechaussee** 'military police'

Words where the first syllable contains an **é** also drop the accent:

etage 'floor, storey', **etalage** 'shop window', **rechaud** 'warmer'

The acute accent is otherwise used on Dutch words to indicate emphasis where in an English text we would normally italicize or underline the word:

een té behoudende koers
a *too* conservative approach

werklozen én studenten
both the unemployed *and* students

Dit woord wordt gewoonlijk zónder, maar ook wel mét klemtoon uitgesproken.
This word is usually pronounced *without*, but sometimes *with* stress.

Where a vowel sound is rendered by more than one letter, an accent is put on both vowel symbols where possible, e.g. **ééuwig** 'eternal', **vóórkomen** 'to occur', **búíten** 'outside'. The grave is used only on the letter **e** in Dutch words where it indicates how that **e** is pronounced;[3] in the sentence **Je doet het, hè?** 'You're going to do it, aren't you?' the grave distinguishes the word **hè** (= **niet waar**) from **hé** 'hey'.

---

[3] The rules given here are those according to the **Woordenlijst** but in practice many Dutch people write **èn** and **tè**, for example, where **én** and **té** are given above, because the grave on **èn** for example corresponds to the way this **e** is pronounced.

Note the difference in meaning the acute accent gives to the following words:

een 'a', **één** 'one'; **voor** 'for', **vóór** 'in front of, before'

Even when these two words have the second meaning they are written with accents only when the meaning could be ambiguous, otherwise they are left off:

Hij heeft één kind.	He has one child.
Er staat één boom voor het huis.	There is one tree in front of the house.
een van mijn vrienden	one of my friends (accents not necessary)[4]

but

Er staat een boom vóór het huis, niet erachter.
There is a tree in front of the house, not behind it.

The acute can be used in other instances to avoid ambiguity:

vérstrekkend 'far-reaching', **verstrekkend** 'issuing'

2.3.2   DIERESIS (het deelteken, het trema)

The dieresis (¨) is used in Dutch in non-compound words to indicate that the vowel it is placed on belongs to a separate syllable from the vowel that immediately precedes it:

geërgerd 'irritated', **geïnteresseerd** 'interested', **ruïne** 'ruin', **financiën** 'finances', **zeeën** 'seas'

A dieresis is not required in **geamuseerd** 'amused' and **buiig** 'showery', for example, as there is no ambiguity as to where the division between the syllables is. Nor is it required in the endings of words of Latin or French origin like **museum** 'museum' and **opticien** 'optician'.

The latest spelling reform differs from the previous reform in its prescription of where to use a dieresis only in the following respect:[5] the second vowel of two adjacent vowels in separate syllables now only gets a dieresis in derived words, as illustrated in the above examples; formerly it was also used in compound words (e.g. **meeëten** 'to dine with', **zeeëgel** 'sea urchin'), but has now been replaced by a hyphen in such cases (i.e. **mee-eten, zee-egel**) (see 2.6). Nevertheless, numerals compounded with **twee** and **drie** still retain the dieresis, e.g. **tweeëntwintig** '22', **drieëndertig** '33'.

---

[4] The rule for the use of accents on **een** as given here is heeded more in the breach than in the observance – it is exceedingly common to write **één** even where no ambiguity exists.
[5] The main differences between the 1947 and the 1996 spelling reform are only referred to here to avoid students becoming confused, as for quite some time to come there will be a great deal of printed matter in circulation where the old rules still apply.

2.4   APOSTROPHE (**de apostrof, het weglatingsteken**)

Unlike English, the apostrophe is not used to show possession:

Karels boek 'Charles's book', **mijn moeders auto** 'my mother's car'

Only when the proper noun ends in **a**, **o**, **u**, **y** or a sibilant is the apostrophe used (see 7.2.1.4):

Helma's woordenboek, Hans' boek

The above is in keeping with the principle that the apostrophe in Dutch is literally a **weglatingsteken**, i.e. where no letter has been left out, no punctuation is required. Thus **Shell's woordvoeder** is wrong, although commonly seen, and the above **Hans'** and **Helma's** are right because in the former case an additional **s** has been omitted and in the latter a hypothetical **a** (in a closed syllable the long vowel would normally be indicated by a doubling of the vowel, i.e. **Helmaas**, but Dutch has opted to omit the second **a** in this case and show it has been dropped by replacing it with an apostrophe) (see use of the apostrophe in plurals 7.2.1.4). In the following words, which are in fact abbreviations, letters have also been omitted and replaced by an apostrophe: **'s morgens** (historically < **des**), **'s-Hertogenbosch** (historically < **des**).

The abbreviated forms of **ik**, **het**, **mijn**, **zijn**, i.e. **'k**, **'t**, **m'n**, **z'n** which use an apostrophe, are best avoided in writing except in certain standard expressions where the abbreviated form is accepted:

met z'n drieën 'the three of them', **op z'n Frans** 'à la française'
(always abbreviated in these two cases), **in m'n eentje** 'on my own',
Ik heb 't koud 'I am cold', **over 't algemeen** 'in general' (commonly abbreviated)

2.5   CAPITAL LETTERS (**hoofdletters**)

The Dutch regard the diphthong **ij** as one letter (it is a separate key on a typewriter, for example) and thus if a word starts with **ij** and has to be capitalised, both the **i** and the **j** are affected:

Het IJ, **het IJsselmeer**, **IJsland** 'Iceland'

Several expressions in Dutch start with **'s** (see 2.4). If such an expression stands at the beginning of a sentence, the first letter of the next word is capitalized:

's Avonds is zij nooit thuis. 'She is never at home in the evening.'

In Dutch family names with **van**, **den**, **der**, **ten** and **ter** one usually writes such particles separately and small letters are used when a first name or initials precede:

Piet van den Berg, **H. van der Molen**

When the first name or initials are not mentioned, a capital letter is used:

een brief van Van den Berg
We hebben het over De Bruijn.
meneer Van der Plank

Note: When looking up a name in a Dutch telephone book or bibliography, it is written as follows: **Berg, P. van den.**[6]

Dutch titles and their abbreviations, i.e. the equivalents of 'Mr.', 'Mrs.' 'Dr.' etc., are usually written with small letters in Dutch except on envelopes:

meneer Smit,[7] **mevrouw Kuiper, drs. A. Smit** (see also Appendix 1)

It will be noticed that in some avant-garde publications (student newspapers, some modern literature, etc.) adjectives of nationality are often written with small letters, e.g. **nederlands**, **amsterdams**. The *Woordenlijst* does not advocate this practice.

2.6   HYPHEN (**het liggend streepje**)

The hyphen in compound words (**het liggend streepje**) is not as common in Dutch as in English because the rules for compound words are on the whole more clearly defined than in English. For example, hesitation about 'kitchen-door' or 'kitchen door', 'race-car' or 'race car' does not arise in Dutch, i.e. **keukendeur**, **raceauto** etc. But a hyphen *is* commonly used when listing compound nouns that share a component of the compound:

maag-, hoofd- en kiespijn 'stomach, head and tooth-ache'
voor- en namiddag 'morning and afternoon'
mond- en klauwzeer 'foot and mouth disease'

Under the spelling rules in force from 1947, where two vowels in compound words belonging to separate syllables ended up side by side and confusion could arise, a dieresis was placed on the second vowel to aid the eye, e.g. **naäpen** 'to mimic'. Under the most recent rules a hyphen

---

[6] It should be noted that in addition to all personal and street names not being capitalized in a Dutch phone book, the personal names are alphabetized according to streetname, not initials.

[7] When a man is addressed directly, **meneer** precedes his name, but if he is being talked about, **de heer** will often precede his name rather than **meneer**; this is particularly the case in formal style:

Mag ik de heer Van Staden even spreken?
May I speak to Mr. Van Staden?

will now be used in compounds, e.g. **na-apen**; use of the dieresis is now to be limited to derivatives (see 2.3.2). Note too the use of the hyphen in the following compounds to assist the eye: **radio-omroep** 'radio broadcasting network', **auto-ongeluk** 'car accident'.

There is one more change concerning the use of hyphens in the new spelling which one should note. Previously in geographical names like **Nieuw-Zeeland** and **Oost-Groningen** the hyphen was dropped in adjectival derivatives and they were written as one word, i.e. **Nieuwzeelands**, **Oostgronings**, but **Nieuw-Zeelands** and **Oost-Gronings** are now being advocated.

Note the use of a hyphen in the two placenames **'s-Gravenhage** and **'s-Hertogenbosch**, both more commonly referred to in speech, and even in writing, as **Den Haag** and **Den Bosch** respectively.

2.7 MEDIAL LETTERS IN COMPOUNDS WORDS (de tussenletter in samenstellingen)

This has long been one of the most confusing issues in Dutch spelling and it remains to be seen whether the new recommendations in this respect will alleviate the situation. Because of the tendency of most speakers to drop their final n's (see 1.3.1), it was not always evident from the pronunciation of a compound word, whether the **e** sound between its constituent parts was to be written **e** or **en**, e.g. **kippepoot** 'chicken leg', **kippenhok** 'chicken pen'. One decided on the correct spelling, so the theory went, by determining whether the first half of the compound conveyed the idea of plurality. In the given examples the leg belongs to one chicken, thus **-e-**, but a pen holds several chickens, thus **-en-**. But in practice there were many inconsistencies, e.g. **pereboom** 'pear tree'. The new spelling now advocates that one write **en** in all cases except:

(a) where the first part of the compound is not a noun, e.g. **hogeschool** 'tertiary institution'.
(b) where the first part is a noun that has a plural in **-en** or **-s** (see 7.2.2.7), e.g. **hoogtevrees** 'fear of heights' not *****hoogtenvrees** as the plural of **hoogte** can be either **hoogten** or **hoogtes**.
(c) where the first part is a noun that has no plural, e.g. **rijstepap** 'rice pudding'.
(d) where the first part, although a noun, is acting as an adjective, e.g. **hondeweer** 'awful weather', **luizebaan** 'dreadful job'.
(e) where the first part is a noun of which only one item exists, e.g. **Koninginnedag** 'Queen's Birthday holiday', **zonneschijn** 'sunshine'.

There are a few more categories but these are the major ones. These rules may seem a little complicated but they amount to the following: if in doubt, write **-en-** and you won't often be wrong.

More difficult for foreigners, but not for native-speakers, is knowing
where a medial sound is required at all in such compounds, given that in
English we simply put two nouns together, as the translations of the above
examples illustrate. Thus why one says **kinderbed** 'child's bed' and **broek-
spijp** 'trouser leg' is impossible to give consistent prescriptive rules for –
it is merely a matter of sound and as the Dutch always know what *sounds*
right, for them there is no problem here. It should be mentioned, however,
that whether a medial **s** sounds right in certain words is a matter of opinion,
and in such cases one is free to write what one says, i.e. either **voorbe-
hoedmiddel** or **voorbehoedsmiddel** 'contraceptive', either **geluidhinder** or
geluidshinder 'noise pollution'.

2.8   TRENDY SPELLINGS

Avant-garde publications sometimes apply a 'phonetic' spelling to foreign
words although this is not condoned by the *Woordenlijst*:

> **bureau – buro** 'office, desk', **cadeau – kado/kadootje** 'gift', **niveau –
> nivo** 'level', **historisch – histories** 'historical', **theater – tejater**
> 'theatre'

The spellings with **o** instead of **eau** are very widespread.

2.9   THE ALPHABET

The letters of the alphabet are pronounced as follows (read the words in
the second column as Dutch words):

a	**a**	n	**en**
b	**bee**	o	**o**
c	**see**	p	**pee**
d	**dee**	q	**ku**
e	**ee**	r	**er**
f	**ef**	s	**es**
g	**gee**	t	**tee**
h	**ha**	u	**u**
i	**ie**	v	**fee**
j	**jee**	w	**wee**
k	**ka**	x	**iks**
l	**el**	y	**ij** or **ie grec** or **upsilon**
m	**em**	z	**zet**

The Dutch are much more comfortable than English speakers in spelling
out a word aloud, for example over the phone, by giving names to the
letters of the alphabet. English speakers tend to choose any personal
name starting with the appropriate letter, but this alphabet has been

standardized in Holland, although there can be slight variations from speaker to speaker. This can be handy to know as it is very commonly used:

Anton	Otto
Bernhard	Pieter
Cornelis	Quirinus
Dirk	Richard/Rudolf
Edward	Simon
Ferdinand	Theodor
Gerard	Utrecht
Hendrik	Victor
Izaak	Willem
Johan/Jacob	Xantippe
Karel	Upsilon
Lodewijk/Leo	IJsbrand (**ij**)
Marie	Zacharias
Nico	

This alphabet is used as follows:

alph: **de a van Anton, de l van Lodewijk, de p van Pieter en de h van Hendrik** or **Anton, Lodewijk, Pieter, Hendrik**

3 **PUNCTUATION** (interpunctie, leestekens)

Generally speaking Dutch punctuation does not differ greatly from that of English. Only the comma is used somewhat differently – usually more sparingly than in English – and thus only the comma is dealt with here. For a complete account of Dutch punctuation see H. M. Hermkens, **Spelling en interpunctie**, Malmberg, Den Bosch.

3.1 THE COMMA (**de komma**)

Only those uses that differ from English are dealt with here.

3.1.1 It may be used between two adjectives before a noun when no conjunction is used (see 9.8.7), as in English, but is also often omitted in such cases; but it is always used when three or more adjectives precede the noun:

> **een koude(,) natte avond**
> a cold, wet evening

but

> **een koude, natte en stormachtige avond**
> a cold, wet and stormy evening

3.1.2 When a subordinate clause precedes a main clause in a compound sentence, a comma is usually used to separate the verbs of the two clauses:

> **Als je het morgen doet, krijg je iets van me.**
> If you do it tomorrow, you'll get something from me.

> **Omdat hij zo laat thuisgekomen was, was zijn vrouw boos op hem.**
> Because he had got home so late, his wife was angry with him.

> **Omdat ik me misselijk voel, blijf ik thuis en ga ik onmiddellijk naar bed.**
> As I am feeling ill, I'm staying home and I'm going straight to bed.

When the main clause precedes a subordinate clause introduced by **dat**, the comma is usually omitted but with other conjunctions the comma is usually inserted:

Ik geloof dat hij morgen komt.
I think he's coming tomorrow.

Ik had de pan aan mijn moeder gegeven, hoewel ik er toen zelf geen had.
I'd given the pot to my mother, although I then didn't have one myself.

3.1.3   With relative clauses a comma is commonly used at the end of the clause (however usually not when the clause is relatively short), but seldom at the beginning of it, although it *is* sometimes found with longer relative clauses:

De vulpen waar je de brief mee schreef(,) is leeg. (a short clause)
The pen you wrote the letter with is empty.

De universiteit(,) die later in het jaar een aantal nieuwe cursussen had willen invoeren, heeft besloten dat dat niet meer mogelijk is.
The university, which would have liked to introduce a number of new courses later in the year, has decided that that is not longer possible.

The following subtle difference in meaning when the first comma is omitted or used should be noted: with a comma the relative clause relates back to the entire group, whereas without a comma it refers to only a section of the group; strictly speaking this is the same in English (called non-restrictive and restrictive relative clauses respectively) although many people are unaware of the distinction:

De jongens, die te laat waren, moesten schoolblijven.
The boys, who were late, had to stay behind at school.
(i.e. There were only boys and all had to stay behind.)

De jongens die te laat waren, moesten schoolblijven.
The boys who were late had to stay behind at school.
(i.e. There were other boys and perhaps girls who were not late.)

3.1.4   Note that the following English commas, which merely indicate a reading pause within a clause, are not used in Dutch:

Het is echter erg moeilijk.
It is, however, very difficult.

Hij heeft het helaas niet gedaan/Helaas heeft hij het niet gedaan.
He has, unfortunately, not done it/Unfortunately, he hasn't done it.

3.1.5   See 14.1.1.2 and 14.7.1.3 for use of the comma with numerals.

4 CASES (naamvallen)

Case, once so prevalent in Dutch – especially in the written language, even right up to 1947[1] – is to all intents and purposes dead nowadays. Remnants of the cases will still be found chiefly in standard expressions, official titles and occasionally in very formal writing, as well as in all pre-war printed matter. Articles, demonstratives, possessives, adjectives and nouns can all be affected by case (see chapters 5–9).

It is traditional in English-speaking countries to refer to the four cases in the following order: nominative (subject), accusative (direct object), genitive (possessive) and dative (indirect object). In Holland, however, the classical order used in the learning of Latin and Greek is more common, i.e. nominative, genitive, dative and accusative. This has resulted in the Dutch naming the cases after their number in the above sequence, i.e. nominative **de eerste naamval**, genitive **de tweede naamval** etc.

Some common expressions preserving archaic case endings are given below to illustrate the concept, but the number is actually infinite. Only the genitive and the dative, apart from the nominative of course, are recognizable nowadays:

EXPRESSIONS PRESERVING THE GENITIVE

wiens hoed, wier jurk? (arch.)	whose hat, whose dress?
's middags	in the afternoon
blootshoofds	bare-headed
desnoods	in case of need
het teken des kruises	the sign of the cross
's lands wijs, 's lands eer	when in Rome, do as the Romans do
het Leger des Heils	the Salvation Army
in naam der wet	in the name of the law
het Koninkrijk der Nederlanden	the Kingdom of The Netherlands

---

[1] Masculine living beings in the accusative and dative case were still indicated in writing although the 'n' endings were not pronounced, e.g. **Hij schoot op den/eenen ouden leeuw** 'He shot at the/an old lion'. The 1947 spelling reform did away once and for all with these archaic endings that bore little resemblance to natural speech, except in standard expressions where the endings are pronounced.

EXPRESSIONS PRESERVING THE DATIVE

ter wille van (see 13.1)	for the sake of
ten einde raad	at one's wits' end
tenslotte	finally
op heterdaad	red-handed
op den duur	in the long run
van ganser harte	from the bottom of one's heart
om den brode	for a living

5 ARTICLES (lidwoorden)

5.1 THE INDEFINITE ARTICLE (**het onbepaald lidwoord**)

The indefinite article 'a/an' in English is **een** in Dutch, which is pronounced **'n** and is sometimes written as such in direct speech. The numeral 'one' is also **een**, pronounced with a long **e** and written **één** where ambiguity can arise (see 2.3.1 and 14.1, footnote 1). Occasionally in standard expressions and archaic or poetic style older case forms of **een** are found:

enerzijds	on the one hand
het leed ener moeder	the sorrow of a mother

5.1.1 OMISSION OF THE INDEFINITE ARTICLE

The indefinite article is sometimes omitted in Dutch where it is used in English.

(a) It is usually omitted after the preposition **als** (see 13.0):

Hij gebruikt zijn schoteltje als (een) asbak.
He's using his saucer as an ashtray.

Ik doe Duits als bijvak.
I'm doing German as a secondary subject.

but

Ze heeft zich als een dame gedragen.
She behaved like a lady. (standard idiom)

(b) It is commonly omitted after the preposition **zonder**:

Ik zag een lijk zonder hoofd.
I saw a corpse without a head.

Hij ging uit zonder hoed.
He went out without a hat.

(c) It is usually omitted before professions (when the verb is **zijn**, **worden** or **blijven**), but is always inserted when the profession is preceded by an adjective:

Hij is leraar.
He is a teacher.

Hij is een zeer goede leraar.
He is a very good teacher.

Also:

Hij is vader geworden.
He has become a father.

Hij is enig kind.
He is an only child.

(d) It is commonly omitted before nationalities (when the verb is **zijn**, **worden** or **blijven**), but is always inserted when the nationality is preceded by an adjective:

Hij is (een) Nederlander.
He is a Dutchman.

Hij is een rasechte Nederlander.
He is a genuine Dutchman.

(e) It is omitted in various standard expressions:

Het was jammer.
It was a pity.

maag-/ kiespijn hebben/krijgen
to have/get a stomach-ache, tooth-ache

oog om oog, tand om tand
an eye for an eye, a tooth for a tooth

kwart voor/over drie
a quarter to/past three

5.2 THE DEFINITE ARTICLE (**het bepaald lidwoord**)

The definite article used before singular common gender nouns is **de**, and **het** is used before neuter nouns. Both genders employ **de** in the plural:

de man, de deur, het kind, het gat – de mannen, de deuren, de kinderen, de gaten

There are many remnants of former cases in the definite article (see 13.1). The most common are **der** (genitive singular feminine or plural), **des** or **'s** (genitive masculine or neuter singular) and **den** (dative masculine and neuter singular). Many case forms of the definite article have been preserved in standard expressions:

in de loop der tijd   in the course of time
Beatrix, Koningin der Nederlanden Beatrix, Queen of The Netherlands

's morgens	in the morning
in naam des konings	in the name of the king
het Leger des Heils	the Salvation Army
desondanks	in spite of it/that
op den duur	in the course of time

The genitive feminine singular and plural **der** in particular is still productive, but it is rather formal.

5.2.1 OMISSION OF THE DEFINITE ARTICLE

In certain idioms the definite article is omitted where it is used in English:

aan tafel	at the table
op tafel	on the table
op kantoor	at the office
naar kantoor	to the office
op straat	in the street
op zolder	in the attic
in bad	in the bath
in huis	in the house
naar zee	to the seaside
aan zee	at the seaside
op Internet	on the Internet
met mes en vork	with a knife and fork
in staat van oorlog	in a state of war
op antwoord wachten	to wait for an answer
piano/gitaar enz. spelen	to play the piano/guitar etc.
koningin en prins	the queen and (the) prince
in eerste instantie	in the first place
ik ben van mening dat	I am of the opinion that
in naam van de koning	in the name of the king

It is also commonly omitted before nouns in apposition:

Clinton, (de) president van de VS, is momenteel op staatsbezoek in Japan.

Clinton, the president of the USA, is on a state visit to Japan at the moment.

5.2.2 INCLUSION OF THE DEFINITE ARTICLE

There are many more cases in which the definite article is used where it is not in English. Some cases are situations where its use can be defined, others are individual idioms.

(a) It is always used before certain abstract nouns:

de mens	mankind
de natuur	nature
de liefde	love
de moderne kunst	modern art
de (vaderlandse) geschiedenis	(Dutch) history
de dood	death
het leven	life
de hemel	heaven
de hel	hell
het paradijs	paradise

De natuur is mysterieus.
Nature is mysterious.

De belangrijkste gebeurtenis in de geschiedenis.
The most important event in history.

Zo is het leven.
Such is life.

(b) It is always used before names of towns and countries when they are preceded by adjectives:

het mooie Amsterdam	beautiful Amsterdam
het toenmalige Duitsland	Germany in those days

(c) It is always used before seasons:

in de lente	in spring
Ze was in de winter in Australië.	She was in Australia in winter.

(d) It is always used with meals after the prepositions **na** and **vóór**:

na/vóór het avondeten	after/before dinner
tijdens de lunch	during lunch

(e) It is always used before the names of streets, parks and squares:

Ik woon in de Hoofdstraat.
I live in Main Street.

Hij woont op de Erasmusweg.
He lives in Erasmus Road.

Ze sliep in het Vondelpark.
She slept in Vondel Park.

Op het Waterlooplein.
At Waterloo Square.

(f) Religions and names of airlines are always preceded by the definite article:

Hij vloog met de KLM.
He flew with KLM.

Waar is het hoofdkantoor van de TWA?
Where is TWA's main office?

De islam is een godsdienst uit het Midden-Oosten.
Islam is a Middle Eastern religion.

het christendom door de eeuwen heen
christianity through the ages

(g) It is used after **meneer** and **mevrouw** when the profession (not the personal name) follows – usually a form of direct address:

meneer de Voorzitter	Mr. Chairman
mevrouw de President	Madame President
meneer De Kat/Hond	Mr. Cat/Dog (in a fairy-tale)
Sprookjes van Moeder de Gans	Mother Goose's fairy-tales

(h) It is used in various idioms:

in de stad	in town
naar de stad	to town
in de kerk	in church
in de gevangenis	in jail
aan de universiteit	at university
in de praktijk	in practice
onder de zeespiegel	below sea level
in het Duits	in German
uit het Frans vertalen	to translate from French
op het tweede net	on channel two (tv)
de school begint om ...	school begins at ...
in de tweede versnelling	in second gear
tussen de 12 en de 15	between 12 and 15 (items or age)
boven/onder de 50	over/under 50 (items or age)
voor de lol	for fun
in het rood gekleed	dressed in red
de een na de ander	one after another, one by one
met de auto/tram etc.	by car, tram etc.
met de hand	by hand
de volgende keer	next time
op het eerste gezicht	at first sight

(i) In Dutch it is not possible for one definite article to do service for two nouns that follow if they are of different gender; the article should be repeated for each noun. If the same article is required by both nouns, the article can be omitted, as it can be when both nouns are in the plural:

De tafel en het vloerkleed waren duur.
The table and floor-rug were expensive.

om de hals en (de) handen
around the neck and hands

de jongens en meisjes van deze klas
the boys and girls from this class

6 DEMONSTRATIVES
(aanwijzende voornaamwoorden)

6.1 The demonstrative, like the definite article, varies according to the gender of the noun it precedes:

common gender:	**deze**	this	**die**	that
neuter gender:	**dit**	this	**dat**	that
plural (both genders):	**deze**	these	**die**	those

deze deur	this door	**die deur**	that door
dit huis	this house	**dat huis**	that house
deze deuren	these doors	**die deuren**	those doors
deze huizen	these houses	**die huizen**	those houses

Note: **de**   **het**

          deze   common gender and plural   **dit**   neuter singular

          die   **dat**

6.2 Other case forms of the demonstratives are found in standard expressions:

(een) dezer dagen	one of these days[1]
op de 18de dezer	on the 18th of this month (in letters)
destijds	at that time
dientengevolge	as a result of that

The genitive form **diens** sometimes replaces the English possessive adjective 'his', see 8.2, footnote 9.

6.3 In higher style 'the former' and 'the latter' can be rendered in Dutch by **deze** and an archaic demonstrative **gene** although **eerstgenoemde** and **laatstgenoemde** are more everyday expressions (all four words can take an **-n** ending when referring to plural persons:

---

[1] In Dutch this expression refers to the near future, not to any point in the future as it does in English. Thus 'one of these days' is not really the correct translation of this expression, but rather 'in the not too distant future'.

Cruyff en Merckx zijn door de sport beroemd geworden, deze als wielrenner, gene als voetballer.

C. and M. gained fame through sport, the latter as a cyclist, the former as a footballer.

Gene is also used in other contexts as a very formal sounding alternative to **die:**

Zij wonen aan deze zijde van de rivier, de vijand aan gene.

They live on this side of the river, the enemy on that (side).

6.4 The pronominal use of demonstratives is dealt with under pronouns, see 8.4.

7 NOUNS (zelfstandige naamwoorden)

GENDER (geslacht)

Dutch nouns are of one of two genders, common gender and neuter. The former is an amalgamation of what were formerly masculine and feminine. Only in some archaic case forms is any distinction between the two still made (see 5.2). In the south of Holland and in Belgium the difference between masculine and feminine is still heeded in the use of pronouns (see 8.1.2.3(b)).

Dutch dictionaries usually indicate gender by placing an **m** (**mannelijk**), a **v** (**vrouwelijk**) or an **o** (**onzijdig**) after the noun.

Every new Dutch noun must be learnt together with the appropriate definite article. There are a few reasonably reliable rules for learning the gender of nouns but there are nevertheless many words which do not fit the rules and for which the gender simply has to be learnt by heart. The following is a list of rules, some hard and fast, others a little vague, to assist in learning genders.

7.1 RULES FOR THE GENDER OF DUTCH NOUNS

7.1.1 COMMON GENDER NOUNS

7.1.1.1 The names of men and women

de burgemeester 'mayor', **de dochter** 'daughter', **de moeder** 'mother', **de koningin** 'queen', **de vader** 'father', **de verpleger** 'male nurse', **de verpleegster** 'nurse', **de zoon** 'son'

Exceptions: **het mens** 'woman', **het wijf** 'woman'

7.1.1.2 The names of most animals, including birds and fish

de haring 'herring', **de leeuw** 'lion', **de mus** 'sparrow'

For exceptions see 7.1.2.3.

7.1.1.3   The names of trees, flowers and fruit

de anjer 'carnation', **de eik** 'oak', **de perzik** 'peach'

7.1.1.4   The names of stones, considered as objects (see 7.1.2.4)

de baksteen 'brick', **de diamant** 'diamond', **de robijn** 'ruby'

7.1.1.5   The names of days, months and seasons (except compounds with *jaar*)

de laatste maandag in oktober 'the last Monday in October', **de lente** 'spring', **de zomer** 'summer'

7.1.1.6   The names of mountains and large rivers

de Mont Blanc, de Nijl 'Nile', **de Rijn** 'Rhine', **de Vesuvius**

7.1.1.7   The names of objects whose names end in *-aard, -aar, -erd*

de standaard 'standard', **de lessenaar** 'desk', **de mosterd** 'mustard'

7.1.1.8   The names of tools or instruments, derived from verbs, and ending in *-el* and *-er*

de beitel 'chisel', **de sleutel** 'key', **de gieter** 'watering-can'

7.1.1.9   Words ending in *-em, -lm* and *-rm*

de bezem 'broom', **de helm** 'helmet', **de term** 'term', **de storm** 'storm'

Exception: **het scherm** 'screen'

7.1.1.10   Words ending in *-ing* and *-ling*

de regering 'government', **de leerling** 'school student'

7.1.1.11   Most monosyllabic words derived from verbs

de lach 'laugh', **de loop** 'walk, gait', **de val** 'trap, fall', **de zucht** 'sigh'

7.1.1.12   The names of letters of the alphabet

de a, **de b**, **de c**

7.1.1.13   The names of numerals

de een, **de zeven**, **de honderd**

7.1.1.14   The names of musical instruments

de hobo 'oboe', **de piano** 'piano', **de viool** 'violin'

Exceptions: **het klavecimbel** 'harpsichord', **het orgel** 'organ', **het spinet** 'spinet'

7.1.1.15   The names of virtues and vices

de nijd 'anger, envy', **de woede** 'rage', **de genade** 'mercy', **de liefde** 'love'

7.1.1.16   Words with the suffix -e

de kou(de) 'cold', **de vrede** 'peace', **de zonde** 'sin'

Exception: **het einde** 'end'

7.1.1.17   Words derived from adjectives ending with the suffix -te

de duurte 'expensiveness', **de hoogte** 'height', **de lengte** 'length'

7.1.1.18   Words ending in -heid and -nis

de vrijheid 'freedom', **de waarheid** 'truth', **de gebeurtenis** 'event', **de geschiedenis** 'history'

7.1.1.19   Words ending in -age, -ij, -ei, -ie, -iek, -teit and -theek

de plantage 'plantation', **de batterij** 'battery', **de pastei** 'pie', **de harmonie** 'harmony', **de fabriek** 'factory', **de elektriciteit** 'electricity', **de bibliotheek** 'library'

Exceptions: **het publiek** 'public', **het schilderij** 'painting'

7.1.1.20   Words ending in an unaccented -(t)ie and -uw

de productie 'production', **de schaduw** 'shadow, shade'

Exceptions: **het concilie** 'council', **het evangelie** 'gospel'

7.1.1.21 Adjectives uses as nouns referring to persons

de rijke 'rich one', **de verminkte** 'crippled one', **de zieke** 'sick one'

7.1.1.22 Words ending in **-schap** signifying a condition (see 7.1.2.15)

de dronkenschap 'drunkenness', **de verwantschap** 'relationship', **de vriendschap** 'friendship', **de zwangerschap** 'pregnancy'

but also the following:

de boodschap 'message', **de broederschap** 'brotherhood', **de eigen-schap** 'quality', **de nalatenschap** 'inheritance', **de wetenschap** 'science'

7.1.2 NEUTER NOUNS

7.1.2.1 All diminutives

het kindje 'child', **het koekje** 'biscuit'

7.1.2.2 All infinitives used as nouns

het eten 'food, eating', **het geven** 'giving', **het werken** 'working'

7.1.2.3 The names of young animals

het kalf 'calf', **het kuiken** 'chicken', **het veulen** 'foal'

Exception: **de big** 'piglet'

7.1.2.4 A great number of minerals

This group includes:

(a) *Stones*, where the name denotes the matter in general, or is a collective noun (see 7.1.1.4)

het diamant 'diamond', **het steen** 'stone', **het kwarts** 'quartz'

(b) *All well-known metals*

het blik 'tin', **het goud** 'gold', **het ijzer** 'iron', **het koper** 'copper', **het nikkel** 'nickel', **het radium** 'radium', **het staal** 'steel', **het tin** 'pewter', **het zilver** 'silver'

(c) *Other minerals*

het asbest 'asbestos', **het barium** 'barium', **het erts** 'ore', **het gips** 'gypsum, plaster'

Exception: **de kalk** 'calcium, lime'

7.1.2.5   The names of countries and provinces (the article is only used when the name is qualified)

het mooie Australië 'beautiful Australia', **het België van toen**
'Belgium as it was then', **het oude Friesland** '(the) old Friesland'

7.1.2.6   The names of cities and villages (including those which have **den** in the name)

het mooie Amsterdam 'beautiful Amsterdam' (although **de Dam**),
het fraaie Den Haag 'charming The Hague'

7.1.2.7   Words formed with the ending **-sel**

het deksel 'lid', **het stelsel** 'system', **het verschijnsel** 'phenomenon',
het voedsel 'food'

Exceptions: nouns whose -sel is not a true suffix, e.g. **de mossel**
'mussel', **de oksel** 'armpit', **de wissel** 'postal note'

7.1.2.8   All collective nouns with the prefix **ge-** and suffix **-te**

het gebergte 'mountain range', **het gebladerte** 'foliage', **het geboomte**
'trees'

7.1.2.9   Collective nouns with the prefix **ge-** and no suffix

het gebroed 'brood', **het gepeupel** 'populace, rabble'

7.1.2.10   Nouns formed from verbal stems beginning with the unstressed prefixes **be-, ge-, ont-, ver-**

het belang 'importance', **het gesprek** 'conversation', **het ontbijt**
'breakfast', **het verbod** 'prohibition'

Exceptions: **de (uit)verkoop** 'sale', **de verhuur** 'hiring out, letting'

7.1.2.11   Adjectives ending in **-e** used as abstract nouns

het goede 'that which is good', **het kwade** 'that which is evil', **het
genotene** 'that which was enjoyed'

7.1.2.12   All colours

het blauw 'blue', **het groen** 'green'

7.1.2.13   All words ending in **-um**

het album 'album', **het gymnasium** 'grammar school'

Exception: **de datum** 'date'

7.1.2.14   Most words ending in **-dom**

het christendom 'Christianity', **het eigendom** 'property', **het mensdom** 'humanity'

Exceptions: **de adeldom** 'nobility', **de ouderdom** 'old age', **de rijkdom** 'riches, wealth'

7.1.2.15   Words ending in **-schap** signifying a function (see 7.1.1.22)

het priesterschap 'priesthood', **het vaderschap** 'fatherhood'

but also the following that do not signify a function:

het genootschap 'society', **het gereedschap** 'tools', **het gezelschap** 'company', **het graafschap** 'county', **het landschap** 'landscape'

7.1.2.16   All words ending in **-isme**

het communisme 'communism', **het germanisme** 'germanism', **het socialisme** 'socialism'

7.1.2.17   All words ending in **-aat**

het consulaat 'consulate', **het internaat** 'boarding school', **het resultaat** 'result', **het secretariaat** 'secretariat'

7.1.2.18   Points of the compass

het noorden 'north', **het noordoosten** 'north-east'

7.1.2.19   Bisyllabic French loanwords seem to be predominantly neuter

het plafond 'ceiling', **het station** 'station', **het toilet** 'toilet', **het trottoir** 'footpath'

Exceptions to this rule end in typically French feminine endings: **de kapel** 'chapel', **de puree** 'mash, pulp'.

7.1.3 COMPOUND NOUNS

Compound nouns always take the gender of the last noun in the compound:

het ontbijt 'the breakfast' + **de tafel** 'the table' = **de ontbijttafel**
de zieken 'the sick people' + **het huis** 'the house' = **het ziekenhuis**

The following are exceptions to this rule:

de blik 'glance'	**het ogenblik** 'moment'
de draad 'wire'	**het prikkeldraad** 'barbed wire'
de kant 'side'	**het vierkant** 'square'
de stip 'dot, point'	**het tijdstip** 'point in time, period'
het stuk 'piece'	**de biefstuk**[1] 'steak'
het weer 'weather'	**de brandweer**[2] 'fire brigade'
het zegel 'seal'	**de (post)zegel** 'stamp'

7.1.4 NOUNS WITH TWO GENDERS

There are many nouns that can have two genders: there are those that have two genders with no difference in meaning and those that do have a difference in meaning:

7.1.4.1 *Nouns with two genders with no difference in meaning*
(The more common gender is given first. This list is not complete – there are more nouns in this category)

de/het aanrecht 'sink'	**de/het omslag** 'envelope'
het/de affiche 'poster'	**het/de poeder** 'powder'
het/de draad 'wire'	**de/het rooster** 'toaster, timetable'
de/het kaneel 'cinnamon'	**de/het schort** 'apron'
de/het kauwgom 'chewing gum'	**de/het sloop** 'pillow case'
het/de knoflook 'garlic'	**de/het soort** 'sort'
de/het matras 'mattress'	

Note: **de keer** 'time' but **deze** or **dit keer** 'this time'

---

[1] In fact this is a corruption of the English word 'steak'.
[2] Actually of different origin as it is derived from the verb **weren** 'to avert'; compare also **het paard** 'horse' and **de luipaard** 'leopard', which are unrelated.

Note the peculiarities of gender in the following expressions:

het been but **Hij is weer op de been** 'He is up and about again'
het weer but **Hij is in de weer** 'He is up and about/busy'
het meer but **de Bijlmermeer, de Haarlemmermeer** (i.e. polder not lake)
het hout but **de Haarlemmerhout** (a forest, not the material)

7.1.4.2 Nouns with two genders with a difference in meaning

de bal 'ball' (pl. **ballen**)	**het bal** 'ball, dance' (pl. **bals**)
de band 'ribbon, tape' (i.e. object)	**het band** 'ribbon, tape' (i.e. material)
de blik 'glance'	**het blik** 'tin' (i.e. metal and tin can)
de bos 'bouquet'	**het bos** 'forest'
de bot 'flounder'	**het bot** 'bone'
de doek 'cloth'	**het doek** 'canvas, curtain, film screen'
de hof 'courtyard'	**het hof** 'court' (of a king)
de hoorn 'horn' (object)	**het hoorn** 'horn' (material)
de idee 'idea'	**het idee** 'plan, thought'
de jacht 'hunting'	**het jacht** 'yacht'
de eerste maal 'first time, occasion'	**het maal** 'meal'
de mens 'man, mankind'	**het mens** 'woman'
de pad 'toad' (pl. **padden**)	**het pad** 'path' (pl. **paden**)
de patroon 'patron, sponsor'	**het patroon** 'pattern'
de portier 'doorkeeper'	**het portier** 'door' (of a vehicle)
de punt 'point' (i.e. of a needle)	**het punt** 'point, mark, place'
de Heilige Schrift 'Bible'	**het schrift** 'exercise book'
de soort 'species'	**het soort** 'kind, sort'
de stof 'material'	**het stof** 'dust'
de veer 'feather, spring'	**het veer** 'ferry'

Note that the names of all precious stones have two genders: they are common gender when the noun refers to the individual stones, and neuter when it refers to the stone as a material:

de smaragd	'the emerald' (jewel)
het smaragd	'the emerald' (material)

7.2 PLURAL OF NOUNS (**meervoudsvorming**)

Dutch nouns form their plural by addition of either **-s** or **-en** to the singular, the latter ending being more common. The basic rule for plural formation is always to add **-en** unless the word belongs to one of the following **-s** plural categories.

7.2.1   -s PLURALS (i.e.: -s OR -'s)

7.2.1.1   *All nouns ending in the unstressed endings -el, -em, -en and -er*

This is a very large group:

appels[3] 'apples', **bezems** 'brooms', **jongens** 'boys', **tafels** 'tables', **spijkers** 'nails', **wapens** 'weapons'

Exceptions: **aderen**[4] 'veins', **artikelen** 'articles', **christenen** 'Christians', **engelen** 'angels', **maatregelen** 'measures', **middelen** 'means', **mosselen**[5] 'mussels', **redenen** 'reasons', **wonderen** 'wonders'

Also nouns ending in the suffix -**sel** and compounds with -**stel**:

verschijnselen 'phenomena', **beginselen** 'principles'; **opstellen** 'essays', **toestellen** 'appliances'

In older writings and more formal style nouns in this group are often found with an -**en** ending:

appelen[3] apples, **wapenen** weapons

The following nouns take on a new meaning when given an -**en** plural:

hemelen	heavens	**tafelen**	tablets (biblical)
hemels	canopies	**tafels**	tables (for food)
hersenen	brains (organ, food)	**vaderen**	forefathers[6]
hersens	brains (food)	**vaders**	fathers
letteren	literature[7]	**wateren**	waterways
letters	letters (of the alphabet)	**waters**	waters
middelen	means	**wortelen**	carrots
middels	waists	**wortels**	roots, carrots

Note: The -**el**, -**en** and -**er** in words like **wiel** 'wheel', **schoen** 'shoe' and **mier** 'ant' are not formal endings and thus they take -**en** in the plural, not -**s**. **Model** has a stressed -**el** ending and goes **modellen**.

---

[3] The compound nouns **aardappel** 'potato' and **sinaasappel** 'orange' are commonly heard with both an -**s** and an -**en** plural.
[4] **Aders** is also possible.
[5] **Mossels** is also possible.
[6] *Note*: **de vroede vaderen** 'the city fathers'.
[7] *Note*: **de Faculteit der Letteren** 'the Arts Faculty'.

7.2.1.2   Nouns ending in *-erd* and *-aard* and designating masculine beings

sufferds 'idiots', **grijsaards** 'old men'

Exception: **Spanjaarden** 'Spaniards'

7.2.1.3   All diminutives ending in *-je*

koekjes 'biscuits', **huisjes** 'houses'

Note: **kind** 'kiddie' but **kindertjes** 'kiddies', **kleertjes** 'clothes' (both derived from the plural of the non-diminutive forms).

7.2.1.4   Nouns ending in *-a*, *-o* and *-u* (all are of foreign origin)

firma's 'firms', **auto's** 'cars', **paraplu's** 'umbrellas'

The apostrophe is inserted because **auto's**, for example, would otherwise be pronounced with a short o; a long o sound can be preserved in a closed syllable only by doubling the letter. The Dutch would find the spelling **autoos** strange and thus replace the second o with an apostrophe. Thus it is not necessary in **cadeaus**, **cafés** and **Hindoes**, for example, but it is used in words ending in **y** and **i** (e.g. **baby's**, **ski's**), although strictly speaking nothing has been omitted.

7.2.1.5   Many foreign words ending in unstressed *-e*

actrices 'actresses', **dames** 'ladies', **garages** 'garages', **secretaresses** 'secretaries', **studentes** 'female students'

For Dutch words ending in **-e** see 7.2.2.7.

7.2.1.6   Foreign words ending in unstressed *-ie*

families, **petites**, **provincies**, **studies**

In higher style the words in this group are found with **-en**, e.g. **de Zeven Provinciën** 'The Seven Provinces' (name of The Netherlands in the Middle Ages).

7.2.1.7   Many loanwords (usually of English or French origin) that are still regarded as foreign words

clubs 'clubs', **films** 'films', **perrons** 'platforms', **restaurants** 'restaurants', **tanks** 'tanks', **telefoons** 'telephones', **trottoirs** 'footpaths'

Nouns of French origin ending in **-eur** and **-trice** belong here too:

> **auteurs** 'authors', **automonteurs** 'mechanics', **ingenieurs** 'engineers', **kapiteins** 'captains', **actrices** 'actresses', **directrices** 'female directors'

Exception: **directeuren** (also with **-s**)

7.2.1.8   *Words ending in -ier and -oor take -s when referring to people and -en when referring to things*

> **kruideniers** 'grocers', **winkeliers** 'shop-keepers', **portiers** 'doormen', **pastoors** '(R.C.) priests'; **formulieren** 'forms', **scharnieren** 'hinges', **portieren** 'doors', **kantoren** 'offices'

Exceptions: **officieren** 'officers', **scholieren** 'school-children'

7.2.1.9   *A few native Dutch words denoting male beings*

> **broers** 'brothers', **bruidegoms** 'bridegrooms', **knechts** 'manservant' (also **-en**), **koks** 'cooks', **maats** 'mates', **ooms** 'uncles', **zoons** 'sons'

Note: **Zoons** also has a plural **zonen** which is often found in names of firms, e.g. **Van Goor en Zonen.**

The military ranks **generaal, kolonel, korporaal** and **luitenant** also take **-s** (all take the stress on the final syllable).

7.2.2   -en PLURALS (-n AND -en)

7.2.2.1   *When the -en suffix is added to nouns to form the plural, the following spelling changes apply*

(a) Nouns with **aa, ee, oo** or **uu** drop one vowel in the open syllable produced by the suffixing of **-en**

> **maan** 'moon' – **manen, peer** 'pear' – **peren, brood** 'bread' – **broden, muur** 'wall' – **muren.**

(b) Nouns with long vowels or diphthongs ending in **-s** change to **z** (i.e. voicing of **s** in intervocalic position):

> **Chinees** 'Chinese' – **Chinezen, huis** 'house' – **huizen, kies** 'molar' – **kiezen, prijs** 'price, prize' – **prijzen, reis** 'journey' – **reizen, roos** 'rose' – **rozen**

> Exceptions: **eis** 'demand' – **eisen, kous** 'stocking' – **kousen, kruis** 'cross' – **kruisen** or **kruizen, paus** 'Pope' – **pausen, Pruis** 'Prussian' – **Pruisen, saus** 'sauce' – **sausen** or **sauzen, zeis** 'scythe' – **zeisen**

(c) Nouns ending in **-ms**, **-ns** and **-rs** change **s** to **z**:

gems 'chamois' – **gemzen, gans** 'goose' – **ganzen, grens** 'border'
– **grenzen, lens** 'lense' – **lenzen, vers** 'poem, stanza' – **verzen**

Exceptions: **dans** 'dance' – **dansen, kikvors** 'frog' – **kikvorsen, koers**
'rate, course' – **koersen, krans** 'wreath' – **kransen, lans** 'lance' –
lansen, mars 'march' – **marsen, mens** 'person' – **mensen, pers** 'press'
– **persen, prins** 'prince' – **prinsen, tendens** 'tendency' – **tendensen,
wals** 'waltz' – **walsen, wens** 'wish' – **wensen**

(d) Nouns with long vowels or diphthongs ending in **-f** change to **v** (i.e.
voicing of **f** in intervocalic position):

brief 'letter' – **brieven, graaf** 'count' – **graven, kloof** 'gap' – **kloven,
neef** 'nephew, male cousin' – **neven**

Exceptions: nouns of Greek origin ending in **-graaf**:

fotograaf 'photographer' – **fotografen, paragraaf** 'paragraph' –
paragrafen, filosoof 'philosopher' – **filosofen**

(e) Nouns ending in **-lf** and **-rf** change to **v**:

golf 'wave' – **golven, wolf** 'wolf' – **wolven, werf** 'wharf' – **werven**

Exception: **elf** 'elf' – **elfen**

(f) Nouns containing a short vowel and ending in a consonant double the
consonant to preserve the short vowel:

bok 'billy-goat' – **bokken, fles** 'bottle' – **flessen, hor** 'wire-screen' –
horren, mus 'sparrow' – **mussen, pot** 'pot' – **potten, straf** 'punish-
ment' – **straffen, stuk** 'piece' – **stukken**[8]

Note: The two stressed feminine endings **-es** and **-in** belong here, e.g.
boerin 'farmer's wife' – **boerinnen, lerares** 'female teacher' – **leraressen**.

(g) Nouns ending in **-ee** add **-ën**:

orchidee 'orchid' – **orchideeën, zee** 'sea' – **zeeën**

Exceptions: words still regarded as French: e.g. **soiree** 'party' –
soirees. Also the Latin word **dominee** 'reverend' – **dominees**

7.2.2.2 *There is a group of very common nouns that have a short
vowel in the singular but a long vowel in the plural*, i.e. nouns which

---

[8] **Stuks** occurs too but with the meaning of items, e.g. **Ik heb tien stuks gekocht** 'I bought
ten (pencils, balls etc.)'.

one would expect to find under (f) above which do not double the consonant and thus the vowel is pronounced long.

Common gender

dag	day	**dagen**
god	God	**goden**
hertog	duke	**hertogen**
hof	court, yard	**hoven**
oorlog	war	**oorlogen**
slag	blow, battle	**slagen**
staf	staff	**staven**[9]
weg	road	**wegen**

Neuter

bad	bath	**baden**
bedrag	amount	**bedragen**
bevel	order	**bevelen**
blad	leaf of a book, magazine	**bladen**[10]
dak	roof	**daken**
dal	valley	**dalen**
gat	hole	**gaten**
gebed	prayer	**gebeden**
gebod	commandment	**geboden**
gebrek	failing	**gebreken**
glas	glass	**glazen**
graf	grave	**graven**[11]
hol	cave	**holen**
lot	lottery ticket	**loten**
pad	path	**paden**[12]
schot	shot	**schoten**[13]
slot	lock, castle	**sloten**
spel	game	**spelen**[14]
vat	barrel	**vaten**[15]
verbod	prohibition	**verboden**
verdrag	treaty	**verdragen**

---

[9] **Staven** is also the plural of **de staaf** 'stick'.
[10] **Het blad** 'leaf of a tree' becomes **bladeren**.
[11] **Graven** is also the plural of **de graaf** 'count'.
[12] **Het pad** 'toad' becomes **padden**.
[13] **De Schot** 'Scot' becomes **Schotten**.
[14] **Het spel** 'game of cards' becomes **spellen**.
[15] **Het handvat** 'handle' becomes **handvatten**.

7.2.2.3   *There is a small group of nouns with a short vowel in the singular that both lengthen and change their vowel in the plural*

gelid 'joint' – **gelederen**, **lid** 'member, limb' – **leden** 'members', but **ledematen** 'limbs', **schip** 'ship' – **schepen**, **smid** 'smith' – **smeden**, **stad** 'city' – **steden**

7.2.2.4   *Nouns ending in* **-aar** *usually take* **-en** *but are found with* **-s**

adelaar 'eagle' – **adelaren** (but **adelaars** is more common), **ambtenaren** 'official' – **ambtenaren**, **leraar** 'teacher' – **leraren**

7.2.2.5   *Nouns ending in stressed* **-ie** *add* **-en**

melodie 'tune' – **melodieën**, **symfonie** 'symphony' – **symfonieën**

Exception: **bougie** 'spark-plug' – **bougies**

Those ending in unstressed **-ie** usually take **-s** (see **-s** plurals, 7.2.1.6) but some are found with **-n** in higher style:
kolonies/koloniën 'colonies', **provincies/provinciën** 'provinces', **studies/studiën** 'studies' (compare **melodieën** etc.), but **financiën** 'finances' can only take **-n**

7.2.2.6   *Foreign nouns ending in* **-or** *usually take* **-en** *with a shift in stress to the penultimate syllable*

professor 'professor' – **professoren**, **lector** 'lecturer, reader' – **lectoren**, **motor** 'motor/engine, motorcycle' – **motoren** 'motors, engines', but **motors/motoren** means 'motorcycles', **organisator** 'organizer' – **organisatoren**, **tractor** 'tractor' – **tractors** or **tractoren** (but usually the former)

The spelling **doctor** is used for the academic title and has a plural **doctoren** or **doctors**; the physician is usually spelt **dokter** and has a plural in **-s**.

7.2.2.7   *Nouns ending in* **-e** *cause difficulty: there are those that always take* **-s** *(see* **-s** *plurals, 7.2.1.5) and there are a few that always take* **-n**

seconde 'second' **sekonden**, **echtgenote** 'female spouse' **echtgenoten**

There are also those that take either, both endings being very common – this is particularly the case for nouns formed from adjectives by the addition of **-te**:

ziekte 'sickness, disease', **hoogte** 'height', **vlakte** 'plain', **type** 'type'

7.2.2.8   *Many Dutch nouns that originally ended in -de in the singular (and still do in formal style) add -n to the -de in the plural*

bladzij(de) 'page' – **bladzijden, la(de)** 'drawer' – **laden, tree/trede** 'step' – **treden** (also **trees** or **treeën**)

7.2.2.9   *The nouns koe 'cow' and vlo 'flea' insert an -i- before -en*

koeien, vlooien (colloquially one also hears **vlooi** in the singular)

7.2.2.10   *Nouns (usually abstracts) ending in -heid form their plural in -heden*

moeilijkheid 'difficulty' – **moeilijkheden, schoonheid** 'beauty' – **schoonheden**

7.2.3   -eren PLURALS

There is a small group of neuter nouns that preserve an old plural ending in -**eren** (compare Eng. *children*):

been	bone	**beenderen**[16]
blad	leaf	**bladeren**[17]
ei	egg	**eieren**
gelid	joint	**gelederen**[18]
gemoed	mind	**gemoederen**
goed	goods, wares	**goederen**
hoen	fowl	**hoenderen**[19]
kalf	calf	**kalveren**
kind	child	**kinderen**
lam	lamb	**lammeren**
lied	song	**liederen**
rad	wheel	**raderen**
rund	cow, ox	**runderen**
volk	nation, people	**volkeren**[20]

Kleren 'clothes' is a contracted form of **klederen** (an archaic plural form of **kleed**).

---

[16] **Been** 'leg' goes **benen**.
[17] **Blad** 'leaf of a book, magazine' goes **bladen**, e.g. **dagbladen** 'daily newspapers'.
[18] See -**en** plurals, i.e. 7.2.2.3.
[19] Also **hoenders**, which is more common than **hoenderen**.
[20] Also **volken**.

7.2.4 IRREGULAR PLURAL FORMATIONS

7.2.4.1 *Words ending in **-man** have a plural in **-lieden** or **-lui**, the former being more formal:*

zeeman 'sailor' – **zeelieden/zeelui**; **koopman** 'merchant' – **kooplieden/ kooplui.**

Some words never employ **-lui**, only **-lieden** by virtue of their elevated meaning:

edelman 'nobleman' – **edellieden, raadsman** 'councillor' – **raadslieden**

Exceptions: **muzelman** 'Muslim' – **muzelmannen, Noorman** 'Viking' – **Noormannen, vuilnisman** 'rubbishmen' – **vuilnismannen**; **Engelsman** 'Englishman' – **Engelsen, Fransman** 'Frenchman' – **Fransen**; **buurman/-vrouw** 'neighbour' – **buren** (males and females combined)

7.2.4.2 *Words of Greek and Latin origin*

(a) Nouns ending in **-um** can take **-s** or **-a**, the former being more common:

album 'album' – **albums** (never **alba**), **atheneum** 'high school' – **atheneums, datum** 'date' – **datums, decennium** 'decade' – **decennia** (never **decenniums**), **museum** 'museums'– **museums** or **musea**

(b) Nouns ending in **-us** referring to people take **-i**:

doctoràndus 'Dutch academic title' – **doctoràndi/doctoràndussen, històricus**[21] 'historian' – **històrici, mùsicus**[21] 'musician' – **mùsici, neerlàndicus**[21] 'graduate in Dutch' – **neerlàndici**; also **catàlogus** 'catalogue' – **catàlogi/catàlogussen** (the accents are not normally written – they are only used here to show the stress)

(c) The nouns **examen** 'examination' and **tentamen** 'preliminary exam' can take **-s** or **-ina**, i.e. **tentamens** or **tentamina**, the former being more common.

7.2.5 ENGLISH PLURALS WHICH ARE SINGULAR IN DUTCH

The following nouns are singular in Dutch and are followed by a verb in the singular when one item is referred to; those with an asterisk can of course be used in the plural when more than one item is referred to:

---

[21] The letter **c** of the singular is pronounced **k** and that of the plural is pronounced **s** (see note under 7.3.7). The words **cactus** and **circus** add **-sen**.

ashes	**de as**	politics	**de politiek**
binoculars	**de verrekijker***	pyjamas	**de pyjama***
economics	**de economie**	scissors	**de schaar***
holidays	**de vakantie***	spectacles	**de bril***
The Netherlands	**Nederland**	tongs	**de tang***
pants	**de broek***	vegetable(s)	**de groente***[22]

Note that when referring to the lives, noses, hats, coats etc. of more than one person, Dutch, unlike English, puts such nouns in the singular as each person has only one:

Die jongens hebben ons (het) leven gered.
Those boys saved our lives.

Ze hebben allemaal hun jas aangetrokken.
They all put on their coats.

7.3   FEMINIZING MASCULINE AGENTS

Dutch has a variety of endings used to denote the female of certain professions, nationalities and animals. There are actually very few rules for their use and on the whole one can best simply learn the feminine equivalents by heart. The following will, however, serve to illustrate the endings in question.

Note: There is an ever increasing tendency for the masculine form to be used even with reference to a female, e.g. **Ze is leraar (i.e. lerares) Duits op een middelbare school in Veghel** 'She is a German teacher at a secondary school in Veghel'.

7.3.1   -e

(a) This ending is commonly used with foreign words where the masculine form has a stressed ending (plural in **-n** or **-s**):

studente 'student', **docente** 'lecturer', **sociologe** 'sociologist', **telefoniste** 'telephonist', **typiste** 'typist'

(b) Also indigenous words ending in **-genoot** (plural in **-n** or **-s**):

echtgenote 'spouse', **tijdgenote** 'contemporary'

(c) The female inhabitant of most countries is designated by the adjective of nationality plus **-e** (these forms are never used in the plural, see Appendix 2, n. (a)):

---

[22] Also pl. **groentes** or **groenten**.

Australische 'Australian', **Engelse** 'English woman', **Nederlandse** 'Dutch woman'

7.3.2   -es (stressed) (plural in -sen)

lerares 'secondary teacher', **onderwijzeres** 'primary teacher', **zangeres** 'singer', **barones** 'baroness', **prinses** 'princess'

7.3.3   -esse (stressed) (plural in -s)

This ending is used to feminize masculine professions ending in **-aris**:

secretaresse 'secretary', **bibliothecaresse** 'librarian'

7.3.4   -euse (stressed) (plural in -s)

This ending is only found in words of French origin of which the masculine ends in **-eur**:

ouvreuse 'usherette', **masseuse** 'masseuse', **coupeuse** '(tailor's) cutter'

7.3.5   -in (stressed) (plural in -nen)

(a) Just a few nationalities take this ending:

Friezin 'Frisian woman', **Russin** 'Russian woman'

(b) A few animals take this ending:

berin 'bear', **leeuwin** 'lioness', **wolvin** 'wolf'

(c) Several other nouns:

boerin 'farmer's wife', **godin** 'goddess', **gravin** 'countess', **jodin** 'Jewess', **keizerin** 'empress', **kokkin** 'cook', **negerin** 'negress', **vorstin** 'monarch', **vriendin** 'friend'

7.3.6   -ster

(a) Nouns derived from verb stems take this ending (plural in **-s**):

kapster 'hairdresser', **schrijfster** 'authoress', **toneelspeelster** 'actress', **verkoopster** 'shop assistant', **verpleegster** 'nurse', **werkster** 'cleaning lady'

(b) Nouns ending in **-stander** and **-ganger** take this ending (plural in **-s**):

voorstandster 'supporter', **voorgangster** 'predecessor'

7.3.7   -trice

Nouns of French origin ending in **-teur** take this ending (plural in **-s**):

actrice 'actress', **directrice** 'director'

Note: Some nouns of Latin origin ending in **-us** formerly took an **-a** ending to denote the female; nowadays, however, the masculine form is usually used (plural in **-i**, where formerly the plural of feminine forms in **-a** was **-ae** or **'s**); the **-a** ending is still occasionally used:

musicus (formerly **musica**) 'musician', **neerlandicus** (formerly **neer-landica**) 'graduate in Dutch'

7.4   POSSESSION

The English possessive 's' is known in Dutch but is not used as extensively as in English. Generally it is only commonly used after proper nouns:

Annekes boek, Vaders auto

Close relatives preceded by a possessive can employ this **s** too:

mijn moeders keuken 'my mother's kitchen', **zijn broers brommer** 'his brother's moped'

All other nouns are better used with a **van** construction:

de auto van mijn oom 'my uncle's car', **de hoofdstad van Duitsland** 'Germany's capital/the capital of Germany'

Note: **Een vriend van mijn broer** 'a friend of my brother's'. The above is a safe guide to correct spoken and written forms, but in practice the **s** forms are commonly heard in instances not recommended here.

The apostrophe is only used to denote possession when the proper noun ends in a vowel, **s** or **z**:

Otto's boek, Rubens' schilderijen, Liz' fiets

Colloquially one will often hear **Hans z'n vriend, mijn oom z'n auto, Anneke d'r vriend, de buren d'r/hun hond** (see 8.2.2).

Note: The official names of phenomena derived from people's names as in the following examples employ a **van** construction rather than using a genitive s as is the case in English: **de komeet van Halley** 'Halley's comet', **de wet van Grimm** 'Grimm's law', **de ziekte van Parkinson** 'Parkinson's disease'.

7.5   DIMINUTIVES (**verkleinwoorden**)

The diminutive is used extensively in Dutch with many connotations of meaning. The mechanics of diminutizing a noun are dealt with here first and then the semantic implications of the diminutive. The various ways of forming the diminutive are generally speaking a question of phonetics, i.e. assimilation of the ending to the sound at the end of the noun.

7.5.1   FORMATION

7.5.1.1.   -je

The basic form is the addition of **-je** to the end of the noun:

aap	– **aapje**	**huis**	– **huisje**
boek	– **boekje**	**oog**	– **oogje**
fornuis	– **fornuisje**[23]	**pet**	– **petje**
hand	– **handje**	**zak**	– **zakje**

7.5.1.2   -tje

(a) Words containing a long vowel or diphthong, either final or followed by **l**, **n** or **r**, add **-tje** to the noun:

ei	– **eitje**	**stoel**	– **stoeltje**
ui	– **uitje**	**schoen**	– **schoentje**
vrouw	– **vrouwtje**	**deur**	– **deurtje**

(b) Words ending in **-el**, **-en** and **-er** also take **-tje**:

tafel	– **tafeltje**	**kamer**	– **kamertje**
deken	– **dekentje**	**jongen**	– **jongetje**

7.5.1.3   -etje

(a) Words containing a short vowel and ending in **l**, **r**, **m**, **n** and **ng** (but not **-ing**, see below), add **-etje**:

bel	– **belletje**	**kam**	– **kammetje**
ster	– **sterretje**	**pan**	– **pannetje**
bloem	– **bloemetje**[24]	**ding**	– **dingetje**

---

[23] **Sj** is pronounced [ʃ] i.e. like English 'sh'.
[24] A little flower is either **bloemetje** or **bloempje** but the former can also mean 'a bunch of flowers', e.g. **Ik heb een bloemetje voor haar meegenomen** 'I took along a bunch of flowers for her'.

(b) A few nouns containing a short vowel ending in **b**, **g** and **p** add **-etje** (but most will be found in the first group):

krab	– krabbetje	big	– biggetje
rib	– ribbetje	vlag	– vlaggetje
slab	– slabbetje	kin	– kinnetje

Some nouns with these characteristics have two diminutive forms (one as described in the first group (7.5.1.1) and one as described here):

brug	– brugje, bruggetje
rug	– rugje, ruggetje
weg	– wegje, weggetje
pop	– popje, poppetje[25]

7.5.1.4   -pje

(a) Words ending in **m** add **-pje**:

boom	– boompje	arm	– armpje
duim	– duimpje	bezem	– bezempje

(b) Many of those monosyllabic neuter nouns which have a short vowel in the singular but a long vowel in the plural (see 7.2.2.2) also have a long vowel in the diminutive form:

blad (pl. bladeren)	– blaadje	pad (pl. paden)	– paadje[27]
gat (pl. gaten)	– gaatje[26]	schip (pl. schepen)	– scheepje
glas (pl. glazen)	– glaasje	vat (pl. vaten)	– vaatje

but

dak (pl. daken)	– dakje	spel (pl. spelen)	– spelletje

Three nouns in this category have two forms:

dag (pl. dagen)	– dagje, daagje(s)
lot (pl. loten)	– lotje, lootje
rad (pl. raderen)	– radje, raadje (also radertje)

The nouns **kind** and **kleren** (a plural) have a special form:

kindje 'little child' (can also take a plural **-s**)
kindertjes 'little children' (always plural)
kleertjes 'little clothes' (always plural)

---

[25] There is a semantic difference between these two – the former means 'dolly' whereas the latter refers to drawn stick figures.
[26] **Gatje** = little backside/bottom, **gaatje** = little hole.
[27] **Paadje** = little path, **padje** = little toad.

7.5.1.5 -kje

Nouns ending in **-ing** change the **g** to **k** before adding **-je**, but nouns ending in **-ling** take **-etje**:

koning	**– koninkje**		**wandeling**	**– wandelingetje**
regering	**– regerinkje**		**leerling**	**– leerlingetje**
		also	**tekening**	**– tekeningetje**

7.5.1.6 Spelling peculiarities

Nouns ending in long vowels (i.e. an open syllable) need to double the vowel when the diminutive ending is added (i.e. making a closed syllable) to preserve the long sound:

oma	**– omaatje**
auto	**– autootje**
paraplu	**– parapluutje**
café	**– cafeetje**

7.5.1.7 Variant forms of the diminutive

In the west of The Netherlands a colloquial variant of the diminutive exists which is sometimes also used in cultured speech for humorous effect – the ending is **-ie**, e.g.:

huisie, jochie, koekie, lichie (from **licht**), **meisie**

In the south of The Netherlands and in Belgium the **-je** form is often colloquially replaced by **-ke**, with the phonetic variant **-ske**:

huiske, meiske, slakske

This ending is common in female first names, even in the north:

Anneke, Aafke

Note: In Frisian first names the **-ke** ending indicates a male, e.g. **Jouke**.

An archaic variant found in names is **-ken**:

Manneken Pis, Duyfken

7.5.2 SEMANTIC IMPLICATIONS OF THE DIMINUTIVE

It is particularly the nuances of meaning expressed by the diminutive which make it so peculiarly unique in Dutch but also so difficult for non-native speakers to master. The following can only serve as a guide to its main uses; its potential is infinite as it is very much a productive ending and it is not merely restricted to nouns (see 7.5.3). On the whole the connotation of a diminutive form is a positive one, but sometimes it fulfils a derogatory function (see (f) below).

(a) The diminutive's basic function is to make things small:

huis 'house'   > **huisje** 'little house, cottage'
kap 'hood'   > **Roodkapje** 'Little Red Riding Hood'

But even when the diminutive merely indicates that something is small, the diminutized noun is commonly preceded by the adjective **klein**.

De sprinkhaan zit onder een klein struikje.
The grasshopper is sitting under a little shrub.

Hij woont op een heel klein kamertje.
He's living in a teeny weeny room.

(b) The diminutive is also used as a form of endearment; first names (and not just of children, but particularly women's names) are often diminutized:

Jantje, **Frankje**, **Marietje**, **Annetje**

(c) Often the diminutive form of a noun renders a completely separate lexical item in English:

brood	loaf of bread	**broodje**	bread roll
kaart	map	**kaartje**	ticket
koek	cake	**koekje**	biscuit
koop	buy	**koopje**	bargain
lepel	spoon	**lepeltje**	teaspoon
Mongool	Mongol	**mongooltje**	mongoloid child
neef	cousin (male)	**neefje**	nephew
nicht	cousin (female)	**nichtje**	niece
scheermes	razor	**scheermesje**	razor blade
schotel	dish	**schoteltje**	saucer
viool	violin	**viooltje**	violet, pansy

The diminutives of **broer** and **zuster** are **broertje** and **zusje** (not **zustertje**, which refers to a nurse) respectively; these forms often render 'younger brother/sister', but this is not necessarily always the case:

Mijn broertje heeft er een.
My younger brother has one.

The diminutive forms of **man** and **wijf** or **vrouw** are used for male and female with reference to animals:

Is het een mannetje of een wijfje/vrouwtje?
Is it a male or a female?

Het is een wijfjesaap/vrouwtjesaap, geen mannetjesaap.
It is a female monkey, not a male monkey.

The latter forms are used chiefly for animals for which there is no separate word for male and female, i.e. not for **paard** 'horse', for example, where one can use the words **hengst** 'stallion' and **merrie** 'mare', but English is much the same as Dutch in this respect.

(d) The diminutive is used to itemize some quantitative nouns, i.e. nouns that stand for a collective quantity (particularly varieties of food and drink) which take on the meaning of one item of that substance when they bear the diminutive ending:

advocaat	advocaat	**een advocaatje**	a glass of advocaat
bier	beer	**een biertje**	a glass of beer
chocola	chocolate	**een chocolaatje**	a chocolate
gebak	pastry, cakes	**een gebakje**	a pastry, little cake
hout	wood	**een houtje**	a bit of wood
ijs	ice-cream	**een ijsje**	an ice-cream
kauwgom	chewing gum	**een kauwgommetje**	a piece of gum
krijt	chalk	**een krijtje**	a piece of chalk
likeur	liqueur	**een likeurtje**	a glass of liqueur
muziek	music	**een muziekje**	a piece of music
snoep	confectionery	**een snoepje**	a sweet
worst	sausage	**een worstje**	a sausage

These endings can have other connotations, however:

een lekker wijntje 'a very nice wine' (not a glass of wine)

(e) A few nouns exist only as diminutives:

meisje	girl (derived from **meid**)
lachertje	ridiculous suggestion, situation etc.
dubbeltje	10 cents
kwartje	25 cents
op het nippertje	in the nick of time

The names of children's games contain the diminutive (a productive ending):

krijgertje spelen	to play tag
verstoppertje spelen	to play hide and seek
touwtje springen	to skip
vadertje en moedertje spelen	to play mummies and daddies

(f) Occasionally the diminutive can give a derogatory connotation to a noun:

een burgermannetje	a petit bourgeois
een raar taaltje	a strange lingo
een boertje van buten[28]	a yokel

7.5.3 DIMINUTIVES OF OTHER PARTS OF SPEECH

It is possible for words other than nouns to take a diminutive ending, thus giving a new connotation to the words concerned or even a completely new meaning.

7.5.3.1 Adverbs are the most notable example of words other than nouns that have this potential; the ending used is **-jes** (with phonetic variants **-tjes** and **-pjes**). Its function is one of toning down the intensity of meaning. In the spoken language it is still productive (see 10.8.2):

eventjes	just a minute	**stilletjes**	quietly, secretively
gezelligjes	cosily	**stiekempjes**	secretively
knusjes	cosily	**strakjes**	in a moment
losjes	loosely	**warmpjes**	warmly
netjes	neatly	**zachtjes**	quietly, softly

Het is hier erg knusjes, hè?
It is very cosy here, isn't it?
Wij zitten er warmpjes bij. (fig.)
We're well-off.

7.5.3.2 Adjectives used as nouns can have a diminutive ending; this form of the adjective is commonly used where we say in English 'a white one', 'a little one' where the 'one' cannot be translated literally (see 9.6.1):

een witje (= **een wit**), **een kleintje** (= **een klein**)

also

de kleintjes	the little ones (children or things)
een nieuwtje	a piece of news

7.5.3.3 Numerals can also take the ending in certain expressions; 'on my/your/his own' etc. is always **in m'n/je/z'n eentje**. A more familiar form

---

[28] **Buten** is a dialectal form of **buiten** and adds to the yokel image of the expression by being used instead of the standard form.

of **met z'n tweeën/drieën** etc. is **met z'n tweetjes/drietjes** etc. (see 10.8.2). Also: **Geef me (er) nog eentje** 'Give me another one'.

7.5.3.4   The expressions **een onderonsje** 'a tête-à-tête' and **ietsje** 'a little' show the diminutive being suffixed to *pronouns*.

Mag het ietsje meer zijn? (shopkeeper to customer when putting something on a scale)
It's a bit over – is that all right?

The adverb **iets** 'somewhat' can also take it:

Ik ben ietsje moe. (colloquially also: **ietsjes moe**)
I am somewhat tired.

7.5.3.5   **Een moetje** 'a shotgun marriage' is a quaint example of a noun formed from a *verbal particle* by addition of the diminutive.

7.5.3.6   There are a few expressions derived from *prepositions* incorporating the diminutive:

toetje 'dessert', **uitje** (from **uitstapje)** 'excursion', **een ommetje maken** 'to go for a short walk', **rondje** 'round (of drinks)'

8 PRONOUNS
(voornaamwoorden)

8.1 PERSONAL PRONOUNS (persoonlijke voornaam woorden)

There are two series of personal pronouns: subject and object pronouns. The forms in the right-hand columns are the unemphatic forms; those that are not normally written are given in brackets. Some pronouns do not have unemphatic forms.

Subject				*Object*		
Singular	1.	**ik**[1]	(**'k**)	**mij**	**me**	
	2.	**jij**	**je**	**jou**	**je**	
		u		**u**		
	3.	**hij**[2]	(**ie**)	**hem**[2]	(**'m**)	
		zij[2]	**ze**	**haar**[2, 3]	(**'r, d'r**)	
		het[2, 4]	(**'t**)	**het**[2]	(**'t**)	
Plural	1.	**wij**	**we**	**ons**		
	2.	**jullie**	**je**	**jullie**	**je**	
		u		**u**		
	3.	**zij**[4, 5]	**ze**	**hen/hun**[5]	**ze** (people)	
				die	**ze** (things and people)	

8.1.1 UNEMPHATIC PRONOUNS

The distinction between emphatic and unemphatic pronouns, which also exists in English in the spoken language (but not in the written: compare

---

[1] An extra emphatic form **ikke** also exists in the spoken language only, e.g. **Jij hebt mijn fiets gestolen, niet waar? Wat, ikke?** 'You stole my bike, didn't you? Who, me?'

[2] Neuter words referring to male or female beings (e.g. **het jongetje, het meisje, het wijf**) are replaced by masculine or feminine pronouns (see also 8.5.2, n. 14), e.g. **Het jongetje is ziek geworden maar hij wordt zeker beter** 'The little boy is sick but he's sure to get better'.

[3] Whether **haar** is pronounced unemphatically as **'r** or **d'r** depends on its phonetic environment, e.g. **Ik heb 'r in de stad gezien** 'I saw her in town', **Ik hou d'r in de gaten** (i.e. after a vowel) 'I'm keeping an eye on her'. But the unemphatic form of **haar** as a possessive adjective (see 8.2) is always **d'r**. Common in speech but rare in writing is the form **ze** for unemphatic **haar** meaning 'her'. Usually the context will indicate whether **ze** means 'her' or 'them'.

[4] **Het** can also be used to translate English 'they' (see 8.1.2.3(c)).

[5] In colloquial Dutch **hun** also occurs as a subject pronoun meaning 'they' but it can only refer to people. This practice, which is becoming very common these days, is better avoided as many still regard it as substandard, and it is certainly never written, e.g. **Hun liggen in bed** 'They are lying in bed'.

'you/ya'), is very important in Dutch. One important difference from English is that many, but not all the unemphatic forms, are written. If no particular stress is required, it is of no consequence whether one writes the emphatic or unemphatic form of the subject pronoun:

Heb je je vrouw gesproken? Heb jij je vrouw gesproken?
Did you speak to your wife? (no particular emphasis)

or

Heb jij je vrouw gesproken of heeft Marie je vrouw gesproken?
Did you speak to your wife or did Marie speak to your wife?
   (emphasis on 'you' and Marie)

but not

Heb jij/je jouw vrouw gesproken? (unless a stress on **jouw** is implied)

(a) The unemphatic form of the possessive **zijn** is written only in such expressions as **met z'n tweeën, op z'n best/hoogst/minst** where it must be used (see 10.1.2.4). Also the colloquial forms **mijn broer z'n auto** and **mijn zuster d'r man**, if ever written, require the unemphatic form (see 8.2.2).

(b) The unemphatic form of **jullie** can be used when **jullie** has already been employed as the subject of the sentence; **jullie** can then be followed by an unemphatic possessive or reflexive form:

Jullie kunnen je onmogelijk vergissen. (where **je** is a reflexive)
You can't possibly make a mistake.

Jullie moeten je snoepjes in je zak stoppen. (where **je** is a possessive)
You should put your sweets in your pocket.

The unemphatic subject form **je** can only be used when a previous clause or sentence has indicated that this **je** stands for **jullie** and not for **jij**. In this case a singular verb is used even though **je** is standing for **jullie**:

Jullie kunnen morgenavond komen en als je gegeten hebt, kunnen we naar de bioscoop gaan.
You can come tomorrow night and when you've eaten, we can go to the movies.

It is very common in spoken Dutch to begin a sentence with **jullie** to indicate that one means you-plural, and then to continue the conversation with **je** + singular verb; more than one **jullie** in a sentence sounds clumsy.

(c) **U** is officially both a singular and a plural pronoun. However, often **jullie** is used as an unemphatic or rather neutral form of plural **u**. Because

u demands a singular verb it can sound as if it refers to one person and for this reason is often replaced by **jullie**, but not in contexts where one must mind ones p's and q's with regard to the form of address.

(d) Unemphatic **hij** is pronounced **ie** only when it follows the verb and the **-t** ending can act as a glide. If it is ever written, which is rare, it is usually hyphenated to the verb:

Heeft-ie dat gedaan?
Did he do that?

Vandaag gaat-ie naar Polen.
He's going to Poland today.

The difference between this and the referential **die** (see 8.1.2.5(c)) is often not heard.

heeft-ie, heeft die

Ie will also be heard after other words ending in **-t**, e.g. **Weet-ie wat ie vandaag moet doen?** 'Does he know what he has to do today?' It sometimes occurs after consonants other than **-t**, e.g. **Vertel me waar ie woont** 'Tell me where he lives'. Only in avant-garde publications will one find **ie** sometimes written.

In natural speech an **n** is commonly inserted before an **ie** or an **ik** after a verbal form ending in **-de** or **-te** (i.e. in the imperfect singular of weak verbs):

Toen rookte-n-ie/ik een sjekkie.
He then smoked a roll-your-own.

Vorig jaar woonde-n-ie/ik nog in Amsterdam.
Last year he was still living in Amsterdam.

(e) Just as in English where the somewhat stilted pronoun 'one' is usually replaced by unemphatic 'you', so in Dutch **men** is replaced by **je** (never **jij**) in general speech and can also be used with this meaning to people one otherwise says **u** to; the emphatic form **jij** can only mean 'you', i.e. the person one is talking to. Similarly **ze** can replace **men** just as in English 'they' replaces 'one'; the difference between **je** and **ze** in such contexts is the same as between 'you' and 'they' in English, i.e. in the latter case the speaker and the person being addressed are not included in the action:

Men heeft de onafhankelijkheid van dat land erkend.
Ze hebben de onafhankelijkheid van dat land erkend.
One has/they have recognized that country's independence.

The pronoun **we** is often used in an impersonal sense too, just as in English.

Hier hebben we het Paleis op de Dam.
Here we have the Palace on the Dam.

See also 11.12.4.9.

8.1.2   REMARKS ON SUBJECT AND OBJECT PRONOUNS

8.1.2.1   *Second person forms of address:* **jij, u, gij, jullie**

Anyone who has attempted to learn another European language will be acquainted with the existence of two forms of second person address. In the ABN of The Netherlands the two forms are **jij** and **u**. Broadly speaking one can compare the usage of the two with similar couplets in other languages, i.e. French **tu/vous**, German **du/Sie**, but in some cases usage sometimes differs quite dramatically from those languages, as some of the following examples illustrate.

The verb **tutoyeren**, borrowed from French, means to be on **jij** terms with someone. The expression **jijen en jouen** means the same thing but is pejorative:

Ken je de directeur goed? Ja wel, we tutoyeren elkaar al lang.
Do you know the manager well? For sure, we've been on first name
    terms for ages.

Ze hebben iedereen zitten jijen en jouen en daar hield ik niet van.
They were addressing everybody with jij and I didn't approve of it.

(a) Use of **u**:

In addition to the usual usage of the polite form of address for strangers, elders, etc., **u** is also employed in the following cases where it would not be used in German, for instance.

1   A minority of people still say **u** to their parents. This was very common prior to the war and can still be found in some upper-middle-class families.
2   It is commonly used for grandparents and aunts and uncles, and is always used for God.

U/uw are still sometimes written with capital letters in very formal letters, but this tradition is fast waning and is certainly no longer the norm.

(b) Use of **jij**

Generally speaking **jij** is used for friends, relatives (with the above exceptions), children and animals. Teachers use **jij** for schoolchildren of all ages, but the student must say **u** to his teachers, but individual teachers may have a preference for mutual use of first names and thus **jij**. Young people of comparable age often call each other **jij** even if they are unacquainted and university students or members of a club will automatically say **jij** to each other; in such cases it is an expression of solidarity and equality.

Generally speaking, however, knowing exactly who to say **jij** to or when in an **u** relationship it is appropriate to start saying **jij**, is a matter of feeling and is not an issue that even the Dutch are always comfortable with.

The following are two common ways of suggesting to your interlocutor that you have no objection to them calling you **jij**:

Zeg maar je!	Say jij to me.
Ik heet Piet/Joke.	My name is Piet/Joke. (in other words, use my first name and thus also **jij**)

(c) Use of **gij**:

In Belgium **gij** (unemphatic **ge**) commonly replaces **jij**, but the latter is becoming increasingly popular as the south begins to follow the north more and more in linguistic matters. Dialectally **gij** is also used in the plural. The object and possessive forms of **gij** are **u** and **uw** respectively.

Note: Historically this form is older than **jij** and **u** and for this reason it was the standard written form for centuries, even in Holland, while in Flanders it never died out. It is this form that was used in the seventeenth century States Translation of the Bible and thus, if it is used in the north at all, it usually has a biblical connotation. **Gij** has the same ring about it to the Dutch as 'thou' to the English. **Gij** has its own specific form of the verb: **ge zijt, ge waart, ge zoudt** (see 11.1.1 note), i.e. old plural forms. An even more antiquated form, **gijlieden**, a plural form used to clearly distinguish singular from plural **gij**, is sometimes encountered in older texts.

(d) Use of **jullie**:

For the use of **jullie** as the plural of **u** see 8.1.1(c). The origin of this form is **jelie(den)** (i.e. you people) and is often found as **jelui** (stress on second syllable) in some older literary works.

8.1.2.2   The object pronouns *hen* and *hun*

Historically there is no distinction between **hen** and **hun**. The two were originally simply phonetic variants of the one word predominating in separate dialects. The distinction made between the two in present-day written ABN is an artificial one imposed upon the language by early grammarians. The artificiality of the distinction is reflected in Dutch speech today where hardly anybody uses the two according to the rules prescribed. It should be noted, however, that the Dutch always use **hun** where grammar strictly speaking demands **hen**, a form which is actually seldom used in the spoken language. In writing one should attempt to use them correctly, as to do otherwise suggests one is illiterate, whereas to use **hen** in everyday speech sounds pedantic.

The official rule is:

hen is the direct object and is also used after prepositions.

hun is the indirect object, the only personal pronoun to have a separate dative form.

Hij heeft hen later in de stad gezien.
He later saw them in town.

Ik heb de informatie aan hen gegeven.
I gave the information to them.

but

Ik heb hun de informatie gegeven.

The distinction is similar to the following in English:

I gave the information to them. (**aan hen**)
I gave them the information. (**hun**)

One is well advised in all the above cases to use **ze** if one is in doubt, but **ze** can of course only be used as an unemphatic pronoun:

Ik heb de informatie aan ze gegeven.
Ik heb ze de informatie gegeven.

It is particularly difficult to distinguish whether **hen** or **hun** is required in cases like the following:

Wij wensten hun geluk.
We congratulated them. (lit. We wished them luck.)

Het lukte hun de top van de berg te bereiken.
They succeeded in getting to the top of the mountain.

Hun werd toen verboden bij deze verkiezingen te stemmen.
They were forbidden to vote in these elections.

Ik beloofde hun dat ik zou komen.
I promised them that I would come.

Ik heb het hun beloofd.
I promised them it.

Ik zei hun dat ik morgen zou komen.
I told them that I'd be coming tomorrow.

In all these cases **hun** should be used because the indirect object is required; this is clearly illustrated by the last two examples where the sentence can be rephrased with prepositions:

Ik heb het aan hen beloofd.
Ik zei tegen hen dat ik morgen zou komen.

When in doubt, always use **hun** as this is at least in line with what is said, regardless of what 'should' be written, and the Dutch themselves are very insecure on this point.

8.1.2.3   'It' as a subject pronoun

(a) It should be noted that singular common gender nouns (whether persons or things) are regarded as being masculine when a pronoun replaces them:

Die stoel heb ik gisteren gekocht. Hij is erg mooi, vind je niet?
I bought that chair yesterday. It's very nice, don't you think?

(b) In Belgium the old distinction between masculine and feminine is still very much alive (see 8.1.2.4(b) below):

Doe de deur dicht! Nee, ik wil dat ze open blijft.
Shut the door. No, I want it to stay open.

Even in Holland abstract nouns are replaced in formal style by **zij**. This applies to abstract common gender nouns ending in:

-heid	**waarheid, eenheid**, etc.
-ie	**commissie, politie**, etc.
-erij	**uitgeverij, bakkerij**, etc.
-nis	**kennis, erfenis**, etc.
-ing	**regering, regeling**, etc.
-st	**kunst, winst**, etc.
-schap	**wetenschap, verwantschap**, etc.[6]
-de, -te	**liefde, begeerte**, etc.

De regering heeft vandaag haar besluiten bekendgemaakt.
The government made its decisions known today.

De discussie vond haar hoogtepunt dertig jaar geleden.
The debate attained its climax thirty years ago.

---

[6] Note that some nouns ending in **-schap** are neuter: **landschap, lidmaatschap** (see 7.1.1.22 and 7.1.2.15).

Female animals, e.g. **koe**, **merrie** etc., can be replaced by **zij** but one does commonly hear the Dutch using **hij** with reference to such animals:

Zie je die kat? Hij heeft net gejongd.
Do you see that cat? She/it has just had kittens.

(c) There is an added complication in the translation of an 'it' referring to common gender nouns. There are instances where an 'it' which one would expect to be **hij** is in fact **het**. The rule is as follows: As subject of the verb **zijn** (and less frequently of **blijken**, **blijven**, **lijken**, **schijnen** and **worden**) the pronoun **het** is used to refer to all nouns and persons (singular and plural) when:

1 the predicate contains a noun; or
2 the predicate contains an adjective used as a noun, but not when the predicate contains simply an adjective on its own; then **het** is used only for singular neuter nouns:[7]

Deze stoel heb ik gisteren gekocht. Het was een heel dure.
I bought this chair yesterday. It was a very expensive one.

but

Deze stoel heb ik gisteren gekocht. Hij was erg duur.
I bought this chair yesterday. It was very expensive.

De stem van mijn zusje is erg zacht, maar het is wel een mooie.
My sister's voice is very soft, but it is a very nice one.

but

De stem van mijn zusje is erg zacht, maar hij is wel erg mooi.
My sister's voice is very soft, but it is very nice.

Het zijn Duitsers die naast ons wonen.
They are Germans living next-door to us.

but

Ze zijn Duits, de mensen die naast ons wonen.
They are German, the people living next-door to us.

Ik heb twee glazen gebroken. Het waren antieke glazen.
I broke two glasses. They were antique glasses.

but

Ik heb twee glazen gebroken. Ze waren antiek.
I broke two glasses. They were antique.

---

[7] This is similar to the use of 'ce' versus 'il/elle' and 'ils/elles' in French.

Note that when the subject is a person, **hij/zij** (i.e. both singular and plural **zij**) are also possible:

Ik weet dat hij/het een vriendelijke man is.
I know he is a nice man

Ik weet dat ze/het vriendelijke mensen zijn.
I know they are nice people.

(d) In addition to the cases mentioned under (c) where an 'it' which one would expect to be **hij** is **het**, there are also other instances where **het** is used instead of **hij**, but for which no concrete rules can be given (see also 8.1.2.4(c) below). The pronoun in such cases refers to an action or state rather than to a noun in the first clause, or sometimes the antecedent is an abstract concept:

Je moet de oostkust bezoeken. Het is er prachtig. (but **Die is prachtig.**)
You should visit the east coast. It is beautiful there. (It is beautiful.)

Hij liet de auto langs de weg staan, want hij wist dat het daar veilig zou zijn.
(see 8.1.2.5(c) below)
He left the car on the side of the road because he knew it would be safe there.

De boerderij van mijn oom is vlakbij Zwolle. Het is ongeveer een kwartier met de auto.
My uncle's farm is close to Zwolle. It is about a quarter of an hour by car.

Is de tandpasta op? Ja, het is op. (uncountable material noun)[8]
Is the tooth-paste finished? Yes, it is finished.

Is de tube tandpasta leeg? Ja, hij is leeg. (countable object)
Is the tube of tooth-paste empty? Yes, it is empty.

8.1.2.4 'It' as an object pronoun

(a) When an object pronoun 'it' refers to a common gender noun, **hem** is used in Dutch, not **het**:

Ik heb een antieke kast gekocht. Wil je hem zien?
I've bought an antique cupboard. Would you like to see it?

---

[8] Such nouns, called **stofnamen** in Dutch, are regarded by some speakers as feminine and are replaced by **ze**, but this practice is fast waning.

Ik had een tafel voor mijn moeder gekocht maar ze wilde hem niet hebben.

I bought a table for my mother but she doesn't want it.

(b) Those speakers for whom certain non-personal nouns are still regarded as feminine (see 8.1.2.3(b) above) **ze** is used as an object pronoun instead of **hem** (and never **haar/d'r**, which can only be used with reference to people):

Wat heb je met je oude tafel gedaan? Ik heb ze verkocht.
    (Southern Dutch)
What have you done with your old table? I've sold it.

(c) On occasions one will hear **het** as an object pronoun where one would expect **hem**. As in 8.1.2.3(d) above, the reference here is to an action or state rather than to the common gender noun in the previous sentence:

Wat een rare lucht! Nou, ik vind het lekker. (i.e. **Ik vind het lekker ruiken.**)

What a strange smell. Well, I like it.

Er klonk een vlugge stap op de trap, maar zij hoorde het niet. (i.e. **het stappen**)

There was a quick footstep on the staircase, but she didn't hear it.

Ik hou morgen een lezing, maar ik weet nog niet of ik het in het Engels of in het Nederlands doe. (i.e. **het houden van de lezing**)
I am giving a talk tomorrow but I don't yet know whether I'll do it in English or Dutch.

(d) 'It' as a prepositional object (i.e. 'in it', 'on it' etc.) is neither **het** nor **hem**, but **er** + preposition. The form is analogous to English 'therein', 'thereon' etc.

Ik heb er mijn geld in gestopt.
I put my money in it.

The above separation of an **er** from its preposition is generally more common in colloquial Dutch than the following:

Ik heb mijn geld erin gestopt.

When separated, the **er** must go immediately after the finite verb and the preposition to the end of the clause, but it precedes infinitives and past participles.

De studenten hebben er de hele dag aan gedacht.
The students were thinking about it all day long.

Negatives precede the preposition:

Wij willen er de bladeren niet in doen.
We don't want to put the leaves into it.

It should be noted that a form such as **erop** etc. can also be translated by 'on them'. Whenever 'them' preceded by a preposition refers to things, it must be translated in this way:

Hier hebben jullie drie mesjes. Wil je er de aardappels mee schillen?
Here are three knives. Will you peel the potatoes with them?

For further functions of **er** see chapter 15.

(e) Note the use of an object **het** in the following expressions where no object is required in English:

Ik geloof/hoop het.   **Ik hoop het.**
I think so.   I hope so.

Ik weet het wel.   **Ik weet het niet.**
I know.   I don't know.

Ik heb het gemoeten/gekund/gemogen.
I had to/was able to/was allowed to. (see. 11.8.2)

8.1.2.5 *Die* as a referential pronoun

(a) The demonstrative **die** is very commonly used in Dutch as a substitute for **hij/hem**, **zij/haar**, **zij/hen/hun** (i.e. it can replace all third person pronouns, singular and plural) with varying connotations of meaning. Except in questions, the clause always begins with **die**; sometimes it is stressed and thus serves as an emphatic pronoun, and in other cases it acts as an unemphatic pronoun:

Is Bob er nog niet? Nee, die komt niet. (unstressed) = **hij**
Isn't Bob here yet? No, he's not coming.

Ik weet het niet maar die weten het wel. (stressed) = **zij** (they)
I don't know but *they* do.

Heb je Marie gesproken? Nee, die heb ik vandaag helemaal niet gezien. (stressed or unstressed) = **haar**
Have you spoken to Marie? No, I haven't seen her at all today.

(b) It should be noticed that **die** appears in the list of object pronouns in 8.1 as the stressed form of **ze** 'them' referring to things; the emphatic forms **hen/hun** can refer only to people and **ze**, which can be used for people or things, is by definition unemphatic; when stressing 'them' referring to inanimate objects, one must use **die**:

Hebben jullie nu al de appels opgegeten die ik vanochtend pas heb gekocht? Nee, díé hebben we niet kunnen vinden.
Have you already eaten all the apples I bought only this morning? No, we weren't able to find *them*.

(c) **Die** can also be a handy means of avoiding the difficulties caused by pronominal substitution of **hij/hem** or **het** mentioned under 8.1.2.3(d) and 8.1.2.4(c):

Hij heeft zijn auto aan de kant van de weg laten staan want hij wist dat die daar veilig zou staan.
He left his car on the side of the road because he knew that it would be safe there.

Here **die** replaces **hij**, which could be ambiguous as it might refer to the person, not the car.

8.1.2.6 *English difficulties with subject and object pronouns*

(a) Due to the subject and object forms of 'you' being the same in English, confusion as to whether to use **jij** or **jou** in Dutch can arise in instances like the following:

Hij is groter dan jij.
He is bigger than you (not **jou**, although it does occur in colloquial Dutch).

Ik vind hem aardiger dan jou. (object)
I like him more than (I like) you.

but

Ik vind hem aardiger dan jij. (subject)
I like him more than you (do).

Als ik jou was ...
If I were you ...

(b) Because of the confusion in the usage of 'I' and 'me' in colloquial English, a confusion which does not occur nearly as often in Dutch (although it is not unknown), one must be careful not to confuse **ik** and **mij** in sentences like the following:

Hij is groter dan ik. (not **mij**). (subject)
He is bigger than me (= I).

Robert heeft wat geld aan Jan en mij gegeven. (object)
Robert gave some money to Jan and I (= me).

8.1.2.7   *The use of 'to' in English before pronominal indirect objects*

Note the use or lack of **aan** in the following examples:

She gave it to the man.	**Zij gaf het aan de man.**
She gave him the book.	**Ze gaf hem het boek (de man het boek).**
She gave it to him.	**Zij gaf het hem.**
	Zij gaf het aan hem. (when emphasized)
Note: She gave it to them.	**Zij gaf het hun.**
	Zij gaf het aan hen. (when emphasized)

8.2   POSSESSIVE PRONOUNS (**bezittelijke voornaamwoorden**)

mijn	**(m'n)**	
jouw	**je**	
uw		
zijn[9]	**(z'n)**	
haar[10]	**(d'r)**	See also 8.1.1 for unemphatic forms
zijn	**(z'n)**	
ons/onze		
jullie	**je**	
uw		
hun[11]	**(d'r)**	

Note that the current use of 'their' in English to avoid an unwieldy 'his/her' is not possible in Dutch; indefinite pronouns like **iemand** 'somebody', **niemand** 'nobody', **iedereen** 'everybody' require **zijn/z'n** as their possessive form. There is no easy way in Dutch of avoiding the inherent sexism here:

Iedereen wilde zijn mening geven.
Everyone wanted to give their opinion.

---

[9] In formal style **diens** may replace the masculine possessive **zijn** (see 6.2): **De gouverneur-general van Nederlands-Indië en diens echtgenote** 'The governor-general of the Dutch East Indies and his wife'. But **diens** must be used when ambiguity can arise: **Hij ging wandelen met zijn vriend en zijn zoon** 'He went for a walk with his friend and his son' (= his own son), **Hij ging wandelen met zijn vriend en diens zoon** (= the friend's son).

[10] Neuter words referring to female beings (e.g. **het meisje**, **het wijf**) take feminine possessive pronouns (see 8.5.2, n. 14): **Het meisje heeft haar grootmoeder lekkere dingen gebracht** 'The girl took tasty things to her grandmother'.

[11] In formal (usually archaic) style **haar** can replace the possessive form **hun**, e.g. **Engelands Australische koloniën in haar ontstaan en tegenwoordige toestand** (title of an old book). This explains why the unemphatic form of possessive **hun** is **d'r**.

8.2.1   INFLECTION OF POSSESSIVES

(a) Only **ons** is inflected (i.e. becomes **onze**) before singular common gender nouns and before all plurals:

onze vriend, onze boeken but **ons boek**.

(b) In very formal style all possessives can take **-e** before feminine singular nouns and plural nouns:

Uwe Excellentie	Your Excellency
Hare Majesteit	Her Majesty
Mijne Heren	Dear Sirs

(c) Possessives sometimes take case endings in formal style or in standard expressions that have preserved such archaisms:

een uwer afgevaardigden	one of your representatives (genitive plural)
mijns inziens	in my opinion (masculine genitive singular)
te zijner tijd	in the course of time (feminine dative singular)

8.2.2   COLLOQUIAL POSSESSIVES

Expressions such as **de auto van mijn broer/mijn broers auto, het huis van mijn moeder/mijn moeders huis, de kleren van die mensen,** have an alternative form which one often hears but usually avoids in writing.

mijn broer z'n auto
mijn moeder d'r oom
die mensen d'r kleren/die mensen hun kleren

Masculine antecedents use **z'n** (i.e. **zijn**) and feminine antecedents use **d'r** while plural antecedents use **d'r** or less colloquially **hun** (see 7.4).

8.2.3   In conversational style **die z'n** and **die d'r** can replace **zijn** and **haar**.

Die z'n vriend is een vreemde figuur.
His friend is a strange person.

Die d'r man studeert in Leiden.
Her husband is studying in Leiden.

8.2.4   INDEPENDENT POSSESSIVE PRONOUNS

	Formal	*Usual*
mine	**de/het mijne**	**(die/dat) van mij**
yours	**de/het jouwe**	**(die/dat) van jou**
yours	**de/het uwe**	**(die/dat) van u**
his	**de/het zijne**	**(die/dat) van hem**
hers	**de/het hare**	**(die/dat) van haar**
its	**de/het zijne**	
ours	**de/het onze**	**(die/dat) van ons**
yours		**(die/dat) van jullie**[12]
theirs	**de/het hunne**	**(die/dat) van hen**

(a) The formal forms can be used in conversation too although **de/het hunne** sounds particularly stilted:

Hier staat mijn auto. Waar staat de jouwe?
Here is my car. Where is yours?

or

Waar staat die van jou?

Mijn huis is erg mooi maar heb je het hare gezien?
My house is very nice but have you seen hers?

or

Heb je dat van haar gezien?

Dit is de mijne en dat is de hunne. (stilted)
This is mine and that is theirs.

or

Dit is van mij en dat is van hen. (normal)

(b) When 'mine/yours/his' etc. are used predicatively, they are simply rendered by **van mij/jou/hem** etc.:

Dit boek is van ons en dat is van jullie.
This book is ours and that (one) is yours.

(c) Note that 'a friend of yours/ours/theirs' etc. is rendered in Dutch by using the following construction:

een vriend van jou/van ons/van hen

Compare: **een vriend van mijn moeder** 'a friend of my mother's'

(d) The formal forms are found in higher style with **-n** in the sense of

---

[12] **Jullie** has only the one form.

'you and yours', 'he and his' etc. (i.e. you/he and your/his family, but the reference can be to any group that belongs together):

Hij en de zijnen gingen op reis.
He and his family went travelling.

8.3 REFLEXIVE PRONOUNS (**wederkerende voornaamwoorden**)

Reflexive pronouns, both with and without verbs, plus the use of **zelf** and **eigen** are dealt with under reflexive verbs. (see 11.17)

8.4 DEMONSTRATIVE PRONOUNS (**aanwijzende voornaamwoorden**)

8.4.1   The demonstratives **deze/dit** and **die/dat** (see 6.1) can also be used pronominally just as 'this/these' and 'that/those' can be in English (although we usually say 'this one, these ones' etc.):

Die stoel was duur maar deze was erg goedkoop.
That chair was expensive but this one was very cheap.

Dat (referring to **boek**) **heb ik gisteren gekocht.**
I bought that (one) yesterday.

In very formal style an archaic genitive form of the demonstrative still occurs, e.g. **schrijver dezes** 'the author (of this document)'. (see chapter 6)
   Nadien 'afterwards' (literally 'after that'), **voordien** 'before' (literally 'before that') and **indien** 'if' (literally 'in that [case]') preserve archaic dative forms of **die**, but these are no longer felt to be such (see 10.4.1, 10.4.4, and 12.2.1.5 respectively).

8.4.2   There is also a pronominal usage of **dit** and **dat** (compare also **het**, 8.1.2.3(c)) which differs greatly from English: **dit** and **dat** (and **het**) can be followed by a plural form of **zijn** (as well as **blijken**, **blijven**, **lijken**, **schijnen** and **worden**) and can refer to a plural quantity in which case they replace English 'they', 'these' and 'those':

Dat zijn Italianen.
They are Italians.

Dat (**dit**) **zijn de enige vorken die ik heb kunnen vinden.**
Those (these) are the only forks I was able to find.

As with **het** (see 8.1.2.3(c)), **dit** and **dat** can only be used in this way if the complement following **zijn** etc. is a noun or an adjective used as a noun, otherwise **zij** or **die** are used:

Ze (die) zijn erg duur.
They are very expensive.

Ze (die) zijn nu op.
They have all gone now.

8.4.3   Independent demonstrative pronouns are not usually[13] preceded by prepositions; **hier** + preposition replaces **dit**, and **daar** + preposition replaces **dat**:

Stop het hierin.
Put it in this.

Ik heb het daarmee (= daar + met) geschreven.
I wrote it with that.

These forms are also separable:

Daar heb ik het mee geschreven.
I wrote it with *that*. (emphasized)

The adverbial expressions of time **daarna** 'after that, afterwards', **daarop** 'after that, thereupon' and **daarvoor** 'before that' are not separated:

Kort daarna vertrokken wij.
Shortly after that we left.

8.5   RELATIVE PRONOUNS (betrekkelijke voornaamwoorden)

8.5.1   DIFFICULTIES WITH ENGLISH RELATIVES

English very often omits relative pronouns (actually only when they are objects, never when subject pronouns, see 12.2.1.1), but they must always be used in Dutch. In addition, there is often a choice of relative in English:

---

[13] Occasionally they are preceded by prepositions when qualified, and in speech when extra emphasis is required:

Wat jij voorstelt, past niet bij dit alles.
What you are suggesting doesn't fit in with all of this.

Vergeleken met dat van mij ...
Compared with mine ...

Ik heb het met dit (= hiermee) gedaan. (emphatic)
I did it with *this*.

Stop het niet in deze la maar in die.
Don't put it in *this* drawer, but in *that* one. (see 6.1)

The man I helped yesterday is now sick.
The man whom/that/which* I helped yesterday is now sick.
De man die ik gisteren heb geholpen, is nu ziek.

* These days 'which' can now only be used with non-personal antecedents (compare 'Our father which art in heaven . . .').

The person I gave the letter to has now left.
The person that/whom I gave the letter to has now left.
The person to whom I gave the letter has now left.
De persoon aan wie ik de brief heb gegeven, is nu weg.

8.5.2 THE SIMPLE RELATIVE IN DUTCH

Die is the relative pronoun used for common gender nouns in the singular and for both common gender and neuter nouns in the plural. **Dat** is used for neuter nouns in the singular.[14] (see 8.5.4, footnote 15)

De man die hier woont, is ziek. (sing.)   Common gender
De mannen die hier wonen, zijn ziek. (pl.)

Het boek dat ik nu lees, is erg lang. (sing.)   Neuter
De boeken die ik nu lees, zijn erg lang. (pl.)

Note:
1 **Die/dat** are pronouns because within their own clause they stand for a noun. In English they are 'who/which/that'.
2 They are relative because they relate back to the preceding word, the antecedent.
3 The finite verb in relative clauses is sent to the end of that clause.
4 If a comma is used at all, it follows the relative clause. In shorter sentences like the above it is usually omitted. Unlike the Germans, the Dutch do not use a comma after the antecedent.

8.5.3 RELATIVE PRONOUNS PRECEDED BY PREPOSITIONS

(a) When a preposition occurs before a relative pronoun of common gender, the pronoun **wie** is used instead of **die** when it refers to a *person*:

De man met wie ik in de winkel stond te praten, is mijn oom.

This sentence can be translated as follows:

[14] It is not uncommon in very colloquial Dutch for a personal neuter antecedent, e.g. **meisje**, to be followed by **die** rather than **dat** as grammar demands: **Ik ken een meisje die automonteur wil worden** 'I know a girl who wants to become a mechanic'.

1 The man to whom I was talking in the shop is my uncle.
2 The man whom I was talking to in the shop is my uncle.
3 The man that I was talking to in the shop is my uncle.
4 The man I was talking to in the shop is my uncle.

In archaic style a dative form **wie** (even older **wien**) without a preposition also occurs.

(b) When a preposition is used before a relative pronoun relating to a *thing*, whether it be a **de** or a **het** word, **waar-** plus the preposition is used:

De stoel waarop jij zit is van mij.

This can be translated as follows:

1 The chair on which you are sitting is mine.
2 The chair which you are sitting on is mine.
3 The chair that you are sitting on is mine.
4 The chair you are sitting on is mine.

But in this instance there is another possible word order in Dutch. This is in fact the more common of the two, certainly in speech. In this case the preposition is sent to the end of the relative clause where it is placed before the verb, which has also been relegated to the end of the clause:

De stoel waar jij op zit, is van mij.

Here are further examples using a neuter noun and a plural where the construction is precisely the same:

Het brood waar ik van hou, is niet verkrijgbaar. Neuter noun
The bread I like isn't available.

De bedden waar de katten onder slapen, zijn oud.   Plural noun
The beds the cats are sleeping under are old.

(c) In colloquial Dutch it is also common to use the **waar-** + preposition construction referred to in (b) for people as well as things, although purists object:

De man waarmee (= met wie) ik in de winkel stond te praten, is mijn oom.

or

De man waar ik in de winkel mee stond te praten, is mijn oom.

8.5.4 RELATIVES WITH INDEFINITE ANTECEDENTS – USE OF **wat**

niets wat[15]	nothing (which/that) you say ...
iets wat	something (which/that) you say
veel wat	much (of what) you say ...
alles wat	everything (which/that) you say
dat wat[16]	that which you say ... (see 8.5.8)
het enige wat	the only thing (which/that) (see 8.6.8(e))
het laatste wat	the last thing (which/that)

Hij heeft niets in zijn huis wat waardevol is.
He hasn't got anything valuable in his house.

Sometimes the antecedent of **wat** is an entire clause:

Hij heeft zijn auto total loss gereden, wat ik erg jammer vind.
He has written his car off, which I think is a great shame.

8.5.5 WORD ORDER IN RELATIVE CLAUSES

Sending the verb to the end of the relative clause sometimes confuses English speakers who are used to the relative immediately following the noun to which it refers. One *can* keep the antecedent and the relative together in Dutch, as the following examples illustrate, but that is not usually the case.

(a) **Ik heb hem het lijstje gestuurd dat je me hebt gegeven.**
   I sent him the list that you gave me.

This word order is preferable to the following although what follows is not incorrect (but note the obligatory comma in this case):

Ik heb hem het lijstje dat je me hebt gegeven, gestuurd.

(b) **Laat me het hondje eens zien dat je gekocht hebt.**
   Show me the puppy that you've bought.

Here the distance between the relative and its antecedent is greater and the speaker may prefer:

Laat me dat hondje dat je gekocht hebt, eens zien.

But either is possible.

(c) **Ik kan een kast toch moeilijk afsluiten waar jij de sleutel van hebt.**
   I can't really lock a cupboard that you have got the key to.

---

[15] In all cases **dat** is sometimes heard but **wat** is more usual. And it is not uncommon either in colloquial speech for relative **dat** (see 8.5.2) to be replaced by **wat**.
[16] The **dat** can be omitted.

Here the distance is so great that the following would be preferred:

Ik kan een kast waar jij de sleutel van hebt, toch moeilijk afsluiten.

8.5.6   WHOSE

1	2	3
wiens (for masculine antecedents)	**van wie/waarvan**	**wie z'n**
wier (for feminine and plural antecedents)	**van wie/waarvan**	**wie d'r/hun**
welks (for non-personal antecedents)	**waarvan**	**waarvan**

The forms given in column 1 are only found in the written language, **wiens** being somewhat more common than **wier** or **welks** both of which are regarded as being particularly archaic or formal sounding.

Usually the forms in column 2 replace those in 1 in writing and speech and those in column 3 are restricted to the colloquial language but are infrequent:

(written)	**De man wiens boek ik geleend heb, is ziek.**
(spoken and written)	**De man van wie ik het boek geleend heb, is ziek.**
	(note the new word order)
(very colloquial)	**De man wie z'n boek ik geleend heb, is ziek.**
	The man whose book I borrowed is sick.
(written)	**Het huis welks dak ingestort is, is later verkocht.**
(spoken and written)	**Het huis waarvan het dak ingestort is, is later verkocht.**
or	**Het huis waar het dak van ingestort is, is later verkocht.**
	The house whose roof (of which the roof) collapsed was later sold.

8.5.7   PREPOSITION PLUS WHOSE

(a) As we have seen, 'whose' is normally expressed in Dutch by **van wie** or **waarvan**, but a complication arises when one is confronted with a sentence like the following:

The man in whose chair I am sitting is my uncle.

It is impossible to have **op** and **van** together. In such an instance **wiens**, although stilted when used as above, is somewhat more commonly used when a preposition is involved:

De man op wiens stoel ik zit is mijn oom.

But **wier**, as in **De vrouw op wier stoel ik zit, is mijn tante** is very rare indeed, other than in the most formal of contexts.

In speech the following would be used:

De man op wie z'n stoel ik zit ...
De vrouw op wie d'r stoel ik zit ...
De mensen op wie hun stoel ik zit ...

In writing, if one wants to avoid **wiens** and **wier**, the following might be preferable, but it sounds as contorted in Dutch as its literal translation does in English, i.e. 'in the chair of whom':

De man/vrouw/mensen op de stoel van wie ik zit ...

(b) A preposition + whose, when the antecedent is a thing, i.e. not a person, also causes complications if one wishes to avoid using **welks** (or the even rarer **welker** which was once used for non-personal feminine and plural antecedents). Once again, as with **wiens**, **welks** is sometimes found in the formal written language when preceded by a preposition:

Het huis op welks dak de kat de hele nacht had gezeten, is de volgende dag als gevolg van de storm ingestort.
The house whose roof the cat had sat on all night, collapsed the next day as a result of the storm.

Alternatively this could be expressed by **Het huis op het dak waarvan ...** (compare 'the house on the roof of which'), but both alternatives sound very contorted and would certainly never be encountered in the spoken language and would even be avoided in the written language wherever possible. Dutch simply seeks to rephrase the statement and thus avoid the complication. In the case of the above example the following would be more usual:

Het huis waar de kat de hele nacht op het dak gezeten had, is de volgende dag als gevolg van de storm ingestort.

8.5.8 INDEPENDENT RELATIVES

These are relatives that begin sentences and thus have no antecedent: **die/wie**[17] 'he who', **wat** 'what, that which', **hetgeen** 'what, that which'. They could also be regarded as indefinite pronouns:

Wie (die) eens steelt, is altijd een dief.
Once a thief, always a thief.

---

[17] **Die** is rather literary.

Wie (die) komen wil, moet nu betalen.
Whoever[18] wants to come must pay now.

Wat je zegt is allemaal onzin.
What (that which) you're saying is simply nonsense.

In the final example the meaning is **dat wat**. This **wat** is commonly replaced in the written language by **hetgeen** (pronounced **'t geen**):

Hetgeen je doet is gevaarlijk.
What (that which) you are doing is dangerous.

Hetgeen ik zeggen wil is dit ...
What (that which) I want to say is this ...

8.5.9   LESS COMMON RELATIVES

(a) The relative **hetgeen** commonly replaces in writing the **wat** which refers back to a whole clause, but it is an archaic form (see 8.5.4):

Hij heeft zijn auto total loss gereden, hetgeen ik erg jammer vind.
He has written his car off, which I think is a great shame.

In this sense **hetwelk** (also written **'t welk**) can also be used; this use of **hetwelk** too is archaic:

De eendracht is in het land hersteld, hetwelk (hetgeen) de gehele bevolking met vreugde vervuld heeft.
Unity was restored in the country, which filled the entire population with joy.

(b) Historically related to **hetwelk** (and **welks**, which was dealt with earlier) is the relative **welk(e)**, which often replaces **die** in formal writing:

De regering, welke (die) dat pas bekendgemaakt had, is gisteren afgetreden.
The government, which had just announced that, resigned yesterday.

De idealen welke (die) eertijds de jeugd bezielden, doen ons nu vaak glimlachen.
The ideals which used to animate young people now often make us smile.

(c) A further common usage of **welk(e)** which cannot be avoided, even in speech, is the following adjectival relative:

Hij zei dat hij alles begrepen had, welke opmerking ik niet de moeite waard vond tegen te spreken.

---

[18] **Degene(n) die** is common in this sense too (see Indefinite pronouns 8.6.6).

He said that he had understood everything, which remark I did not
consider worth contradicting.

**Max Havelaar, welk boek (welke roman) ik op mijn veertiende
jaar leerde kennen, vind ik nog steeds prachtig.**
I still find Max Havelaar, which book (novel) I got to know when I
was fourteen, fabulous.

8.5.10 EXTENDED PARTICIPIAL PHRASES WHICH REPLACE RELATIVE CLAUSES

In formal style, and often in journalese, one finds an avoidance of relative
clauses by placing the information usually contained in the relative clause
before the noun it refers to, in an extended adjectival phrase. Such phrases
always contain a present or past participle (or occasionally an infinitive
– see the last two examples).

Het boek *dat ik gisteren antiquarisch heb gekocht,* **heb ik aan mijn
beste vriend gegeven.**
I have given the book that I bought second-hand yesterday to my
best friend.
Het *gisteren door mij gekochte antiquarische* **boek heb ik aan mijn
beste vriend gegeven.**

Hij heeft in de boekenkast *die hij gemaakt heeft* **een riks gevonden.**
He found ƒ2.50 in the bookcase which he made.
Hij heeft *in de door hem gemaakte* **boekenkast een riks gevonden.**

Alle bomen *die in dit park staan* **zijn eiken.**
All the trees in this park are oaks.
Alle *in dit park staande* **bomen zijn eiken.**

Het bedrag *dat u nog betalen moet.*
The amount that you are yet to pay.
Het *door u nog te betalen* **bedrag.**

Er schijnt weinig discussie te bestaan over de *te volgen* **weg.**
There seems to be little discussion about the course to be taken.
Er schijnt weinig discussie te bestaan over de weg *die te volgen is.*

Some adjectival adjuncts can be of unwieldy length, as the following
extreme example taken from a newspaper illustrates:

**De in 1949 wegens collaboratie en roven van kunstschatten tot 8
maanden gevangenisstraf veroordeelde nu 77 jaar oude Blaricumse
miljonair Pieter Menten, heeft het land weten te ontvluchten.**
The now 77 year-old Blaricum millionaire, Pieter Menten, who was

sentenced to eight months' prison for collaboration and theft of works of art, has managed to flee the country.

Relative clauses must be used in English when translating such extended participial phrases (see 11.12.4.7).

8.5.11   Under 8.5.10 examples of Dutch participial constructions which are rendered by relative clauses in English are given. There are, however, participial (both past and present) constructions in English which must be rendered by relative clauses in Dutch:

De huizen die in de jaren vijitig gebouwd zijn, zijn gehorig.
The houses built in the fifties are noisy.

This could also be rendered by an adjectival phrase placed before the noun:

De in de jaren vijftig gebouwde huizen zijn gehorig.

De man die in de hoek de krant zit te lezen, is ernstig ziek.
The man reading the paper in the corner of the room is seriously ill.

8.5.12   See 12.2.1.1.

8.6   INDEFINITE PRONOUNS (onbepaalde voornaamwoorden)

8.6.1   'One'

The English pronoun 'one' has an exact equivalent in Dutch which is **men**. Like its English counterpart, **men** belongs more in formal speech and writing than in everyday language. In conversation it is commonly replaced by unstressed **je** or **ze** (i.e. 'they', see 11.12.4.9). It differs from English, however, in that **men** can only serve as a subject pronoun; when the object is needed, **je** (i.e. unstressed **jou**) or **iemand** is used in colloquial style; in formal style a passive is often used (see 11.12.4.9):

Als een leraar je tussen de middag in een klaslokaal vindt, word je gestraft.
If a teacher finds one in a classroom at lunchtime one is punished.

The possessive 'one's' is rendered by **zijn** and the reflexive 'oneself' by **zich**:

Men moet jaarlijks zijn belasting betalen.
One has to pay one's taxes every year.

8.6.2 'EVERYONE', 'EVERYBODY'

The most usual word is **iedereen**. Occasionally just **ieder** (also **ieders** 'everyone's') is used. In more formal style **een ieder** and **elkeen** are also found:

Dit is een 'must' voor een ieder die geïnteresseerd is in de kunst van de 17de eeuw.

This is a must for everybody who is interested in the art of the 17th century.

8.6.3 'SOMEONE', 'SOMEBODY'; 'ANYONE', 'ANYBODY'; 'NO ONE', 'NOBODY'

The subtle distinction between 'someone' and 'anyone' does not exist in Dutch; both are rendered by **iemand**. When 'anyone' is used with a negative in English, Dutch simply uses **niemand** 'nobody':

Heb je iemand gezien?
Did you see anyone?

Ja, ik heb iemand gezien.
Yes, I saw someone.

Nee, ik heb niemand gezien.
No, I didn't see anyone. (i.e. I saw nobody)

Iemand and **niemand** also have a genitive form **iemands** and **niemands**:

iemands pet 'somebody's cap'

'Somebody else' is **iemand anders**, the genitive of which can be expressed in four ways:

iemand anders pet 'somebody else's cap' (spoken and written)
de pet van iemand anders (spoken and written)
iemand anders z'n pet (spoken)
andermans pet (written)

8.6.4 'SOMETHING'; 'ANYTHING'; 'NOTHING'   (see also **ergens**, **nergens** and **overal** 8.6.9)

The situation here is similar to that above: 'something/anything' are rendered by **iets** or more colloquially by **wat**; 'nothing' is **niets** or in the spoken language **niks**:

Heeft ze iets/wat gekocht?
Did she buy anything?

Ja, ze heeft iets/wat gekocht.
Yes, she bought something.

Nee, ze heeft niets gekocht.
No, she didn't buy anything. (i.e. she bought nothing)

For **iets/wat** and **niets** followed by an adjective see 9.1.5.

Note: **iets** and **wat** also render the adverb 'somewhat'. (see 9.1.4 note)

8.6.5 'WHOEVER'; 'WHATEVER' (see 12.6)

Wie ... ook and **wat ... ook** translate the above:

Wie er ook komt, wij zullen voor hen kunnen zorgen.
Whoever comes, we will be able to take care of them.

Alwie 'whoever' and **alwat** 'whatever' are sometimes used in the written language.

Note: **Wie dat zegt is een leugenaar** 'Whoever (= he who) says that is a liar' (see 8.5.8). **Die** is used in formal style instead of **wie.**

8.6.6 'MANY', 'SEVERAL', 'VARIOUS', 'SOME', 'OTHERS', 'A FEW'

veel, vele(n)	much, many
verscheidene(n)	several
ettelijke(n)	several
verschillende(n)	various
sommige(n)	some
andere(n)	others
enkele(n)	a few
een paar	a few
degene(n) die	the one who (those who) [only used with reference to people]
die/dat	that/those which [for non-personal referents]
hetgene dat	that which; what (lit.)

With the exception of **een paar**, all words in this category (plus **alle** and **beide**, see below) add **-n** when they are used independently referring to people. All but the last two can also be used as adjectives before nouns, in which case they do not add **n**, nor when used independently referring to things:

Verscheidene mensen willen niet komen.
Some people don't want to come.

Sommigen blijven thuis maar anderen gaan naar de bioscoop.
Some are staying at home but others are going to the movies.

Ik heb vandaag een paar boeken gekocht. Ik heb er ook enkele vérkocht.

I bought a few books today. I *sold* a few too.

Note that **vele** is rather formal:

Zuid-Afrika is voor vele Nederlanders een land waar men een bijna 'kinderlijk taaltje' praat.

For many Dutch people South Africa is a country where an almost 'childish language' is spoken.

Usually **veel** is used attributively before a plural noun, e.g. **veel kinderen** 'many children', **veel boeken** 'many books'.

The form **veel** can also be used independently when referring to non-animate things:

Veel (winkels understood) **moesten sluiten.**

but

Velen (mensen understood) **moesten gaan.**

Note: In literary style a genitive from **veler** is sometimes found, e.g. **op veler verzoek** 'at the request of many'.

8.6.7 'BOTH'

(a) The basic word for 'both' is **beide**. It is used in the same way as the expressions given above, i.e. **beide mensen; beide boeken; beide (boeken** understood) **waren duur; beiden (mensen** understood) **zijn vertrokken.**

(b) But **beide(n)** can also follow the verb, as in English, but in Dutch this sounds rather formal:

Deze boeken waren beide duurder dan ƒ50.

These books were both more expensive than fifty guilders.

In this case **beide(n)** is interchangeable with **allebei**, which is what is usually heard in the spoken language:

Deze boeken waren allebei duurder dan ƒ50.

(c) In addition, the form **allebei** is used to translate 'both of us/you/them' – also used with nominal subjects and objects:

Mijn ouders gaan allebei naar de markt.

My parents are both going to the market.

Both my parents are going to the market.

Ze gaan allebei naar de markt.
They are both going to the market.
Both of them are going to the market.

Ik heb ze allebei in de stad gezien.
I saw them both in town.
I saw both of them in town.

(d) Expressions such as 'both the brothers' can be translated as follows, but the variant with **allebei** is the most usual in the spoken language:

De twee broers/beide broers gaan naar de markt.
De broers gaan allebei/beiden naar de markt.
Both brothers are going to the market/The brothers are both going to the market.

(e) Note the following expressions: **mijn beide broers** 'both my brothers', **een van beide(n)** 'one of the two', **geen van beide(n)** 'neither of the two', **ons beider vriend** 'a friend of both of us' (a formal genitive form).

8.6.8 'ALL' (see also, **ergens**, **nergens** and **overal** below)

The way in which 'all' is translated into Dutch is similar to the way in which 'both' is translated (see above).

(a) The basic word is **alle** and is used like the expressions dealt with above, i.e. **alle mensen**, **alle boeken**, **alle** (**boeken** understood) **waren duur**, **allen** (**mensen** understood) **moesten gaan**.

(b) But **alle(n)** can also follow the verb, as in English, but this sounds rather formal:

Deze boeken waren alle duurder dan ƒ50.
These books were all more expensive than fifty guilders.

In this case **alle(n)** is interchangeable with **allemaal**, which is the most common word in the spoken language:

Deze boeken waren allemaal duurder dan ƒ50.

(c) In addition, the form **allemaal** is used to translate 'all of us/you/them':

Ze gaan allemaal naar de markt (= **Ze gaan allen naar de markt.**)
They are all going to the market. (or All of them are going to the market)

Ik heb ze allemaal in de stad gezien.
I saw all of them in town. (or them all)

Note: The word **allemaal** is also used very idiomatically in spoken Dutch with a variety of meanings only vaguely related to the literal meaning:

Ik kan dat allemaal niet begrijpen.
I can't understand any of that.

Wat is er allemaal gebeurd? ·
What's happened?

Er hingen allemaal schilderijen aan de muren.
There were a whole lot of paintings hanging on the walls.

(d) Expressions such as 'All the men went there' can be translated in three ways:

Al de mannen/alle mannen gingen ernaartoe.
De mannen gingen er allemaal/allen naartoe.

Note that the variant **al de mannen** can have the connotation 'all the men (but not the women)'.

(e) Note the ambiguity of the following English 'all': That's all I can tell you, i.e. meaning both 'everything' and 'the only thing'. The first meaning is translated as **Dat is alles** (or even **al**) **wat ik je kan vertellen** and the second as **Dat is het enige wat ik je kan vertellen**, but in practice you'll hear **alles** being used in both cases.

(f) Note that **alles** means 'everything' and **al** usually means 'already' (see above for exceptions).

(g) Note that 'all' with reference to periods of time is rendered by the definite article plus **heel**, e.g. **de hele dag/nacht/week/maand** 'all day/night/week/month', **het hele jaar** 'all year'.

8.6.9 PRONOMINAL USE of **ergens**, **nergens** AND **overal**

These three words which are usually used as adverbs rendering English 'somewhere/ somehow', 'nowhere' and 'everywhere' also have a pronominal function: when **iets** 'something', **niets** 'nothing' and **alles** 'everything' are preceded by a preposition, they are often replaced, particularly in speech, by **ergens**, **nergens** and **overal** respectively and the preposition follows these words:

Hij kijkt ergens naar.[19]
He is looking at something.

Ik heb hem nergens over verteld.
I told him about nothing.

Je kunt het overal mee doen.
You can do it with anything.

---

[19] Note the following adverbial use of **ergens**: **Ergens heeft hij gelijk** 'Somehow he is right'.

Should the indefinite pronoun be followed by a relative clause, however, those alternative forms can't be used (see 8.5.4):

Hij kijkt naar iets wat ik gemaakt heb.
He is looking at something I have made.

Je kunt het doen met alles wat je vinden kunt.
You can do it with anything you can find.

Ergens, **nergens** and **overal** also cannot replace i**ets**, **niets** and **alles** when the latter are followed by an inflected adjective in **-s** (see 9.1.5):

Ik zoek iets moois voor haar verjaardag.
I'm looking for something pretty for her birthday.

We zaten naar iets leuks op de televisie te kijken.
We were watching something good on tv.

8.7   INTERROGATIVE PRONOUNS (**vragende voornaamwoorden**)

(for interrogative adverbs see 12.6)

8.7.1   'WHO'; 'TO WHOM', 'FROM WHOM', ETC.

The interrogative pronoun 'who' is **wie**:

Wie is je leraar?
Who is your teacher?

Questions involving 'who' plus prepositions are always posed as follows:

Aan wie heb je het schrift gegeven?
To whom did you give the exercise book?/Who did you give the exercise book to?

English usually employs the word order 'Who(m) did you give the book to?' This is not possible in Dutch:

Van wie heb je olie hoed gekregen?
Who(m) did you get that hat from?

English speakers must be careful not to confuse the *interrogative* 'who' in indirect questions (i.e. **wie** in Dutch) with the *relative pronoun* 'who' (i.e. **die** or **waar** in Dutch, see 8.5.2, n.1):

Ik weet niet wie het gedaan heeft. (indirect interrogative)
I don't know who did it.

Hij is degene die het gedaan heeft. (relative)
He is the one who did it.

8.7.2 'WHOSE'

The possessive interrogative pronoun 'whose' is **wiens** or **van wie**:

Wiens boek is dit? (lit.)
Van wie is dit boek?   Whose book is this?
Wie z'n boek is dit? (spoken language)

When the reference is obviously to a female being or plural beings, the very formal written language also knows the form **wier**, and the spoken language **wie d'r** for feminine beings:

Wie d'r (or **z'n**) **beha is dit?**
Whose bra is this?

8.7.3 'WHAT'

(a) 'What' is **wat**, but when used in combination with a preposition, it is replaced by **waar** + preposition, which can also be separated:

Wat heb je gedaan?
What have you done?

Waarmee heb je het gedaan?/Waar heb je het mee gedaan?
What did you do it with?

(b) 'What kind/sort of a' is rendered by the idiom **wat voor (een)**:

Wat voor (een) auto heb je?/Wat heb je voor (een) auto?
What sort of car do you have?

(c) **Wat** is common in exclamations:

Wat jammer!   What a pity/shame!
Wat een mooi huis!   What a beautiful house!

Note: **Wat een dure boeken!** What expensive books!

(d) Sometimes English 'what' is rendered by **hoe** in Dutch (see 10.6.1):

Hoe laat is het?   What time is it?
Hoe is uw naam?/Hoe heet u?   What is your name?

(e) Sometimes English 'what' means 'which' (see 8.7.4 below).

8.7.4 'WHICH'

Dutch **welk(e)** can be used attributively before nouns or independently. English often uses 'what' in this sense too:

Welk boek (welke film, welke mensen) heb je gezien?
Which/what book (film, people) did you see?

Welke heb je gekocht?
Which/what ones did you buy?

Welk (boek understood) **heb je gekocht?**
Which/what one did you buy?

9 ADJECTIVES (bijvoeglijke naamwoorden)

9.1 RULES FOR INFLECTION (verbuiging)

9.1.1 An adjective used attributively (i.e. before the noun) will always take an **-e** ending except in the following cases, all of them indefinite:

(a) Before a singular neuter noun preceded by **een, elk, enig, geen, genoeg, ieder, menig, veel, welk, zo'n, zulk**:

> **een/geen klein huis** 'a/not a small house', **elk/ieder klein meisje** 'every/each small girl', **genoeg wit papier** 'enough white paper', **welk wit papier** 'which white paper'

It should be noted that in expressions such as 'Jan's large house', Jan's is a possessive (i.e. = **zijn**) and thus the adjective following it is inflected, i.e. **Jans grote huis**.

(b) Before singular neuter nouns preceded by nothing, i.e. **oud brood** 'stale bread', **zoet water** 'fresh water'.[1] Note that in all other cases an ending is required, e.g. **het oude brood** 'the stale bread', **zulke oude huizen** 'such old houses', **stoute kinderen** 'naughty children', **dat stomme ding** 'that stupid thing' etc.

Predicative adjectives (i.e. those not used before nouns as in 'rubies are red') never inflect in Dutch.

9.1.2 There are numerous cases where an adjective does not take an **-e** ending where you would expect one according to the rules above:

(a) Adjectives ending in **-en**, which includes materials (e.g. **open** 'open', **eigen** 'own', **houten** 'wooden', **zilveren** 'silver') and strong past participles (e.g. **gesloten** 'closed', **vertrokken** 'departed', **opgeblazen** 'blown up'). Exception: **verscheidene** 'several' always takes **-e**. When adjectival past participles ending in **-en** are used as nouns, they take **-e** (**-en** in plural), e.g. **de betrokkene** 'the person affected', **volwassene** 'the adult', etc.

---

[1] In expressions such as **Witte Huis te koop** 'white house for sale', **Rode Kruis** 'Red Cross' and **Engelse pond gedevalueerd** 'English pound devalued' the meaning is definite even though the neuter article has been omitted, therefore the adjective is inflected.

(b) A limited number of adjectives do not take **-e** but are affixed to the following noun instead (see 9.8.5).

(c) Some adjectives of foreign origin are indeclinable: **beige, crème, gratis, lila, nylon, oranje, plastic, platina, aluminium, rose/roze** 'pink'.

(d) Place name adjectives in **-er**: **Groninger koek, Haarlemmer olie**.

(e) Comparatives of more than three syllables are commonly left uninflected (see 9.2.2).

(f) A few adjectives take on a figurative meaning if uninflected: **oud-soldaat** 'ex-soldier', **een groot man** 'a great man'.

(g) The adjectives **rechts** and **links** have their own peculiar form in **-er** and are often written as one word, particularly when referring to parts of the body and items of clothing: **de rechterhand** 'the right hand', **de linkerschoen** 'the left shoe', also **de linkeroever** 'the left bank', **de rechterkant** 'the right(-hand) side', **de linkerzijde** 'the left(-hand) side'. Preceding other nouns they behave as normal adjectives: **het rechtse verkeer** 'traffic from the left', **de linkse partijen** 'the left-wing parties'.

(h) It is very common for adjectives preceding nouns referring to human beings (particularly masculine beings indicating a profession or function) to be left uninflected after articles. One is advised only to copy those one has heard or read and otherwise to apply the ending, e.g. **de waarnemend burgemeester** 'the acting mayor', **de tijdelijk zaakgelastigde** 'the temporary chargé d'affaires', **een bekwaam musicus** 'a competent musician', **een vroom man** 'a pious man', **een beroemd schrijfster** 'a famous authoress', **Geyl is een bekend Nederlands historicus** 'Geyl is a famous Dutch historian'.

The adjective does not inflect after **een, geen, zo'n** etc. before the common gender noun **iemand**, e.g. **een belangrijk iemand** 'an important person'.

Note: **een aardig mens** 'a nice person', i.e. with a positive adjective, can only refer to a female although an uninflected adjective + **mens** can refer to a male when there is a negative connotation, e.g. **Willem II was een kil mens** 'William II was a cold person'.

There is a long list of nouns, particularly neuter nouns, which, even when preceded by the singular definite article, do not require that the preceding adjective be inflected as one would expect according to the rules given above. The adjective and the noun are regarded as a sort of compound in such cases. But note that in the plural the adjective is inflected:

het stedelijk museum 'the municipal museum', **de stedelijke museums**

The following list is not by any means complete but will serve to illustrate
the concept:

het academisch ziekenhuis	het menselijk lichaam
het centraal station	het noordelijk halfrond
het cultureel akkoord	het noordoostelijk deel
het dagelijks leven	het oostelijk deel
het economisch herstel	het openbaar vervoer
het Engels Instituut	het sociaal pakket
het geestelijk leven	het stedelijk museum
het Gents Advertentieblad	het stoffelijk overschot
het heilig sacrament	het uitroerend orgaan
het koninklijk gezin	het verzameld werk
het medisch onderzoek	het zelfrijzend bakmeel

The names of the parts of speech also belong in this category, e.g. **het
bijvoeglijk naamwoord** 'adjective', **het wederkerend werkwoord** 'reflexive
verb' etc.

The expression **hartelijk dank** 'many thanks' also dispenses with inflection although **dank** is a common gender noun.

9.1.3   Inflection often causes spelling changes in accordance with the
phonetic spelling rules of Dutch:

(a) Adjectives with **aa**, **ee**, **oo** and **uu** drop one vowel, e.g. **kaal** – **kale**,
    geel – **gele**, **groot** – **grote**, **duur** – **dure**. Those ending in **-ieel** add a
    dieresis, e.g. **officieel** – **officiële**. Note also that past participles used
    adjectivally are also subject to this rule, e.g. **gehaat** (from **haten** 'to
    hate') – **gehate**, **vergroot** (from **vergroten** 'to enlarge') – **vergrote**.

(b) In adjectives with a long vowel or a diphthong and ending in **-f**, the
    f changes to **v** (i.e. the **f** becomes voiced between two vowels), e.g.
    lief – **lieve**, **braaf** – **brave**, **doof** – **dove**.[2] A word such as **laf** goes **laffe**,
    however, because it contains a short vowel (see rule (d)).

(c) In adjectives with a long vowel or a diphthong and ending in **-s**, the
    s changes to **z** (i.e. the **s** becomes voiced between two vowels), e.g.
    vies – **vieze**, **dwaas** – **dwaze**. There are a few isolated exceptions to
    this rule, however, e.g. **kies** – **kiese**, **overzees** – **overzeese**, **hees** – **hese**,
    heus – **heuse**, **kuis** – **kuise**, **histories** – **historiese** (see 2.8), **Parijs** –
    Parijse. Adjectives of nationality ending in **-ees** go **-ese**, e.g. **Chinees**
    – **Chinese**, also **Fries** – **Friese** (but as plural nouns they take **z**, e.g.
    Chinezen, **Friezen**).

---

[2] Both rules (a) and (b) apply here.

(d) Adjectives with a short vowel ending in a consonant double the consonant to keep the vowel short, e.g. **dik – dikke, laf – laffe, wit – witte,
tam – tamme, dun – dunne, fris – frisse**. Exception: **grof – grove** (but
usually pronounced **grovve**, also in the comparative, **grovver**).

(e) Adjectives with a long vowel or diphthong ending in **-d** are often
pronounced with a vocalised **d** (see 1.2), e.g. **rode – rooie, goed –
goeie, oud – ouwe**. They are sometimes written like this too in informal
style.

(f) Note the adjective **bijdehand** 'smart, bright' which goes **bijdehante**.

9.1.4   A limited number of adjectives denoting location take **-ste** instead
of simply **-e**, e.g. **bovenste, middelste, onderste; binnenste, buitenste;
achterste, voorste**.

Note: **binnenstebuiten** 'inside out', **ondersteboven** 'upside down', **achter-
stevoren** 'back to front'.

In colloquial language one often hears **enigst** instead of **enig**, but the
former is an analogical form and is better avoided:

Hij is enigst kind.
He is an only child.

Dat is de enigste mogelijkheid.
That is the (one and) only possibility.

The words **laatste, zoveelste, hoeveelste** belong here too (see 14.2.1.4 and
14.9).

9.1.5   -s INFLECTION OF THE ADJECTIVE

There is also an **-s** inflection of the adjective in Dutch. It is used nowadays in only a limited number of cases. It is always used after **iets/wat**
(i.e. something), **niets** (see 8.6.4), **veel, allerlei, weinig, een heleboel, wat
voor, genoeg**, e.g. **iets nieuws** 'something new', **niets sterkers** 'nothing
stronger' (added here to the comparative), **een heleboel moois** 'a lot of
nice things'. **Wat heb je nou voor lekkers gekocht?** 'What delicious things
have you bought now?' **Er is nog genoeg fraais te bedenken** 'There are
enough nice things to think of.' Adjectives that already end in **-s** (e.g. **vies,
Belgisch**) do not of course take another s.

Note: **Wat** and **iets** can mean 'something' or 'somewhat'; with the latter
meaning followed by an adjective, no **-s** is added to the adjective, e.g. **Het
ziet er wat nieuw uit** 'It looks somewhat new'.

9.1.6   Formerly there was a complete paradigm of strong and weak adjectival endings for all four cases and all three genders (see chapter 7 (Gender)), as is still the case in German. The above rules for -e and -s inflection are in fact all that is left of these declensions except for those endings preserved in standard expressions and those found in older literary texts, e.g. **op heterdaad** 'red-handed' (dative), **te allen tijde** 'always' (dative), **in koelen bloede** 'in cold blood' (dative); **blootsvoets** 'bare-footed' (genitive), **grotendeels** 'on the whole' (genitive). The fact that these adjectives are often written together with the noun indicates that they are no longer regarded as inflected adjectives plus a noun, but more as compound nouns.

9.2   THE COMPARATIVE OF THE ADJECTIVE (**de vergrotende trap**)

9.2.1   FORMATION OF THE COMPARATIVE

The comparative is formed, as in English, by adding **-er** to the adjective whereby the same spelling changes apply as for **-e** inflection (see 9.1.3):

groot – groter, doof – dover, vies – viezer, dik – dikker.

Adjectives ending in **-r** take **-der**:

puur – puurder, zuiver – zuiverder, ver – verder.

There are two adjectives that have an irregular comparative form, as in English:

goed – beter 'good – better', **kwaad – erger** 'bad – worse'

Note: **Kwaad** meaning 'angry' becomes **kwader**. **Moe** 'tired' uses **vermoeider** as its comparative, but in speech **moeër** and **meer moe** occur.

9.2.2   INFLECTION OF THE COMPARATIVE

When used attributively, comparatives follow the rules for the inflection of simple adjectives, e.g. **een grotere jongen** 'a bigger boy', **een kleiner huis** 'a smaller house'.

Comparatives of more than three syllables are often not inflected because of the resulting sequence of unstressed syllables when an **-e** is added to the existing **-er** ending and the combination is thus difficult to pronounce, e.g. **een uitvoeriger(e) beschrijving** 'a more detailed description', **verstandiger(e) gedachten** 'more sensible thoughts'.

It is also quite common for some comparatives of two syllables not to inflect, but here one has the choice, e.g. **na korter(e) of langer(e) tijd**. The rules for **-s** inflection also apply to comparatives, e.g. **iets groters** 'something bigger', **niets duurders** 'nothing more expensive'.

9.2.3   USE OF **meer** WITH THE COMPARATIVE

In English the comparative of longer adjectives is formed by placing 'more' before the word rather than by adding '-er', e.g. 'more important,' 'more interesting'. As a general rule one can say that this is not the case in Dutch, e.g. **belangrijker** 'more important', **interessanter** 'more interesting'. The comparative with **meer** is known in Dutch but is not often compulsory and should thus be avoided if in doubt, e.g. **succesvoller** or **meer succesvol**, **typischer** or **meer typisch** (sometimes used with adjectives ending in **-isch**). It is often used before adjectives of nationality too, e.g. **meer Hollands** (= more Dutch, Dutcher), although the latter sounds somewhat peculiar in English too) and is also usually used before past participles functioning as adjectives, e.g. **meer geïnteresseerd** (also **geïnteresseerder**) 'more interested', **meer gewend aan** 'more used to', **meer opgewonden** (also **opgewondener**) 'more excited'. On occasions **-er** is possible in such cases, e.g.:

Een vervallenr/meer vervallen huis dan dit hebben we nog nooit gezien.
We have scarcely seen a more dilapidated house than this.

Die acties waren nog uitgebreider.
The campaigns were even more extensive.

9.2.4   'MORE AND MORE' CONSTRUCTIONS

Dutch too can say **meer en meer**, **dieper en dieper**, but it is more common to use **steeds/alsmaar** + comparative, e.g. **De hemel wordt steeds blauwer** 'The sky is getting bluer and bluer'. Another common alternative is **hoe langer hoe** + comparative, e.g. **De hemel werd hoe langer hoe blauwer** 'The sky turned progressively bluer', **Hij werd hoe langer hoe brutaler** 'He got more and more cheeky' (as time passed).

9.2.5   ATTRIBUTIVE USE OF COMPARATIVE FORMS

Note the following difference between English and Dutch: **De beste van de twee jongens/De beste van de drie jongens** 'The better of the two boys/The best of the three boys', i.e. no such distinction is made in Dutch. This is not the case after **een**, e.g. **Ik heb een betere oplossing gevonden** 'I have a better solution', but **Mijn oplossing was de beste van de twee** 'My solution was the better of the two'.

But the comparative is found after both indefinite and definite articles and demonstratives in expressions like the following where no direct comparison is being made: **een oudere heer** 'an elderly gentleman', **de jongere generatie** 'the younger generation', **de hogere standen** 'the upper classes'.

9.2.6 'MORE THAN' AND 'AS BIG AS' CONSTRUCTIONS

Comparatives of the sort 'He is bigger than I' are expressed as **Hij is groter dan ik**. Colloquially one often hears **als** instead of **dan**, but some people disapprove of this (see 12.2.1.8(e). The very English 'error' of saying 'She is richer than me' should be avoided in Dutch, although it is not unknown there either – the Dutch would nearly always say **ik**. Similarly in 'He is more important than you', the 'you' is **jij** not **jou**, i.e. a subject pronoun. But: **Ik vind hem aardiger dan jou**, i.e. an object pronoun. (see 8.1.2.6(a)). Also note **Hij is nog langer dan ik** 'He is even taller than I'.

Conversationally one hears a superfluous **wat** after **dan/als** with such comparatives which is identical to 'what' in colloquial English:

Hij is groter dan/als (wat) ik dacht.
He's bigger than (what) I thought.

Despite what was said about **als** above, it is used in expressions such as **(net) zo groot als** '(just) as big as'. There is also the alternative form **even groot als**:

Hij is net zo groot als ik/Hij is even groot als ik.
He is just as big as I.

And when negating one says:

Hij is niet zo groot als ik/Hij is niet even groot als ik.
He is not as big as I.

9.3 THE SUPERLATIVE OF THE ADJECTIVE (de overtreffende trap)

9.3.1 FORMATION OF THE SUPERLATIVE

The superlative of the adjective is formed by adding **-st** whereby no change in the spelling takes place, e.g. **groot – grootst, doof – doofst, dik – dikst**.
Adjectives ending in **-s** simply add a **-t**, e.g. **vies – viest, fris – frist**.

The two adjectives that have an irregular comparative also have an irregular superlative: **goed – beter – best** 'good – better – best', **kwaad – erger – ergst** 'bad/evil – worse – worst'.

9.3.2 INFLECTION OF SUPERLATIVES

Superlatives used attributively are always inflected regardless of their length, unlike comparatives (see 9.2.2), e.g. **de belangrijkste man** 'the most important man', **het interessantste verhaal** 'the most interesting story'.

9.3.3   USE OF **meest** WITH SUPERLATIVES

There are certain parallels between the use of **meest** in superlatives and the use of **meer** in comparatives. Generally speaking all adjectives, however long, add **-st**, unlike English, e.g. **interessantst** 'most interesting', **opwindendst** 'most exciting'. But the superlative with **meest** is preferable in Dutch with adjectives ending in **-isch** and **-st**, e.g. **typisch – meest typisch, juist – meest juist, robuust – meest robuust**.

As with comparatives, some longer adjectives such as **succesvol** and **opwindend** will be heard in the superlative with **meest**, although an **-st** ending is also correct and the more usual. One should, however, only copy examples one has heard or read·except for adjectives of nationality and for past participles used as adjectives, e.g. **meest Hollands** 'most Dutch', **Ik ben de meest geïnteresseerde** 'I am the most interested', **Hij is de meest opgewondene van de groep** 'He is the most excited of the group'. There are in addition some adjectives of foreign origin which can't take an **-st** ending and thus use **meest**, e.g. **meest sexy, meest beige**.

9.3.4   USE OF THE SUPERLATIVE

There is one use of the superlative in Dutch which replaces an English comparative (see 9.2.5); otherwise it is used as in English.

9.3.5   ABSOLUTE SUPERLATIVES

Dutch has an adjectival intensifier formed by the prefix **aller-** plus a superlative ending, e.g. **een alleraardigst(e) man** 'a very nice man', **een allerbeste vriend** 'a very good friend'.

Hoogst and **uiterst** (actually adverbs) are used to intensify adjectives:

Dat was een hoogst interessant verhaal.
That was a most interesting story.[3]

Dit is uiterst belangrijk.
This is extremely important.

Here **hoogst** and **uiterst** simply replace 'very'. (see 10.2.1)

The word **best** is used as an adjectival modifier:

Ik vond het best leuk bij hem.
I found it quite nice at his place.

Het is best moeilijk.
It's quite difficult.

---

[3] Not to be confused with 'the most interesting story' which is **het interessantste verhaal** (see 9.3.2).

Also note the following use of this **best** where it does not qualify an adjective but is an adjective in itself:

Ik vind het best, hoor.
I have no objections.

Het is een beste fiets.
It is a great bike.

Beste is also used in letters, e.g. **Beste Wim** 'Dear Wim' (see Appendix 1).

9.3.6 NOTES ON SUPERLATIVES

(a) Note the following compound adjectives incorporating superlatives: **dichtstbijzijnde** 'closest', **dichtstbijgelegen** 'closest', e.g. **de dichtstbijzijnde/dichtstbijgelegen brievenbus** 'the nearest letter-box'.
(b) There is a small group of adjectives of location which take an **-ste** inflection instead of **-e** and do not thus belong to the realm of superlatives, e.g. **middelste, benedenste** etc. (see 9.1.4). And see 14.2.1.7 for 'second best', 'third most important' etc.

9.4 ADJECTIVES USED ONLY PREDICATIVELY OR ATTRIBUTIVELY

9.4.1 There is a small number of adjectives which can never precede a noun and thus are never inflected, e.g. **anders** 'different', **zoek** 'lost'. One says for example **Mijn pen is zoek**, but if one wanted to express this with an attributive adjective, one would need to use another word, e.g. **mijn zoekgeraakte pen**. Similarly **verschillend** could replace **anders**. In addition the word **stuk** 'broken' is only used predicatively and can be replaced by **kapot** if an attributive adjective is required, e.g. **Mijn radio is stuk/mijn kapotte radio**.

9.4.2 The material adjectives **betonnen** 'concrete', **gouden** 'golden', **houten** 'wooden', **ijzeren** 'iron', **marmeren** 'marble' etc. can only be used attributively. Predicatively one says **van beton, van goud** etc., e.g. **dit houten huis** 'this wooden house', **Dit huis is van hout** 'This house is made of wood'.

9.5 PREDICATIVE ADJECTIVES FOLLOWED BY PREPOSITIONS

It is impossible to give a complete list of such adjectives, particularly of those derived from verbs, but the list below will serve as a guide. Many have the same preposition as in English. If in doubt, a good dictionary should indicate which preposition to use. An asterisk indicates those which can either precede or follow the object to which they refer, most of them being derived from verbs (i.e. past participles):

Ik was zeer in zijn verhaal geïnteresseerd or
Ik was zeer geïnteresseerd in zijn verhaal.
I was very interested in his story.

Hij is met haar getrouwd or
Hij is getrouwd met haar.
He is married to her.

By following the objects they govern such adjectives stand at the end of the clause in the usual position for a past participle.

The other adjectives in this list can also follow the object they refer to but usually only for particular emphasis:

Met jóú ben ik tevreden.
I am satisfied with *you.*

Tegen míj was hij aardig.
He was nice to *me.*

Some others, not derived from past participles, can also be found following the object they govern:

Hij is financieel afhankelijk van zijn vader or
Hij is van zijn vader financieel afhankelijk.
He is financially dependent on his father.

Note that Dutch **vol** 'full of' does not require any preposition, e.g. **De emmer was vol water** 'The bucket was full of water', **een huis vol mensen** 'a house full of people'; it is sometimes found with **met**, in which case it would seem to be somewhat emotive, e.g. **De trein zat vol met kinderen en ik kon niet eens zitten** 'The train was full of children and I couldn't even sit down'; **een kamer vol met rook** 'a room full of smoke'. **Moe** 'tired of' and **zat** 'fed up with' do not require a preposition either but they follow the noun to which they refer, e.g. **Ik ben het alleenzijn moe/zat** 'I am tired of/fed up with being alone'.

aardig voor	nice to	**afkomstig uit**	originating from
aardig tegen	nice to	**allergisch voor**	allergic to
* **aannemelijk voor**	acceptable to	**analoog aan**	analogous to
		anders dan	different from
* **(on)afhankelijk van**	dependent on, (independent of)	**arm aan**	poor in
		bang van/voor[4]	afraid of
		* **bedekt met**	covered in/with

begerig naar	desirous of	evenwijdig aan	parallel to
* begroeid met	overgrown with	* gedoemd tot	doomed to
* bekend met	acquainted/	* gehecht aan	attached to (fig.)
	familiar with	* gehuwd met	married to
* bekend om	known for		(formal)
* bekommerd	worried about	* geïnteresseerd in interested in
over (lit.)		gek op	mad about,
* belast met	in charge of		keen on
* bemind om	loved for	gelijk aan	identical to
benieuwd naar	curious about	gelukkig met	happy with
* beroemd om	famous for	* geneigd tot	inclined to
* bestemd voor	intended for	* gepikeerd over	sore at
* bewust van	aware of	* getrouwd met	married to
* bezeten van	obsessed with	(on)gevoelig	(in)sensitive to
* bezorgd over	anxious about	voor	
blauw van	blue with	* gewend aan	used to[5]
bleek van	pale with	goed in	good at
blij met	pleased with	goed voor	good to (s.o.)
boos op	angry with	identiek aan	identical to
dankbaar voor	grateful for	* ingenomen met	pleased/taken
dol op	mad about,		with
	keen on	* ingesteld op	oriented/geared
enthousiast	enthusiastic		to
over	about	karakteristiek	characteristic of
* ervaren in	experienced in	voor	
(omgekeerd)	in (inverse)	jaloers op	jealous/envious
evenredig	proportion/		of[6]
met	proportionate	kenmerkend	characteristic of
	to	voor	

[4] **Bang voor** is the usual expression, whereas **bang van** is used in a more figurative sense and does not normally correspond literally to 'afraid of'

Hij had een pistool in zijn hand en ik was bang voor hem.
He had a pistol in his hand and I was afraid of him.

Ik ben bang voor slangen.
I'm afraid of snakes.

Kernergie – daar word ik bang van.
Nuclear energy – it frightens me.

[5] **Aan** is quite commonly omitted from **gewend aan** 'used to':

In Denemarken zijn we (aan) dit soort weer gewend.
In Denmark we are used to this sort of weather.

[6] **Jaloers** is ambiguous; if one specifically wants to express envy, the verb **benijden** must be used:

Ik benijd hem.
I envy him/I am envious of him.

kwaad op	angry with	* **teleurgesteld over**	disappointed in/with
lelijk tegen	nasty to	**tevreden met/ over**	pleased/satisfied with
links van	to/on the left of		
medeplichtig aan	accessory to	**toegankelijk voor**	accessible to
nijdig op	angry with, mad at	**trots op**	proud of
* **omgeven door**	surrounded by	**trouw aan**	faithful to
* **omringd door**	surrounded by	**typerend voor**	typical of
* **omsingeld door**	surrounded by	**typisch voor**	typical of
onderhevig aan	liable/subject to	**veilig voor**	safe from
* **ongerust over**	anxious/worried about	**verantwoor- delijk voor**	responsible for
onverschillig voor	indifferent to, regardless of	* **verbaasd over**	amazed at
		* **verbannen uit**	banished from
onzichtbaar voor	invisible to	* **vergeleken bij/met**	compared to/with
* **opgewassen tegen**	(to be) a match for, (to be) up to	* **verliefd op**	in love with
		* **verrast door**	surprised by
		verschillend van	different from/to
* **opgewonden over**	excited about	* **verslaafd aan**	addicted to
		* **vervangen door**	replaced by
optimistisch over	optimistic about	* **verwant aan**	related to (languages, issues)
* **overtuigd van**	convinced of		
pessimistisch over	pessimistic about	* **verwant met**	related to (people)
rechts van	to/on the right of	* **verwonderd over**	amazed at
rijk aan	rich in	**vol (met)**	full of
schadelijk voor	harmful to	**vriendelijk tegen**	friendly towards
schuldig aan	guilty of		
slecht in	bad at	**woedend op**	furious with
* **teleurgesteld in**	disappointed in/with s.o.	**zwak in**	weak at

9.6   ADJECTIVES USED AS NOUNS

9.6.1   Very often in English we use constructions such as 'large shoes and little ones'. The 'ones' cannot be translated into Dutch and is expressed by the adjective alone, e.g. **grote schoenen en kleine**. Whether the adjective is inflected or not in Dutch depends on whether it would be inflected if the noun that is understood were mentioned, e.g. **een groot**

huis en een klein (huis) 'a large house and a small one', **een grote schoen en een kleine (schoen)** 'a large shoe and a small one'. Because the meaning of **klein** permits it, the above would also be commonly expressed as **een groot huis en een kleintje, een grote schoen en een kleintje** (see 7.5.3).

9.6.2 **De rijke, de blinde** etc. can stand alone for **de rijke man, de blinde man**. Similarly in the plural **de rijken, de blinden** mean 'the rich' and 'the blind'.

9.6.3 The inflected adjective preceded by the neuter definite article renders an abstract noun, e.g. **het goede** 'good', **het kwade** 'evil', **het mooie** 'the nice thing', **het stomme** 'the stupid thing':

Het leuke is dat ze een studiebeurs gekregen heeft.
The nice thing is she got a scholarship.

Het mooie van schaatsen is dat iedereen het kan doen.
The nice thing about skating is that everyone can do it.

9.6.4 Colours are **het groen, het geel** etc.:

Het groen van jouw trui bevalt me niet.
The green of your pullover doesn't appeal to me.

9.6.5 Note that adjectives of nationality are used in almost all cases to form the name of the feminine inhabitant, e.g. **Chinees** = Chinese, **de Chinese** = the Chinese woman (see Appendix 2).

9.7 FORMATION OF ADJECTIVES

9.7.1 SUFFIXES

It should be noted that the endings **-aardig, -kundig, -matig, -talig, -waardig** and **-zijdig** take the stress, e.g. **plantáárdig** 'vegetable', **veelzíjdig** 'versatile'.

Note: Sometimes the same word can take a number of the endings given below, each new combination giving a new word, e.g. **kinderachtig** 'childish, puerile', **kinds** 'senile', **kinderlijk** 'child-like'.

-(e)loos is equivalent in every way to English '-less', e.g. **doelloos** 'aimless', **ouderloos** 'parentless', **hopeloos** 'hopeless'

Note: **Werkloos** 'unemployed' is often pronounced **werkeloos** and can be written that way too.

-end(e)   actually the addition of **-d(e)** to the infinitive to form a present-participle (see 11.15) that can act as an adjective, e.g. **kokend** 'boiling', **de arbeidende klasse** 'the working class'.

-achtig   a very common and useful ending and one that is still productive. It often renders English '-like', e.g. **katachtig** 'cat-like', **bladachtig** 'leaf-like'. The possibilities are infinite, e.g. **Dat kind doet zo grote-mensen-achtig** 'That child behaves so much like an adult', **oudevrijsterachtig** 'old-maidish'. It can also be suffixed to colours to render '-ish', e.g. **groenachtig** 'greenish'. But the literal meaning is often no longer evident, e.g. **twijfelachtig** 'doubtful', **regenachtig** 'rainy'. In many cases the stress has even shifted to the ending, e.g. **reusachtig** 'gigantic', **woonachtig** 'resident', **waarachtig** 'true(ly)'.

-baar   a common ending added to the stems of verbs often corresponding to English '-able', e.g. **draagbaar** 'portable', **onuitstaanbaar** 'unbearable', **leesbaar** 'readable', **dankbaar** 'grateful', **zichtbaar** 'visible'.

-en   this ending is suffixed to nouns denoting materials, similar to the English ending in the first two examples (see 9.4.2), e.g. **houten** 'wooden', **gouden** 'golden', **kartonnen** 'cardboard', **betonnen** 'cement', **papieren** 'paper', **stenen** 'stone', **gipsen** 'plaster'.

-rijk   means 'rich in', 'endowed with', e.g. **fantasierijk** 'imaginative', **belangrijk** 'important', **schaduwrijk** 'very shady', **glorierijk** 'glorious'.

-talig   a handy ending for rendering '-speaking', e.g. **Engelstalig** 'English-speaking' (**Engelssprekend** is also possible), **Nederlandstaligen** 'Dutch-speaking people', **een anderstalige** 'someone who speaks a different language'.

-ig   a common ending often suffixed to nouns meaning 'having, characterised by', e.g. **machtig** 'mighty', **ijverig** 'industrious', **buiig** 'showery', **levendig** 'lively'. It is also used colloquially just like English '-ish' for approximation, e.g. **groenig** 'greenish', **viezig** 'dirtyish', **nattig** 'wettish'. This ending is also commonly applied to scientific disciplines ending in **-kunde** to form adjectives, e.g. **taalkundig** 'linguistic', **letterkundig** 'literary', **plantkundig** 'botanical' (all taking penultimate stress). From those adjectives are then formed the names of the people who practise the respective science, e.g. **taalkundige** 'linguist', **verloskundige** 'obstetrician'.

-erig	is not a very common ending and it often has a pejorative meaning, e.g. **petieterig** 'tiny', **slaperig** 'sleepy', **winderig** 'windy', **zanderig** 'sandy', **kitscherig** 'kitschy', **hebberig** 'greedy', **puisterig** 'pimply', **paniekerig** 'panicky'.
-isch	(occasionally spelt **-ies**, see 2.8) is chiefly found in foreign, often scientific words and is equivalent to English '-ic, -ical', e.g. **historisch**, **socialistisch**, **logisch**.
-s	(formerly **-sch** and still found in pre-war books as such, see 2.1(a)) 1 common ending for nationalities, e.g. **Nederlands**, **Zweeds**, **Engels**, **Frans**. 2 for adjectives derived from placenames, e.g. **Amsterdams**, **Leids**, **Londens**, **Gouds**, **Gronings**. 3 it is sometimes added to nouns other than proper nouns, e.g. **kerks** churchy, **hemels** 'heavenly', **duivels** 'devilish', **aards** 'earthly', **kinds** 'senile', **schools** 'pedantic', **speels** 'playful'.

It is this ending which one employs in the very commonly used expressions formed with **op z'n** + adjective + **s** which are similar in meaning to the French 'à la + adjective', e.g. **op z'n Frans** 'à la française' (i.e. as the French do, in the French way).

Colloquially one can invent such adjectives forming them from the names of people or firms, e.g. **op z'n McDonalds** 'as McDonalds would do it'.

-(e)lijk	a very common suffix which has no adverbial qualities despite its historical connections with English '-ly' (compare 'lovely', 'homely').[7] The **e** is usually included but not always, e.g. **onafhankelijk**[8] 'independent', **vriendelijk** 'friendly', **maatschappelijk** 'social', **menselijk** 'human(e)', **ongelooflijk** or **ongelofelijk**[9] 'unbelievable', **vreeslijk** or **vreselijk**[9] 'terrible' (usually the latter), **gevaarlijk** 'dangerous', **persoonlijk** 'personal'.
-zaam	a common ending usually added to verbal stems, e.g. **langzaam** 'slow', **buigzaam** 'flexible', **gehoorzaam** 'obedient'.
-vol	similar to English '-ful', e.g. **succesvol** 'successful', **talentvol** 'talented', **waardevol** 'valuable'.

[7] Only the couplet **gewoon/gewoonlijk** 'ordinary/ordinarily' makes a distinction between the adjective and the adverb by means of this ending. It is otherwise most unusual for any distinction to be made between the adjective and the adverb in Dutch (see chapter 10).
[8] Note the change to **k** when this ending is added to a root ending in **g**: **aanvankelijk** 'initially', **koninklijk** 'royal'.
[9] Notice that the final consonant of what was the verbal stem remains unvoiced, despite the fact that it stands between two vowels.

-vormig   corresponds to English '-shaped' and is still a very productive ending, e.g. **trechtervormig** 'funnel-shaped', **bolvormig** 'spherical-shaped', **tegelvormig** 'tile-shaped'.

-waardig   equivalent to English '-worthy'. e.g. **bezienswaardig** 'worth seeing', **bewonderenswaardig** 'praiseworthy', **betreuren-swaardig** 'lamentable', **zeewaardig** 'seaworthy', **merkwaardig** 'remarkable'. This ending is always stressed.

-aardig   not a very common ending and no longer productive, e.g. **plantaardig** 'vegetable', **kwaadaardig** 'malignant', **goedaardig** 'benign'. This ending is always stressed.

-matig   this ending denotes a conformity with what is expressed in the noun it is suffixed to. It is quite a common ending and is always stressed, e.g. **regelmatig** 'regular', **kunstmatig** 'artificial', **instinctmatig** 'instinctively'.

-vrij   this corresponds to the English endings '-free' and '-less' and is still very productive, e.g. **boomvrij** 'treeless', **autovrij** 'free of cars', **loodvrij** 'unleaded'.

9.7.2   PREFIXES

on-   is the most common means of negating adjectives and is used in a similar way to English 'un-', e.g. **onvriendelijk** 'unfriendly', **ondankbaar** 'ungrateful'. **On-** is always unstressed. There are a few compounds with **on-** whose principal component does not exist as a separate word, e.g. **onnozel** 'silly', **ondeugend** 'naughty'.

in-   Some foreign words, as in English, are negated by the addition of **in-** (**im-**), e.g. **inconsequent** 'inconsistent, **inefficiënt** 'ineffi-cient', **immoreel** 'immoral', **intolerant** 'intolerant'.

Dutch has a number of adjectival intensifiers which are very commonly used:

aarts-   **aartsdom** 'really stupid', **aartslui** 'very lazy'.

dood-   very common, e.g. **doodarm** 'very poor', **doodgewoon** 'quite ordinary', **doodeenvoudig** 'simple', **doodstil** 'very quiet', **dood-moe** 'very tired'.
          Note: **doodsbang** 'very afraid', **doodsbleek** 'very pale'.

oer-   **oerdom** 'very stupid', **oeroud** 'very old', **oerlelijk** 'very ugly', **oersaai** 'terribly boring'.

over-   has the same force as English 'over-', e.g. **overrijp** 'overripe', **overgevoelig** 'over-sensitive', **overgaar** 'over-cooked'.

poep-	vulgar, but more so is **stront-**, e.g. **poepduur** 'very dear', **poepdeftig** 'very posh'; **stronteigenwijs** 'as stubborn as a mule'.
reuze-	still productive, e.g. **reuze populair** 'very popular', **reuze vervelend** 'very annoying'. **Reuze** is usually not written as one word with the adjective it qualifies but **reuzeleuk** 'really nice' is a notable exception.
stapel-	only used in combination with words for 'mad', e.g. **stapelgek**, **stapelidioot**.
super-	**superfijn** 'very fine', **superknap** 'very clever', **superveilig** 'very safe'.
ultra-	usually with loanwords, e.g. **ultraradicaal**, **ultraconservatief**.

The intensifiers given above are particularly common and are to a degree still productive. In addition to them are others, many of them nouns, which occur in only one compound adjective. Sometimes these can be translated almost literally, e.g. **ijskoud** 'ice-cold', **spotgoedkoop** 'dirt-cheap', but very often in English they are rendered by an 'as ... as ...' phrase, e.g. **stokdoof** 'as deaf as a post'. Beware when confronted with an English 'as ... as ...' expression which you want to translate because more often than not it will be a compound adjective in Dutch, but **zo ... als** expressions do exist too, e.g. **zo mager als een lat** 'as thin as a rake', **zo blind als een mol** 'as blind as a bat', **zo trots als een pauw** 'as proud as a peacock'.

The following list of compound adjectives is by no means complete.

apetrots	as proud as a peacock
broodnuchter	as sober as a judge
drijf-, klets-, zeiknat	soaking wet, wet through
glashelder	as clear as a bell
gloedheet	red hot, as hot as hell
gloednieuw	brand new
haarfijn	as fine as hair
haarscherp	very sharp
hemelsbreed	very wide
hondsbrutaal	very cheeky, bold
ijskoud	ice-cold
keihard[10]	rock hard
kerngezond	as fit as a fiddle
kersvers	very fresh, new; hot off the press
kurkdroog	as dry as a bone

---

[10] **Keihard**, like the adjective **hard**, can mean 'hard', 'fast' or 'loud' and can thus be translated in various ways.

loodrecht	perpendicular, vertical
loodzwaar	as heavy as lead
morsdood	as dead as a doornail
peperduur	very expensive
piekfijn	very spruce, smart
piemelnaakt	stark naked, as naked as the day he was born
pijlsnel	very quick
pikdonker	pitch-dark
poedelnaakt	stark naked, as naked as the day he was born
roodgloeiend	red-hot
rotsvast	as steady as a rock
schatrijk	very wealthy
smoorverliefd	head-over-heels in love
snikheet	sweltering hot, as hot as hell
spiegelglad	as smooth as silk
splinternieuw	brand new
spotgoedkoop	dirt cheap
springlevend	alive and kicking
stampvol	chock-full
snik-, stikheet	sweltering hot, as hot as hell
steenkoud	stone-cold
stokdoof	as deaf as a post
stokoud	as old as the hills
stomdronken	dead-drunk
straatarm	as poor as a church-mouse
tjok-, propvol	chock-full
vlijmscherp	razor sharp
wagenwijd (open)	wide (open)
wildvreemd	utterly strange

9.7.3 COLOURS

beige	beige	**orange**	orange
blauw	blue	**paars**	purple
bruin	brown	**purper**	purple
geel	yellow	**rood**	red
grijs	grey	**rose**	pink
groen	green	**wit**	white
lila	lilac	**zwart**	black

-kleurig is often used to form new colours from nouns, for example from metals, e.g. **goudkleurig** 'gold', **zilverkleurig** 'silver'.

licht- and **donker-** prefixed to any colour render (light) and (dark), e.g. **lichtgroen, donkerrood.** *Note:* **lichtpaars** 'mauve'.

-ig and **-achtig** (most usually the latter) can be suffixed to the names of colours to render '-ish', e.g. **groenachtig** 'greenish'.

All colours can be compounded with each other to render shades, e.g. **grijsgroen** 'greyish green', **geelbruin** 'yellowish brown'. Note: **zwartwit** 'black and white',[11] e.g. **een zwartwit (televisietoestel)** 'a black and white television set'.

Sometimes nouns are prefixed to the colours as is done in English, e.g. **smaragdgroen** 'emerald green', **kastanjebruin** 'chestnut brown', **scharlakenrood** 'scarlet', **okergeel** 'ochre', **pikzwart** 'black as pitch', **roetzwart** 'as black as soot', **bloedrood** 'blood red', **hemelblauw** 'sky blue', **grasgroen** 'as green as grass', **spierwit** 'as white as a sheet'.

Note: **Wat voor kleur is het?** 'What colour is it?'

9.8 NOTES ON SOME PECULIARITIES OF ADJECTIVES

9.8.1 The adjective **wijlen** 'late' (as of deceased persons) precedes the title as in English but is not used together with the definite article, unlike English 'late', e.g. **wijlen Prof. T. H. Elsschot** 'the late Prof. T. H. Elsschot', **wijlen Koning Karels zoon** 'the late King Charles' son'.

9.8.2 There are a number of standard expressions in which the adjective follows the noun. English has such cases too, e.g. **moederlief, vaderlief, meisjelief** 'mother dear' etc., **God almachtig** 'God almighty', **gouverneurgeneraal** 'governor-general', **Staten-Generaal** 'States-General', **moederoverste** 'mother-superior'.

9.8.3 Some adjectives are now joined to the noun and are seen as forming a new concept; the shifted stress in such cases (indicated here by acute accents) illustrates the degree to which such words are considered compound nouns, e.g. **plattelánd** 'country', **jongemán** 'young man', **jongelúi** 'young people, youth', **hogeschóol** 'tertiary educational establishment', **hoogléraar** 'professor', **vrijgezél** 'bachelor'. But there are some which retain the stress on the adjective, e.g. **zúúrkool** 'sauerkraut' (but **rodekóól** 'red-cabbage'), **wíttebrood** 'white bread'. There does not seem to be any rule for inflection in such compounds – they must simply be learnt as they are met. Often one sees **halfdrie** etc. (i.e. time) written as one word as well as **een halfpond**.

---

[11] **Het zwart op wit hebben** 'to have it in black and white (i.e. on paper)'.

9.8.4   Adjectives of nationality (see Appendix 2) are always written with capitals although some modern writers ignore this (see 2.5). Note that geographical regions, and adjectives derived from them, are written as hyphenated nouns; adjectives derived from such nouns were not hyphenated in the pre-1996 spelling, e.g. **West-Duitsland** > **West-Duits** 'West German', **Midden-Europa** > **Midden-Europees** 'Central European' (previously **Westduits** and **Middeneuropees**). Similarly prefixes which are in themselves adjectives are hyphenated, e.g. **Zeeuws-Vlaanderen** but **Zeeuws-Vlaams**, **Kaaps-Hollands** 'Cape Dutch', **Brits-Amerikaans** 'British American'. Also many learned compounds made up of two adjectives, e.g. **literair-kritisch**.

9.8.5   The adjectives **eerstejaars** 'first-year', **eersterangs** 'first-class', **tweedehands** 'second-hand' and **volbloed** 'full-blood' are never inflected and are frequently found prefixed to the noun, e.g. **een eerstejaars student** 'a first-year student', **een eersterangs hotel** 'a first-class hotel', **een tweedehands piano** 'a second-hand piano', **een volbloed Europeaan** 'a full-blood European'.

The adjective **rot** 'awful, dreadful, horrible', which is rather colloquial but very commonly heard in colloquial Dutch, is also prefixed to the noun, e.g. **een rotauto** 'a dreadful car', **een rotdag** 'a ghastly day'. But there is also the adjective **rottig**, which has a similar meaning but can also be used predicatively, e.g. **Dat moet wel rottig voor je geweest zijn** 'That must have been awful for you', **Hoe is die auto van jou? Rottig, hoor** 'What's that car of yours like? Dreadful'. Also **Het is een rottige auto.**

9.8.6   **De** and **het** are prefixed to **-zelfde**, e.g. **dezelfde man** 'the same man', **Dat is mij allemaal hetzelfde** 'That is all the same to me'. Also **ditzelfde**, **datzelfde** and **diezelfde**, but **deze zelfde man** 'this very same man'. Note that in higher style **zelfde** can be used together with **een** rendering 'one and the same':

> **Deze voorbeelden laten zien dat een zelfde regel soms tot verschillende uitkomsten kan leiden.**
> Such examples illustrate that one and the same rule can sometimes produce different results.

9.8.7   On occasions when using more than one adjective before a noun in English we join the two by 'and', but this is not done in Dutch, e.g. **prachtige, buitengewone dingen** 'beautiful (and) unusual things'.

9.8.8   The adjectives **heel**, **geheel** and **gans**, all of which mean 'whole' although the last two are somewhat formal, can precede the definite article, e.g. **heel/geheel de wereld** 'the whole world', **gans het volk** (lit.) 'the entire nation'.

10 ADVERBS (bijwoorden)

Defining exactly what constitutes an adverb is difficult. They are those words which shed information on the when, where, why and how of the action (i.e. the verb) of the sentence, but they can also qualify adjectives (e.g. 'very good') and other adverbs (e.g. 'quite slowly'). They can be individual words or complete phrases. The approach adopted here is to look at the simplest adverbs, i.e. those derived from adjectives, and to list the most common adverbs of time and place (see TMP rule, 10.3) as well as interrogative adverbs and finally to look briefly at the formation of adverbs. Otherwise mastering adverbs is really chiefly a matter of extending one's vocabulary.

The adverb and adjective are identical in Dutch, i.e. Dutch does not have any equivalent of the English '-ly' ending (exception: **gewoon** 'usual'; **gewoonlijk** 'usually'), e.g. **Hij is snel**; **hij rent snel** 'He is quick; he runs quickly'. But adverbs, unlike adjectives, do not inflect, which is why in the following sentences **ontzettend**, **verschrikkelijk** and **typisch** have no ending but **leuk**, **oud** and **Nederlands** do:

een ontzettend leuke tas	an awfully nice bag
een verschrikkelijk oude man	a terribly old man
een typisch Nederlandse hoed	a typically Dutch hat

Compare:

een verschrikkelijke(,) oude man   a terrible old man

10.1 COMPARATIVE AND SUPERLATIVE OF ADVERBS

As there is no distinction made between the adjective and the adverb in Dutch, the rules for forming the comparative and superlative of adverbs are basically as for adjectives, i.e. by the addition of **-er** and **-st** (see 9.2.1, 9.3.1).

The predicative superlative is preceded by the article **het** and ends in **-st**, e.g. **het mooist** '(the) prettiest', **het grootst** '(the) biggest'. Occasionally one meets superlative adverbs that end in **-ste** instead of **-st**, e.g. **het dichste bij** or **het dichtstbij** '(the) closest', **tenminste** 'at least'.

This use of **het** has a parallel in English although the use of 'the' in the superlative of the adverb is optional in English:

Wanneer zijn de bloemen het mooist?
When are the flowers (the) prettiest?

Wie heeft het langst gezongen?
Who sang (the) longest?

This contrasts with the superlative of the adjective, which is **de/het/de mooiste** 'the prettiest (one)' or **de/het/de langste** 'the tallest (one)' where the choice of **de**, **het** or **de** depends on whether the implied noun is common gender, neuter or plural respectively, e.g. **Hij is de langste van de drie jongens** 'He is the tallest (one) of the three boys'.

At times it is difficult to decide whether it is the superlative of the adjective or the adverb that is required; in such cases usually both are correct but the use of the article varies (if 'the' can be left out in English, it is the adverb one is dealing with):

Welke vrouw is het mooist?	adverb
Welke vrouw is de mooiste?	adjective
Which woman is (the) prettiest?	

Die weg is het breedst.	adverb
Die weg is de breedste.	adjective
That road is (the) widest.	

Dit meisje is het aardigst.	adverb
Dit meisje is het aardigste.	adjective
This girl is (the) nicest.	

10.1.1   IRREGULAR COMPARATIVES AND SUPERLATIVES

goed	**beter**	**best**	good, better, best
graag[1]	**liever**	**liefst**	willingly, more/most willingly
veel	**meer**	**meest**	much, more, most
weinig	**minder**	**minst**	little, less, least

In addition one should note that although **dikwijls** and **vaak** 'often' are interchangeable, only **vaak** has a comparative and a superlative form, i.e. **vaak – vaker – vaakst**. Also with **dichtbij** and **vlakbij** 'nearby' only the former can be inflected, i.e. **dichterbij (het dichtste bij/het dichtstbij)** (see 9.3.6):

Hij woont dichtbij/vlakbij, maar zij woont dichterbij/het dichtstbij.
He lives nearby but she lives nearer/nearest.

For the use of **meer/meest** to form the comparative and superlative grades of adverbs see 9.2.3, 9.3.3; the same rules apply as for adjectives:

---

[1] See 11.8.3.1.3 and 11.8.5.4(b) for uses of **graag**. Note that in higher style **gaarne** can replace **graag**.

Zij is het meest geëmancipeerd van allemaal.[2]
She is the most emancipated of all.

10.1.2   NOTES ON THE SUPERLATIVE OF ADVERBS

10.1.2.1   There is a difference in meaning between 'the most important meeting' and 'a most important meeting'; the former is the superlative of the adjective 'important' and is rendered in Dutch as **de belangrijkste vergadering**, whereas the latter is simply an adverb (= very, very), formed from a superlative, which is qualifying the adjective 'important' and is rendered by **een hoogst belangrijke vergadering**.

10.1.2.2   **Minder/minst** 'less/least' are commonly used before adjectives in this way too:

Dit is een minder interessant boek dan dat.
This is a less interesting book than that.

Maar dit boek is het minst interessant.[3]
But this book is the least interesting.

But **minst** and derivatives of it also occur in other adverbial expressions:

niet in het minst   not in the least
minstens, tenminste, op z'n minst   at least

Note that **althans** commonly renders 'at least' as an adverbial conjunction, but as a simple adverb it is usually interchangeable with **tenminste**:

Hij is niet gekomen, althans ik heb hem niet gezien (or ... **ik heb hem althans niet gezien**)
Hij is niet gekomen. Ik heb hem tenminste niet gezien.
He hasn't arrived, at least I haven't seen him.

10.1.2.3   A common alternative to the superlative formed from **het + st** is that formed from **op z'n/hun mooist**, where **z'n** is more usual in the spoken language (see 8.1.1(a)):

Deze tulpen zijn in mei op z'n/hun mooist.
The tulips are prettiest in May.

---

[2] The superlative of the adjective here would read **Zij is de meest geëmancipeerde van allemaal** where a word like **vrouw** is implied after **geëmancipeerde**.
[3] Without the **e** ending, this is an adverb, but with it it can be perceived as either an adverb or an adjective, i.e. **het minst interessante boek** understood.

op z'n best 'at best', **op z'n vroegst** 'at the earliest'

Also: **laatst, op het laatst** 'at last, in the end'; **laatst** can mean 'lately' too.

10.1.2.4 In the written language the following adverbial superlatives occur which are not translatable as such into English:

Ik zou dat ten zeerste betreuren.
I would regret that very much.

Dat is ten strengste verboden.
That is strictly forbidden.

Het moet ten spoedigste worden afgeleverd.
It must be delivered immediately.

Hij heeft het ten stelligste ontkend.
He flatly denied it.

10.2   INTENSIFYING ADVERBS

There is a variety of these, as indeed there is in English too, which are used to emphasize other adverbs and adjectives (see 9.3.5).

10.2.1   'VERY': heel, erg, zeer (lit.), hartstikke

The three are completely synonymous but **zeer** is rather formal or particularly emphatic and only **erg** can be used with negatives, e.g. **Hij was niet erg groot** 'He wasn't very big'. **Heel**, as an adjective, can also mean 'whole' and **erg** can mean 'terrible', e.g. **Het was heel erg** 'It was quite awful', **een erge aardbeving** 'a terrible earthquake'. Occasionally one gets a doubling up of **heel** and **erg** as adverbs, e.g. **Het is heel erg moeilijk** 'It is very, very difficult'. It is also common for the adverbs **erg** and particularly **heel** to inflect when preceding an inflected attributive adjective, but this should be avoided in writing, e.g. **een hele mooie boom** = **een heel mooie boom** 'a very beautiful tree'.

Hartstikke, although seldom ever written, is frequently used to qualify adjectives in colloquial Dutch, e.g. **hartstikke leuk** 'very nice', **hartstikke duur** 'very expensive', **hartstikke stom** 'very stupid'.

10.2.2 The following adverbs are very commonly used to intensify adjectives and other adverbs:

akelig[4]	awful(ly)
vreselijk	terrible(-y)
verschrikkelijk	frightful(ly)

ontzaglijk	awful(ly)
ontiegelijk	extremely (coll.)
afschuwelijk[4]	horrible (-y)

These adverbs must never be inflected when occurring before attributive adjectives:

een ontzettend leuke jurk	an awfully nice dress
een verschrikkelijk lief kind	a terribly nice child
een afschuwelijk lelijk gezicht	a horribly ugly face

Ontiegelijk, which was in fashion a few years ago, although seldom written, now seems to be waning in popularity, but the word **enorm** is very 'in' at the moment (see also **reuze**, 9.7.2):

een enorm duur gebouw	a tremendously expensive building
Ik heb enorm veel verkocht.	I sold an enormous amount.

10.2.3

bijzonder	especially (pronounced **biezonder**)
buitengewoon	exceptional(ly)
te	too
veel te	much too (colloquially also **veels te**)

One should take care with English 'especially': when it is used as an adjectival or adverbial intensifier **bijzonder** is the appropriate word:

Het was bijzonder interessant.
It was especially (particularly) interesting.

But in 'especially when it rains' or 'especially in summer' etc. the word **vooral** is required, i.e. in contexts where 'especially' can be substituted by 'above all' (i.e. when 'especially' is not qualifying an adjective):

Vooral wanneer het regent
Especially when it rains

vooral 's zomers
especially in (the) summer

10.3 ADVERBS OF TIME

10.3.1 It is good style in Dutch to begin clauses with adverbs of time. It is particularly advisable to do this when there are also adverbs of manner

---

[4] **Akelig** and **afschuwelijk** can only be used in pejorative situations, e.g. **akelig zoet** 'sickly sweet', **afschuwelijk duur/lelijk** 'terribly expensive/ugly'; compare **vreselijk leuk/lelijk** 'really nice/ugly'.

and place in the same clause. Dutch insists on the order Time, Manner, Place whereas English usually has the reverse order:

	P	M	T
He goes	to school	by bus	every day.
	T	M	P
Hij gaat	**elke dag**	**met de bus**	**naar school.**

By beginning clauses with time in Dutch, one then needs only concentrate on putting manner and place in the correct order:

Elke dag gaat hij met de bus naar school.

Notice that if one begins the clause with time, inversion of subject and verb takes place.

Only statements can of course begin with time, never questions, where the verb must be in first position:

Kom je morgen met de fiets of de tram?
Are you coming by bike or tram tomorrow?

The only exceptions to time always preceding manner and place are the short commonly occurring adverbs **er**, **hier** and **daar**. Er (unemphatic 'there') always precedes time and **hier** and **daar** can stand at the beginning of the clause for emphasis and thus precede time; otherwise they usually follow time, but do not have to (see 10.3.7):

Ik ben er al geweest. (only possible order)
Daar ben ik al geweest/Ik ben al daar geweest/Ik ben daar al geweest.
I've already been there.

Hier heb ik vanochtend brood gekocht/Ik heb vanochtend hier brood gekocht/
Vanochtend heb ik hier brood gekocht/Ik heb hier vanochtend brood gekocht.
I bought bread here this morning.

10.3.2 When there are two expressions of time in a clause, the less definite always precedes the more definite:

Ik sta iedere zondag om tien uur op/Iedere zondag sta ik om tien uur op.
I get up at 10.00 a.m. every Sunday.

Hij leest altijd tot middernacht.
He always reads till midnight.

10.3.3   Note that in the previous English sentence the adverb of time occurs between the subject and the finite verb. This is very common in English but is impossible in Dutch because of the necessity of the verb always standing in second position:

Hij belt me zelden op.
He seldom rings me up.

Hij heeft me het geld nooit gegeven.
He never gave me the money.

10.3.4   When an expression of time occurs in a sentence with a nominal direct object, it precedes the object, not however, when the object is a pronoun:

Jullie moeten vanavond dit hoofdstuk lezen.
You must read this chapter tonight.

but

Jullie moeten het vanavond lezen.

Ik heb hem gisteren het geld gegeven.
I gave him the money yesterday.

Note that this problem can be avoided by beginning with time:

Vanavond moeten jullie dit hoofdstuk lezen.
Gisteren heb ik hem het geld gegeven.

The same commonly occurs with an expression of place:

Hij zat in de tuin een boek te lezen.
He was sitting in the garden reading a book.

Zij zag overal vreemde dingen.
She saw strange things everywhere.

but

Zij zag ze overal.
She saw them eveywhere.

10.3.5   Do not let the word order in co-ordinate clauses containing an adverb of time confuse you. Remember that the co-ordinating conjunctions **en**, **of**, **want** and **maar** do not affect the word order. Thus in the following example **morgen** is taken as the first idea in the new clause and consequently inversion of subject and verb takes place:

Gisteren is hij naar Amsterdam gevlogen maar morgen komt hij terug.
Yesterday he flew to Amsterdam but he is coming back tomorrow.

A stylistic variant of the above, not placing time at the beginning of the two clauses, is:

Hij is gisteren naar Amsterdam gevlogen maar (hij) komt morgen terug.

10.3.6   There can be a slight difference in the word order in subordinate clauses too:

Zij ging vroeg naar bed, omdat ze die dag een lange wandeling had gemaakt.
She went to bed early because that day she had gone for a long walk, or:
She went to bed early because she had gone for a long walk that day.

The only possible place for the adverb is after the subject. This is not the case in English as the above translations illustrate.

10.3.7   Note the presence or absence of 'for' in expressions of time:

(a) **(Voor) hoe lang ga je? Ik ga er (voor) twee weken naartoe.**
    How long are you going for? I'm going there for two weeks.
(b) **Ik ben er twee weken geweest/Ik was er twee weken.**
    I was there for two weeks.
(c) **Ik woon hier al twee jaar.**
    I have been living here for two years.

(a) **voor** (when in the future, but it can also be omitted in such cases)
(b) nothing (when in the past)
(c) **al** (when in the past in English but lasting up till the present with the verb in the present in Dutch, see 11.2.1.3, 11.2.2.3)

Note the word order with **al twee maanden/weken/jaar/uur** type constructions:

Ik woon er/hier/daar al twee jaar or: **Ik woon al twee jaar hier/daar.**

but only

Ik woon al twee jaar in Amsterdam.
Ik wacht al twee uur op je.

10.3.8　DAYS OF THE WEEK

on Sundays	**'s zondags** or **op zondagen** etc.
on Mondays	**'s maandags**
on Tuesdays	**dinsdags**
on Wednesdays	**'s woensdags**
on Thursdays	**donderdags**
on Fridays	**vrijdags**
on Saturdays	**zaterdags**
on Sunday (past and coming)	**(op) zondag**
the Sunday after	**de zondag daarna**
Sunday morning, afternoon, evening/night	**zondagochtend/-morgen, -middag, -avond**
on Sunday evenings	**op zondagavond**
by Sunday	**vóór zondag**
next Sunday	**aanstaande/komende zondag volgende week zondag**
last Sunday	**afgelopen zondag vorige week zondag**
Sunday week	**zondag over een week**
Sunday fortnight	**zondag over twee weken**
from Sunday (on)	**vanaf zondag**
on Sundays and holidays	**op zon- en feestdagen**

10.3.9　YESTERDAY, TODAY, TOMORROW, ETC.

yesterday	**gister(en)**
yesterday morning, afternoon	**gisterochtend/-morgen, -middag**
yesterday evening or (more usually) last night	**gisteravond**
the day before yesterday	**eergisteren**
the evening of the day before yesterday	**eergisteravond/-nacht (eergisterochtend/-morgen)**
today	**vandaag**
today	**heden** (lit.)
from today on	**vanaf vandaag**
this morning, afternoon	**vanochtend, -morgen, -middag**
tonight, this evening	**vanavond**
tonight (after midnight)	**vannacht**
last night (after midnight)	**vannacht**
tomorrow	**morgen**
tomorrow morning	**morgenochtend (not *morgenmorgen)**
tomorrow afternoon, evening/night	**morgenmiddag, -avond**
the day after tomorrow	**overmorgen**

10.3.10   PERIODS OF THE DAY

in the morning(s)	**'s morgens**
in the morning(s)	**'s ochtends**
in the afternoon(s)	**'s middags**
in the evening(s)	**'s avonds**
at night	**'s nachts**
during the day	**overdag**
late in the evening	**'s avonds laat**
early in the morning	**'s ochtends vroeg**
at lunch-time	**tussen de middag**
at one o'clock in the morning/a.m.	**om één uur 's nachts** (see 14.8.1.4)
at five o'clock in the morning/a.m.	**om vijf uur 's ochtends**

10.3.11   WEEKEND

this/next weekend	**dit/volgend/komend weekend**
last weekend	**vorig/afgelopen weekend**
at/on the weekend	**in het weekend/weekeinde**

10.3.12   SEASONS

next summer, winter, autumn, spring	**volgende/aanstaande/(aan) komende zomer, winter, herfst, lente**
last summer	**vorige/afgelopen zomer**
this summer (i.e. both past and coming)	**van de zomer**
in summer	**'s zomers, in de zomer**
in winter	**'s winters, in de winter**
in autumn	**in de herfst, in het najaar**
in spring	**in de lente, in het voorjaar**

10.3.13   NOW

now	**nu** (colloquial **nou**)
now	**thans** (lit.)
from now on	**van nu af aan, vanaf nu, voortaan**
until now, up to now	**tot nu toe,**[5] **tot nog toe, tot dusver, tot op de dag van vandaag, tot op heden**
nowadays	**vandaag de dag, tegenwoordig, hedentendage**

[5] Note that in this expression **nu** cannot be pronounced **nou**.

now and then	**(zo) nu en dan, af en toe**
now and then, every so often	**om de zoveel tijd**

10.3.14   HOUR

for hours	**urenlang**
hours ago	**uren geleden**
two hours ago	**twee uur geleden**[6]
in two hours' time	**over twee uur**

10.3.15   DAY

one day, morning, evening	**op een dag, morgen, avond**
that day, morning, evening	**die dag, morgen, avond**
the day after	**de dag daarna**
the next day	**de dag daarop**
the day before	**de dag daarvoor/ervoor/tevoren**
all day, evening, night	**de hele dag, avond, nacht**
for days	**dagenlang**
days ago	**dagen geleden**
one of these days[7]	**een dezer dagen**
(on) the same day	**(op) dezelfde dag**
once/twice a day	**een/twee keer per dag**
daily	**dagelijks**
three times a day	**drie keer per dag**
	drie keer daags (lit.)
the day after (that)	**de dag daarna/erna**
	daags nadien (lit.)
	daags daarna (lit.)
the day before	**de dag tevoren**
	daags tevoren (lit.)

10.3.16   WEEK

this week	**deze week, van de week**
next week	**volgende/aanstaande/komende week**
last week	**vorige/verleden/afgelopen week**
in a week, in a week's time	**over een week**
in a fortnight, in a fortnight's time	**over twee weken, over veertien dagen**

[6] **Uur** is always in the singular after numerals (see 14.8.1.6).
[7] In English this expression can mean at any time in the future but the Dutch expression refers to the not too distant future, i.e. soon, shortly = **binnenkort**.

within a week	**binnen een week**
a week ago	**een week geleden**
a fortnight ago	**twee weken geleden**
Friday week, a week from Friday	**vrijdag over een week**
during the week, on weekdays	**door de week, op werkdagen**
at the beginning/end of next/ last week	**begin/eind volgende/vorige week**
the week after	**de week daarop**
all week (long)	**de (ge)hele week (door)**
from next week on	**vanaf volgende week**
once a week	**een keer in de week/per week**
twice a week	**twee keer in de week/per week**
every other/second week	**om de (andere) week**

10.3.17 MONTH

this month	**deze maand, van de maand**
next month	**volgende/aanstaande/komende maand**
last month	**vorige/verleden/afgelopen maand**
from next month (on)	**vanaf volgende maand**
in a month's time	**over een maand**
within a month	**binnen een maand**
a month ago	**een maand geleden**
for months	**maanden(lang)**
	maanden achtereen (lit.)
once a month	**een keer in de maand/per maand**
the month after, the next month	**de maand daarop**
at the beginning of January	**begin januari**
in the middle of January	**half januari**
	medio januari (official)
at the end of January	**eind januari**
in June	**in juni**

10.3.18 YEAR

this year	**dit jaar**
from this year (on)	**vanaf dit jaar**
next year	**volgend/komend jaar**
last year	**vorig/verleden/afgelopen jaar**
in two years' time	**over twee jaar**[8]
two years ago	**twee jaar geleden**

[8] **Jaar** is always in the singular after numerals (see 14.8.1.6).

years ago	**jaren geleden**
	jaren her (lit.)
the last three years	**de afgelopen drie jaar**
all year long/through	**het hele jaar door**
the year after	**het jaar daarop**
once a year	**een keer per/in het jaar**

10.3.19   HOLIDAYS

on public holidays	**op feestdagen**
on Ascension Day	**op hemelvaartsdag**[9]
on the Queen's Birthday (holiday)	**op Koninginnedag**[10]
at Christmas time	**met (de) Kerst/Kerstmis**
at Easter	**met Pasen**
at Whitsuntide	**met Pinksteren**

10.3.20   GENERAL

always	**altijd**
still	**steeds**
	nog
	nog altijd
	nog steeds
not yet	**nog niet**
still not	**nog steeds niet**
for good	**voor altijd**
	voor goed
for ever (and ever)	**voor eeuwig (en altijd)**
seldom	**zelden**
ever	**ooit**
never	**nooit**
mostly	**meestal**
sometimes	**soms**
now and again	**af en toe**
meanwhile	**intussen**
	in de tussentijd
	ondertussen
	inmiddels

---

[9] Note that although the names of such festivities are capitalized (e.g. **Hemelvaart, Kerstmis, Pasen**), when used in compounds these words are written with a small letter: **kerstboom** 'christmas tree', **paasvakantie** 'Easter holidays'.

[10] April 30th is not in fact the Queen's birthday, although it was Juliana's, but the day on which Beatrix was inaugurated (Dutch monarchs are not crowned) as queen.

often	**vaak**
	dikwijls
more often	**vaker** (see 10.1.1)
usually	**gewoonlijk**
usually, generally	**doorgaans**
recently	**onlangs**
	kort geleden
lately	**laatst**
	de laatste tijd
at the latest	**op z'n laatst**
at the latest, not later than	**uiterlijk**
at the earliest	**op z'n vroegst**
late	**te laat**
these days	**tegenwoordig**
in the future	**in de toekomst**
	vervolgens
henceforth	**in het vervolg**
in the course of time	**in de loop der tijd**
	op den duur
	na verloop van tijd
	mettertijd
in due course	**te zijner tijd** (**t.z.t.**)
high time	**hoog tijd**
	(**de**) **hoogste tijd**
for the time being, provisionally	**voorlopig**
temporarily	**tijdelijk**
since, since then	**sindsdien**
	sedertdien (lit.)
of old	**vanouds** (**her**)
from way back, from childhood	**van jongs af** (**aan**)

10.4   ADVERBS OF TIME WITH ALTERNATIVE TRANSLATIONS IN DUTCH

10.4.1   'AFTERWARDS'

afterwards	**toen, daarna, naderhand**
afterwards, after that	**nadien** (lit.)
afterwards, later	**later**
shortly afterwards	**kort daarna**

10.4.2   'AGAIN'

again	**weer**

(yet) again	**alweer**
(once) again	**opnieuw**
again and again	**steeds weer**
	telkens (weer)

10.4.3 'ALREADY'

| already | **al** |
| | **(al)reeds** (lit.) |

10.4.4 'BEFORE'

before, earlier, formerly, previously	**vroeger**
(never) before	**(nooit) eerder**
before that	**voordien** (lit.)
as never before	**als nooit tevoren**

10.4.5 'FINALLY'

finally	**tenslotte**[11]
finally, at last	**eindelijk**
eventually	**uiteindelijk**[12]
finally, at the end	**op 't laatst**
finally, lastly	**ten laatste** (following **ten eerste**, **ten tweede** etc.) (lit.)

10.4.6 'FIRSTLY'

firstly	**eerst**
for the first time	**voor 't eerst, de eerste keer**
firstly (followed by secondly, thirdly etc.)	**in de eerste/tweede/derde plaats ten eerste (ten tweede, ten derde, etc.)**
first (as in 'Show me the letter first', i.e. before you send it)	**eerst van tevoren**
at first	**in het begin**

---

[11] **Tenslotte** also translates 'after all'.

[12] Note that **eventueel**, which is both an adjective and an adverb, means 'possible(ly)', not 'eventual(ly)':

Men kan eventueel met een cheque betalen.
It is possible to pay by cheque.

10.4.7 'IMMEDIATELY'

immediately   **onmiddellijk**
                                     meteen

10.4.8 'IN A MOMENT'

as in 'I'll do it in a moment'.   **zo meteen**
                                     straks[13]
                                     dadelijk
                                     zo
                                     direct

10.4.9 'JUST'

just   **net**
                                     pas[14]
                                     zojuist[15]

10.4.10 'SOON'

soon   **gauw**
soon, quickly   **spoedig**
soon afterwards   **kort daarna**
soon, shortly   **binnenkort, straks**
sooner   **vroeger**
sooner or later   **vroeger of later, vroeg of laat**
                                     op een gegeven ogenblik/moment
as soon as possible   **zo gauw mogelijk**[16]

Note: I'll do it soon (see 'in a moment').

10.4.11 'THEN'

then   **dan**

---

[13] **Straks** can refer to both the near future and the very recent past:

Tot straks!
See you in a little while/later.

Ik heb je horloge straks op je bed zien liggen.
I saw your watch lying on your bed a moment ago.

[14] **Pas** also means 'only' and 'not until' (see 14.6).

[15] Despite appearances **juist** 'correct' does not usually mean 'just', only **zojuist** does.

[16] All expressions of this type, i.e. 'as (adj./adv.) as possible' take the form **zo** + adj./adv. + **mogelijk** where the second 'as' is not translated: **zo laat/groot/dik mogelijk** 'as late/large/fat as possible'.

then (verb in past tense)	**toen**
then, at that time	**destijds**
	toentertijd
	indertijd
then, after that, next	**vervolgens**

Note: **Dan** can occur in sentences in both the past and present tenses:

> **Ze waren van plan (om) elkaar in de stad te ontmoeten. Ze wilden dan ...**
> They intended meeting each other in town. They then wanted to ...

Here the verb is in the past but the action is not. It did not occur.

Compare:

> **Ze hebben elkaar in de stad ontmoet. Toen gingen ze ...**
> They met in town. Then they ...

Toen refers to one occasion. The word **altijd** (repeated occasions) necessitates the use of **dan** in the following sentence, even if the verb is in the past:

> **Ik keek altijd eerst naar het nieuws en dan (= vervolgens) las ik de krant.**
> I would always watch the news and then read the paper.

Compare the use of **wanneer** when the verb is in the past. (see 12.2.1.6)

10.4.12   'TIME'

at the same time	**tegelijk**
	tegelijkertijd
	terzelfdertijd
some time ago	**een tijd(je) geleden**
a little while/moment ago	**straks** (see footnote 13)
a little while	**een tijdje**
	een poosje
	eventjes
all the time	**de hele tijd**
for a long time	**(al) lang**
(exactly) on time	**(stipt) op tijd**
	bijtijds
at all times/any time	**te allen tijde**
once; one time	**één keer, eenmaal**
twice	**twee keer, tweemaal**
a few/several times	**een paar keer**
last time	**de vorige keer**

next time	**de volgende keer**
this time	**deze/dit keer**[17]
two times (twice) a day	**twee keer per dag/op een dag**
in the course of time	**in de loop der tijd**
	op den duur
	na verloop van tijd
	mettertijd

10.5 ADVERBS OF PLACE AND DIRECTION

It will be noticed that in many of the groups set out below there is a form with and without the preposition **naar**. In English there is usually only one word to express both place and motion towards a place; in the latter case Dutch must express the motion with **naar** after verbs of motion.

Wanneer komt hij hiernaartoe?	When is he coming here?
Zij ging naar buiten.	She went outside.
Zij gingen naar boven.	They went upstairs.

hier	here
daar	there
er	there (**er** is an unemphatic form of **daar**. See 15.4)

hiervandaan, van hier	from here
daar-, ervandaan, van daar	from there
hiernaartoe	(to) here
daar-, ernaartoe	(to) there

hiernaast	next-door
hierop	on this/these
hierin	in this/these
hierachter	behind this/these etc.

Similarly:

daarop	on that/those
daarin	in that/those
daarachter	behind that/those etc.
erop	on it/them
erin	in it/them
erachter	behind it/them (see 15.3)

links	on the left

---

[17] Take note of the double gender of **keer** in the above expressions (see 7.1.4.1); **keer** is always used in the singular after numerals.

rechts	on the right
linksaf	(turn) left
rechtsaf	(turn) right
naar links	to the left
naar rechts	to the right
die/deze kant op/uit	that way, this way
in het midden	in the middle
rechtdoor	straight ahead
verderop	further on
naar voren (toe)	forward, ahead
naar achteren (toe)	back(wards)
voorin	in the front
voorop	up the front
vooraan	at the head/front
achterin	in the back
achterop	on the back
achteraan	at the end (see 13.2.3)
boven	upstairs
beneden	downstairs
naar boven, de trap op	(to) upstairs
naar beneden, de trap af	(to) downstairs
bovenop, bovenaan	at the top (of)
onderaan	at the bottom (of)
binnen, binnenshuis	inside
buiten, buitenshuis	outside
naar binnen	(to) inside
naar buiten	(to) outside
naar huis	home
thuis	at home

Note the exception **thuiskomen** 'to come home', not ***naar huis komen**.

weg	away
ver weg	far away
onderweg	underway, on the way
bergop(waarts)	uphill
bergaf(waarts)	downhill
stroomop(waarts)	upstream
stroomaf(waarts)	downstream
alhier (lit.)	here, at this place
aldaar (lit.)	there, at the place mentioned
te uwent (lit.)	at your place

10.5.1   INDEFINITE ADVERBS OF PLACE AND DIRECTION

overal	everywhere
ergens	somewhere (also an adverb of manner meaning 'somehow'; see 8.6.9)
nergens	nowhere (see 8.6.9)
ergens anders, elders	somewhere else
nergens anders	nowhere else
overal vandaan	from everywhere (see 8.6.9)
overal naartoe	(to) everywhere
ergens vandaan	from somewhere
ergens naartoe	(to) somewhere
nergens vandaan	from nowhere
nergens naartoe	(to) nowhere

10.5.2   ADVERBS OF MANNER AND DEGREE

Adverbs of manner and degree are too numerous and diverse to list. The student is advised to consult a dictionary for these.

10.6   INTERROGATIVE ADVERBS (**vragende bijwoorden**)

Interrogative adverbs are those words that introduce questions asking when, where, how and why etc. (see also Interrogative pronouns, 8.7). For interrogative adverbs in indirect questions see 12.6.

waarom	why
wanneer	when
sinds wanneer	since when
waar	where
waar ... naartoe/heen	where ... to
waar ... vandaan	where ... from
hoe	how

10.6.1   Hoe sometimes renders English 'what', e.g. **Hoe is uw naam?** 'What is your name?' **Hoe heet u?** 'What is your name?' Also the question 'What is the date?' is **De hoeveelste is het vandaag? Hoe** is often followed by other adverbs as in English, common combinations being written as one word:

hoelang	how long
hoeveel	how much/many

hoe vaak	how often

Note the interrogative clause **Hoe komt het dat . . .?** 'How come . . .?'

10.6.2 Whenever **waar** occurs in a question with a verb of motion designating direction to or from a place, Dutch must use the compounds **waar . . . naartoe/heen** or **waar . . . vandaan** respectively (compare the use of 'whither' and 'whence' in archaic English):

Waar woont u?	Where do you live?

but

Waar gaat u naartoe?	Where are you going? (= whither)
Waar komt hij vandaan?	Where does he come from? (= whence)

10.7   ADVERBIAL CONJUNCTIONS (bijwoordelijke voegwoorden)

See 12.3, 12.6.

10.8   FORMATION OF ADVERBS

10.8.1   -s

The addition of a final **-s** to various words is a common adverbial formation:

heelhuids	unscathed, without a scratch
onverwachts	unexpectedly
(te)vergeefs	in vain

The **op z'n** noun + **s** constructions are still productive:

op z'n Frans	à la française
op z'n Hollands	as the Dutch do, à la hollandaise
op z'n Wims	as Wim does (any person's name)
op z'n janboerenfluitjes	in a slapdash way

10.8.2   -jes

There is also a group of adverbial diminutives that are very commonly used in the spoken language, but most are permissible in the written language too. This ending is still productive (see 7.5.3.1):

eventjes	just a moment (also pron. **effentjes**)

frisjes	coolish, fresh, nippy
gezelligjes	cosy, cosily
kalmpjes (aan)	calmly
knusjes[18]	cosily, snugly
losjes	loosely
netjes[18]	nice, nice(ly), properly
slapjes[18]	weak, gutless
stiekempjes	secretly
stilletjes	quietly
strakjes	in a moment, soon
zachtjes	quietly, gently

10.8.3 -gewijs

This is rather literary; its basic meaning is something like 'according to, by':

groepsgewijs	in groups
steekproefsgewijs	by taking random samples
verhoudingsgewijs	relatively, proportionately

10.8.4 -halve

Basic meaning 'for the sake of':

gemakshalve	for convenience('s sake)
volledigheidshalve	for the sake of completeness
veiligheidshalve	for safety's sake

10.8.5 -lijks

No longer productive. Actually an adverbial **-s** suffixed to the adjectival ending **-lijk.** Found only in the words **dagelijks** 'daily', **maandelijks** 'monthly', **jaarlijks** 'yearly'. All these words are also used as adjectives: e.g. **ons dagelijks brood** 'our daily bread'.

10.8.6 -lings

No longer productive:

blindelings	blindly

---

[18] Some of these words are occasionally used as predicative adjectives:

Jij ziet er netjes uit.
You look nice (i.e. nicely dressed).

beurtelings	in turns
ijlings	in haste
schrijlings	astride

10.8.7   -waarts

Comparable to English -'ward(s)' and still productive:

bergopwaarts	uphill
bergafwaarts	downhill
stroomopwaarts	upstream
stroomafwaarts	downstream
huiswaarts	home, homewards
stadwaarts	towards the city

10.8.8   -weg

This is quite a common ending for making adverbs of certain adjectives and is still productive to a degree, particularly in the spoken language:

brutaalweg	coolly, barefacedly
domweg	(quite) simply
gewoonweg	(quite) simply
kortweg	in short
pakweg	about, approximately, say

11 VERBS (werkwoorden)

Dutch verbs can be weak, strong, mixed or irregular; modal auxiliary verbs and **zijn** and **hebben** can be seen as belonging to separate categories again.

WEAK VERBS

Weak verbs are simply regular verbs, the term 'weak' having been invented by Jacob Grimm and being peculiar to Germanic languages. Weak verbs are those that form their past tenses by the addition of a dental suffix, as is the case in English: compare 'work*ed*' (with a 't' sound) – **werk*te***, **gewerk*t***, 'play*ed*' (with a 'd' sound) – **speel*de***, **gespeel*d***.

STRONG VERBS

Colloquially strong verbs are often referred to as irregular verbs, but strictly speaking there is a difference between strong and irregular verbs. Strong verbs are those belonging to the seven original ablaut series common to all Germanic languages, i.e. they follow one of seven basic patterns (see 11.1.3.2). Irregular verbs, on the other hand, are those that show irregularities that are at odds with the seven ablaut series (see 11.5). The term 'mixed verb' is used to describe those verbs which have a strong past participle and a weak imperfect (see 11.4). Strong verbs form their present tense exactly as weak verbs. Only in the past tenses does it become obvious whether a verb is strong. All strong verbs have in common (a) a change in the vowel of the stem in the imperfect and/or the past participle and (b) all past participles end in **-en**.

TENSE

The various tenses or 'times of action' of both weak and strong verbs will be looked at one by one in the following chapter. The complicated issue of tense is twofold: first it entails the formation of the various tenses and second, the use of those tenses. The two are dealt with separately here.

11.1   FORMATION OF TENSES

11.1.1   PRESENT TENSE (**de onvoltooid tegenwoordige tijd – o.t.t.**)

With the exception of **komen**, **zijn**, **hebben** and the modals, all verbs are regular in the present tense and the irregularities of strong verbs are only evident in the past tenses.

Example: **werken** 'to work':

Singular	*Plural*
1 **ik werk**	1 **wij werken**
2 **jij werkt**	2 **jullie werken, werkt**
u werkt	**u werkt**
3 **hij, zij, het werkt**	3 **zij werken**

Note: Nowadays the form in **-en** with **jullie** is the more usual. In Belgium **gij** 'you', both a singular and a plural, is in general use and it takes the plural **-t** ending. This form is also found in Holland in older texts and particularly in the Bible (see 8.1.2.1(c))

11.1.1.1   Interrogative

The interrogative is formed simply by inverting the subject and the object:

| **ik werk** | I work, I am working, I do work |
| **werk ik?** | am I working?, do I work? |

The **jij** form drops its **-t** when inversion occurs, e.g. **jij/je werkt** but **werk jij/je?**

Note that the present progressive or continuous tense (i.e. 'I am running' etc.) is not usually rendered in Dutch (for exceptions see 11.16)

11.1.1.2   Rules for the formation of the present tense of all verbs (i.e. weak and strong)

The plural is always identical to the infinitive; the singular is formed by isolating the stem of the verb and then adding **-t** to the second and third persons; the first person singular and the stem are always identical. The rules that apply for the spelling of the stem are the same as for the plural of nouns and the inflection of adjectives, but are in reverse, i.e. the **-en** ending of the infinitive is dropped and the spelling rules of Dutch necessitate that certain consonants be written singularly instead of double, certain vowels be written double instead of singularly, and **v** and **z** be written **f** and **s**:

Examples:

liggen 'to lie'	**lopen** 'to walk'
ik lig	**ik loop**
jij ligt	**jij loopt**
hij ligt	**hij loopt**
wij liggen	**wij lopen**
jullie liggen	**jullie lopen**
zij liggen	**zij lopen**
geloven 'to believe'	**reizen** 'to travel'
ik geloof	**ik reis**
jij gelooft	**jij reist**
hij gelooft	**hij reist**
wij geloven	**wij reizen**
jullie geloven	**jullie reizen**
zij geloven	**zij reizen**

Sometimes, as with nouns and adjectives, a combination of these rules is applicable (see **geloven** above). If the stem already ends in **-t**, no further **t** is required, but if the stem ends in **-d** (pronounced t), then a **t** is added for the sake of form:

Examples:

bijten 'to bite'	**rijden** 'to drive, ride'
ik bijt	**ik rij(d)**
jij bijt	**jij rijdt**
hij bijt	**hij rijdt**
wij bijten	**wij rijden**
jullie bijten	**jullie rijden**
zij bijten	**zij rijden**

The interrogative of **jij bijt** is **bijt jij?**, whereas that of **jij rijdt** is **rij(d) jij?**

Note: Common verbs whose stem ends in **-d** and which have an **ij** or **ou** in the stem always drop the **d** in the first person singular and the inter-rogative of the second person singular; it may be written but is never pronounced: **ik rij(d)**, **ik hou(d)**; **rij(d) je**, **hou(d) je?** Less common verbs merely drop the **t**, which means there is no change in the way they are pronounced, e.g. **ik lijd** (< **lijden** = to suffer), **ik vermijd** (< **vermijden** = to suffer); **lijd je**, **vermijd je?**

There are five monosyllabic verbs that should be noted:

staan 'to stand'	**gaan** 'to go'	**slaan** 'to hit'
ik sta	**ik ga**	**ik sla**
jij staat	**jij gaat**	**jij slaat**

(sta je?)	(ga je?)	(sla je?)
hij slaat	**hij gaat**	**hij slaat**
pl. **staan**	pl. **gaan**	pl. **slaan**

zien 'to see'	**doen** 'to do'
ik zie	**ik doe**
jij ziet	**jij doet**
(**zie je?**)	(**doe je?**)
hij ziet	**hij doet**
pl. **zien**	pl. **doen**

The verb **komen** 'to come' shows a slight irregularity in the present tense:

ik kom (not **koom**)	**wij komen**
jij komt	**jullie komen**
hij komt	**zij komen**

11.1.2   IMPERFECT TENSE (**de onvoltooid verleden tijd – o.v.t.**)

The imperfect or simple past in English is 'I worked' (a weak verb), 'I sang' (a strong verb). The progressive and emphatic forms 'I was working', 'I did work' are not usually rendered in Dutch (for exceptions see 11.14).

11.1.2.1 Weak verbs

The imperfect is formed, as in English, by the addition of a dental ending to the stem of the verb. The rules for the isolation of the stem are given above. The only difficulty with the formation of the imperfect of weak verbs in Dutch is deciding whether to add **-te/-ten** or **-de/-den** to the stem. The two possible conjugations are as follows:

werken 'to work'

ik werkte	**wij werkten**
jij werkte	**jullie werkten**
u werkte	**u werkte**
hij, zij, het werkte	**zij werkten**

Gij forms end in **-tet**.

horen 'to hear'

ik hoorde	**wij hoorden**
jij hoorde	**jullie hoorden**
u hoorde	**u hoorde**
hij, zij, het hoorde	**zij hoorden**

Gij forms end in **-det**.

Those stems that end in the voiceless consonants **p, t, k, f, s, ch** add the voiceless ending **-te/-ten**, e.g. **hoopte** 'to hope' – **hoopte**, **blaffen** 'to bark' – **blafte**, **lachen** 'to laugh' – **lachte** etc. The word **'t kofschip** can serve as a mnemonic. Stems ending in any other sound including those ending in a vowel, take **-de/-den**, e.g. **bestellen** 'to order' – **bestelde**, **bouwen** 'to build' – **bouwde**, **gooien** 'to throw' – **gooide** etc.

Note what happens with the many verbs of recent English origin. The **'t kofschip** rule is applied according to the final sound, not letter, of the stem: **faxen** – **faxte**, **joggen** – **jogde**, **rugbyen** – **rugbyde**, **racen** – **racete**, **updaten** – **updatete**, **upgraden** – **upgradede**.

The endings **-te/-ten** and **-de/-den** are added to the stems of all weak verbs, regardless of whether they already end in **t** or **d**, e.g:

praten 'to talk'	– **praatte, praatten**
branden 'to burn'	– **brandde, brandden**

Because of the tendency in ABN to drop final **n**'s in speech, the following verbal forms are all pronounced identically: **wij praten, ik praatte, wij praatten**.

Sometimes the difference between the present and the past tense is not evident, e.g. **zetten** 'to put':

present tense:	**ik zet, wij zetten**
past tense:	**ik zette, wij zetten** (i.e. **-ten** added to the stem **zet-**)

Verbs with **v** or **z** in the infinitive:
The rule given above that states that the decision between **-te/-ten** and **-de/-den** is based on the final sound of the stem is in fact a slight over-simplification, but it retains its validity if one remembers this one exception: verbs such as **reizen, verhuizen, geloven** and **leven**, which contain a voiced consonant in the infinitive which becomes **s** and **f** in the stem, (i.e. **reis, verhuis, geloof, leef**), add **-de/-den** to this stem, i.e. **reisde, verhuisde, geloofde, leefde**. But the **s** and **f** in such cases are pronounced voiced.

One should be careful of verbs ending in **-eren**. Those with the stress on the ending are of French origin and add **-de/-den** after doubling the **e** of the ending, e.g. **reservéren** 'to reserve' – **reservéérde(n)**. Those of Dutch origin with the stress on the stem vowel do not double the **e**, e.g. **lúisteren** 'to listen' – **lúisterde**, **herínneren** 'to remind' – **herínnerde**. (These accents are not normally written; they are used here merely to indicate the difference in stress.)

(See 8.1.1(d) for the use of an enclitic **n** with **ik** and **ie** (i.e. **hij**) after verbs ending in **-de/-te**.)

11.1.2.2 Strong verbs

There is but one form for the singular and one for the plural:

binden 'to tie'

ik bond	**wij bonden**
jij bond	**jullie bonden**
hij bond	**zij bonden**

One should learn both the singular and the plural (as well as the past participle of course) by heart because in some ablaut series the two differ; note groups 4 and 5 below where the singular contains a short vowel and the plural a long vowel:

			Singular	*Plural*
1	**schrijven**	'to write'	**schreef**	**schreven**
2	**schieten**	'to shoot'	**schoot**	**schoten**
	buigen	'to bend'	**boog**	**bogen**
	wegen	'to weigh'	**woog**	**wogen**
3	**drinken**	'to drink'	**dronk**	**dronken**
4	**nemen**	'to take'	**nam**	**namen**
5	**eten**	'to eat'	**at**	**aten**
	zitten	'to sit'	**zat**	**zaten**
6	**dragen**	'to wear'	**droeg**	**droegen**
7	**hangen**	'to hang'	**hing**	**hingen**
	slapen	'to sleep'	**sliep**	**sliepen**

11.1.3 PERFECT TENSE (de voltooid tegenwoordige tijd – v.t.t.)

The perfect tense is a compound tense, i.e. it is formed from an auxiliary verb (either **hebben** or **zijn**, see 11.7.2) plus a derivative of the verb known as the past participle, e.g. 'He has lived'. In English the imperfect and the past participle of weak verbs are identical (e.g. 'I worked', 'I have worked'); in Dutch they are different and must not be confused. As is the case with the present and imperfect tenses, Dutch does not usually express the progressive or continuous form, i.e. 'I have been working' (for exceptions see 11.13).

11.1.3.1 Weak verbs

(a) Formation of the past participle: as for the imperfect of weak verbs the stem of the verb must be isolated; to this stem **ge-** is prefixed and **-t** or **-d** is suffixed: the rules for the choice of the latter are the same as for **-te/-ten** or **-de/-den** in the imperfect (see 11.1.2.1), e.g. **werken – gewerkt, horen – gehoord, reizen – gereisd, leven – geleefd.**

With the past participle, unlike the imperfect, if the stem already ends in **-t** or **-d**, no further **-t** or **-d** is added, e.g. **zetten – gezet, branden – gebrand**. The rules of Dutch spelling do not permit a consonant to be doubled at the end of a word.

Note what happens with the many verbs of recent English origin. The **'t kofschip** rule is applied according to the final sound, not letter, of the stem: **faxen – gefaxt, joggen – gejogd, rugbyen – gerugbyd, racen – geracet, updaten – geüpdatet, upgraden – geüpgraded**.

One should be careful with verbs ending in **-eren**. These are of two types:

1 those where the suffix is of French origin with the stress on -**eren** and which thus double the **e** in the past participle to preserve the long vowels, e.g. **reservéren** 'to reserve' – **gereservéérd, waardéren** 'to appreciate' – **gewaardéérd**. (These accents are not normally written; they are used here merely to indicate the difference in stress.)

2 those native Dutch words with the stress on the stem vowel which do not double the **e**, e.g. **lúisteren** 'to listen' – **gelúisterd, herín-neren** 'to remind' – **herínnerd**. (These accents are not normally written; they are used here merely to indicate the difference in stress.)

(b) The past participle is invariable for all persons; only the auxiliary verb is conjugated, e.g.:

ik heb gewerkt	**wij hebben gewerkt**
jij hebt gewerkt	**jullie hebben gewerkt**
hij heeft gewerkt	**zij hebben gewerkt**

For the use of **zijn** as an auxiliary verb in the perfect tense see 11.7.2.1.

(c) Those verbs beginning with any of the following unstressed prefixes do not add **ge-** (which would be yet another unstressed prefix, which the Dutch like to avoid):

be-, er-, ge-, her-, ont-, ver-

Examples: **beloven** 'to promise' – **beloofd, erkennen** 'to recognize' – **erkend, geloven** 'to believe' – **geloofd, herhalen** 'to repeat' – **herhaald, ontmoeten** 'to meet' – **ontmoet, vertalen** 'to translate' – **vertaald**.

(d) Past participles of weak verbs can be used as adjectives, as in English, and are inflected as normal adjectives, e.g. **het vertaalde boek** 'the translated book', **de gehate man** 'the hated man' (note the spelling change).

11.1.3.2 Strong verbs

(a) The past participle of strong verbs is formed by the prefixing of **ge-** to a root that may or may not have the same vowel as the stem of the imperfect (depending on the ablaut series), and the suffixing of **-en**. The past participles of those verbs given in 11.1.3.2, for example, are as follows:

1	**schrijven**	**geschreven**
2	**schieten**	**geschoten**
	buigen	**gebogen**
	wegen	**gewogen**
3	**drinken**	**gedronken**
4	**nemen**	**genomen**
5	**eten**	**gegeten**
	zitten	**gezeten**
6	**dragen**	**gedragen**
7	**hangen**	**gehangen**
	slapen	**geslapen**

(b) As with weak verbs, the past participle of strong verbs in conjunction with an auxiliary verb (either **hebben** or **zijn**) is invariable.

(c) As with weak verbs, there are also strong verbs with the unstressed prefixes **be-, er-, ge-, her-, ont-** and **ver-**. Such verbs simply add no **ge-** but otherwise behave as strong verbs in the perfect:

verdrinken	'to drown'	**verdronken**	(derived from **drinken**)
bewegen	'to move'	**bewogen**	(derived from **wegen**)
ontvangen	'to receive'	**ontvangen**	(derived from **vangen**)

(d) Past participles of strong verbs, like those of weak verbs, can be used as adjectives, but there is one difference: as these all end by definition in **-en**, they are treated as adjectives like **open** and **eigen**, for example, and do not take an **-e** ending when used attributively (see 9.1.2):

de gesloten deur	the closed door
de geschreven brief	the written letter

But when used as nouns they take both **-e** and **-en**:

de betrokkene(n)	the one(s) concerned
de verbannene(n)	the exiled one(s)

11.1.4 PLUPERFECT TENSE (de voltooid verleden tijd – v.v.t)

The pluperfect, a compound tense like the perfect, is formed from the imperfect of an auxiliary verb (either **hebben** or **zijn**, see 11.7.2) plus the past participle which remains invariable. The pluperfect can be described as the past in the past:

Hij wist dat ik gewerkt had.   He knew that I had worked.
Wij hadden genoeg gedronken.   We had drunk enough.
Hij was naar huis gegaan.   He had gone home.

11.1.4.1 *Word order in perfect and pluperfect tenses in subordinate and relative clauses*

In a subordinate or relative clause, i.e. in a clause where the finite verb does not stay in second position, the usual word order is as follows:

Je weet waarom ik het niet gedaan heb. or
Je weet waarom ik het niet heb gedaan.
You know why I did it.

Ik heb je verteld dat ik haar opgebeld had. or
Ik heb je verteld dat ik haar had opgebeld. or
Ik heb je verteld dat ik haar op had gebeld.
I told you that I had rung her.

Purists have a preference for the finite verb preceding the past participle, but common practice in standard Dutch would seem to suggest that both word orders are extremely common; a split form like **op had gebeld** is more likely to be said than written.

Compare the position of finite modal verbs in subordinate or relative clauses on 11.8.

11.1.5 FUTURE TENSE (**de onvoltooid tegenwoordig toekomende tijd – o.t.t.t**)

11.1.5.1 The auxiliary used for the future tense which corresponds to English 'will' is the verb **zullen**; it is not the verb **willen** although there are occasions when an English non-temporal 'will' is translated by **willen** (see 11.8.5.4). **Zullen** is conjugated like a modal verb in the present tense:

ik zal = I will	**wij zullen**
jij zult, zal	**jullie zullen, zult**
u zult, zal	**u zult**
hij zal	**zij zullen**

Jij can take either **zult** or **zal** and both are equally common. When inverted, **jij zult** becomes **zul jij**. **Jullie zullen** is more common than **jullie zult**.

U can take either **zult** or **zal** but the former is more common.

Zullen can have modal as well as temporal qualities (see 11.2.6, 11.8.5.5). The future tense of all verbs is formed by the use of **zullen** plus the infinitive of the verb concerned; this infinitive is sent to the end of the clause:

Ik zal het brengen.   I will bring it.
Wij zullen hem zien.   We will see him.

11.1.5.2   The future can also be rendered by the verb **gaan** instead of **zullen**, as is the case in English:

Ik ga volgend jaar een huis kopen.
I am going to buy a house next year.

Gaat het regenen?
Is it going to rain?

Never use **gaan** with **komen**, modal verbs (e.g. He's going to have to give it back)[1] or in contexts where it does not refer to an imminent action.

11.1.5.3   A third possible way of rendering the future, which also has a parallel in English, is by using the simple present tense:

Hij koopt binnenkort een nieuwe auto.
He is buying a new car soon.

Hij vliegt morgen naar Amsterdam.
He is flying to Amsterdam tomorrow.

This form of the future is somewhat more common in Dutch than in English. It is always used when the sentence contains an adverb of time which is sufficient to indicate that the action will take place in the future; compare the two sentences above with the previous four sentences. There are numerous occasions where we might use 'will' where the Dutch would give preference to the present tense:

Dat doe ik morgen.
I'll do it tomorrow.

Hij komt volgende week.
He'll be coming next week.

11.1.6   FUTURE PERFECT TENSE (**de voltooid tegenwoordig toekomende tijd – v.t.t.t.**)

The future perfect tense in Dutch corresponds exactly to that in English:

---

[1] But constructions of the sort **Hij gaat het moeten teruggeven** do occur in Flanders.

Hij zal het gedaan hebben (or **hebben gedaan**)
He will have done it.

Zij zal naar huis gegaan zijn (or **zijn gegaan**)
She will have gone home.

Zij zullen het mij hebben laten zien.
They will have shown it to me.

Note that the auxiliary 'have' is rendered by either **hebben** or **zijn** depending on which auxiliary the main verb normally takes in the perfect and pluperfect tenses, i.e. **Hij heeft het gedaan** 'He's done it', **Zij is naar huis gegaan** 'She has gone home'.

11.1.7   CONDITIONAL TENSE (**de onvoltooid verleden toekomende tijd – o.v.t.t.**)

11.1.7.1   The conditional can be described as the past in the future. It is the tense that employs 'would + infinitive' in English. Just as English uses the past tense of its future auxiliary 'will' to form the conditional, i.e. 'would', so Dutch employs the past tense of **zullen**, i.e. singular **zou**, plural **zouden**. The **gij** form is **zoudt** but this is sometimes used with **u**, particularly in inverted constructions to facilitate pronunciation as a liaison is formed between the **-dt** and the **u**, e.g. **Zoudt u dat willen?** 'Would you want that?', but the use of **zoudt** instead of **zou** with **u** sounds rather formal.

Als . . ., dan zou zij hem geloven.   If . . ., (then) she would believe him.
Zij zouden het kopen als . . .   They would buy it, if . . .

11.1.7.2   **Zou(den)** is also used in Dutch to express 'was/were going to', i.e. an intention to do something that was not fulfilled:

Ik zou vorig jaar naar Duitsland gaan maar . . .
I was going to go to Germany last year but . . .

11.1.7.3   There is one English 'would' which is not conditional in meaning and is not translated by **zou(den)**, i.e. the one that means 'used to'; the repetitive nature of the action is not expressed by the verb in Dutch, unlike English, but merely by adverbs of time (in the case below by **geregeld**):

Toen ik in Amsterdam woonde, heb ik geregeld mijn tante in Rotterdam bezocht (or **bezocht ik . . .**)
When I lived in Amsterdam I would regularly visit my aunt in Rotterdam.

11.1.7.4 A 'should' which means 'would' is rendered by **zou(den)** but in all other senses 'should' is rendered by a form of **moeten** (see 11.8.5.2(b)):

Ik zou het doen als ik jou was.
I should do it if I were you.

11.1.8   CONDITIONAL PERFECT TENSE (**de voltooid verleden toekomende tijd – v.v.t.t.**)

The conditional perfect is the past of the future perfect:

Hij zou het gezien hebben (or **hebben gezien**).
He would have seen it.

Zij zou gegaan zijn (or **zijn gegaan**).
She would have gone.

Zij zouden het mij hebben laten zien.
They would have shown it to me.

Contracted conditional perfects:
Because the conditional perfect employs two auxiliaries (**zou/zouden** + **hebben/zijn**) in addition to one or two more verbs (i.e. a past participle or two infinitives), there is a tendency to contract the auxiliaries into one form to reduce the overall number of verbs, i.e. as in German **hätte** and **wäre**. This is actually a remnant of the former imperfect subjunctive although the forms are identical to the imperfect of **hebben** and **zijn** nowadays:

Hij *zou* **het gezien** *hebben*	= **Hij** *had* **het gezien (als...)**
Hij *zou* **gegaan** *zijn*	= **Hij** *was* **gegaan (als...)**
Zij *zouden* **het mij** *hebben* **laten zien**	= **Zij** *hadden* **het mij laten zien (als ...)**

Confusion with the imperfect is usually avoided by context, i.e. there is always an 'if' clause preceding, following or implied.

Although it is not compulsory to contract, in cases like the third example where there are four verbs, it is preferable to reduce the number to three by such contraction. (For further verbal contractions see modal verbs, 11.8.3)

11.2 USE OF TENSES

11.2.1 PRESENT TENSE

The present tense is used as in English with the following exceptions:

11.2.1.1 Dutch has its own idiomatic way of expressing the present continuous (i.e. He is reading a book, see 11.13) and the emphatic present (i.e. He does like fish, see 11.14).

11.2.1.2 The present tense is used even more extensively in Dutch than in English to express the future; it is in fact the most usual way of expressing the future. (see 11.1.5.3)

11.2.1.3 An English perfect followed by 'for' plus an expression of time is rendered by the present tense in Dutch as the action of the verb is seen not to have been completed but as still continuing into the present:

Ik woon al tien jaar hier.   I have been living here for ten years.
I have lived here for ten years.

A similar construction is required in sentences introduced by 'how long':

Hoe lang leert hij al Nederlands? How long has he been learning Dutch?

(see 10.3.7(c))

11.2.2 IMPERFECT TENSE

11.2.2.1 Some confusion about when to use the imperfect arises because of the common practice in Dutch of using the perfect where English uses the imperfect (see Perfect Tense, 11.2.3). The real difficulty associated with the use of the imperfect in Dutch is in recognizing the few occasions when it cannot be replaced by the perfect. It is also particularly difficult to give rules for when it must be used. Generally speaking it tends to be used for narrating a series of events in the past. When mentioning isolated actions or listing a sequence of separate actions in the past, the perfect tense is normally preferred, however.

In the following example, the fact that a new topic is being introduced into the conversation is announced by use of the perfect tense. If you then proceed to give further detail, it is likely that you would then switch to the imperfect to relate the further sequence of events:

> **Gisteren ben ik naar Amsterdam gegaan. Ik ging naar een paar boekhandels, lunchte op de Damrak, bezocht het Rijksmuseum en nam de trein om vier uur terug naar Utrecht.**
> I went to Amsterdam yesterday. I visited a few bookshops, had lunch on the Damrak, went to the National Museum and caught the train back to Utrecht at 4.00.

The verbs **zijn** and **hebben** are more commonly used in the imperfect than the perfect:

Wat had je in je hand?	What did you have in your hand?
Hoe was het weer die avond?	What was the weather like that night?

But the perfect would not be wrong in such cases.

In the following examples **hebben** and **zijn** indicate a permanent state rather than an isolated action like **zingen** and **doodgaan** and thus they must be in the imperfect:

> **Zij heeft langer gezongen dan hij en zij had ook een mooiere stem.**
> She sang longer than he (did) and she had a nicer voice too.

> **Onze hond is net doodgegaan, maar ja, hij was dan ook erg oud.**
> Our dog (has) just died but then he was very old too.

The imperfect is always used after the conjunction **toen** 'when', which necessitates the use of the same tense in the main clause:

> **Hij lag nog altijd in bed toen ik bij hem kwam.**
> He was still lying in bed when I got to his place.

11.2.2.2 Dutch has its own idiomatic ways of expressing the imperfect continuous and emphatic, i.e. He was reading a book, He did like fish (see 11.13 and 11.14).

11.2.2.3 There is one imperfect in Dutch which replaces an English pluperfect:

> **Hij lag er al uren toen ik bij hem kwam.**
> He had been lying there for hours when I got to his place.

Here, as with the present tense (see Present Tense, 11.2.1.3), the action of the first clause is seen as still continuing when the action of the second occurs and thus an imperfect must be used for the first action; a pluperfect (in Dutch) would imply that he was no longer lying there when I arrived, but that he *had* been lying there.

11.2.2.4   Two variant forms of the imperfect in English which often cause confusion are those indicating habit or custom which employ the auxiliaries 'used to' and 'would':

> We used to live in Amsterdam.
> When we lived in Amsterdam we would often go to the National Museum.

In the first example the Dutch use either the imperfect or the perfect and express the habitual aspect with the adverb of time **vroeger** 'previously, formerly':

> **Wij woonden vroeger in Amsterdam.**
> **Wij hebben vroeger in Amsterdam gewoond.**

In the second example the conjunction **toen** determines the use of the imperfect in the first clause, and the 'would', which is equivalent in meaning to 'used to', is rendered as in the first example with an adverb of time, **dikwijls** (see Conditional Tense 11.1.7.3):

> **Toen wij in Amsterdam woonden, gingen we dikwijls naar het Rijksmuseum.**

Such sentences expressing an habitual action may employ the verb **plegen** 'to be accustomed to' in very formal style:

> **Het karretje waarmee hij naar de stad placht te rijden, ...**
> The cart in which he would (= used to) ride to town, ...

11.2.2.5   One should also beware of what seem to be imperfects in Dutch but which are in fact contracted conditionals (see 11.2.7, 11.8.3.2.1). Imperfects in such 'if' clauses cannot be replaced by perfects.

11.2.3   PERFECT TENSE

11.2.3.1   It is in the use of the perfect that Dutch tenses differ most from those of English. The basic rule for the use of the perfect is as follows:

All perfects in English are rendered by perfects in Dutch (with one exception, see Present Tense, 11.2.1.3), but most imperfects in English may be rendered by imperfects or perfects in Dutch, the perfect tense being more common, particularly in speech (for the few instances where English imperfects must be imperfects in Dutch, see Imperfect Tense above).

For example, the sentence 'He bought a car yesterday' can only use an imperfect in English as the time of the action is mentioned, whereas 'He has bought a car', without any mention of the time, is possible. In Dutch the latter would also always use a perfect but the former could employ either an imperfect or a perfect.

Hij heeft gisteren een auto gekocht or
Hij kocht gisteren een auto but only
Hij heeft een auto gekocht.

Remember this: a perfect in English is always a perfect in Dutch!

11.2.4 PLUPERFECT TENSE

11.2.4.1   The pluperfect tense is used as in English (with one exception – see Imperfect Tense, 11.2.2.3).

11.2.4.2   Dutch has its own idiomatic ways of expressing the pluperfect continuous, i.e. He had been reading a book for hours (see 11.13).

11.2.5 FUTURE TENSE

The use of the future tense is very similar in Dutch and English, including the tendency to use the verb 'to go', **gaan**,[2] and the present tense for actions in the future (see 11.1.5.2). The main difference is that Dutch uses the present tense more than English does to express the future (see 11.1.5.3, 11.2.1.2).

English 'will' often does not denote future action and in such instances Dutch uses **willen**, not **zullen** (see 11.8.5.4(a)).

11.2.6 FUTURE PERFECT TENSE

There is no difference between English and Dutch in the use of this tense except for the tendency for Dutch to use **zullen** in a modal sense with no connotation of the future, as illustrated by the following examples:

Dat zal in andere landen ook wel gedaan zijn.
That's sure to have been done in other countries too.

Hij zal het zeker gedaan hebben.
He did it for sure.

It is possible to use a perfect where semantically a future perfect is implied:

---

[2] It should be noted, however, that **gaan**, unlike 'going to' in English, cannot be used in combination with modal verbs to express future action: ***Ik ga dat niet kunnen doen** 'I am going to be able to do that'. Here one must use **zullen: Ik zal dat niet kunnen doen** (see 11.1.5.2).

Tegen die tijd heb ik het wel gedaan (= zal ik het wel gedaan hebben).
I will have done it by then.

11.2.7   CONDITIONAL TENSE

The conditional is used as in English except that the verb in the 'if' clause of a conditional sentence, which in English is often in the imperfect (actually an imperfect subjunctive), can be either a conditional or an imperfect in Dutch.

Als je meer geld zou hebben (had), ...
If you had more money, ...

Als hij minder zou drinken (dronk), ...
If he drank less, ...

By using the conditional in such instances the Dutch are trying to compensate for an historical simplification that has affected both English and Dutch, i.e. the falling together of the imperfect subjunctive with the imperfect. Compare:

Als ik rijk was (zou zijn) ...
If I were rich ... (see 11.2.2.5)

The contracted form **was** (or **had**) can also replace the conditional in the 'would' clause, not just in the 'if' clause:

Als hij vroeger gewerkt had, dan zou hij nu rijk zijn =
Als hij vroeger gewerkt had, dan was hij nu rijk.
If he had worked previously, he'd now be rich.

Als hij vroeger gewerkt had, dan had hij nu meer geld.
If he had worked previously, he would now have more money.

The periphrastic forms with **zou/zouden** in an 'if' clause are close in literal meaning and feeling to English 'were to':

If he were to drink less ...
If I were to be rich ...
If he were to have worked hard ...

Zou(den) is often used to render English 'was/were going to' or 'intended to':

Vader zou mij voor Sinterklaas een brommer geven, maar ik kreeg een fiets.
Father was going to give me a moped for St. Nicholas but I got a bike.

11.2.8   CONDITIONAL PERFECT TENSE

There are no differences between English and Dutch in the use of this tense but beware of contractions (see 11.1.8).

11.3   ALPHABETICAL LIST OF STRONG AND IRREGULAR VERBS

The Roman numerals refer to the class to which the verbs belong. The abbreviation 'm.v.' stands for mixed verbs, 'i.v.' for irregular verbs and 'mo.' for modal verbs. All these verbs are listed again according to class in 11.3.1.

bakken	m.v.	**druipen**	II
barsten	m.v.	**duiken**	II
bederven	III	**dunken**	i.v.
bedriegen	II	**durven**	mo.
beginnen	III	**dwingen**	III
begrijpen	I	**eten**	V
belijden	I	**fluiten**	II
(op)bergen	III	**gaan**	i.v.
bevelen	IV	**gelden**	III
bewegen	II	**genezen**	V
bezwijken	I	**genieten**	II
bidden	V	**geven**	V
bieden	II	**gieten**	II
bijten	I	**glijden**	I
binden	III	**glimmen**	III
blazen	VII	**graven**	VI
blijken	I	**grijpen**	I
blijven	I	**hangen**	VII
blinken	III	**hebben**	i.v.
braden	m.v.	**heffen**	VII
breken	IV	**helpen**	III
brengen	i.v.	**heten**	m.v.
brouwen	m.v.	**hijsen**	I
buigen	II	**houden**	VII
delven	III, m.v.	**houwen**	VII
denken	i.v.	**jagen**	VI, m.v.
dingen	III	**kiezen**	II
doen	i.v.	**kijken**	I
dragen	VI	**kijven**	I
drijven	I	**klimmen**	III
dringen	III	**klinken**	III
drinken	III	**kluiven**	II

knijpen	I	schijnen	I
komen	IV	schrijden	I
kopen	i.v.	schrijven	I
krijgen	I	schrikken	III
krimpen	III	schuiven	II
kruipen	II	slaan	VI, i.v.
kunnen	mo.	slapen	VII
kwijten	I	slijpen	I
lachen	m.v.	slijten	I
laden	m.v.	slinken	III
laten	VII	sluipen	II
lezen	IV	sluiten	II
liegen	II	smelten	III
liggen	V	smijten	I
lijden	I	snijden	I
lijken	I	snuiten	II
lopen	VII	snuiven	II
malen	m.v.	spannen	m.v.
melken	III, m.v.	spijten	I
meten	IV	spinnen	III
mijden	I	splijten	I
moeten	mo.	spreken	IV
mogen	mo.	springen	III
nemen	IV	spruiten	II
nijpen	I	spugen	II
ontginnen	III	spuiten	II
overlijden	I	staan	i.v.
plegen	i.v.	steken	IV
pluizen	II	stelen	IV
prijzen	I	sterven	III
raden	VII, m.v.	stijgen	I
rijden	I	stijven	I
ridgen	I	stinken	III
rijten	I	stoten	VII, m.v.
rijzen	I	strijden	I
roepen	VII	strijken	I
ruiken	II	stuiven	II
scheiden	m.v.	treden	V
schelden	III	treffen	III
schenden	III	trekken	III
schenken	III	vallen	VII
scheppen	VII	vangen	VII
scheren	II	varen	VI
schieten	II	vechten	III

verbieden	II	**weven**	m.v.
verdelgen	III	**wijken**	I
verdrieten	II	**wijten**	I
verdwijnen	I	**wijzen**	I
vergelijken	I	**willen**	mo.
vergeten	V	**winden**	III
verliezen	II	**winnen**	III
vermijden	I	**worden**	i.v.
verraden	VII	**wreken**	m.v.
verschuilen	II, m.v.	**wrijven**	I
verslijten	I	**wringen**	III
verslinden	III	**zeggen**	i.v.
verwijten	I	**zenden**	III
verwijzen	I	**zien**	IV, i.v.
verzinnen	III	**zijn**	i.v.
verzwelgen	III	**zingen**	III
vinden	III	**zinken**	III
vlechten	III	**zinnen**	III
vlieden	II	**zitten**	V
vliegen	II	**zoeken**	i.v.
vragen	VI, m.v.	**zouten**	m.v.
vouwen	m.v.	**zuigen**	II
vreten	IV	**zuipen**	II
vriezen	II	**zullen**	mo.
waaien	VI, m.v.	**zwelgen**	III
wassen	VII, m.v.	**zwellen**	III
wegen	II	**zwemmen**	III
werpen	III	**zweren**	II, m.v.
werven	III	**zwerven**	III
weten	i.v.	**zwijgen**	I

11.3.1 STRONG AND IRREGULAR VERBS

The bolded Roman numerals heading the groups of verbs that follow, refer to the class, or ablaut series, to which these verbs belong historically (see chapter 11 (Introduction), 11.1.3.2).

* = verbs conjugated only with **zijn** (see 11.7.2.1).

⁺ = verbs conjugated with **hebben** or **zijn** (see 11.7.2.2).

I All verbs with **ij** in the stem belong in this group except for a few formed from non-verbal parts of speech, which are weak:

benijden   **benijdde**   **benijdden**   **benijd**   to envy also

bevrijden 'to liberate', **kastijden** 'to chastise', **verblijden** 'to gladden', **verslijken** 'to silt up', **wijden** 'to consecrate, to devote'.

Note that the verb **vrijen** 'to kiss and cuddle; to make love (a euphemism)' is officially weak, but in practice is usually treated as a strong verb, i.e. not **vrijde/vrijden/gevrijd** but **vree/vreeën/gevreeën**.

begrijpen	begreep	begrepen	begrepen	to understand
belijden	beleed	beleden	beleden	to confess
bezwijken*	bezweek	bezweken	bezweken	to succumb
bijten	beet	beten	gebeten	to bite
blijken*	bleek	bleken	gebleken	to appear
blijven*	bleef	bleven	gebleven	to remain, stay
drijven⁺	dreef	dreven	gedreven	to float, drive
glijden⁺	gleed	gleden	gegleden	to glide, slide
grijpen	greep	grepen	gegrepen	to seize, grab
hijsen	hees	hesen	gehesen	to hoist, lift
kijken	keek	keken	gekeken	to look
kijven	keef	keven	gekeven	to quarrel
(k)nijpen	(k)neep	(k)nepen	ge(k)nepen	to pinch
krijgen	kreeg	kregen	gekregen	to get, receive
zich kwijten	kweet	kweten	gekweten	to acquit oneself
lijden	leed	leden	geleden	to suffer
lijken	leek	leken	geleken	to seem, resemble
overlijden*	overleed	overleden	overleden	to pass away
prijzen	prees	prezen	geprezen	to praise
rijden⁺	reed	reden	gereden	to ride, drive
rijgen	reeg	regen	geregen	to string (beads), tack
rijten	reet	reten	gereten	to tear
rijzen*	rees	rezen	gerezen	to rise
schijnen	scheen	schenen	geschenen	to seem, shine
schrijden⁺	schreed	schreden	geschreden	to stride
schrijven	schreef	schreven	geschreven	to write
slijpen	sleep	slepen	geslepen	to sharpen
smijten	smeet	smeten	gesmeten	to throw
snijden	sneed	sneden	gesneden	to cut
spijten	speet	speten	gespeten	to be sorry
splijten	spleet	spleten	gespleten	to split
stijgen*	steeg	stegen	gestegen	to rise, climb
stijven	steef	steven	gesteven	to stiffen
strijden	streed	streden	gestreden	to fight
strijken	streek	streken	gestreken	to iron, lower (flag)

verdwijnen*	**verdween**	**verdwenen**	**verdwenen**	to disappear
vergelijken	**vergeleek**	**vergeleken**	**vergeleken**	to compare
(ver)mijden	**(ver)meed**	**(ver)meden**	**(ver)meden**	to avoid
(ver)slijten⁺	**(ver)sleet**	**(ver)sleten**	**(ver)sleten**	to wear (out)
(ver)wijten	**(ver)weet**	**(ver)weten**	**(ver)weten**	to reproach
(ver)wijzen	**(ver)wees**	**(ver)wezen**	**(ver)wezen**	to (refer), show
(ver)zwijgen	**(ver)zweeg**	**(ver)zwegen**	**(ver)zwegen**	to keep quiet
wijken⁺	**week**	**weken**	**geweken**	to yield, retreat
wrijven	**wreef**	**wreven**	**gewreven**	to rub

II   Not all verbs with **ui** and **ie** are irregular:

huilen	**huilde**	**hulden**	**gehuild**	to cry
spieden	**spiedde**	**spiedden**	**gespied**	to spy

also

bruisen 'to fizz', **gebruiken** 'to use', **getuigen** 'to testify', **kruisen** 'to cross', **verhuizen** 'to shift', **wuiven** 'to wave', **geschieden** 'to happen', **wieden**, 'to weed'.

buigen	**boog**	**bogen**	**gebogen**	to bend, bow
druipen	**droop**	**dropen**	**gedropen**	to drip
duiken⁺	**dook**	**doken**	**gedoken**	to dive
fluiten	**floot**	**floten**	**gefloten**	to whistle
kluiven	**kloof**	**kloven**	**gekloven**	to pick a bone
kruipen⁺	**kroop**	**kropen**	**gekropen**	to crawl, creep
pluizen	**ploos**	**plozen**	**geplozen**	to give off fluff
ruiken	**rook**	**roken**	**geroken**	to smell
schuiven⁺	**schoof**	**schoven**	**geschoven**	to push, shove
sluipen	**sloop**	**slopen**	**geslopen**	to steal, sneak
sluiten	**sloot**	**sloten**	**gesloten**	to close
snuiten	**snoot**	**snoten**	**gesnoten**	to blow one's nose
snuiven	**snoof**	**snoven**	**gesnoven**	to sniff
spuiten	**spoot**	**spoten**	**gespoten**	to spout, squirt, spray
spruiten	**sproot**	**sproten**	**gesproten**	to sprout
stuiven	**stoof**	**stoven**	**gestoven**	to be dusty, rush
verschuilen	**verschool**	**verscholen**	**verscholen**	to hide
	verschuilde	**verschuilden**		
zuigen³	**zoog**	**zogen**	**gezogen**	to suck
zuipen	**zoop**	**zopen**	**gezopen**	to booze
spugen	**spoog**	**spogen**	**gespogen**	to spit

³ But **stofzuigen** 'to vacuum' is regular: **stofzuigde, gestofzuigd**.

bedriegen	bedroog	bedrogen	bedrogen	to deceive
bieden	bood	boden	geboden	to offer
genieten	genoot	genoten	genoten	to enjoy
gieten	goot	goten	gegoten	to pour
kiezen	koos	kozen	gekozen	to choose
liegen	loog	logen	gelogen	to lie, tell lies
schieten	schoot	schoten	geschoten	to shoot
verbieden	verbood	verboden	verboden	to forbid
verdrieten	verdroot	verdroten	verdroten	to vex; sadden
verliezen[4]	verloor	verloren	verloren	to lose
vlieden+ (lit.)	vlood	vloden	gevloden	to flee
vliegen+	vloog	vlogen	gevlogen	to fly
vriezen	vroor	vroren	gevroren	to freeze
wegen	woog	wogen	gewogen	to weigh
bewegen	bewoog	bewogen	bewogen	to move
scheren	schoor	schoren	geschoren	to shear, shave (see 11.4.3)
zweren[5]	zweerde	zweerden	gezworen	to fester
archaic:	zwoor	zworen		

III The vowel in the infinitive of all the following verbs is either **e** or **i** and in all but five cases (**treffen; trekken, schrikken; vechten, vlechten**) this vowel is followed by either **m**, **n**, **l** or **r** plus another consonant:

beginnen*	begon	begonnen	begonnen	to begin
(op)bergen	borg (op)	borgen (op)	(op)geborgen	to store
binden	bond	bonden	gebonden	to bind
blinken	blonk	blonken	geblonken	to shine
delven	delfde	delfden	gedolven	to dig
archaic:	dolf	dolven		
dingen	dong	dongen	gedongen	to haggle
dringen+	drong	drongen	gedrongen	to push, crowd
drinken	dronk	dronken	gedronken	to drink
dwingen	dwong	dwongen	gedwongen	to force
gelden	gold	golden	gegolden	to be valid
glimmen	glom	glommen	geglommen	to glimmer, shine
klimmen+	klom	klommen	geklommen	to climb
klinken	klonk	klonken	geklonken	to sound
krimpen+	kromp	krompen	gekrompen	to shrink

[4] One will hear both **Ik ben mijn pen verloren** and **Ik heb mijn pen verloren** with no difference in meaning (see 11.7.2.2(d)). See also **vergeten** in group V.
[5] See group VI for **zweren** 'to swear'.

melken	molk	molken	gemolken	to milk
	melkte	melkten		
ontginnen	ontgon	ontgonnen	ontgonnen	to open up, reclaim (land)
schelden	schold	scholden	gescholden	to abuse
schenden	schond	schonden	geschonden	to violate
schenken	schonk	schonken	geschonken	to pour, give
schrikken*6	schrok	schrokken	geschrokken	to be frightened
slinken*	slonk	slonken	geslonken	to shrink
smelten+	smolt	smolten	gesmolten	to melt
spinnen	spon	sponnen	gesponnen	to spin
springen+	sprong	sprongen	gesprongen	to jump
stinken	stonk	stonken	gestonken	to stink, smell
treffen	trof	troffen	getroffen	to hit
trekken+7	trok	trokken	getrokken	to pull
vechten	vocht	vochten	gevochten	to fight
verslinden	verslond	verslonden	verslonden	to devour
verzwelgen	verzwolg	verzwolgen	verzwolgen	to swallow up
vinden	vond	vonden	gevonden	to find
vlechten	vlocht	vlochten	gerlochten	to plait
winden	wond	wonden	gewonden	to wind
winnen	won	wonnen	gewonnen	to win
wringen	wrong	wrongen	gewrongen	to wring
zenden	zond	zonden	gezonden	to send
zingen	zong	zongen	gezongen	to sing
zinken*	zonk	zonken	gezonken	to sink
(ver)zinnen	zon	zonnen	gezonnen	to ponder, muse
zwelgen	zwolg	zwolgen	gezwolgen	to guzzle
zwellen*	zwol	zwollen	gezwollen	to swell
zwemmen+	zwom	zwommen	gezwommen	to swim
bederven+	bedierf	bedierven	bedorven	to spoil
helpen	hielp	hielpen	geholpen	to help
sterven*	stierf	stierven	gestorven	to die
werpen	wierp	wierpen	geworpen	to throw
werven	wierf	wierven	geworven	to recruit
zwerven	zwierf	zwierven	gezworven	to wander, roam

IV

bevelen	beval	bevalen	bevolen	to order, command

---

[6] The derived verbs **verschrikken** and **opschrikken** are regular.
[7] **Trekken** takes **zijn** in various compounds: **vertrekken** 'to depart', **wegtrekken** 'to go away'.

breken	brak	braken	gebroken	to break
komen*	kwam	kwamen	gekomen	to come
nemen	nam	namen	genomen	to take
spreken	sprak	spraken	gesproken	to speak
steken	stak	staken	gestoken	to stab
stelen	stal	stalen	gestolen	to steal

V

bidden	bad	baden	gebeden	to pray
eten	at	aten	gegeten	to eat
genezen+	genas	genazen	genezen	to heal
geven	gaf	gaven	gegeven	to give
lezen	las	lazen	gelezen	to read
liggen	lag	lagen	gelegen	to lie
meten	mat	maten	gemeten	to measure
treden*	trad	traden	getreden	to tread, step
vergeten+8	vergat	vergaten	vergeten	to forget
vreten	vrat	vraten	gevreten	to eat (of animals)
zien	zag	zagen	gezien	to see
zitten	zat	zaten	gezeten	to sit

VI

dragen	droeg	droegen	gedragen	to carry
graven	groef	groeven	gegraven	to dig
jagen	joeg	joegen	gejaagd	to chase
	jaagde	jaagden	gejaagd	to hunt
slaan9	sloeg	sloegen	geslagen	to hit
varen+	voer	voeren	gevaren	to sail, go (by ship)
vragen	vroeg	vroegen	gevraagd	to ask
archaic:	vraagde	vraagden		
waaien	woei	woeien	gewaaid	to blow (wind)
	waaide	waaiden	gewaaid	
zweren	zwoer	zwoeren	gezworen	to swear (an oath)

---

[8] The criteria for the use of **zijn** or **hebben** with **vergeten** are different from other verbs marked +: when the meaning is 'to have left something behind' **hebben** may be used, but when a fact etc. has been forgotten, only **zijn** can be employed; but in practice **zijn** is more commonly used in both cases (see 11.7.2.2(d)): **Ik ben (heb) mijn regenjas vergeten** 'I have forgotten my raincoat', **Ik ben zijn naam vergeten** 'I have forgotten his name'.

[9] **Slaan** should not be confused with the regular verb **slagen** 'to succeed; pass an exam'. Note the past participle is **geslagen**, not *geslaan*, while that of **gaan** and **staan** is **gegaan** and **gestaan**.

VII

blazen	**blies**	**bliezen**	**geblazen**	to blow
hangen	**hing**	**hingen**	**gehangen**	to hang
heffen	**hief**	**hieren**	**geheven**	to lift
houden	**hield**	**hielden**	**gehouden**	to hold
houwen[10]	**hieuw**	**hieuwen**	**gehouwen**	to hew
laten	**liet**	**lieten**	**gelaten**	to let, leave
lopen+	**liep**	**liepen**	**gelopen**	to walk
raden[11]	**raadde**	**raadden**	**geraden**	to guess, advise
archaic:	**ried**	**rieden**		
roepen	**riep**	**riepen**	**geroepen**	to call
scheppen[12]	**schiep**	**schiepen**	**geschapen**	to create
slapen	**sliep**	**sliepen**	**geslapen**	to sleep
stoten	**stootte**	**stootten**	**gestoten**	to push, shove
archaic:	**stiet**	**stieten**		
vallen*	**viel**	**vielen**	**gevallen**	to fall
vangen	**ving**	**vingen**	**gevangen**	to catch
verraden	**verried**	**verrieden**	**verraden**	to betray
wassen*[13]	**wies**	**wiesen**	**gewassen**	to grow, wax
wassen	**waste**	**wasten**	**gewassen**	to wash
archaic:	**wies**	**wiesen**		

11.3.2 MIXED VERBS

bakken	**bakte**	**bakten**	**gebakken**	to bake
barsten*	**barstte**	**barstten**	**gebarsten**	to burst
braden	**braadde**	**braadden**	**gebraden**	to roast
brouwen	**brouwde**	**brouwden**	**gebrouwen**	to brew
heten	**heette**	**heetten**	**geheten**	to be called
lachen[14]	**lachte**	**lachten**	**gelachen**	to laugh
laden	**laadde**	**laadden**	**geladen**	to load
malen	**maalde**	**maalden**	**gemalen**	to grind
scheiden	**scheidde**	**scheidden**	**gescheiden**	to separate
spannen	**spande**	**spanden**	**gespannen**	to stretch
vouwen	**vouwde**	**vouwden**	**gevouwen**	to fold
weven	**weefde**	**weefden**	**geweven**	to weave

---

[10] The compound **beeldhouwen** 'to sculpt' is weak; **beeldhouwde, gebeeldhouwd**.
[11] Nowadays **raden** is mostly used in the meaning of 'to guess'. 'To advise' is rendered by **aanraden**.
[12] There is also a regular verb **scheppen** 'to scoop, ladle'.
[13] **Wassen** 'to grow' (intransitive) is archaic and is usually replaced by **groeien**, except in standard expressions, e.g. **de wassende maan** 'the waxing moon'.
[14] Note that **glimlachen** 'to smile' is regular: **glimlachte, geglimlacht**.

| wreken | wreekte | wreekten | gewroken | to avenge, revenge |
| zouten | zoutte | zoutten | gezouten | to salt |

Verbs in this sub-group also have an archaic strong imperfect. See list of strong verbs.

delven	delfde	delfden	gedolven	to dig
melken	melkte	melkten	gemolken	to milk
raden	raadde	raadden	geraden	to advise, guess
stoten	stootte	stootten	gestoten	to push, shove
wassen	waste	wasten	gewassen	to wash
zweren	zweerde	zweerden	gezworen	to fester

Jagen and **waaien** also have a weak imperfect; in the case of **jagen** the weak imperfect has a different meaning, i.e. 'to hunt'.

jagen	joeg	joegen	gejaagd	to chase
waaien	woei	woeien	gewaaid	to blow (wind)
vragen	vroeg	vroegen	gevraagd	to ask

11.3.3   IRREGULAR VERBS

brengen	bracht	brachten	gebracht	to bring
denken	dacht	dachten	gedacht	to think
dunken[15]	docht			to think, seem (see 11.19.1.2)
kopen	kocht	kochten	gekocht	to buy
plegen[15]	placht	plachten		to be used to
zoeken	zocht	zochten	gezocht	to look for, seek
doen	deed	deden	gedaan	to do
gaan*	ging	gingen	gegaan	to go
slaan	sloeg	sloegen	geslagen	to hit
staan	stond	stonden	gestaan	to stand
zien	zag	zagen	gezien	to see
hebben	had	hadden	gehad	to have
weten	wist	wisten	geweten	to know
worden*	werd	werden	geworden	to become
zeggen	zei	zeiden	gezegd	to say
zijn*	was	waren	geweest	to be

[15] See 11.5.1.

11.3.4   MODAL VERBS

durven	**durfde**	**durfden**	**gedurfd**	to dare
archaic:	**dorst**	**dorsten**		
hoeven	**hoefde**	**hoefden**	**gehoeven**	to be necessary, need
kunnen	**kon**	**konden**	**gekund**	to be able
moeten	**moest**	**moesten**	**gemoeten**	to have to
mogen	**mocht**	**mochten**	**gemogen**[16]	to be allowed to
willen	**wilde**	**wilden**	**gewild**	to want to
	wou	(see 11.8.1.4)		
zullen	**zou**	**zouden**	**gezuld**	will

11.4   MIXED VERBS

11.4.1   Mixed is the name given to those verbs which for historical reasons have a weak imperfect and a strong past participle (or occasionally vice versa):

bakken	**bakte**	**bakten**	**gebakken**	to bake

For a complete list of such verbs see 11.3.2.

11.4.2   There are five verbs which have a strong imperfect which is now archaic (see 11.3.2):

delven	**dolf**	**dolven**	to dig
raden	**ried**	**rieden**	to guess, advise
stoten	**stiet**	**stieten**	to push
wassen	**wies**	**wiesen**	to wash
zweren	**zwoor**	**zworen**	to fester

Also **verschuilen** 'to hide' but its strong imperfect is not archaic ·(see 11.3.1.II).

11.4.3   **Jagen** 'to hunt, chase', **vragen** 'to ask' and **waaien** 'to blow (wind)' are exceptional mixed verbs in that they all have a strong imperfect and a weak past participle. **Jagen** and **waaien** also have a weak imperfect which is current, whereas that of **vragen** is archaic:

jagen	**joeg/joegen, jaagde/jaagden**	**gejaagd**
waaien	**woei/woeien, waaide/waaiden**	**gewaaid**
vragen	**vroeg/vroegen, vraagde/vraagden**	**gevraagd**

---

[16] See 11.8.1.3.

But it should be noted that there is a difference in meaning between the weak and strong imperfects of **jagen**: **joeg/joegen** 'chased away'; **jaagde/jaagden** 'hunted'.

Scheren 'to shave, shear [a sheep]' is usually regarded as a strong verb (see 11.3.1.II) but as the imperfect of 'to shave' one commonly hears **scheerde**.

Ervaren 'to experience, discover' should follow **varen** (see 11.3.1.VI) but **ervaarde** is frequently heard in the imperfect by analogy with **aanvaarden** 'to accept', e.g. **Hij ervaarde** (= **ervoer**) **het als een eer uitgenodigd te worden** 'He regarded it as an honour to be invited', **Hij aanvaardde de eer uitgenodigd te worden** 'He accepted the honour of being invited'.

11.5 IRREGULAR VERBS

Colloquially the term 'irregular' is used as a synonym for 'strong' with reference to verbs. Strictly speaking, however, irregular verbs are those that show irregularities that do not follow any of the seven basic patterns of strong verbs, i.e. classes I to VII.

There are three groups of irregular verbs:

11.5.1 Those that are historically weak verbs that all show a change of vowel in the past tenses, which they have in common with strong verbs, and also a dental ending, which they have in common with weak verbs. There are only six such verbs, two of which are not used in the spoken language, i.e. **dunken** and **plegen** (see 11.3.3). All derivatives of these verbs have the same irregularities, e.g. **verkopen** 'to sell' derived from **kopen** 'to buy' and **verzoeken** 'to request' derived from **zoeken** 'to search'. There is also a verb **plegen**, which means 'to commit', but it is a regular verb, i.e. **pleegde, gepleegd**.

11.5.2 There are five monosyllabic verbs that belong historically to one of the seven groups of strong verbs (except **doen**), but which show certain peculiarities other strong verbs do not. (see 11.1.1.2, 11.3.3)

11.5.3 There are a few isolated verbs that follow no particular pattern at all. (see 11.3.3) **Zeggen** also has a singular form **zeide**, which is occasionally found in literature, and the analogical formation **zegde** is common in Belgium. But compounds of **zeggen** are all regular:

ontzeggen	**ontzegde**	to deny
opzeggen	**zegde ... op**	to recite; cancel

11.6   Hebben 'TO HAVE'

11.6.1   FORMS OF hebben

The verb **hebben** shows several irregularities that the other irregular and strong verbs do not:

Present tense
ik heb 'I have' etc.	**wij hebben**
jij hebt	**jullie hebben, hebt**
u hebt, heeft	**u hebt, heeft**
hij heeft	**zij hebben**

The **gij** form is **hebt**. As with **zijn**, **u** can take either a second or third person verb and both are equally common. **Jullie hebben** is more common nowadays than **jullie hebt**. In **'plat'** Dutch the form **hij heb** is often heard, but should not be copied.

Imperfect tense	singular: **had**	plural: **hadden**
Perfect tense	**ik heb gehad**	I have had
Pluperfect tense	**ik had gehad**	I had had
Future tense	**ik zal hebben**	I will have
Future perfect tense	**ik zal gehad hebben**	I will have had
Conditional tense	**ik zou hebben**	I would have (or contracted to **ik had**, see 11.2.7)

Conditional perfect tense	**ik zou gehad hebben** I would have had (or contracted to **ik had gehad**, see 11.1.8)
Imperative	**heb!**
	The imperative forms **hebt u** and **hebben jullie** exist but are not common, as indeed is the imperative of **hebben** generally.
Subjunctive:	The third person of the present subjunctive occurs in certain standard expressions, e.g. **God hebbe zijn ziel** '(May) God rest his soul'.
	Occasionally in older literature the past subjunctive form **hadde** is also found.

11.6.2   USES OF hebben

For **hebben** as an auxiliary verb in perfect tenses see 11.1.3, 11.7.2.2.

The following expressions comprising the verb 'to be' in English are expressed with **hebben** in Dutch:

dienst hebben	to be on duty
dorst hebben	to be thirsty
(on)gelijk hebben	to be (wrong) right
geluk hebben	to be in luck
haast hebben	to be in a hurry (see 16.1.4.4)
honger hebben	to be hungry
pech hebben	to be unlucky
slaap hebben	to be sleepy
vakantie hebben	to be on holidays
vrij hebben	to be off (from work)

Note:

erge dorst/honger hebben	to be very thirsty/hungry etc.
geen dorst/honger hebben	to be not thirsty/hungry etc.

The following **hebben** constructions, which employ 'to be' in English, contain an idiomatic **het** which is usually written '**t**. They are only used with personal subjects, e.g. **Ik heb het druk** 'I am busy', but **Het is erg druk** 'It is very busy'.

't benauwd hebben	to feel off/sick
't druk hebben	to be busy
't koud hebben	to be cold
't moeilijk hebben	to be in trouble
't warm hebben	to be hot
't hebben over	to be talking about

11.7   Zijn 'TO BE'

11.7.1   FORMS OF THE VERB zijn

The verb 'to be', as in all European languages, is extremely irregular:

Present tense

ik ben 'I am'	**wij zijn**
jij bent 'you are' etc.	**jullie zijn, bent**
u bent, is	**u bent**
hij is	**zij zijn**

The **gij** form is **zijt**. **U** can take a second or third person verb, but **bent** is more common, and certainly in the plural. **Jullie zijn** is more common than **jullie bent**.

Imperfect tense   singular: **was**   plural: **waren**

The **gij** form is **waart**.

Perfect tense
The past participle is **geweest** and is formed from another infinitive
wezen (see below). The perfect tense of **zijn** takes **zijn** i.e. **ik ben
geweest** etc. I have been

There is an adjective formed from the past participle but it is strong in
form: **de gewezen burgemeester** 'the former mayor'

Pluperfect tense	**ik was geweest**	I had been
Future tense	**ik zal zijn**	I will be
Future perfect tense	**ik zal geweest zijn**	I will have been
Conditional tense	**ik zou zijn**	I would be
	(or contracted to **ik was**, see 11.2.7)	
Conditional perfect tense	**ik zou geweest zijn**	I would have been
	(or contracted to **ik was geweest**)	
Imperative	In the imperative a derivative of the second infinitive **wezen** is used for all persons: **wees!**	
	The forms **weest u, wezen jullie** also occur.	
Subjunctive	Subjunctive forms of 'to be' are still found in some standard expressions:	
	God zij dank! 'Thank God!'[17]	
	Volledigheidshalve zij hier vermeld dat ... 'For the sake of completeness let it be said that . . .' **als het ware** 'as it were'	

11.7.1.1   Notes on *wezen*

Wezen, which is historically a synonym of **zijn**, is used (other than in the
imperative as described above) in two ways:

1 to replace **zijn** when the latter stands in the infinitive (rather colloquial):

Het zou erg leuk kunnen wezen.   It could be really nice.
Weg wezen!   Be off with you!

2 to replace **zijn** in double infinitive constructions (i.e. it replaces the past
participle, see 11.9.2.5(b)):

Ik ben wezen kijken.   I have been to look.
Hij is wezen vissen.   He has been fishing.

---

[17] But this is more commonly expressed as **goddank!**

11.7.2   USES OF THE VERB zijn

Zijn as an auxiliary verb in compound tenses.

Many verbs in Dutch, unlike in English, employ the verb 'to be' as the auxiliary in compound tenses:

I have bought a car.	**Ik heb een auto gekocht.**

but

He has gone home.	**Hij is naar huis gegaan.**
The trees had fallen over.	**De bomen waren omgevallen.**

Verbs that denote a change from one position or state to another belong to this category.

komen 'to come', **vallen** 'to fall', **stijgen** 'to rise'

which all denote a motion from one point to another.

worden 'to become', **sterven** 'to die', **groeien** 'to grow'

which all denote a change from one state to another. But it is not always immediately evident to English speakers that the verbs concerned imply a change of position or state, e.g. **blijven** 'to stay, remain', **verdwijnen** 'to disappear'.

The verbs in this group are all intransitive (for exceptions see 11.7.2.1, n. 18, 11.7.2.2(b)–(c)).

Both weak and strong verbs can be conjugated with **zijn**. This raises another problem: most Dutch-English dictionaries and grammars will indicate in the list of strong verbs (see 11.3.1) whether those verbs take **zijn** in their compound tenses, but as weak verbs are never listed, those weak verbs that take **zijn** are more difficult to isolate and learn. For this reason the list given below is incomplete.

11.7.2.1   *Verbs that always take* zijn

The following verbs always take **zijn** in the perfect, pluperfect, future perfect and conditional perfect tenses:

We shall take **vallen** 'to fall' as an example of how such verbs form their tenses:

perfect	**ik ben gevallen**	I have fallen
pluperfect	**ik was gevallen**	I had fallen
future perfect	**ik zal gevallen zijn**	I will have fallen
conditional perfect:	**ik zou gevallen zijn/**	
	ik was gevallen	I would have fallen

It is impossible to give a complete list but the following will suffice to give an indication of the sort of verb that takes **zijn**, both weak and strong:

aanbreken	to dawn	**gebeuren**	to happen
afslaan	to stall (of a car)	**geschieden**	to happen
af-, toenemen	to decrease/ increase	**groeien**	to grow
		immigreren	to immigrate
barsten	to burst	**kelderen**	to plummet
bedaren	to calm/die down (wind)	**komen**[19]	to come
		krimpen	to shrink
beginnen[18]	to start	**landen**	to land (plane)
belanden	to land, end up	**meevallen**	to exceed expectations
bevallen	to like (impersonal) to give birth	**(mis)lukken**	to succeed (fail)
bevriezen	to freeze	**ontsnappen**	to escape
blijken	to appear	**ontstaan**	to originate
blijven	to remain, stay	**opgroeien**	to grow up
dalen	to descend	**ophouden**	to stop
doorschieten	to go to seed	**opschieten**	to make progress
emigreren	to emigrate	**opstaan**	to get up, stand up
gaan[19]	to go		

---

[18] There are just a few transitive verbs that use **zijn**; **beginnen** 'to begin', **naderen** 'to approach', **nagaan** 'to follow up', **oversteken** 'to cross' (a road etc.), **tegenkomen** 'to bump into s.o.', **vergeten** 'to forget' (see 11.3.1.V), **verliezen** 'to lose' (see 11.3.1.II).

Beginnen (see 11.9.2.4) usually turns the direct object into an indirect object by the use of a preposition:

Hij is een zaak in de stad begonnen.	He's started a business in town.
Ik begin (aan/met) een nieuw hoofdstuk van mijn leven.	I'm starting a new chapter in my life.
Zij is al aan (met) haar huiswerk begonnen.	She's already started her homework.
Ik ben er al aan (mee) begonnen.	I've already started it.

The verbs **aankomen** 'to gain weight' and **afvallen** 'to lose weight' take **zijn** although they seem to be used transitively in expressions such as **Ze is twee kilo afgevallen** 'She has lost 2 kilos' (see 14.10). For other transitive verbs that use **zijn** see 11.7.2.2(b)–(c).

[19] Many derivatives of these and other verbs also take **zijn**, e.g. **ondergaan** 'to set (of the sun'), **vergaan** 'to pass'., **binnenkomen** 'to come in', **opvallen** 'to strike' but not all derivatives do: sometimes the prefixes make transitive verbs of these otherwise intransitive verbs and then **hebben** is used, e.g. **ondergaan** 'to undergo', **nagaan** 'to check, trace', **voorkomen** 'to prevent', **betreden** 'to tread on', **bestijgen** 'to ascend (the throne)'. **Schoolgaan** 'to go to school' also takes **hebben**. On the other hand there are sometimes derivatives that take **zijn** when the root verb in its literal sense does not (see 11.20):

opstaan 'to get up' – **Ik ben opgestaan,**
but **staan** 'to stand' – **Ik heb twee uur gestaan.**
afbranden 'to burn down' – **Het huis is afgebrand,**
but **branden** 'to burn' – **Het huis heeft urenlang gebrand.**
dichtvriezen 'to freeze up' – **De rivier is dichtgevroren,**
but **vriezen** 'to freeze' – **Het heeft gevroren.**

opstijgen	to take off (plane)	verbleken[21]	to turn pale
overlijden	to pass away	verdorren[21]	to wither
rijzen	to rise	verdwijnen[21]	to disappear
slagen	to succeed	verkleuren[21]	to change colour
spruiten	to sprout	verouderen[21]	to get old, age
stappen (in-, uit-, over-)	to step (get in, out, change)	verschieten[21]	to fade, run (colours)
sterven	to die	verschijnen[21]	to appear
stijgen[19]	to rise	vertrekken[21]	to leave, depart
stikken	to suffocate	verwelken[21]	to wither
stoppen	to stop	vluchten	to flee
tegenvallen	to be disappointing	(uit)wijken	to give way to
		worden	to become
treden[19]	to tread	zakken	to fail (exams)
uitslapen[20]	to sleep in	zijn	to be
vallen	to fall	zinken	to sink
		zwellen	to swell

11.7.2.2 VERBS THAT TAKE EITHER hebben OR zijn

There is also a group of verbs that can take either **hebben** or **zijn** as the auxiliary in the perfect tenses. There are four categories of such verbs:

(a) The following verbs are conjugated with **zijn** if a motion to or from a particular place is mentioned (in which case they do not differ from the verbs given in 11.7.2.1 above); but if there is no motion but merely an action, they are conjugated with **hebben** (the asterisks are explained below):

dansen	to dance	hollen	to run
fietsen	to cycle	joggen	to jog
glijden	to slide	klimmen	to climb

[20] Many Dutch verbs can take the prefix **uit** giving the meaning 'to be finished doing'. These compound verbs all take **zijn** even if the verbs from which they are formed do not:

uitslapen	to sleep in, have one's fill of sleep
uitpraten	to finish saying what one has to say
uitkijken	to finish looking

Ik was nog niet uitgepraat of hij begon al te boeren.
I had hardly finished talking when he began to burp.

Ben je uitgekeken?
Have you seen enough/finished looking?

[21] The prefix **ver-** basically means 'change' (see 11.20.2.1.6) and thus many **ver-** verbs are found in this group, but not all **ver-** verbs belong here as many are transitive:

| verstaan | to understand |
| vertalen | to translate (i.e. to change from one language to another) |

kruipen	to crawl	**stappen**	to step
lopen	to walk	**trappen**	to pedal, tread
reizen	to travel	**varen***	to go (by sea)
rennen	to run	**vliegen***	to fly
rijden*	to drive, ride	**wandelen**	to walk, stroll
roeien*	to row	**zeilen***	to sail
springen	to jump	**zwemmen**	to swim

lopen 'to run'	**Hij is naar huis gelopen.**
	He walked home.
	Hij heeft de hele dag gelopen.
	He (has) walked all day.
rijden 'to drive'	**We zijn in drie kwartier naar Rotterdam gereden.**
	We drove to Rotterdam in three quarters of an hour.
	Ik heb vandaag erg veel gereden.
	I drove (have driven) a lot today.
zwemmen 'to swim'	**Gisteren is er een Engelsman van Dover naar Calais gezwommen.**
	Yesterday an Englishman swam from Dover to Calais.
	Heb je ooit in de Oostzee gezwommen?
	Have you ever swum in the Baltic Sea?

(b) Some of the verbs mentioned above can also be used transitively, in which case they take **hebben**, as do all transitive verbs. They are marked *:

rijden	**Heb je ooit een Mercedes gereden?**
	Have you ever driven a Mercedes?
roeien	**Hij heeft haar naar de overkant van de rivier geroeid.**
	He rowed her to the other side of the river.

(c) There is in addition a small group of verbs that take **zijn** when used intransitively, but **hebben** when used transitively, but they have nothing to do with motion like those under point (b), but indicate a change of state:

bederven	to spoil	**ontdooien**	to defrost
breken	to break	**veranderen**	to change
genezen	to heal, cure		

Het is bedorven.	It has spoiled.
Jij hebt het bedorven.	You've spoilt it.

De stoel is gebroken.	The chair has broken.
Jij hebt hem gebroken.	You broke it.
De wond is genezen.	The wound has healed.
De dokter heeft me genezen.	The doctor (has) cured me.
De kip is ontdooid.	The chicken has defrosted.
Ik heb de kip ontdooid.	I have defrosted the chicken.
Het weer is veranderd.	The weather has changed.
Ik heb het veranderd.	I altered it.

It should be noted that when such verbs are used intransitively in Dutch, they are conjugated with **zijn** and the past participles can be indistinguishable from predicative adjectives:

De stoel is gebroken.
The chair has broken/The chair is broken.
(also The chair has been broken, see 11.12.4.1)

Note that with a verb like **ontdooien** 'to defrost', when an object is involved you have the choice of saying **Ik heb de kip ontdooid** (for example in a microwave) or **Ik heb de kip laten ontdooien** (see 11.18.2) where the defrosting has been allowed to occur naturally.

(d) The verbs dealt with here can be conjugated with **zijn** or **hebben** but the criteria for their use are separate in each case:

vergeten 'to forget': with **hebben** the meaning is 'did not think of something', 'neglected to do something' or 'left something behind':

Ik heb vergeten te schrijven.
I forgot to write.

Ik heb mijn paraplu vergeten.
I've forgotten my umbrella

With **zijn** the meaning is 'has gone from one's memory':

Ik ben glad vergeten waar ik het gelaten heb.
I have completely forgotten where I left it.

Ik ben je naam vergeten.
I have forgotten your name.

In practice most Dutch speakers use **zijn** in all cases as even they find the distinction too subtle to remember.

verleren 'to forget something learnt': this verb can be conjugated with **hebben** or **zijn** with no difference in meaning:

Ik heb/ben het Frans geheel verleerd.
I have totally forgotten French.

verliezen 'to lose': should always be conjugated with **hebben** but in the sense of mislaying something is commonly heard with **zijn** either by analogy with **vergeten** or with **kwijt zijn**:

Ik ben mijn sleutels kwijt.
Ik heb mijn sleutels verloren
I have lost my keys.

but only

Zij hebben de verkiezing verloren.
They lost the election.

volgen 'to follow': when this verb means 'to pursue' it is conjugated with **zijn**:

Onze hond is de buurman gevolgd.
Our dog followed the neighbour.

Otherwise **hebben** is used:

Ik heb colleges bij hem gevolgd.
I did courses with him.

Zij heeft de politieke ontwikkelingen in Zuid-Afrika gevolgd.
She has followed the political developments in South Africa.

The verb **opvolgen** 'to succeed, follow' is found with both auxiliaries:

Beatrix heeft/is haar moeder in 1980 opgevolgd.
Beatrix succeeded her mother in 1980.

Note: Because only one auxiliary (i.e. 'have') is used in the perfect and pluperfect tenses in English, one can often have several past participles following, all dependent on the one 'have'. In Dutch this is only possible if all past participles require **hebben** or all require **zijn**; the auxiliary must be repeated if one or more requires **hebben** and the other(s) **zijn**:

Hij heeft een vliegtuig gehuurd en is naar Moskou gevlogen.
He has hired a plane and flown to Moscow.

11.7.2.3 *TRANSLATING 'TO BE' WITH REFERENCE TO POSITION*

Very often the English verb 'to be', when referring to the position of something, is rendered in Dutch by the verbs **hangen** 'to hang', **liggen** 'to lie', **lopen** 'to run', **staan** 'to stand' and **zitten** 'to sit'. They are usually found in constructions with repletive **er** (see 15.1) and thus commonly render 'there is/are':

Er staan hier veel bomen.	There are many trees here.
Achter ons huis loopt een gracht.	Behind our house (there) is a canal.
Er hangt een schilderij aan de muur.	There is a picture (hanging) on the wall.
Wat zit er in dat glas?	What is in that glass?

11.8 MODAL AUXILIARY VERBS (**modale hulpwerkwoorden**)

Modal verbs form a special class of their own because they show a variety of irregular forms and, due to their auxiliary nature in expressing attitude, also a variety of meanings. There are four true modals (**kunnen, moeten, mogen, willen**) plus the verbs **durven, hoeven,** and **zullen** which share one or more modal characteristics.

One feature common to both Dutch and English modals is the lack of a **te** or 'to' before the infinitive for which they are acting as an auxiliary, e.g. **Hij kan het doen** 'He can do it'.

Note than when a modal verb followed by one or more infinitives is the finite verb in a subordinate or relative clause, i.e. in a clause where the finite verb does not stay in second position, the usual word order is as follows:

Hij wist al lang dat ze niet kon komen. (komen kon is possible but unusual)
He had known for ages that she couldn't come.

Hij wist al lang dat ze niet zou kunnen komen.
He had known for ages that she would not be able to come.

Ze vroeg of ik haar op zou bellen. (opbellen zou is possible but unusual) or
Ze vroeg of ik haar zou opbellen.
She asked whether I'd ring her.

11.8.1 FORMS

11.8.1.1 *Kunnen* 'to be able to, can'

Present:

ik kan = I am able, can	**wij kunnen**
jij kunt, kan	**jullie kunnen, kunt**
u kunt, kan	**u kunt**
hij kan	**zij kunnen**

Jij can take either **kunt** or **kan** and both are equally common. When inverted, **jij kunt** becomes **kun jij**. **Jullie kunnen** is more common than

jullie kunt. In 'plat' Dutch **kennen** 'to know' and **kunnen** are often confused, e.g. **Dat ken niet, hoor** 'That is not possible'.

U can take either **kunt** or **kan** but the former is more common.

Imperfect:
> **ik, jij, u, hij kon** = I was able, could   **wij, jullie, zij konden**

Past participle:
> **gekund** (see Perfect tenses of modal verbs, 11.8.2)

11.8.1.2   *Moeten* 'to have to, must'

For the negative of **moeten** using **hoeven** see 11.8.5.2.

Present:
> **ik moet** = I have to, must   **wij moeten**
> **jij, u moet**   **jullie moeten, moet**
> **hij moet**   **zij moeten**

Jullie moet is not common.

Imperfect:
> **ik, jij, u, hij moest** = I had to   **wij, jullie, zij moesten**

Past participle:
> **gemoeten** (see Perfect tenses of modal verbs, 11.8.2)

11.8.1.3   *Mogen* 'to be allowed to, may'

Present:
> **ik mag** = I am allowed, may   **wij mogen**
> **jij, u mag**   **jullie mogen, mag**
> **hij mag**   **zij mogen**

Jullie mag is not common. The **gij** form is **moogt**.

Imperfect:
> **ik, jij, u, hij mocht** = I was allowed to   **wij, jullie, zij mochten**

Past participle:
> **gemogen, gemocht** or **gemoogd**

One finds all three forms but in practice most people use **gemogen** (see Perfect tenses of modal verbs, 11.8.2).

11.8.1.4   *Willen* 'to want to'

Present:
> **ik wil** = I want to   **wij willen**

jij wilt, wil	jullie willen, wilt
u wilt, wil	
hij wil	zij willen

Jij can take either **wilt** or **wil** and both are equally common; when inverted **jij wilt** becomes **wil jij**. **Jullie wilt** is not common.

U can take either **wilt** or **wil** but the former is more common.

Imperfect:
ik, jij, u, hij wilde/wou = I wanted to   **wij, jullie, zij wilden**

One often hears a plural form **wouwen** but this is never written and should be avoided in more careful speech; the singular form **wou** is permissible in both writing and speech, however, and is completely interchangeable with **wilde** as an imperfect form (see also Contracted modals in conditional tenses, 11.8.5.4 where the two are not interchangeable).

Past participle:
gewild (see Perfect tenses of modal verbs, 11.8.2)

11.8.2 PERFECT TENSES OF MODAL VERBS

The past participle of modal verbs is not often used. Because of the auxiliary functions of modals, a perfect tense (including pluperfects, future perfects and conditional perfects) is usually followed by another infinitive and in this case the so-called 'double infinitive rule' applies, i.e. if one has an English sentence where the past participle of a modal verb is followed by an infinitive, Dutch does not use the past participle but the infinitive of the modal concerned (see also 11.9.2.5(a)):

Ik heb hem niet *kunnen* bezoeken.	I have not *been able to* visit him.
Ze hadden *mogen* gaan.	They had *been allowed to* go.
Zij zal het hebben *moeten* uitgeven.	She will have *had to* spend it.

Only when the infinitive for which the modal is acting as auxiliary is not mentioned (but simply implied), is the past participle used; note the obligatory use of **het** in such cases:

Ik heb het niet gekund.	I have not been able to (see him).
Zij hadden het gemogen.	They had been allowed to (go).
Zij zal het hebben gemoeten.	She will have had to (spend it).

The following is commonly done by Dutch people with the perfect tense of modals: modals all take **hebben** as their auxiliary verb in the perfect tense but the speaker is often misled by the infinitive that follows the perfect of the modal:

Hij is niet kunnen komen.	He hasn't been able to come.

Here the speaker anticipates the verb of motion which follows the modal and which requires **zijn** in its perfect tense, but in actual fact it is the perfect of **kunnen** which is required here and **kunnen** requires **hebben**, e.g. **Hij heeft niet kunnen komen**. Similarly **Hij is weggemoeten**, which is an abbreviated form of **Hij heeft moeten weggaan** where **gaan** is not mentioned but simply implied (see also 11.8.4).

11.8.3   CONTRACTED MODALS IN CONDITIONAL TENSES

11.8.3.1   Conditional tense:

The modal auxiliary verbs have in common with the auxiliaries **hebben** and **zijn** the fact that they have contracted forms in the conditional (see 11.1.8). There is one example of the concept in English too: 'I could do it' can mean either 'I was able to do it' (an imperfect) or 'I would be able to do it' (a conditional).

11.8.3.1.1   *kunnen*

Similarly the Dutch sentence **Ik kon het doen** is ambiguous without a context and in the latter meaning it replaces **Ik zou het kunnen doen**, where **kon** is the contracted form of **zou kunnen**. Either form is permissible but the latter avoids any ambiguity.

11.8.3.1.2   *moeten*

In the same way **moest/moesten** can mean 'should, ought to' (a conditional) as well as 'had to' (an imperfect), e.g. **Je moest meer eten** 'You should eat more'. **Je zou meer moeten eten** is equally correct and preferable if ambiguity is likely.

11.8.3.1.3   *willen*

Willen has a contracted form too which means 'would like to, want to' and which is also identical to the past tense:

Ik wou graag twee kilo appels (hebben) =
Ik zou graag twee kilo appels willen (hebben).
I would like two kilos of apples.

The adverb **graag** is usually used in such 'would like' constructions but not in questions:

Wil je een kopje koffie?
Would you like a cup of coffee?

Note the following use of **wou** which is also derived from a contracted conditional:

Ik wou dat ik rijk was.
I wish I were rich.

Wilde(n) can never be used in any of the above conditional senses.

11.8.3.1.4 *mogen*

There is a contraction of **mogen** in the conditional which is rather formal style and which is translated by 'should' in English:

Mocht het regenen, dan komen we niet.
Should it rain, we won't be coming.

Use of **dan** in the second clause in this construction with **mocht** is compulsory (see 12.2.1.5) but note its position in the clause compared with the above when used together with an imperative:

Mocht uw instelling inmiddels gefuseerd zijn, wilt u dan aangeven waarmee?
Should your institution have been amalgamated in the meantime, would you mention with what?

11.8.3.2 *Conditional perfect of **kunnen** and **moeten** (see also 11.12.4.4*

11.8.3.2.1 *kunnen*

The English phrase 'could have done' is a contraction of 'would have been able to do' and as such can be rendered in Dutch by **Hij zou het hebben kunnen doen** but the following contracted form is more commonly used: **Hij had het kunnen doen** (for contraction of **zou ... hebben** to **had/hadden**, see 11.1.8).

It is best to learn **had/hadden kunnen doen** parrot-fashion and to apply it as follows:

Zij had het liedje beter kunnen zingen.
She could have sung the song better.

11.8.3.2.2 *moeten*

The construction 'should have done' is similar to the above but is impossible to rephrase sensibly in 'would' terms in English. In this case it is advisable to learn **had/hadden moeten doen** parrot-fashion and to apply it as follows:

Zij hadden de krant moeten lezen.
They should have read the newspaper.

Note that the contracted conditional perfect forms **had(den) kunnen doen**
and **had(den) moeten doen** are identical to the pluperfect (as a result of
the double infinitive rule, see 11.8.2), but context always makes the
meaning clear:

Als ik het had moeten doen, zou ik geweigerd hebben.
If I had had to do it, I would have refused. (pluperfect)

Ik had het moeten doen maar ik had er geen zin in.
I should have done it but I didn't feel like it. (conditional perfect).

See uses of **zullen** on 11.8.5.5.

11.8.4   USE OF INDEPENDENT MODALS

There is one use of modals which differs considerably from English:
kunnen, moeten, mogen and **willen** often stand alone and the verb that
follows in English is simply implied in Dutch; this is particularly the case
when the implied verbs are **doen, gaan, komen, hebben** and **worden**:

Ik kan het niet.	I can't do it.
Dat moet.	It's necessary.
Je mag naar binnen.	You may go inside.
Hij zou het niet willen.	He wouldn't want to do (or to have) it.
Kan dat?	Is that possible?
Mag dat?	Is that allowed?
Dat hoeft niet.	That's not necessary (see **hoeven**, 11.8.5.2)

11.8.5   SEMANTIC DIFFICULTIES WITH MODALS

11.8.5.1   *kunnen*

(a) As in English, **kunnen** 'can' and **mogen** 'may' are often confused, e.g.
'Can I borrow your bicycle?' should in prescriptive grammar read
'May I borrow your bicycle?' but in practice the semantic distinction
between the two is ignored, which is the case in Dutch too; **Kan ik
je fiets even lenen?** will often be heard instead of **Mag ik je fiets even
lenen?**

Also in other contexts English 'may' is sometimes rendered by **kunnen** in
Dutch:

Dat kan wel waar zijn maar ...
That may be true but ...

De koning kan elk ogenblik komen.
The king may/might come at any moment.

(b) **Kunnen** is commonly used in polite requests:

**Kunt u het raam even dichtdoen?/Zou u het raam even dicht
   kunnen doen?**
Could you close the window?

(c) **Kunnen** + **beter** renders English 'had better':

Je kan beter geen auto kopen.
You had better not buy a car/You're better off not buying a car.

(d) Note that **kunnen** is not used with verbs of perception unlike English:

Ik zie/hoor niets.
I can't see/hear anything.

Ik versta je niet.
I can't understand you.[22]

(e) A conditional of **kunnen** is often used to render 'might' (see
   11.8.5.3(d)).

11.8.5.2   moeten

(a) **Moeten** has two meanings:
   1 to be obliged to, have to
   2 to be advised to

Je moet je vader helpen.
You must (are obliged to) help your father.
You must (i.e. I advise you to) help your father.

English has the same ambiguity. When the above English examples are
negated, the following occurs:

   meaning 1: You don't have to help your father = You needn't help
         your father.
   meaning 2: You mustn't help your father. (i.e. I advise you not to/
         forbid you to)

Similarly in Dutch a different verb is used to negate the former:

---

[22] Note that this means 'I can't hear you/what you are saying' (e.g. on the phone). 'I don't
understand you' with reference to your behaviour would be **Ik begrijp je niet**.

meaning 1: **Je hoeft je vader niet te helpen.**
meaning 2: **Je moet je vader niet helpen.**

Hoeven (hoefde/hoefden/gehoeven) is a semi-modal verb. Firstly, it replaces **moeten** in the above sense and it can be used independently like **moeten**, e.g. **Dat hoeft niet** 'That's not necessary', **Dat had niet gehoeven** 'That wasn't neccessary'. But there are cases when **hoeven** must be followed by **te** (an unmodal trait) and others where one has the option, i.e. **te** is always used in the present and imperfect tenses (see examples above), but may be omitted in compound tenses where double infinitive constructions occur, for example:

Dat zul je nooit hoeven (te) doen.
You'll never have to do that.

Dat heeft hij nooit hoeven (te) doen.
He's never needed to do that.

Note the following use of **hoeven** with the conjunction **zonder dat/te** (see 12.5.1.4 for the distinction) where a negative is merely implied; **moeten** is possible here too:

Je kon daar naar binnen gaan zonder dat je hoefde te wachten.
You could enter without having to wait.

(b) 'Should, ought to' are expressed by **moeten** in Dutch (see also **mogen**, 11.8.3.1.4). Although the contracted conditional form **moest(en)** (see 11.8.3) is often used in this sense, the present tense is also very common and is certainly simpler:

Je moet (moest) vaker schrijven.
You should write more often.

Dat moet (moest) verboden worden.
That should be forbidden.

Note that 'should' which means 'would' is expressed by **zou/zouden**:

Ik zou het doen als ik jou was.
I should do it, if I were you.

(c) In formal style the verbs **dienen** and **(be)horen** can replace **moeten** in the sense of 'to be obliged to'. They are always followed by **te**:

Alle passagiers dienen zich vóór acht uur bij loket vier te melden.
All passengers should register at counter four before eight o'clock.

Bij het binnengaan van een kerk, behoren de heren hun hoed af te nemen.
On entering a church, gentlemen must remove their hats.

11.8.5.3 mogen

(a) In addition to the basic meaning of 'to be allowed to', **mogen** also renders the verb 'to like' (of people), e.g. **Ik mag hem graag** 'I like him a lot', as distinct from **ik hou van hem** 'I love him'; otherwise one must say **Ik vind hem aardig** to express 'to like'.

(b) There is a **mogen** commonly used with the adverb **wel eens** which means 'could, would be better if':

Je mag je kamer wel eens opruimen.
You could tidy up your room (to begin with).

Hij mag zich wel eens omkleden.
He could change his clothes (for once).

(c) There is a polite, obsolete first person present subjunctive form of **mogen** that occurs in formal letters:

Naar aanleiding van uw schrijven van 21 december jl. moge ik u mededelen ...
With reference to your letter of the 21st Dec. last I would like to inform you ...

A third person present subjunctive form **moge** meaning 'may' occurs in standard idioms expressing a desire:

Moge hij rusten in vrede (= Hij ruste in vrede).
May he rest in peace.

Note also the following use of subjunctive **moge** which lingers on as a standard expression:

Waar hij ook moge zijn op de wereld, hij is dankzij zijn mobiele telefoon altijd te bereiken.
Wherever he may be in the world, thanks to his mobile phone he can always be contacted.

(d) English 'might', a form derived from 'may', is usually expressed in Dutch simply by the addition of **misschien** 'perhaps' to the sentence, but the conditional of **kunnen** is also possible:

Hij komt misschien morgen/Hij zou morgen kunnen komen.
He might come tomorrow.

Dat zal misschien moeilijk zijn/Dat zou moeilijk kunnen zijn.
That might be difficult.

'Might' in the following example is semantically different, however, and **misschien** cannot be used:

Hij had mij kunnen vragen of ik het hebben wilde.
He might have asked me if I wanted it (i.e. he could have asked).

(e) Note the following idiomatic use of **mocht(en)** which expresses a lack of ability:

Ik heb alles geprobeerd om af te vallen maar niets mocht lukken.
I tried everything to lose weight but nothing worked.

Zijn inspanningen om het dier te redden mochten niet lukken.
His efforts to save the animal were to no avail.

11.8.5.4   willen

(a) In addition to the meaning 'want (to)', the Dutch verb **willen** also often renders English 'will'; in such cases no futurity is expressed but a polite imperative (as in English 'would you mind . . .').

Wilt u het raam even dichtdoen?
Will you please shut the window?

(b) English 'would like' is expressed by the conditional of **willen** (see 11.8.3.1.3):

Ik zou u graag willen ontmoeten.
I would like to meet you.

Ik zou graag een kopje koffie willen/Ik wou graag een kopje koffie.
I would like a cup of coffee.

But colloquially **Ik zou graag een kopje koffie hebben**, without **willen**, is very common.
   Note also the idiom **Hoe wou u het gehad hebben?** 'How would you like it?' (i.e. How would you like it done/to see it happen etc.)

(c) **Ik wil dat jij** . . . etc. renders 'I want you to . . . etc.':

Moeder wil dat ik mijn broertje meeneem.
Mother wants me to take my little brother along.

11.8.5.5   zullen

In addition to being the auxiliary used to form the future tense (see 11.1.5), **zullen** can also have other connotations:

Zullen we gaan? Shall we go? (= **Laten we gaan!** Let's go!)

It also renders biblical 'shalt' (i.e. 'must'):

Gij zult niet stelen.
Thou shalt not steal.

The idiom **Dat zal wel** 'That's probably so/the case' is very common. (see 11.2.6)

The past participle of **zullen**, **gezuld**, is quite rare and can be forgotten, but **zullen** does occur in double infinitive constructions (see 11.8.2). In such cases it is very close in meaning to **moeten** (see 11.8.3.2.2) although with **zullen** the emphasis is on the intention rather than the obligation, which is the case with **moeten**.

Ze had het zullen doen maar ze deed het niet.
She intended/was going to do it but she didn't (do it).

Compare:

Ze had het moeten doen maar ze deed het niet.
She should have done it but she didn't (do it).

Note the following idiomatic use of **zullen** in the infinitive:

Ze hebben beloofd om bombardementen niet te zullen hervatten.
They promised not to resume bombing (= that they would not resume bombing).

Ze vreesden uit het land gezet te zullen worden.
They feared being deported from the country (= that they would be deported).

In addition to rendering 'would', the past tense of **zullen**, **zou/zouden**, is used in journalese above all in a quotative sense, i.e. to report a fact without committing yourself as to whether what is being reported is true or not (compare the use of the subjunctive in reporting speech in German):

De brand zou zijn aangestoken door een vluchteling.
The fire was started by a refugee (= It is claimed/believed that ... / allegedly)

11.9 THE INFINITIVE (**de onbepaalde wijs**)

11.9.1 CHARACTERISTICS OF THE INFINITIVE

The infinitive or basic undeclined form of the verb always ends in **-en** in Dutch, **lopen** 'to run', **jagen** 'to hunt' etc. There are only six monosyllabic verbs whose infinitives end in **-n**: **doen**, **gaan**, **slaan**, **staan**, **zien**, **zijn**.

English always puts 'to' before the infinitive in isolation; one should learn each new verb as follows: **lopen** = to run. In context, however, there are occasions when this 'to' may or may not be used. Similarly in Dutch, although the infinitive in isolation is never preceded by **te**, in context there are rules for when **te** is and is not used before an infinitive.

11.9.2   RULES FOR THE USE OF **te**

As a general rule one can say that an infinitive at the end of a clause is always preceded by **te** except in the following cases:

11.9.2.1   When the infinitive is used as a general impersonal imperative (see 11.10.3):

> **niet roken** 'don't smoke', **geen lawaai maken** 'don't make any noise', **niet zo langzaam lopen** 'don't walk so slowly', **weg wezen** 'get lost/scram'.

11.9.2.2   It is never used after modal verbs, i.e. when a modal is the finite verb in the clause. Dutch often shares this feature with English:

> **Hij kan het niet doen.**
> He can't do it/He isn't able to do it.

> **Wij hebben tien boeken moeten lezen.**
> We had to read ten books.

Note the English modal 'to want to', where a 'to' is used (compare 'to be able to' and 'to have to' above), unlike Dutch.

> **Hij wil gaan.**   He wants to go.
> **Hij moet gaan.**   He has to go.

11.9.2.3   The auxiliary **hoeven**, which is used to form the negative of **moeten**, is commonly followed by **te**, unlike the true mòdals. (see 11.8.5.2).

11.9.2.4   The verbs **durven** 'to dare', **staan** 'to stand', **liggen** 'to lie', **lopen** 'to walk', and **zitten** 'to sit' behave in a similar way to **hoeven**, i.e. in the present and imperfect tenses they require a **te** to precede any infinitive dependent on them, but not in the perfect (i.e. not in double infinitive constructions, see 11.8.2):

> **Durf je dat te doen?**
> Do you dare (to) do that?

> **Dat heb ik nooit durven (te) zeggen.** (**te** is optional with the perfect of **durven**)
> I never dared (to) say that.

> **Hij zit een boek te lezen.**
> He's sitting reading a book.

Hij heeft de hele dag een boek zitten lezen.
He has been (sitting) reading a book all day.

Zij stond naar een koe te kijken.
She stood looking at a cow.

Ze kan urenlang naar koeien staan kijken.
She can stand looking at cows for hours.

The verbs **proberen** and **trachten** 'to try' can occur in a double infinitive construction like that of the above verbs but they always require **te**:

Hij probeerde mij te helpen.
He tried to help me.

Hij heeft mij proberen te helpen.
He (has) tried to help me.

A double infinitive can be avoided here by employing the following construction, which is in fact just as commonly used as the above:

Hij heeft geprobeerd mij te helpen.

The verb **beginnen**, when used in the perfect tense and followed by another infinitive, usually follows the regular pattern of past participle + **te** + infinitive but it can also follow the same pattern as **proberen**, using the infinitive instead of the past participle:

Toen is het kind begonnen te schreeuwen/
Toen is het kind beginnen te schreeuwen.
Then the child started to scream/screaming.

Hij is begonnen een brief te schrijven/
Hij is een brief beginnen te schrijven.
He began to write/writing a letter.

Similarly the verb **weten**, which literally means 'to know' but renders English 'to manage' in such constructions:

Hij wist te ontsnappen.
He managed to escape.

Hij heeft het weten te vinden.
He (has) managed to find it.

11.9.2.5 When the following verbs are used as finite verbs and are followed by an infinitive, the infinitive is not preceded by **te**:

horen	gaan	helpen	laten	hebben	blijven
zien	komen	leren	doen	wezen	vinden
					voelen

Zij hoorde mij komen.
She heard me coming.

Ik vond het potlood bij het raam liggen.
I found the pencil lying near the window.

(a) All these verbs (except **hebben**, see (e) below) employ a double infinitive construction in the perfect tense, i.e. they use an infinitive, not a past participle when followed by another infinitive (see also Perfect tenses of modal verbs, 11.8.2). Such constructions are very common because of the tendency in Dutch to use the perfect tense instead of the imperfect, as illustrated by the translations of the following examples:

Ik heb hem horen komen.
I heard him coming.

Hij is gaan kijken.[23]
He has gone (went) to look.

Hij heeft zijn hart voelen kloppen.
He felt his heart beating.

Ik heb mijn zoontje leren zwemmen.[24]
I taught my son to swim.

We hebben er urenlang naar staan kijken.
We stood watching it for hours.

Hij heeft zijn handen leren gebruiken.
He has learnt to use his hands.

Hij is blijven doorpraten.
He went on talking.

(b) **Zijn** has a special alternative infinitive used only in such double infinitive constructions:

Ze zijn wezen kijken.
They have been to have a look. (see 11.7.1.1)

This means essentially the same thing as **Ze zijn gaan kijken** 'They went and had a look'.

(c) **Laten** in such constructions expresses 'to have something done by someone else':

---

[23] Note the use of **zijn** to render the perfect tense of **gaan**, a verb of motion.
[24] Compare **Hij heeft leren schrijven** 'He (has) learnt to write' and **Hij heeft lezen en schrijven geleerd** 'He (has) learnt to read and write' where **lezen** and **schrijven** are acting as nouns.

Hij heeft een huis laten bouwen.
He has had a house built.

Ik heb mijn haar laten knippen.
I (have) had my hair cut.

Doen often replaces **laten** in more formal style and in certain standard expressions:

De regering heeft het parlementsgebouw doen ontruimen.
The government (has) had parliament house evacuated.

De zon heeft de gewassen vroeger dan gewoonlijk doen rijpen.
The sun made the plants ripen earlier than usual.

Dat was de druppel die de emmer deed overlopen.
That was the straw that broke the camel's back.

Note: **Doen** can be used as a sort of auxiliary in combination with another infinitive provided the sentence begins with that infinitive:

Lezen doet ze wel.
She does read.

(d) There are some pairs of infinitives incorporating the above verbs which render a new concept in English:

blijven zitten	to fail, stay down (at school)
gaan zitten	to sit down
blijven staan	to stop still, stop walking
doen denken aan	to remind (someone of something)

(e) Note the following idiomatic use of **hebben** which requires no **te** before the infinitive that follows it:

Ik heb een tante in Friesland wonen.
I have an aunt living in Friesland.

Zij heeft een prachtige lamp in de hoek staan.
She has a beautiful lamp (standing) in the corner.

11.9.3 USE OF **om ... te** BEFORE INFINITIVES

This is a complicated issue in Dutch. There are a few instances where only **te** can be used (see 11.9.2) and a few cases where only **om ... te** can be used:

11.9.3.1 When in English 'to' means 'in order to' (compare the archaic English form 'She went to town for to buy a bonnet', which comes close to the literal meaning and feeling of Dutch **om ... te**):

Ik ga naar de stad om een jas te kopen.
I am going to town to buy a coat.

Het is niet nodig (om) de weg over te steken om bij de winkels te komen.
It is not necessary to cross the road to reach the shops.

11.9.3.2   When a sentence begins with an infinitive clause:

Om een taal goed te leren moet je het land bezoeken.
To learn a language well, you must visit the country. (= in order to)

11.9.3.3   When an infinitive construction follows a noun that it is describing; in such cases **om** is always followed by a preposition:

Een pad om op te fietsen.
A path to ride on.

Een surfboot is een boot om mee door de branding te gaan.
A surfboat is a boat for going through the surf.

Nieuwe huizen zijn niet prettig om in te wonen.
New houses are not nice to live in.

Ik heb al mijn kinderen om voor te zorgen.
I have all my children to look after.

Note: There is one specific use of **om ... te** which renders English 'only to ...' (see 12.5):

Het vliegtuig steeg op om een half uur later neer te storten.
The plane took off only to crash half an hour later.

In all other cases the use of **om ... te** is optional but nowadays there is a tendency to include **om** wherever possible:

Ze weigerde (om) mee te gaan.[25]
She refused to go along.

Het is niet (om) uit te houden.
It is impossible to bear.

Het is stom (om) een tweedehands auto te kopen.
It is stupid to buy a second-hand car.

---

[25] **Te** used with a separable verb goes between the prefix and the verb and the three words are written separately, not as one word as in German.

Ik ben vergeten (om) te vragen of hij zijn regenjas meeneemt.
I forgot to ask whether he's taking his raincoat.

Zij was van plan (om) een uitstapje naar Marken te maken.
She intended making a trip to Marken.

Dat is niet (om) te doen.
That can't be done.

11.9.4   THE INFINITIVE AS A NOUN

The infinitive is also used as a neuter noun:

blaffen 'to bark', thus **het blaffen** 'the barking'
behangen 'to wall-paper', thus **het behangen** 'the wall-papering'

Ik ben tegen roken.
I am against smoking.

Het uit je hoofd leren van werkwoorden valt tegen.
Learning verbs by heart isn't easy.

Vermijd het te veel drinken van wodka als je in Rusland bent.
Avoid drinking too much vodka when you're in Russia.

11.10   THE IMPERATIVE MOOD (de gebiedende wijs)

11.10.1   As the imperative is an order or command form addressed to another person or persons, there is a **jij**, **jullie** and **u** form. It is common to put an exclamation mark after a command in Dutch if the sentence is relatively short:

werk!
werken jullie!   work
werkt u!

The form derived from the simple stem can actually be used for all persons whether singular or plural, familiar or polite:

Kom binnen en ga zitten!
Come in and sit down.

Ontsteek uw lichten! (traffic sign)
Turn your headlights on.

The **u** form is used only when being particularly polite:

Komt u binnen en gaat u zitten!

The simple stem can sound a little harsh and it is often softened by the use of the adverbs **eens** or **even** (or both) which add the connotation of 'would you mind' or 'please', but **alsjeblieft/alstublieft** can also used in combination with imperatives, with or without **eens** and/or **even**. In natural speech **eens** is nearly always pronounced **'s**:

Geef me eens je boek!
Give me your book.

Doe het raam eens even dicht!
Shut the window.

Lees dat eens even voor, alsjeblieft.[26]
Please, read that out.

Wacht eens even!
Wait a moment.

Sometimes **jij**, **u** or **jullie** is added for emphasis (compare 'You sit there' and see the use of **u** in the imperative above):

Ga jij nou daar zitten!
Sit there/You sit there.

Note the following common colloquial imperatives employing the particle **ze**, which has no meaning outside of such imperatives:

werk ze!	work hard
slaap ze!	sleep well
eet ze!	bon appetit

11.10.2   In formal written style (and often in advertisements too) one meets an imperative formed from the stem + **t**, actually a plural form in origin:

Leest de Bijbel!   Read the Bible.

11.10.3   The infinitive is also commonly used as a general hyper-impersonal imperative; this is particularly common on signs and is also used in recipes (the simple stem is common in recipes too).

signs: **Niet roken**
                         Don't smoke
                         Voorrang verlenen
                         Give way (i.e. in traffic)

---

[26] Note that you can never start a sentence with **alsjeblieft**, unlike English 'please'. It either stands at the end of the clause or in the middle, e.g. **Lees dat alsjeblieft eens even voor.**

recipes: **Het vlees met kruiden inwrijven en dan twee**
                             dagen op een koele plaats laten staan.
                             Rub spices into the meat and let it stand in
                             a cool place for two days.

11.10.4   Occasionally the past participle is used as a general impersonal
imperative, particularly with the verbs **opletten** and **oppassen**:

Opgelet/Opgepast!   **Ingerukt mars!**
Watch out/Take care.   Dismiss.

11.10.5   The imperative form 'let' as in 'Let's go home' etc. can be
expressed in two ways in Dutch:

(a) either by the simple imperative formed from the stem plus the object
     pronoun as in English:

     Laat ons naar huis gaan!   **Laat me het zo zeggen.**
     Let's go home.   Let me put it this way.

(b) or by using the subject pronoun and the appropriate form of the verb:

     Laten we naar huis gaan!
     Laat ik het zo zeggen.

11.11   THE SUBJUNCTIVE MOOD (de aanvoegende wijs)

The subjunctive mood, which was formerly quite common in Dutch and may
still be met in older literature, is not actively used any more. It has suffered
the same fate in Dutch as in English – it is only preserved in certain standard
expressions. As in English, it is used to express actions that are wished for,
feared, doubted or are conditional on other occasions. (see 11.7.1)

The *present subjunctive* only differs from the present indicative in that
the first and third persons singular end in **-e**, e.g. **ik werke**, **hij worde**. **Jij**,
being a familiar form, is never found with a subjunctive form of the verb.

The *past subjunctive* of weak verbs is the same as the imperfect indicative, but that of strong verbs ends in **-e** in the first and third persons
singular and is otherwise the same as the imperfect indicative, e.g. **ik
hadde, hij kwame**.

The monosyllabic verbs **doen, gaan, slaan, staan** and **zien** add no **-e** but
employ the stem only. **Zijn** has the irregular forms **zij** (first and third persons
present subjunctive) and **ware** (first and third persons past subjunctive).

Examples of some commonly used subjunctives:

Leve de koningin!	Long live the Queen. (present)
Het koste wat het kost.	Cost what it may. (present)
Het ga u goed!	May all go well for you. (present)
God zij dank!	Thanks be to God. (present)
Wat hij ook moge doen.	Whatever he may do. (present)
Moge de Heer u zegenen.	May the Lord bless you. (present)
Verblijve met de meeste	I remain yours respectfully
hoogachting	(present)
Als het ware.	As it were. (past)

Note the final example has a parallel in English, but the English imperfect subjunctive preserved in 'If I/he were rich...' no longer exists in Dutch, i.e. **Als ik/hij rijk was ...**

There is one present subjunctive that is still productive: in formal writing a third person singular subjunctive with the subject pronoun **men** renders an imperative, e.g.

Men lette hierop.
Take note of this (= one should take note of this).

Men herleze mijn openingswoord ter gelegenheid van het derde colloquium.
Reread my introductory speech on the occasion of the third congress.

This form is sometimes also used in recipes.

11.12 THE PASSIVE (de lijdende vorm)

11.12.1 THE TENSES OF THE PASSIVE

Present	**De auto wordt (door hem) gewassen.**
	The car is [being] washed (by him).
Imperfect	**De auto werd (door hem) gewassen.**
	The car was [being] washed (by him).
Perfect	**De auto is (door hem) gewassen [geworden].**[27]
	The car has been washed (by him).

---

[27] Because of the Dutch tendency to use the perfect tense where English uses the imperfect, this can also be translated with 'was washed'. As **zijn** is also used to form the active perfect tense of some intransitive verbs, there is no formal difference between the active perfect of those verbs and the passive perfects of all other verbs, but there is never any confusion as intransitive verbs cannot normally be used in the passive:

Hij is gisteren in Amsterdam aangekomen.	**Hij is gisteren in Amsterdam gezien.**
He arrived in Amsterdam yesterday.	He was seen in Amsterdam yesterday.

Pluperfect	**De auto was (door hem) gewassen [geworden].**
	The car had been washed (by him).
Future	**De auto zal (door hem) gewassen worden.**
	The car will be washed (by him).
Conditional	**De auto zou (door hem) gewassen worden.**
	The car would be washed (by him).
Future perfect	**De auto zal (door hem) gewassen [geworden] zijn.**
	The car will have been washed (by him).
Conditional perfect	**De auto zou (door hem) gewassen [geworden] zijn.**
	The car would have been washed (by him).

11.12.2 WHAT IS THE PASSIVE?

The passive is a so-called voice, not a tense, because all tenses of the active extend to the passive too. A passive construction is one where the object of the active sentence becomes the subject of the finite verb:

active	**Hij wast de auto.**
	He washes/is washing the car.
passive	**De auto wordt (door hem) gewassen.**
	The car is [being] washed (by him).

In the passive the agent of the action may be left unmentioned if so desired, but it is always implied.

11.12.3 HOW TO CONSTRUCT THE PASSIVE

The passive is constructed in English by a form of the verb 'to be' plus a past participle plus an optional agent introduced by the preposition 'by':

| subject | + to be | + past participle | (+ by + noun/pronoun) |
| The car | is being | washed | by him. |

The Dutch passive differs in that the verb **worden** is used, not **zijn**, to translate the verb 'to be' and 'by' is translated by **door**:

| subject | + **worden** | (+ **door** + noun/pronoun) | + past participle |
| **De auto** | **wordt** | **door hem** | **gewassen.** |

11.12.4   DIFFICULTIES WITH THE PASSIVE

11.12.4.1   *Perfect and pluperfect passive*

A complication arises where the auxiliary **worden** is required in the perfect tense, i.e. The car has been washed. Here one would expect:

*De auto	**is**	**gewassen**	**geworden.**
The car	has	washed	been.

This double participle is not liked, however, and the Dutch simply drop the **geworden**, reasoning that if a car 'has been washed' then it 'is washed', i.e. **is gewassen**.

Similarly in the pluperfect: 'the car had been washed' might be expected to be **De auto was gewassen geworden**, but the **geworden** is dropped because if the car 'had been washed' then it 'was washed', i.e. **was gewassen**.

It should be noted that this use of **geworden**, which is considered superfluous to meaning in standard Dutch, is nevertheless commonly heard in Belgium and Flemish Dutch is thus similar to German in this respect. For this reason **geworden** is given in square brackets in the paradigm under 11.12.1.

But these two forms **is/was gewassen** lead the English speaker to think that a sentence like 'The car is/was washed by him' is **De auto is/was door hem gewassen**, but these translate as 'The car has/had been washed'. Be careful here. In this case the present or past of **worden** is required: **De auto wordt/werd door hem gewassen**.

Note: The perfect tense is more common in Dutch than in English because of the tendency to render English imperfects with perfects in Dutch. This applies just as much to the passive as the active (see 11.2.3.1):

De auto werd gisteren door hem gewassen.
De auto is gisteren door hem gewassen.
The car was washed by him yesterday.

The active of the above is:

Hij waste gisteren de auto.
Hij heeft gisteren de auto gewassen.

11.12.4.2   *Action versus state with the past participle*

A further difficulty arises with a sentence like 'The door is closed'. If one is describing an action, i.e. if the sentence is 'The door is (being) closed (by him)', then the present tense of **worden** must be used: **De deur wordt (door hem) gesloten**.

Similarly, in the past 'The door was shut'; if it means 'The door was (being) shut (by him)', it will be in Dutch **De deur werd (door hem) gesloten**.

But perhaps only a state, not an action, is implied, i.e. The door is/was closed. Here the past participle can be regarded as an adjective as in 'The door is/was red' and no agent is implied. If this is the case then the sentence is translated: **De deur is/was gesloten**. Thus both 'The door has (had) been closed' and 'The door is (was) closed' are **De deur is (was) gesloten** and the context makes clear what is intended.

11.12.4.3 Passives with indirect objects

A special difficulty arises in passive sentences such as the following: 'I was given a book (by them)'. If one looks firstly at the active of this sentence 'They gave a book to me' one sees that the English 'I' is an indirect object in meaning: I was not given, but a book was given to me. Such indirect objects in passive sentences can be rendered in three ways in Dutch:

Er werd een boek aan mij gegeven/Er werd mij een boek gegeven.
(Aan) mij werd een boek gegeven. (less common)
Een boek werd aan mij gegeven. (less common)
I was given a book.

The first alternative, which utilizes a repletive **er**, is very common in the passive in Dutch, especially when the agent is not mentioned. (see 15.1)

Er werden gisteren veel auto's gewassen.
Many cars were washed yesterday.

Er moet wat gedaan worden.
Something must be done.

Er werden felicitaties aan hen gestuurd.
They were sent congratulations.

11.12.4.4 Use of modals with the passive

Modal verbs often act as auxiliaries in the passive too as in English and should simply be translated literally; take note that the infinitive 'to be' is of course rendered by **worden**, not **zijn**:

Het moet gedaan worden.
It must be done.

Het kon niet schoongemaakt worden.
It couldn't be cleaned.

The following modal constructions differ considerably from English (see 11.8.3.2):

Dat had gedaan kunnen worden.
That could have been done.

Dat had gedaan moeten worden.
That should have been done.

Een beslissing had nu al genomen kunnen/moeten zijn.
A decision could/should have been taken by now.

11.12.4.5   Word order with modals

In main clauses the order of the constituent parts of the passive with a modal verb can be either:

Dat kan gedaan worden/Dat kan worden gedaan.
That can be done.

Dat zou gedaan moeten worden/Dat zou moeten worden gedaan.
That should be done.

In subordinate clauses the following alternatives exist (the finite verb is never placed after the verbal cluster).

Ik weet dat het gedaan kan worden/
Ik weet dat het kan worden gedaan. (never *gedaan worden kan)
Hij zei dat het gedaan zou moeten worden/
Hij zei dat het zou moeten worden gedaan.

11.12.4.6   Contracted conditionals in the passive

Contracted forms of **zijn** are common in the passive (see 11.1.8):

De stad was vernietigd als ... /De stad zou vernietigd zijn als ...
The city would have been destroyed if ...

Het boek was eerder gelezen als ... /Het boek zou eerder gelezen
zijn als ...
The book would have been read sooner if ...

11.12.4.7   Passives rendered by extended participial phrases
(see 8.5.10)

It is common in journalese and other written style to replace clauses containing a passive with adjectival phrases containing a participle (either a past or a present participle, or occasionally an infinitive) placed before the relevant noun:

De rekening die gisteren door hem werd betaald.
The bill which was paid by him yesterday.
De gisteren door hem betaalde rekening.

Het bedrag dat nog door hem betaald moet worden.
The amount that still has to be paid by him.
Het door hem nog te betalen bedrag.

Such constructions must be translated into English with relative clauses in the passive.

11.12.4.8 There are some impersonal English passives which are rendered in Dutch by an infinitive construction, thus avoiding the passive altogether:

Er was niemand te zien.	There was nobody to be seen.
Dat was te verwachten.	That was to be expected.
Dat is te hopen.	That is to be hoped.
Waar is het boek te verkrijgen?	Where can that book be obtained?

11.12.4.9   Use of *men/je/ze* instead of the passive

It should be noted that the passive in all its forms is more common in English than in Dutch. Very often the Dutch use an active form of the verb with **men** 'one' or **je** 'you' as its subject.

Men spreekt hier Nederlands.
Dutch is spoken here.

Men/je kan koeien met de hand melken.
Cows can be milked by hand/You can milk cows by hand.

Men is as formal in Dutch as 'one' is in English. In everyday speech **je** (never **jij**) is used, just as in English, as illustrated by the previous example. English can also use a non-personal 'they' instead of the passive; Dutch has this too and uses **ze** (never **zij**):

Ze zeggen dat het gaat regenen.
They say it's going to rain.

11.13   PROGRESSIVE OR CONTINUOUS TENSES

When first learning Dutch verbs one is told that a form such as 'I am working' is **ik werk**, 'I was working' is **ik werkte** and 'I have been working' is **ik heb gewerkt**. This is indeed usually the case but there are instances where the continuous aspect needs to be expressed and there are three ways of doing so in Dutch:

11.13.1   Zijn aan 't + infinitive

Ik ben druk aan 't koken.
I am busy cooking.

Ik was de hele middag aan 't timmeren.
I was hammering away all afternoon.

Ik ben urenlang aan 't koken geweest.
I have been cooking for hours (and have finished, see 11.2.1).

This is the most common way.

11.13.2   Zitten, staan, liggen or lopen + te + infinitive

Ze zit al een hele tijd televisie te kijken.
She's been watching television for ages.

Hij stond buiten met de buurman te praten.
He was (standing) talking to the neighbour outside.

Jantje ligt te slapen.
Jantje is sleeping.

Note the use of the present tense in this construction in the following example as the action is still on-going (see 11.9.2.4):

Zij zit al een hele tijd dat boek te lezen.
She has been reading that book for ages.

These verbs all utilize a double infinitive construction in the perfect tense (see 11.9.2.4):

Hij heeft urenlang liggen slapen.
He was asleep for hours.

Ik heb ernaar lopen zoeken.
I have been looking for it.

This is also a very common construction.

11.13.3   Zijn bezig te + infinitive

Ik ben bezig een boek te schrijven.
I am (busy) writing a book.

Zij waren bezig het hele appartement te verven.
They were (busy) painting the whole flat.

This is not as common as 11.13.1 and 11.13.2.

11.14 EMPHATIC PRESENT AND IMPERFECT TENSES FORMED WITH 'TO DO'

One usually learns that a form such as **ik werk** renders three English forms, i.e. I work, I am working, I do work and the imperfect **ik werkte** renders I worked, I was working, I did work. This is so, but just as the 'am/was working' forms are expressed in a different way in Dutch (see 11.13), so too the emphatic forms 'do/did work' have an equivalent in Dutch. In this case the adverbs **toch** and **wel**, which are not synonymous, accompany the verb to give it the required emphasis:

Let er toch goed op!
Do take note of it.

Ik heb het wel gedaan.
I did do it (which is the opposite of **Ik heb het niet gedaan**).

11.15 THE PRESENT PARTICIPLE (**het tegenwoordig deelwoord**)

The present participle in Dutch is formed by adding **-d** or **-de** to the infinitive; the former is the more usual but in many standard expressions the latter form is found, e.g. **lopend** 'walking', **kijkend** 'looking'. The present participle is not commonly used in Dutch as most English '-ing' constructions are expressed in other ways (see 11.17). It is used in the following instances:

11.15.1 Many adjectives are formed from the present participle, in which case an **-e** is of course added to the form in **-d** wherever the adjective needs to be inflected:

een lachende vrouw	a laughing woman
een roerend verhaal	a moving story
Dit is uitstekend.	This is excellent.
volgende week	next week
volgend jaar	next year
bij wassende maan	while the moon is waxing

11.15.2 It is commonly used as an adverb of manner, in which case it often has a direct parallel in English:

Het kind kwam huilend binnen.	The child came in crying.
Ik ging er lopend naartoe.	I went there on foot.
de zaak draaiende houden	to keep the business going

11.15.3   It renders some English '-ing' forms in certain standard expressions:

jou kennende ...	knowing you ...
zodoende ...	by so doing ...

In addition, the form **al ...-d(e)**, meaning 'while -ing', is quite common in higher style:

Al reizend(e) leert men veel.	One learns a lot while travelling.
Al lezend(e) ontdekte hij dat ...	While reading he discovered that ...

11.15.4   In the written language it is often used in much the same way as '-ing' in English (see 11.16 for alternative constructions commonly used in the spoken language):

Aankomende op de Grote Markt in Brussel verbaasde hij zich dat ...
Arriving at the Grand' Place in Brussels he was amazed that ...

Uitgaande van wat hier geschreven staat ...
Going on what is written here ...

Daar stond een ruine, bestaande uit een toren en een gedeelte van de stadsmuur.
There was a ruin there consisting of a tower and a section of the city wall.

11.15.5   It can also be used to form nouns, in which case it always ends in **-de** (actually the form in **-d** plus an adjectival ending) and takes a plural in **-n**:

de overlevende(n)	the survivor(s)
de inzittende(n)	the passenger(s) (in a car)

11.15.6   A few present participles have assumed the function of prepositions:

gedurende	during
aangaande	concerning, with regard to
betreffende	concerning, with regard to

11.16   HOW TO RENDER ENGLISH '-ING' FORMS IN DUTCH

The use of '-ing' constructions in the formation of the progressive continuous form of the present and imperfect tenses (i.e. I am/was buying a book) is described in 11.1.1 and 11.1.2 and is thus not discussed here.

Although there is the possibility of expressing the English present participle literally in Dutch on occasions, this is rarely done in colloquial speech and such forms are reserved for literary or more formal style (see 11.5).

The present participle is usually avoided in Dutch. It is generally necessary to paraphrase an English sentence containing an '-ing' construction in order to translate it into natural Dutch. The following are the most common ways of doing so. (When seeking the appropriate translation, skim the phrases in italic for the construction which most resembles the one you have to put into Dutch).

11.16.1 With the infinitive plus **te**:

It is lovely *being here*.
Het is heerlijk hier te zijn.

I *succeeded in seeing* the queen.
Het lukte mij de koningin te zien.

I *like staying* at home.
Ik hou ervan thuis te blijven. (also: **Ik blijf graag thuis**, see 11.16.11)

He left *without saying* a word.
Hij vertrok zonder een woord te zeggen. (see 11.16.3)

He remained seated *instead of standing* up.
Hij bleef zitten in plaats van op te staan. (see 11.16.3 and also 12.5.1.4)

11.16.2 English '-ing' clauses introduced by 'by' or 'from' are rendered in Dutch by infinitive clauses introduced by **door** or **van** (see 12.5):

I'm trying to lose weight *by eating* less.
Ik probeer af te vallen door minder te eten.

By doing that you'll achieve nothing.
Door dat te doen zul je niets bereiken.

You get tired *from reading* so much.
Je wordt erg moe van zo veel te lezen.

11.16.3 Some '-ing' clauses are avoided by using **dat** constructions in Dutch:

They had already arrived there *without our knowing* it.
Ze waren er al aangekomen zonder dat wij het wisten.
(Compare: **We waren er al aangekomen zonder het te weten** where the subject of both parts is the same, see 11.16.1 and 12.5.1.4)

Instead of him doing it I had to do it. (compare 11.16.1)
In plaats (van) dat hij het deed, moest ik het doen. (see 12.5.1.4)

11.16.4   Some '-ing' clauses can be paraphrased by 'since/because'
clauses which are rendered in Dutch by the conjunctions **daar/omdat**, the
former being rather formal:

Being sick he could not come. (i.e. Since he was sick ...)
Daar/doordat hij ziek was, kon hij niet komen.

Being students we didn't need to pay anything. (i.e. Because we were
   students ...
Omdat wij studenten waren, hoefden we niets te betalen.

11.16.5   When there is a temporal sense expressed in the English '-ing'
construction, subordinating conjunctions of time are used in Dutch:

Before going to bed we drank a cup of tea.
Voordat we naar bed gingen, dronken we een kopje thee.

(After) having written a letter to his mother he went and sat in front
   of the television.
**Na een brief aan zijn moeder te hebben geschreven, ging hij voor de
   televisie zitten.** This could also be translated as follows: **Nadat hij
   een brief aan zijn moeder geschreven had, ging hij ...** (see 12.5)

When writing such an official letter you should be polite.
Wanneer je zo'n officiële brief schrijft, moet je beleefd zijn.

But the following are also expressed with a temporal subordinating
conjunction:

Finding the house uninhabited, he didn't want to ...
Toen hij merkte dat het huis onbewoond was, wilde hij niet...

Having recovered he went home.
Toen hij hersteld was, ging hij naar huis.

11.16.6   Some '-ing' clauses can be paraphrased with 'while' and these
are rendered in Dutch by a subordinate clause introduced by **terwijl**:

Saying that he smiled.
Terwijl hij dat zei, glimlachte hij.

11.16.7 If the English construction is 'to stand, sit or lie doing something', Dutch translates the present participle with an infinitive (see 11.13.2):

He *stood waving* at the window.
Hij stond aan het raam te wuiven.

They *were sitting (sat) watching* a film.
Zij zaten naar een film te kijken.

When such constructions are put in the (plu-)perfect tense one is dealing with double infinitives.

We *were standing (stood) talking* the whole time.
Wij hebben de hele tijd staan praten.

Similarly of course the other verbs that occur in double infinitive constructions translate '-ing' in this way (see 11.9.2.5(a)–(b)).

I *saw him coming.*
Ik zag hem komen/Ik heb hem zien komen.

He *heard me singing.*
Hij hoorde mij zingen/Hij heeft mij horen zingen.

Note:

I *have* an aunt *living* in Friesland.
Ik heb een tante in Friesland wonen.

He *has* an etching by Rembrandt *hanging* on the wall. (see
    11.9.2.5(e))
Hij heeft een ets van Rembrandt aan de muur hangen.

11.16.8 Some English '-ing' constructions are disguised relative clauses and must be translated as such into Dutch:

The tree standing in the park is very old.
De boom die in het park staat, is erg oud.

The man in the corner *reading* the paper is my uncle.
De man in de hoek die de krant leest/zit te lezen, is mijn oom.

11.16.9 An infinitive noun construction also exists but can usually be avoided by other means:

You must be *careful when getting in.*
Je moet oppassen bij het instappen.

This could of course be translated as follows:

Je moet oppassen wanneer/als je instapt.

11.16.10   The so-called gerund in English, i.e. the present participle used as a noun, is rendered in Dutch by the infinitive – such nouns are always neuter (see 11.16.9):

The cooking of vegetables is a great art.
Het koken van groente is een grote kunst.

Writing novels doesn't interest me.
Het schrijven van romans/Romans schrijven interesseert me niet.

Going out is very expensive.
Uitgaan is erg duur.

Note: No smoking.
　　　Niet roken. (an imperative in Dutch)

11.16.11   'To like/prefer doing something' is rendered by the very commonly used construction **iets graag/liever doen**:

I like watching him.
Ik kijk graag naar hem.

They *prefer sitting* inside.
Zij zitten liever binnen.

He *likes getting* up early.
Hij staat graag vroeg op.

but also:

Hij houdt ervan vroeg op te staan.

11.16.12   Constructions such as 'to think of doing something' are rendered by a clause containing a prepositional object (i.e. **er** + a preposition) followed by an infinitive clause (see **er**, 15.3):

He is *thinking of buying* a boat.
Hij denkt erover een boot te kopen.

I *suspected* my family *of having sold* the house.
Ik verdacht mijn familie ervan het huis te hebben verkocht.

Does anyone *feel like going* to the cinema?
Heeft iemand zin om naar de bioscoop te gaan?

11.16.13 Occasionally an '-ing' construction introduces a new clause and can be got around by inserting a conjunction and simply making a co-ordinate clause of it:

> As he was very ill he stayed in bed all day, *not getting up* till the evening.
>
> **Omdat hij erg ziek was, bleef hij de hele dag in bed liggen en stond pas 's avonds op.**

11.17 REFLEXIVE VERBS (**wederkerende werkwoorden**)

Reflexive verbs are verbs which have as their object a reflexive pronoun,[28] i.e. the action reflects back on the subject of the verb. The concept is known to English but is not nearly as common. For example, the verb 'to shave' can be used in two ways: 'I shave every day' or 'The barber shaved me'. In Dutch the verb **scheren** must have an object; that is to say, if you are not shaving someone else (e.g. **De kapper schoor me**) then you must be shaving yourself and must thus say so, i.e. **Ik scheer me iedere dag**. To omit this reflexive pronoun would be incorrect and is an error commonly committed by English speakers.

There are basically two sorts of reflexive verb:

(a) those that are always reflexive.

---

[28] Some reflexive verbs can also take a direct object and thus behave as transitive verbs at the same time:

Ik herinnerde me hem erg goed.
I remembered him very well.

Zij kon het zich niet veroorloven.
She could not afford it.

Note: If a reflexive verb governs a direct object **het** (although most reflexive verbs are intransive), the **het** precedes the reflexive pronoun, as it is unstressed:

Hij herinnerde het zich niet meer.
He didn't remember (it) any more.

Ik kan het me niet veroorloven.
I can't afford it.

Compare the following objects where there is greater stress and thus the reflexive precedes the object:

Hij herinnerde zich mijn moeder niet meer.
He didn't remember my mother any more.

Ik kan me geen auto veroorloven.
I can't afford a car.

Ik kan me dat niet veroorloven.
I can't afford that.

(b) those that may be used reflexively but which can also be used as transitive verbs with direct objects (such as **scheren** above).

It is impossible to list all the verbs in both groups but the list under 11.17.1
will serve to illustrate the concept.

The reflexive pronouns are as follows:

	singular		*plural*	
1st person	**me** (lit. **mij**)	myself	**ons**	ourselves
2nd person	**je**	yourself	**je**	yourselves
	u	yourself	**u**	yourselves
	zich		**zich**	
3rd person	**zich**	himself	**zich**	themselves
		herself		
		itself		
		oneself		

Examples:

ik heb me gewassen I washed (myself) etc.   **wij hebben ons gewassen**
jij hebt je gewassen   **jullie hebben je gewassen**
u hebt u gewassen   **u hebt u gewassen**
u heeft zich gewassen   **u heeft zich gewassen**
hij heeft zich gewassen   **zij hebben zich gewassen**
zij heeft zich gewassen
het heeft zich gewassen
men heeft zich gewassen

The reflexive **u** should be used with **hebt** and **zich** with **heeft**, i.e. a second
person reflexive pronoun with a second person verb and a third person
reflexive pronoun with a third person verb, although in practice one will
hear **u hebt zich** (but not **u heeft u**). When the subject pronoun and the
reflexive stand side by side, i.e. when they are not separated by other
words, there is a definite preference for **zich**, **u u** being considered unpro-
nounceable:

Heeft u zich vergist?
Were you mistaken?

Denkt u dat u zich vergist heeft?
Do you think you were mistaken?

Notice also **Heeft u dat boek bij zich? Hebt u dat boek bij u?** 'Do you
have that book on you?'

Note: All reflexive verbs in Dutch are conjugated with **hebben**, unlike in
Romance languages. Exception: **zich rot/kapot schrikken** 'to get a terrible
shock/fright', e.g. **Ik ben me rot geschrokken** 'I got a terrible shock'.

11.17.1   VERBS THAT ARE ALWAYS REFLEXIVE (sample list only)

zich aanstellen	to show off, carry on
zich afvragen	to wonder
zich begeven	to proceed, make one's way
zich bemoeien met	to meddle with
zich bevinden	to find oneself
zich bewust zijn van	to be aware of
zich gedragen, misdragen	to behave, misbehave
zich generen	to be embarrassed
zich haasten	to hurry
zich herinneren	to remember
zich herstellen	to recover
zich indenken	to imagine, visualize
zich inspannen	to exert oneself
zich in acht nemen voor	to be on one's guard against
zich onthouden van	to refrain from
zich realiseren	to realize
zich schamen voor	to be ashamed of
zich uitsloven	to go to trouble (for someone)
zich verbeelden	to imagine
zich verdiepen in	to go (deeply) into (a problem/issue)
zich vergissen	to be mistaken
zich verhangen	to hang oneself
zich verheugen op	to look forward to
zich verkijken	to make a mistake (in looking at s.t.)
zich verschrijven	to make a mistake (in writing)
zich verslapen	to sleep in (by mistake), oversleep
zich verslikken	to choke, swallow (wrong way)
zich voordoen	to happen, occur
zich voorstellen	to imagine

Note that some of the above verbs can also be used as transitive verbs (like those in 11.17.2) but then their meaning is quite different from that given here:

herstellen	to repair	**verdiepen**	to deepen
herinneren	to remind	**voorstellen**	to introduce

Verbs in this group are never used with **-zelf** (see 11.17.3).

11.17.2   TRANSITIVE VERBS THAT CAN BE USED REFLEXIVELY

All the verbs in this group also occur as normal transitive verbs, e.g. **Hij verdedigde zich** 'He defended himself', but also **Het leger verdedigde de stad** 'The army defended the town'. The verbs in this category are actually too numerous to list in their entirety. For instance, one would not normally call the verb **verkopen** 'to sell' a reflexive verb, but there can be occasions when one wants to express 'to sell oneself' and this is rendered by **zich verkopen**. The following list, although very limited, will serve to illustrate (see the end of the list for an explanation of the asterisk):

*	**zich aankleden**	to dress (oneself), get dressed
	zich amuseren	to amuse, enjoy oneself
*	**zich bewegen**	to move
	zich bezighouden met	to busy oneself with
*	**zich ergeren**	to get irritated
*	**zich inschrijven**	to enrol
*	**zich melden**	to report (for duty, sick)
	zich noemen	to call oneself
*	**zich omdraaien**	to turn around
*	**zich omkleden**	to change one's clothes
	zich opgeven	to give oneself up
	zich opofferen voor	to sacrifice oneself for
*	**zich opstapelen**	to pile up, accumulate
	zich opwinden	to get excited
	zich overeten	to overeat
*	**zich overgeven**	to surrender
*	**zich scheren**	to shave
	zich snijden[29]	to cut oneself
*	**zich terugtrekken**	to retreat, pull back
*	**zich uitkleden**	to undress oneself, get undressed
*	**zich verbazen**	to be amazed
*	**zich verbergen**	to hide (oneself)
*	**zich verschuilen**	to hide (oneself)
*	**zich verstoppen**	to hide (oneself)
	zich verdedigen	to defend oneself
*	**zich verkleden**	to get dressed in fancy dress
*	**zich veroorloven**	to afford[30]
*	**zich vervelen**	to be bored

[29] Note the following peculiarity of **zich snijdent**: if the part of the body one has cut is mentioned, it is preceded by **in** and the definite article is used:

Ik heb me in de vinger gesneden but also non-reflexively
Ik heb in mijn vinger gesneden.
I cut my finger.

But one will also hear a combination of the two: **Ik heb me in m'n vinger gesneden**.

[30] There are three ways of expressing 'to afford' (actually always expressed in English and Dutch as 'to be able to afford').

Ik kan het me niet veroorloven.
Ik kan het me niet permitteren.   I can't afford it. (see footnote 28)
Ik kan het niet bekostigen. (*Note*: this is not reflexive)

* **zich voelen**	to feel
zich voorbereiden op	to prepare oneself for
zich voorstellen	to introduce oneself
* **zich wassen**	to wash (oneself)
zich wegen	to weigh oneself
zich wijden aan	to devote oneself to

* The verbs marked with an asterisk illustrate the problem involved with Dutch reflexives: in English these verbs would seldom be reflexive.

Hij kleedde zich aan.	He dressed.
Hij draaide zich om.	He turned around.
Hij herinnerde zich mij.	He remembered me.
Hij verstopte zich.	He hid.

11.17.3   USE OF zichzelf

11.17.3.1   All verbs in group 11.17.2 (i.e. those that can also occur as transitive verbs) can on occasion use **zichzelf** instead of a simple **zich**, but only when one needs to emphasize that one washed or dressed oneself and not somebody else:

Ik kleedde Jantje aan en toen kleedde ik mezelf aan. (stress on **zelf**)
I dressed Jantje and then I dressed myself.

Ik woog de koffers en toen mezelf. (stress on **zelf**)
I weighed the suitcases and then myself.

Haar hebben ze niet verdedigd, alleen zichzelf. (stress on **haar** and
  zelf)
They didn't defend her, only themselves.

11.17.3.2   There is also a group of verbs that one would not normally regard as reflexive verbs but which can be used reflexively, but then always with **zichzelf**. Such verbs cause complications for the English-speaking student who is often inclined to use **zichzelf** with the other more numerous verbs that require only **zich**. All verbs requiring **zichzelf** imply an emphasis on the self:

zichzelf iets aandoen	to do something (harmful) to oneself
bij zichzelf denken	to think to oneself
zichzelf haten	to hate oneself
alleen met zichzelf rekening houden	to take only oneself into account

zichzelf kennen	to know oneself
in zichzelf lachen	to laugh to oneself
in zichzelf praten	to talk to oneself
over zichzelf praten	to talk about oneself
bij zichzelf zeggen	to say to oneself
zichzelf zien als	to see oneself as
zichzelf zijn	to be oneself
voor zichzelf zorgen	to care for, look after oneself

11.17.4   USE OF INDEPENDENT **zelf**

English often uses 'myself', 'yourself' etc. with verbs that would not normally be classified as reflexive verbs. In such cases the reflexive pronoun is used to emphasize who the doer of the action concerned is. In Dutch these pronouns are expressed simply by **zelf**:

Ik heb het zelf gedaan.
I did it myself.

Zij hebben het huis zelf veverfd.
They painted the house themselves.

11.17.5   USE OF INDEPENDENT **zich**

In sentences where the prepositional object and the subject pronouns are one and the same person, the simple reflexive pronoun is used in Dutch:

Ik heb geen geld bij me.
I have no money on me.

Hij keek achter zich.
He looked behind him.

De officieren hadden veel soldaten onder zich.
The officers had a lot of soldiers under them.

The expression **op zich(zelf)**, which grammatically speaking belongs in this category, is usually best translated by 'actually' or 'in fact'; here too the use of **-zelf** adds emphasis:

Op zich is dat niet zo erg. (stress on **zich**)
Actually that's not so bad.

Het is op zich een vreemde uitdrukking. (stress on **zich**)
It's a strange expression in fact.

11.17.6 USE OF **z'n eigen** AS A REFLEXIVE PRONOUN

In substandard speech one often hears **m'n eigen**, **je eigen**, **z'n eigen** etc. instead of the reflexive **me**, **je**, **zich** etc. This practice, although common, should not be copied as it sounds 'plat':

Ik ben m'n eigen kapot geschrokken.
I got a terrible shock.

Jij kent je eigen niet.
You don't know yourself.

Note: Dutch, like English, uses the reciprocal pronoun **elkaar** 'each other' in sentences such as the following, not the reflexive as is the case in French and German:

We hebben elkaar in de stad ontmoet.
We met each other in town.

11.18 TRANSITIVE AND INTRANSITIVE VERBS (**overgankelijke en onovergankelijke werkwoorden**)

11.18.1 Very often difficulties arise with verbs because the distinction between transitive and intransitive is not fully understood: transitive verbs are those that can take a direct object and intransitive verbs are those that can't. Verbs that are transitive in English may not necessarily be so in Dutch. For example, if one wants to translate 'I answered the question' one will find in the dictionary under 'to answer' the words **antwoorden** and **beantwoorden**. A good dictionary will indicate that the former is intransitive and the latter transitive. The above example will thus be translated by either **Ik beantwoordde de vraag** or **Ik antwoordde op de vraag** (intransitive verbs often take prepositional objects, i.e. they are only capable of taking an object if connected to that object by a preposition).

It is not possible to give rules for such difficulties but the following common examples will serve to illustrate what one has to be wary of:

to burn	**branden** (intr.)	**Het hout brandde.**[31]
		The wood was burning.
	verbranden (trans.)	**Hij verbrandde het hout.**
		He burnt the wood.
to leave	**vertrekken** (intr.)	**De trein vertrok om tien uur.**
		The train left at ten o-clock.

---

[31] **Branden** also exists as a transitive verb but only in a more figurative sense, e.g. **zijn tong/vingers branden** 'to burn one's tongue/fingers'.

	verlaten (trans.)	**De trein verliet Ede om tien uur.**
		The train left Ede at ten o'clock.
to taste	smaken (intr.)	**Deze appel smaakt goed.**
		This apple tastes good.
	proeven (trans.)	**Proef deze appel!**
		Taste this apple.

11.18.2   Sometimes a verb which is both transitive and intransitive in English, but only intransitive in Dutch, is made transitive by the use of **laten** as an auxiliary (in more formal style **doen**). This is done when no separate transitive verb exists in Dutch:

to sink	zinken (intr.)	**Het stuk metaal zonk.**
		The piece of metal sank.
	laten zinken (tr.)	**Ik heb het laten zinken.**
		I sank it.
to shrink	krimpen (intr.)	**De trui is gekrompen.**
		The jumper has shrunk.
	laten krimpen (tr.)	**Ik heb hem laten krimpen.**
		I shrank it.
to run	lopen (intr.)	**Het paard liep langs het strand.**
		The horse ran along the beach.
	laten lopen (tr.)	**Ik heb het paard langs het strand laten lopen.**
		I ran the horse along the beach.
to melt	smelten (intr.)	**De boter is gesmolten.**
		The butter has melted.
	laten smelten (tr.)	**Ik heb de boter in de magnetron laten smelten.**
		I melted the butter in the microwave.

Such **laten** constructions are very common in Dutch (see 11.9.2.5(c)).

11.18.3   Transitive verbs are usually conjugated with **hebben** in the perfect tenses (see 11.7.2.1, footnote 18 for the very few exceptions). Intransitive verbs, on the other hand, use either **hebben** or **zijn**, for example:

Hij is gestorven.
He (has) died.

Hij heeft gelachen.
He laughed.

Het huis heeft urenlang gebrand.
The house burnt for hours.

11.18.4 Intransitive verbs cannot be used in the passive as the passive is by definition a construction where the object of the active sentence becomes the subject. (see footnote 27, 11.12.1)

11.19 IMPERSONAL VERBS

Impersonal verbs are those which only occur in the third person (usually only in the singular, but some can occur in the plural too). In the third person singular the subject is always **het**. English has impersonal verbs too but Dutch has more.

11.19.1 VERBS THAT ARE IMPERSONAL IN ENGLISH AND DUTCH

11.19.1.1 Verbs denoting weather conditions which are used only in the third person singular:

Het bliksemt.	There's lightning.
Het dondert.	It's thundering.
Het dooit.	It's thawing.
Het hagelt.	It's hailing.
Het mist.	There's a fog.
Het onweert.	There's a thunderstorm.
Het regent.	It's raining.
Het schemert.	It's dawning, It's twilight.
Het sneeuwt.	It's snowing.
Het stormt.	There's a storm.
Het trekt/tocht.	There's a draught.

11.19.1.2 Several other verbs that can only be used in the third person singular:

gebeuren, geschieden	to happen	**Het gebeurde 's nachts.**
		It happened at night.
betreffen	to concern	**Wat mij betreft, ...**
		As far as I'm concerned, ...
overkomen	to happen to (s.o.)	**Het overkwam mij.**
		It happened to me.
dunken (lit.)	to seem to	**Het dunkt mij dat ...**
		It seems to me that ...

11.19.2   VERBS THAT ARE IMPERSONAL IN DUTCH BUT NOT IN ENGLISH

These verbs often denote a feeling or reaction:

bevallen	to please	**Het bevalt me.**[32] I like it.
spijten	to be sorry	**Het spijt me.** I'm sorry.
lukken	to succeed	**Het lukte me (niet).** I succeeded (didn't succeed).
zwaarvallen	to find difficult	**Het valt me zwaar.** I find it difficult.
meevallen	to please	**Het viel (me) mee.**[32] It wasn't bad. (I didn't mind it.)
tegenvallen	to disappoint	**Het viel me tegen.**[32] I was disappointed with it.
verbazen	to amaze	**Het verbaast me.**[32] I'm amazed.
verheugen	to rejoice	**Het verheugt me.**[32] I'm pleased.
verwonderen	to amaze, surprise	**Het verwondert me.**[32] I'm surprised.

These verbs are very commonly followed by **dat** clauses:

Het speet me dat . . .	I was sorry that . . .
Het verbaasde haar dat . . .	It surprised her that . . .

11.20   VERBAL PREFIXES (werkwoordelijke voorvoegsels)

In Dutch both separable and inseparable verbal prefixes are used to form new words. This is a very economical means of vocabulary building. In many instances there are parallel examples in English, e.g. **gaan** = to go, **ondergáán** = to undergo; **kijken** = to look, **ópkijken** = to look up. (The accents are not normally written but merely serve here to indicate the stress.) Often, however, the addition of a prefix in Dutch renders a totally new word, e.g. **spreken** = to speak, **tegenspreken** = to contradict; **huren** = to hire/rent, **verhuren** = to rent out; **geven** = to give, **toegeven** = to admit, **overgeven** = to vomit.

---

[32] These verbs can be used with other persons, e.g. **Ik beviel hem niet, Hij viel me tegen** etc., but are commonly found in the third person and in such contexts are rendered by personal constructions in English as is illustrated in the above examples. In addition, **bevallen**, as well as **mee-** and **tegenvallen**, take **zijn** in the perfect.

Separable verbs are recognized by the fact that the prefix bears the stress; this is not the case with inseparable verbs, e.g. **vóórstellen** = to introduce, **voorspéllen** = to predict.

A verb that normally takes **hebben** in the perfect tense may, by the addition of a prefix, take on a new meaning which requires **zijn** in the perfect; the reverse is also true, e.g. **staan** 'to stand' takes **hebben** but **opstaan** 'to get/stand up' takes **zijn**; **komen** 'to come' takes **zijn** but **voorkomen** 'to prevent' takes **hebben**. This is so because the use of **zijn** or **hebben** has to do with meaning, i.e. **zijn** is used in the case of all verbs that indicate a movement from one position to another or a change of state (see 11.7.2).

11.20.1 SEPARABLE VERBS (**scheidbare werkwoorden**)

There are three sorts of separable prefixes:

1 Prepositional prefixes, many of which can also be inseparable, e.g. **aan, achter, af, bij, door, in mee***[33] (from **met**), **om, onder, op*, over, tegen*, toe***[33] (from **tot**), **uit*, voor**.
   (* = those that can only be separable)

2 Nominal prefixes formed from what is actually the object of the verb but which has been used so frequently with certain verbs that the object has come to be regarded as a verbal prefix and behaves as a separable prefix, i.e. is joined to the verb in the infinitive and the past participle. It is common to write these prefixes separately, e.g. **koffiedrinken** 'to drink coffee', **haarknippen** 'to cut hair', **boekbinden** 'to bind books', **lesgeven** 'to teach', **gelukwensen** 'to congratulate', **televisiekijken** 'to watch television', **schaatsenrijden** 'to skate'.

3 There are also many verbs whose prefix is adverbial in origin rather than nominal, e.g. **goedkeuren** 'to approve', **misverstaan** 'to misunderstand', **samengaan** 'to go along', **tegemoetkomen** 'to meet, fall in with', **teleurstellen** 'to disappoint', **terechtwijzen** 'to reprimand', **thuiskomen** 'to come home', **volstoppen** 'to cram full', **weergeven** 'to return, reproduce'.

11.20.1.1 *Tenses of separable verbs*

(a) When a separable verb is conjugated in the present and imperfect tenses and in the imperative the prefix goes to the end of the clause:

meegaan 'to go along', e.g.　　**Hij gaat/ging ook graag mee.**
　　　　　　　　　　　　　　　　He wants/wanted to go along too.

---

[33] See 11.21.1.

opstaan 'to get/stand up', e.g.   **Sta onmiddellijk op!**
Get/stand up immediately.

But these prefixes can precede prepositional adjuncts (i.e. any adverbial expression of time, manner or place that begins with a preposition), in which case they do not have to stand at the very end of their clause:

Wij gingen samen na afloop van het programma weg or
Wij gingen samen weg na afloop van het programma.
We left together after the conclusion of the programme.

In formal writing one may be more inclined to find the prefix standing at the end of the clause in such cases, but the second sentence is possibly more usual in speech.

(b) In the future tense or after modals the infinitive of a separable verb remains as one word at the end of the clause:

Ik zal je opbellen.
I'll ring you up.

Hij moest me aan haar voorstellen.
He had to introduce me to her.

When additional verbs stand at the end of the clause, there is a tendency, which is more common in speech than in writing, to split the separable verb and place the prefix before all the verbs:

Ik zou hem op kunnen bellen.
I could ring him up.

Ik begrijp niet waarom je niet vroeger op had kunnen staan.
I don't understand why you couldn't have got up sooner.

This is often avoided in more formal written style.

(c) The past participle of separable verbs is formed by inserting **ge-** between the prefix and the verbal stem, e.g. **voorstellen** 'to introduce' – **voorgesteld**, **opgraven** 'to dig up' – **opgegraven**. Such compound past participles are often split (particularly in speech) just like the infinitives above:

Ik weet dat hij je op heeft gebeld.
I know he rang you up.

Ik begrijp niet waarom hij niet mee is gegaan.
I don't understand why he didn't go along.

(d) When the infinitive of a separable verb is accompanied by **te**, the **te** is placed between the prefix and the verb and the three parts are written separately, unlike German:

Hij hoopt zijn vakantie in Spanje door te brengen.
He's hoping to spend his holidays in Spain.

Hij hoopt zijn vakantie in Spanje door te kunnen brengen.
He's hoping to be able to spend his holidays in Spain.

Probeer vóór middernacht terug te komen.
Try to get back before midnight.

Note: Often confusion arises between separable verbs with prepositional prefixes and verbs followed by prepositional objects:

opkijken	to look up	**kijken op**	to look at (a watch/clock)
overschrijven	to copy	**schrijven over**	to write about
doorlopen	to continue walking	**lopen door**	to walk through

The above is potentially confusing only to the foreign learner but the following is also confusing to the Dutch.

A verb like **lopen door** further complicates the issue because of the tendency for some prepositions to follow the object to which they refer in order to indicate a motion (13.2.1); such cases as **doorlopen** and **lopen door** can look and sound the same in certain contexts but remain semantically different:

doorlopen	**Ik liep gewoon door.**
	Ik ben gewoon doorgelopen.
	I simply walked on.
lopen door	**Ik liep door het bos.**
	I walked through the forest (i.e. in the forest).
	Ik liep het bos door.
	I walked right through the forest (i.e. crossed it).
	Ik ben door het bos gelopen.
	Ik ben het bos door gelopen/doorgelopen.

In the final example strictly speaking **door gelopen** is correct but one is more likely to see **doorgelopen** (see also 15.5.5).

11.20.2   INSEPARABLE VERBS (onscheidbare werkwoorden)

There are four sorts of inseparable prefixes:

1 Prefixes that can only be inseparable: **be-, er-, ge-, her-, ont-, ver-**.
2 Prepositional prefixes which can also act as separable prefixes (see 11.20.1): **aan, achter, door, om, onder, over, voor.**
3 A few adverbs which act as inseparable prefixes: **mis, vol, weer**; (all of these also occur as separable prefixes), e.g. **zich misdrágen** 'to misbehave, **voldóén** 'to suffice', **weerstáán** 'to withstand'.

4 There are just a few compound verbs which do not separate but which, unlike the verbs in the previous three groups, bear the stress:

beeldhouwen	to sculpt	**rangschikken**	to arrange in order
glimlachen	to smile	**stofzuigen**	to vacuum clean
huisvesten	to house	**stroomlijnen**	to streamline
knipogen	to wink	**voetballen**	to play football
raadplegen	to consult	**waarschuwen**	to warn

All the verbs in groups 1, 2 and 3 are conjugated like normal verbs in all tenses, never separate, and because they already contain an unstressed prefix, no **ge-** (which would be a further unstressed prefix) is added to form the past participle:

Hij herstélde de televisie/Hij heeft de televisie herstéld.
He repaired the television set.

Hij voorspélde slecht weer/Hij heeft slecht weer voorspéld.
He predicted bad weather.

Het huis doorstónd het orkaan/Het huis heeft het orkaan doorstáán.
The house withstood the hurricane.[34]

(The above accents should not be copied in writing; they are only to illustrate the stress.)

The verbs in group 4, all of which have a stressed prefix, do take **ge-**, but this does not go between the prefix and the verb as is the case with separable verbs:

Wij hebben de hele dag gevoetbald.
We played football all day.

It is not always possible to isolate the meaning of these prefixes but there are a few patterns which can be described.

11.20.2.1 Meaning of the prefixes in group 1 (those in groups 4 are usually self-evident, which is often the case with those in 2 and 3 too, but not necessarily)

11.20.2.1.1   The prefix **be-** is an extremely common prefix and has a variety of functions:

(a) It can be used to make transitive those intransitive verbs that take a prepositional object (see 11.21), sometimes with a slight change in

---

[34] The English verb 'to withstand' in this example illustrates that a similar phenomenon exists in English too.

meaning. This process is not productive and only applies to a limited number of verbs:

antwoorden op	to answer	**– beantwoorden**	to answer
schieten op	to fire on/at	**– beschieten**	to fire on/at
kijken naar	to look at	**– bekijken**	to look at
luisteren naar	to listen to	**– beluisteren**	to listen to
oordelen over	to judge, assess	**– beoordelen**	to judge, assess
pleiten voor	to argue/plead for	**– bepleiten**	to argue/plead for
spreken over	to talk about	**– bespreken**	to discuss

Also:

eindigen	to finish (intr.)	**– beëindigen**	to finish (trans.)

(b) Sometimes the verb assumes a slightly different meaning, as is often the case in group (a) too, but there is no question here of a preposition being replaced:

denken	to think	**– bedenken**	to think of, devise, concoct
dienen	to serve (God etc.)	**– bedienen**	to serve, attend to guests, wait upon customers
groeten	to greet	**– begroeten**	to receive, welcome
rekenen	to do sums, count	**– berekenen**	to calculate, figure out
studeren	to study (a subject)	**– bestuderen**	to analyse, study (a book)

(c) In a few isolated cases the **be-** has no force at all and is merely a more formal sounding variant of the verb concerned:

hoeven	**– behoeven**	to need (+ a negative, see 11.8.5.2(a))
horen	**– behoren**	to be fitting, proper

Note: The verbs **danken/bedanken** 'to thank' do not differ in meaning but do differ in usage:

Ik dank u, **meneer.** (direct speech, formal)
I thank you, sir.

Zij heeft haar tante bedankt.
She thanked her aunt.

11.20.2.1.2   The prefix **er-** is of German origin and is found in only three words and it is not possible to define a meaning:

zich erbarmen over	to have pity on
erkennen	to acknowledge, recognize [e.g. politically]
ervaren	to experience

Nederland heeft Kroatië erkend.
The Netherlands recognized Croatia.

11.20.2.1.3   The prefix **ge-** is not a common prefix on infinitives and its meaning avoids definition:

gebeuren	to happen	**gelijken**	to resemble
zich gedragen	to behave	**geloven**	to believe

Note how these verbs look in the perfect:

Ik heb hem niet geloofd.
I didn't believe him.

Hij heeft zich slecht gedragen.
He behaved disgracefully.

In the case of **gelukken** 'to succeed' and **geraken** 'to get, attain' the prefix is superfluous and is usually not used; as with **behoeven** and **behoren** (see above) the forms with **ge-** sound rather formal.

11.20.2.1.4   The prefix **her-** is very common and still productive; it is similar in meaning and function to English 're-' (i.e. again):

heradverteren	to readvertise	**herkennen**	to recognize
herbenoemen	to reappoint	**herschrijven**	to rewrite

Ik heb mijn eigen moeder niet herkend.
I didn't recognize my own mother. (compare **erkennen** under **er-** above)

11.20.2.1.5   The prefix **ont-** often means 'away' but its literal meaning is usually hard to isolate; it expresses for example the 'de-' in 'develop' and the 'ex-' in 'explode'. It is a common prefix:

ontkomen	to get away	**ontstaan**	to originate
ontmoeten	to meet	**ontsnappen**	to escape
ontploffen	to explode	**ontwikkelen**	to develop

11.20.2.1.6   The prefix **ver-** is the most common of all inseparable prefixes and has a variety of meanings and functions:

It commonly means 'change':

veranderen	to change	**vernederlandsen**	to Dutchify
verhuizen	to move	**vertalen**	to translate
verhuren	to rent out	**verwisselen**	to confuse
verkopen	to sell		

It also commonly means 'wrong' (in which case the verbs are usually reflexive):

zich vergissen	to make a mistake
zich verkijken	to look wrongly
zich verschrijven	to make a mistake in writing
zich verslapen	to sleep in, oversleep
zich verspreken	to make an error in speech, mispronounce

It is prefixed to existing verbs to indicate that the object of the resulting transitive verb is wasted (always a negative connotation):

de tijd verpraten	to talk away the time
benzine verrijden	to use up petrol by superfluous driving
de/zijn tijd verslapen	to sleep away the/one's time

It is used to make **branden** 'to burn' a transitive verb:

Ik probeerde de kist te verbranden en die brandde niet makkelijk.
I tried to burn the crate and it didn't burn easily.

11.20.2.2 Examples of verbs in groups 2 and 3 with prepositional or adverbial prefixes

It is impossible to give a complete list but the following will illustrate the concept. When the same compound exists as both a separable and an inseparable verb, the meaning of the former is usually more literal than that of the latter, e.g. **óndergaan** 'to go down, set [of the sun]', **ondergáán** 'to undergo'; **óvernemen** 'to take over', **ondernémen** 'to undertake'. Notice how so many of the English translations below don't take the stress on the prefix either (i.e. pur-, con-, mis-, em-, sur-, pre-, re- etc.), but on the second syllable, the stem of the verb; this is similar to what is occurring in the Dutch:

aanvaarden	to accept	**omhelzen**	to embrace
aanbidden	to worship	**omschrijven**	to describe
achterhalen	to catch up with	**omsingelen**	to surround
achtervolgen	to pursue	**omvatten**	to comprise
doordenken	to consider fully	**onderbreken**	to interrupt
doorzoeken	to search	**ondernemen**	to undertake
misbruiken	to misuse, abuse	**overleven**	to survive
zich misdragen	to misbehave	**overtuigen**	to convince

volbrengen	to fulfil	voorspellen	to predict
voldoen	to satisfy	weerspiegelen	to reflect
voorkomen	to prevent	weerstaan	to resist

11.21 VERBS FOLLOWED BY PREPOSITIONAL OBJECTS

Some of the verbs below will be found under more than one preposition with a difference in meaning. Many verbs are followed by the same preposition in English and are thus not necessarily included here. Others require no preposition in English but do in Dutch, e.g. trouwen met 'to marry', genieten van 'to enjoy', houden van 'to love' (see 11.21.1). The verbs are grouped under the Dutch prepositions they are followed by in order to give the learner a feeling for the use of prepositions in Dutch. This approach thereby fulfils a function the dictionary does not.

aan

(zich) aanpassen	to adapt to, assimilate to	meedoen	to take part in
beantwoorden	to correspond to/with	onderwerpen	to subject to
besteden	to spend on	ontkomen	to evade
bijdragen	to contribute to	ontlenen	to borrow (words)
binden	to tie to	ontsnappen	to escape from s.o.
deelnemen	to take part in	(zich) onttrekken	to withdraw from
denken	to think of	overdragen	to transfer to
doen	to take part in, go in for (sport)	overlijden	to die from
doen denken	to remind s.o. of s.t.	overhandigen	to hand over to
zich ergeren	to be irritated by	schrijven	to write to
geloven (also in)	to believe in (God)	sterven	to die from
geven	to give to	sturen	to send to
grenzen	to border on	toeschrijven	to attribute to
behoefte hebben	to be in need of	toevertrouwen	to entrust to
gebrek hebben	to be short of	toevoegen	to add to
hechten	to believe in	twijfelen	to doubt s.t.
herinneren	to remind s.o. of s.t.	vertellen	to tell to s.o.
		voldoen	to satisfy (demands)
horen	to belong to	
zich houden	to stick to (an agreement)	voorafgaan	to precede s.t.
		voorstellen	to introduce to
laten zien	to show to	wennen	to get used to
lenen	to lend to	zich wijden	to devote o.s. to

leveren	to deliver to	**wijten**	to blame s.o. for s.t.
lijden	to suffer from (a disease)	**zenden**	to send to s.o.

bij

aankomen	to arrive at s.o.'s place	**passen**	to match
(be)horen	to belong together	**wonen**	to live with (i.e. at s.o.'s place)

boven

verkiezen	to prefer to

door

vervangen	to replace by

in

aankomen	to arrive at	**veranderen**	to change into
belangstellen	to be interested in	**zich verdiepen**	to go deeply into, lose o.s. in (work)
bijten	to bite (a part of s.o.'s body, see 8.2.4)		
geloven	to believe in s.o.	**geïnteresseerd zijn**	to be interested in
trek/zin hebben	to feel like	**verdelen**	to divide into
slagen	to succeed at, in	**voorzien (in een behoefte)**	to satisfy a need
zich specialiseren	to specialize in		

met (see 11.21.1)

zich bemoeien	to mind (one's own business), interfere in	**overeen-stemmen**	to be in keeping with
condoleren	to condole with s.o. on s.t.	**praten**	to talk to
spotten	to scoff at	**spreken**	to speak to
feliciteren	to congratulate	**trouwen**	to marry
akkoord gaan	to agree with	**vergelijken**	to compare with
gebeuren	to happen to	**wonen**	to live with
gelukwensen	to congratulate on	**het eens zijn**	to agree with s.o.
overeenkomen	to correspond with, agree with s.t.		

naar

aarden	to take after, resemble	**staren**	to stare at
geuren	to smell of	**smachten**	to thirst, long for
gluren	to peep, peer at	**stinken**	to stink of

gooien	to throw at	**streven**[35]	to strive for
graven	to dig for	**sturen**[36]	to send to
grijpen	to grab at	**uitkijken**	to look out for, look forward to
hunkeren	to pine for		
kijken	to look at	**er uitzien**	to look (like)
knikken	to nod at	**uitzien**	to look forward to
luisteren	to listen to	**verlangen**	to long for
oordelen	to judge from	**vertrekken**	to leave, depart for
pikken	to pick at	**verwijzen**	to refer to
rieken	to smack, reek of	**vissen**	to fish for
ruiken	to smell of	**vragen**	to ask for s.o.
schrijven[36]	to write to	**werpen**	to throw at
smaken	to taste of	**wijzen**	to point at
snakken	to yearn, pine for	**zenden**[36]	to send for
solliciteren	to apply for	**zoeken**	to look for[37]

om

bedelen	to beg for	**smeken**	to plead for
benijden	to envy s.o. s.t.	**soebatten**	to implore for
denken	to think of, remember	**treuren**	to grieve, weep for
geven	to care about	**verzoeken**	to ask for s.t., request
huilen	to cry for, about s.t.	**vragen**	to ask for s.t.
(glim)lachen[38]	to (smile) laugh at s.t.	**wenen**	to cry, weep for

onder

| **lijden** | to suffer under, by (e.g. a regime). Compare **lijden aan**. |

op

aandringen	to insist on	**richten**	to direct at
zich abonneren	to subscribe to	**schatten**	to value at
antwoorden	to answer to (a question)	**schieten**	to shoot at
zich beroepen	to appeal to	**staan**	to insist on
berusten	to be founded, based on	**stemmen**	to vote for

[35] Compare **nastreven** 'to pursue, aspire to, strive after'.
[36] **Schrijven, sturen, zenden aan** someone, but **naar** a country, but one will also hear the Dutch saying **naar** someone.
[37] **Naar** is optional in the sense of looking 'for' something lost, but cannot be used, for example, if a firm is looking for a secretary: **De KLM zoekt een secretaresse** 'The KLM is looking for a secretary'.
[38] To laugh at s.o. (i.e. to ridicule) is **iemand uitlachen**.

drinken	to drink to	**storten**	to deposit in
duiden	to point to		(an account)
gokken	to bet on	**terugkomen**	to return to
kritiek hebben	to be critical of		(a point, issue)
toepassen	to apply to	**zich**	to apply o.s. to
		toeleggen	
betrekking	to refer to	**trakteren**	to treat to
hebben			
recht hebben	to be entitled to	**zich**	to look forward
		verheugen	to, rejoice
hopen	to hope for		at
ingaan	to go into (a matter)	**zich verlaten**	to rely, depend
			on
jagen	to hunt (after)	**veroveren**	to conquer from
kijken	to look at (a watch, clock)	**vertrouwen**	to rely, depend
			on
komen	to hit upon, think of	**vestigen**	to fix upon
	(a name etc.)	**vissen**	to fish for
lijken	to look like	**volgen**	to follow after,
			on
letten	to pay attention to	**zich**	to prepare for
		voor-	
		bereiden	
loeren	to lie in wait for	**vuren**	to fire at
attent maken	to draw one's attention to	**vliegen**	to fly to[39]
mikken	to aim at	**wachten**	to wait for
neerkomen	to boil down to	**wedden**	to bet on
passen	to look after	**wijzen**	to point to, out
reageren	to react to	**ja zeggen**	to say yes to
rekenen	to rely on	**zinspelen**	to allude to, hint
			at

over

beschikken	to have at one's disposal	**peinzen**	to ponder on
beslissen	to decide on	**praten**	to talk about
zich ergeren	to get irritated at	**roddelen**	to gossip about
klagen	to complain about	**zich schamen**	to be ashamed of

[39] **Vliegen op** is used for towns and countries regularly serviced by an airline:

De KLM vliegt op Australië.
KLM flies to (= serves) Australia.

Compare:

We vliegen morgen naar Nieuw-Zeeland.
We're flying to New Zealand tomorrow.

zich druk maken	to make a fuss about	**schrijven**	to write about
mopperen	to grumble about	**spreken**	to speak, talk about
nadenken	to think about	**zich verheugen**	to rejoice at
oordelen	to judge	**vertellen**	to tell about

tegen

blaffen	to bark at	**spreken**	to speak to
glimlachen	to smile at	**zich verzetten**	to resist
opzien	to look up to s.o., dread s.t.	**vloeken**	to swear at
ruilen	to exchange for	**zeggen**	to say to

tot (see 11.21.1)

aansporen	to incite, urge to	**aanleiding geven**	to give cause for
aanzetten	to incite, urge to	**kiezen**	to choose as
behoren	to belong to, be part of	**zich richten**	to apply to
bekeren	to convert to	**toelaten**	to admit to (university)
zich beperken	to limit o.s. to		
besluiten	to decide on	**veroordelen**	to condemn to
bidden	to pray	**zich verplichten**	to commit o.s. to
bijdragen	to contribute to	**zich wenden**	to turn to s.o.
leiden	to lead to		

uit

afleiden	to infer from	**ontstaan**	to arise, spring from
bestaan	to consist of	**opmaken**	to conclude from
concluderen	to conclude, infer from	**verbannen**	to banish from
dateren	to date from	**vertalen**	to translate from
drinken	to drink from (a glass)	**voortvloeien**	to result from
komen	to come from (a country, town)		

van

afhangen	to depend on	**leven**	to live on
afstammen	to be descended from	**overtuigen**	to convince of
balen	to be fed up with	**schrikken**	to be shocked by
barsten	to burst with	**stikken**	to suffocate from

beroven	to derive of		swarm with
bevallen	to give birth to	**veranderen**	to change (one's
beven	to tremble with		opinion,
			intention)
bevrijden	to liberate, free from	**verdenken**	to suspect of
blozen	to blush with	**verliezen**	to lose to s.o.
genieten	to enjoy	**verschillen**	to differ from
houden	to like	**voorzien**	to supply with
huilen	to cry with	**wemelen**	to swarm/teem
			with
krioelen	to swarm, teem with	**weten**	to know of

voor

behoeden	to guard, protect from	**zich in acht**	to be on one's
bezwijken	to succumb, yield to	**nemen**	guard against
	(the enemy)	**oppassen**	to look out for
danken	to thank for	**slagen**	to pass (exam)[40]
doorgaan	to pass for	**zich uitgeven**	to pass off for, as
gelden	to count for, be valid for	**verslijten**	to take s.o. for
belangstelling		**vrezen**	to be afraid of
hebben	to be interested in	**waarschuwen**	to warn against
zich hoeden	to beware of	**wijken**	to give way/
			yield to
zich interesseren	to be interested in	**zakken**	to fail (exam)[40]
kiezen	to choose for	**bang zijn**	to be afraid of
in aanmerking		**zorgen**	to take care of,
komen	to be considered for		look after

11.21.1   NOTE 1: met/mee, tot/toe

When verbs followed by **met** or **tot** govern a nominal object there is no complication:

Ik heb jouw fiets met de mijne vergeleken.
I (have) compared your bike to mine.

De vakbond heeft de mannen tot staken aangezet.
The union (has) incited the men to strike.

---

[40] Note how these two verbs are used with **voor** and conjugated with **zijn** in the perfect:

Hij is voor het examen/Engels geslaagd.
He (has) passed the exam/English.

Hij is voor het examen/Engels gezakt.
He (has) failed the exam/English.

But when the noun or pronoun is replaced by a pronominal **er**, **hier** or **daar** (see 8.1.2.4(d), 15.3) or the relative **waar** (see 8.5.3(b)), the alternative forms **mee** and **toe** must be used:

Ik heb de fiets ermee/daarmee/hiermee vergeleken.
I (have) compared it with it/that/this.

Zij hebben haar ertoe aangespoord.
They incited her to it.

De vulpen waar ik de brief mee schreef, is leeg.
The fountain pen I wrote the letter with is empty.

11.21.2 VERBS WITH PREPOSITIONAL OBJECTS WHICH ARE TRANSITIVE IN ENGLISH

A few Dutch verbs are followed by a preposition where English requires none:

bijten in	**De hond heeft hem in zijn been gebeten.** (see footnote 29, 11.17.2) The dog bit his leg.
klappen in	**Ze klapten in hun handen.** They clapped their hands.
lezen in	**Hij zit (in) een boek te lezen.** (preposition optional here) He's reading a book.
snijden in	**Ik heb me in mijn vinger gesneden.** (see footnote 29) I've cut my finger.
trouwen met	**De filmster trouwde met de prins.** The filmstar married the prince.

12 CONJUNCTIONS
(voegwoorden)

The distinction between conjunctions and certain sorts of adverbs is sometimes difficult to make. This section thus deals with those words, whether they be classed as conjunctions or adverbs, that join two or more clauses in a sentence.

Note: The footnote numbers next to the conjunctions in the lists in this chapter do not indicate true footnotes but refer to the notes that follow those lists.

12.1 CO-ORDINATING CONJUNCTIONS (nevenschikkende voegwoorden)

The main distinguishing feature of a co-ordinating conjunction in Dutch is that it does not have any effect on the word order of the following clause:

en[1]	and
want[2]	for, because
of[3]	or
maar	but
doch (lit.)[4]	but, nevertheless
dus[5]	thus, therefore
alleen (lit.)[4]	only, but

Hij is zeer arm maar hij heeft een auto.
He is very poor but he does have a car.

Kom je vandaag of kom je morgen?
Are you coming today or tomorrow?

Hij heeft het beloofd doch hij heeft het niet gedaan.
He promised to but he didn't do it.

12.1.1 NOTES:

12.1.1.1 Note that the following English conjunctional constructions with 'and' are avoided in Dutch:

We gingen zitten.
We went and sat down.

Ze gingen toen samen drop kopen.
They then went and bought licorice together.

Hij zit buiten een boek te lezen.
He is sitting outside (and) reading a book.

12.1.1.2 The conjunction 'for' is rather formal in English and is usually replaced by 'because', but in Dutch the reverse is the case. A sentence such as 'He dropped the cup because it was too hot' would usually be rendered as **Hij liet het kopje vallen want het was te heet**, although **omdat** plus subordinate word order would be quite correct too. Note that just as English 'because' cannot always be replaced by 'for', so **omdat** cannot always be replaced by **want**, i.e. when a compound sentence begins with the subordinate clause, then 'because' and **omdat** must be used:

Omdat het kopje te heet was, liet hij het vallen.
Because the cup was too hot, he dropped it.
Hij liet het kopje vallen want het was te heet.
Hij liet het kopje vallen omdat het te heet was.
He dropped the cup because it was too hot.

12.1.1.3 In the following context, where what follows 'or' is an explanation of what precedes it, i.e. means 'that is', **oftewel** may be used instead of **of**; it is a formal sounding word:

de cobra oftewel brilslang
the cobra or/that is the spectacled snake

Ofwel is a common synonym of **of** in the sense of 'or otherwise/else', but here **of** would suffice too:

Hij gaat (ofwel) morgen terug, ofwel overmorgen
He's returning tomorrow or otherwise/else the day after tomorrow.

This can also express 'either ... or' (see 12.4.1): 'He's either returning tomorrow or the day after tomorrow'.
   The co-ordinating conjunction **of** is commonly found after negative clauses in which case it can be translated in various ways into English:

Het scheelde niet veel of hij was overreden.
He was very nearly run over.

Nauwelijks was ik thuis of ik moest weer weg.
I was hardly home when I had to leave again.

Het duurde niet lang of ze stopten voor een groot ijzeren hek.
It wasn't long before they stopped in front of a large iron gate.

In addition, **of** is used idiomatically in the following expressions to render 'approximately':

een stuk of tien	about ten (pieces, books, apples, etc.)
een man of acht	about eight people
om een uur of acht	at about eight o'clock

Note the idiomatic expression **nou en of**:

Kun je lekker koffie zetten? Nou en of!
Can you make nice coffee? I certainly can/And how!

Het heeft veel geregend, niet waar? Nou en of!
It rained a lot, didn't it. It certainly did/And how!

Of can also be a subordinating conjunction with a further set of complex meanings (see 12.2.1.9).

12.1.1.4 The co-ordinating conjunctions **doch** and **alleen** are usually replaced by the adverbial conjunctions **toch** and **alleen** in the spoken language (see 12.3).

12.1.1.5 **Dus** can act as an ordinary co-ordinating conjunction not affecting word order, but can also cause inversion, in which case it acts as an adverbial conjunction (see 12.3):

Ruud bleef thuis dus Karel ging ook niet uit. (co-ordinating)
Ruud bleef thuis dus ging Karel ook niet uit. (adverbial)
Ruud stayed at home thus Karel didn't go out either.

But note that when **dus** is preceded by **en**, only the adverbial construction is possible – here **en** is the conjunction and **dus** is merely an adverb:

Ruud bleef thuis en dus ging Karel ook niet uit.

12.2 SUBORDINATING CONJUNCTIONS (onderschikkende voegwoorden)

There is a large number of such conjunctions, most of which are listed below. The distinguishing feature of these is that the verb of the dependent clause is sent to the end of that clause. The following pitfalls with subordinating conjunctions should be noted.

Be careful with word order when a subordinating conjunction governs two subordinate clauses which are joined by a co-ordinating conjunction:

Ik bleef thuis omdat ik een beetje ziek was en (omdat) er op mijn werk toch niet veel te doen was.
I stayed home because I felt a bit off and (because) there wasn't much to do at work anyway.

Wat was ze blij, toen ze zijn stem hoorde en (toen ze) zijn gezicht zag.
How glad she was when she heard his voice and (when she) saw his face.

Onze kennissen hadden ons verteld, dat het een zeer interessante plaats was en (dat) we er makkelijk een paar dagen zouden kunnen doorbrengen.
Our friends had told us that it was a very interesting place and (that) we could easily spend a few days there.

It is nearly always possible for stylistic reasons in both English and Dutch to place a subordinate clause in front of the main clause in a compound sentence. In English this has no effect on word order but in Dutch the subordinate clause assumes the role of first idea in the main clause (i.e. in the sentence as a whole) and thus inversion of subject and verb is required in the main clause. It is also usual to insert a comma between the two clauses to keep the finite verbs of each clause apart (see 3.1.23):

Ik maakte de bedden op terwijl zij de afwas deed =
Terwijl zij de afwas deed, maakte ik de bedden op.
While she washed up, I made the beds.

When a co-ordinating conjunction is followed by a subordinating conjunction, the subordinating one governs the word order of the following clause, but not that of the co-ordinate clause in which it is embedded; the subject and verb of the following co-ordinate clause invert as above because the subordinate clause takes on the role of first idea in the overall sentence:

Ik blijf thuis en omdat ik erg slecht geslapen heb, ga ik terug naar bed.
I'm staying home and because I slept really badly, I'm going back to bed.

A subordinate clause can be embedded in another subordinate clause, in which case one must remember to put the verb of the interrupted clause to the end when one returns to it. In the following example, which is stylistically not ideal but nevertheless possible, **als je een vreemde taal leert** has been embedded in the clause **dat je gewoonlijk je eigen taal beter kunt begrijpen**:

Ik vind dat als je een vreemde taal leert, je gewoonlijk je eigen taal beter kunt begrijpen.
I think that if you learn a foreign language you can usually understand your own language better.

dat[1]	that
voordat, **voor**[2]	before (see also 12.5)
eerdat, **eer** (lit.)	before
nadat, **na**[2]	after (see also 12.5)
totdat, **tot**	until
omdat[3]	because, as, since
zodat[4]	so that (result)
opdat[4]	so that (purpose)
doordat	by, because (see also 12.5)
mede doordat	also because
in plaats van dat	instead of (see also 12.5)
zonder dat	without (see also 12.5)
behalve dat	except that
zodanig dat	such that
vandaar dat	for that reason, thus
alsmede dat	as well as (the fact that)
inzover(re) dat	to the extent that
zoals[8]	(just) as
alsof[9]	as if
als[2, 5, 6, 8, 9]	when, if
wanneer[2, 6]	when, whenever
toen[6]	when
indien (lit.)[5]	if
daar (lit.)	since, because
aangezien	since, because, seeing
terwijl[7]	while, whereas
sinds	since (temporal)
sedert	since (temporal)
ofschoon (lit.)	although
schoon (lit.)	although
(al)hoewel	although
nu	now that
zodra (coll. also **zo gauw**)	as soon as
zolang	as/so long as
(voor) zover	(in) as far as
gelijk (lit.)	just as (= **net zoals**)
evenals	just as (= **net zoals**)
evenmin als	just as little as, no more than
tenzij	unless
mits	provided that

vermits (lit.)	whereas, since
of[9]	whether
of dat[9]	or whether
onverschillig of	regardless of whether
naar[10]	as
naarmate	as
naar gelang[1]	as
niettegenstaande[1]	notwithstanding that
ingeval[1]	in case, in the event (that)

The following is a list of commonly used phrases/clauses that introduce subordinate clauses, most of them **dat** clauses:

daar staat tegenover dat	on the other hand
stel/veronderstel/gesteld (lit.) **dat**	let's say/assume (that)
tegen de tijd dat	by the time (that)
dat neemt niet weg dat	that does not alter the fact that
dat wil (niet) zeggen dat	that means (doesn't mean) that
dat maakt dat	that means that, has as a result that
gezien het feit dat	as, in light of the fact that
ondanks het feit dat	in spite of the fact that
voor het geval dat	in case
daar komt (nog) bij dat	in addition
laat staan dat/als/wanneer	let alone that/if/when
het toeval wilde dat	chance would have it that
met dien verstande dat	on the understanding that
het ziet ernaar uit dat	it looks as if

12.2.1 NOTES:

12.2.1.1   dat

Note that 'that' is often omitted in English but never in Dutch:

Hij zei dat hij komen zou.
He said he would come.

De eerste keer dat ze het zei ...
The first time she said it ...

Not only the subordinating conjunction 'that' is dropped in English but also the relative pronoun 'that'; this pronoun, which is either **die** or **dat** in Dutch, may not be omitted either (see 8.5.1).

In uncultivated speech a superfluous **dat** is sometimes used after other subordinate conjunctions and interrogative adverbs in indirect questions (see 12.6):

Ik weet niet waar dat ze wonen.
I don't know where they live.

Nu dat ik rijk ben ...
Now (that) I am rich ...

It is, for example, very common after **naarmate, naar gelang** and **niettegenstaande**.

A rather idiomatic usage of **dat** is the following:

Een stank dat er was!
There was a terrible smell!

En eten dat hij kan!
How he can eat!

Note also the use of **dat** in the following instances where it could be confused with the relative pronoun:

De tweede keer dat hij kwam.
The second time he came.

Dit is een pot uit de tijd dat er hier nog geen blanken leefden.
This is a pot from the time that/before there were any whites living here.

12.2.1.2 The conjunctions **voordat** and **nadat** are commonly used in combination with the following words: by **kort voordat/nadat** 'shortly before/after', **daags voordat/nadat** 'the day before/after' and **lang voordat/nadat** 'long before/after'.

Wanneer and **als** (meaning 'when') are commonly preceded by **pas** 'only when/not until' (see 16.1.4.6), **zelfs** 'even when' and **vooral** 'especially when'.

12.2.1.3 For substitution of **omdat** with **want** see 12.1.1.2. Note that where 'as' or 'since' mean 'because' (see **daar**) they should be translated by **omdat**:

Omdat hij zich misselijk voelt, blijft hij thuis.
As he feels sick, he's staying at home.

12.2.1.4 In colloquial Dutch the subtle distinction between **zodat** and **opdat** is often ignored and **zodat** is used in both senses:

Het heeft de hele dag geregend zodat we niet uit konden gaan.
(It rained all day so that (with the result that) we were not able to go out.

De Russische regering heeft het bedrag van de steun verhoogd opdat de armsten geen honger zullen lijden.
The Russian government has raised the amount of the support so that (with the purpose that) the poorest won't starve.

12.2.1.5 As in English, **als/indien** 'if' in conditional sentences can be omitted in higher style and the clause can begin with the verb; the main clause is then always introduced by **dan** (see 12.3):

Was hij gekomen, dan hadden wij het kunnen doen.
Had he come, we could have done it.

Als hij gekomen was, hadden wij het kunnen doen.
If he had come, we could have done it.

Komt er oorlog, dan zullen we het land verlaten.
Should war come, then we'll leave the country.

Als er oorlog komt, zullen we het land verlaten.
If war comes, we'll leave the country.

See **mogen**, 11.8.3.1.4.

Note: The following syntactical device can occur in higher style where the conjunctionless 'if' clause comes second:

Vakanties moeten uitzonderlijk zijn, willen ze in die brochure staan.
Holidays have to be exceptional if they want to appear in that brochure.

12.2.1.6 The translation of English 'when' into Dutch is a complex issue. There are three words: **wanneer, als, toen.**
   Wanneer is always used in interrogative clauses both direct and indirect:

Wanneer komt hij thuis? Ik weet niet wanneer hij thuiskomt.
When is he coming home? I don't know when he is coming home.

It is also used to translate 'when' in subordinate clauses when the verb is in the present, future or perfect tense. In this case it can be replaced by **als**:

Wanneer (als) het regent, blijf ik thuis.
When it rains I stay at home.

It can only be used in a clause with the verb in the imperfect or pluperfect when it means 'whenever', otherwise **toen** is used (see below). This **wanneer** can also be replaced by **als**:

Wanneer (als) hij dan thuiskwam was zij altijd boos op hem.
Whenever he came home she was always angry with him.

Als, apart from replacing **wanneer** in instances such as the above, also renders 'if' (but not 'if' which means 'whether', see **of**), in which case a slight ambiguity as to whether **als** means 'if' or 'when' can arise, but this does not worry the Dutch:

Als het regent, wil ik thuis blijven.
When/if it rains, . . .

See 12.2.1.9 below for **als** as an abbreviation of **alsof**. See chapter 13 for use of **als** as a preposition.

Toen replaces **wanneer/als** when the verb is in the past, i.e. when the meaning is 'when on one occasion', but **wanneer/als** are used when the verb is in the imperfect and the meaning is 'whenever', i.e. 'when on repeated occasions':

Toen hij thuiskwam, was ik al weg.
When he got home, I had already left.

Compare:

Wanneer (als) hij thuiskwam, was ik altijd al weg.
When(ever) he got home, I had always already left.

Note: There is also an adverb **toen** 'then' which should not be confused with the conjunction **toen** 'when' discussed here (see 10.4.11):

Toen ging hij weg.
He then left.

Toen hij wegging ...
When he left ...

12.2.1.7 **Terwijl** often helps one out of certain difficult English verbal '-ing' constructions (see 11.16.6):

Terwijl ik in de stad rondliep, kwam ik hem tegen.
Walking around in town I bumped into him.

12.2.1.8 **Als** as a subordinating conjunction has a variety of meanings:

(a) 'when, whenever' (see 12.2.1.6)
(b) 'if', in which case it can be omitted (see 12.2.1.5 and 12.2.1.6)
(c) 'as/so long as', in which case it replaces **zolang**:

Het kan me niet schelen hoe, als je het maar doet.
I don't care how, as/so long as you do it.

(d) 'as', in which case it can be confused with **zoals** (see point (h)) but this is not a common usage of **als**:

Het ziet eruit als volgt: . . .
It appears to be as follows: . . .

Compare the following use of **zoals** which stands at the beginning of the sentence:

Zoals al gezegd, . . .
As already mentioned, . . .

(e) 'than', used after comparatives (often followed by simple nouns and pronouns rather than clauses). In this sense it is not approved of by everyone and is thus better replaced by **dan** (see 9.2.6):

Hij is langer als (dan) ik.
He is taller than I.

Hij deed het beter als (dan) ik het had kunnen doen.
He did it better than I could have done it.

(f) **Als** can also be used as an adverbial conjunction replacing the subordinating conjunction **alsof** (see 12.3):

Ze renden als vreesden ze voor hun leven.
They were running as if they were afraid for their lives.

Hij zag eruit als had hij dagenlang niet geslapen.
He looked as if he hadn't slept for days.

The adverbial conjunction **als** with the meaning of **alsof** occurs in very formal style followed by the archaic subjunctive form **ware**:

Het was als ware hij met stomheid geslagen.
It was as if he was struck dumb.

The standard expression **als het ware** 'as it were', where **als** acts as a subordinating conjuncton, can also be used to express 'as if':

Toen lachte hij als het ware om zich te verontschuldigen.
Then he laughed as if to apologize.

(g) **Als** can also function as a preposition meaning 'as' (see 5.1.1):

Als kind werkte hij in een goudmijn.
As a child he worked in a gold mine.

Ik gebruikte het als asbak.
I used it as an ashtray.

Zich gedragen als een heer.
To behave as (like) a gentleman.

Iemand erkennen als koning.
To recognize someone as king.

(h) **Zoals** can only be used as a subordinating conjunction, whereas **als** has both adverbial and prepositional functions in addition to that of a conjunction:

(i) '(such) as, in such a way as'

Hij speelde zoals hij nog nooit gespeeld had.
He played (such) as he had never played before.

(ii) 'as'

Zoals je weet, ga ik ook mee.
As you know, I'm going too.

Net zoals ik gezegd heb, ...
Just as I said ...

(iii) 'as, like'

Je moet doen zoals wij.
You should do as (like) we (do).

Zoals menigeen heeft hij al zijn geld in de oorlog verloren.
Like so many, he lost all his money in the war.

12.2.1.9   Alsof 'as if'

Very often the **als** is dropped and **of** maintains the full meaning of 'as if' (see 15.4.1.4):

Hij deed of hij er niets van wist.
He pretended he didn't know anything about it.

Somewhat less common is just **als** meaning **alsof** but in this case **als** acts as an adverbial conjunction (see 12.3). The option of this alternative construction is not always at your disposal; it seems to be most common when the verb that follows is a form of **hebben** or **zijn**:

De kamer zag eruit als was er een olifant door gelopen
The room looked as if an elephant had gone through it.

Of as a subordinating conjunction can mean:

(a) 'whether' (and note that 'or whether' is **of dat** to avoid a double **of**):

Ik wist niet of hij thuis was.
I didn't know if he was at home.

Of ze zal slagen, is nog de vraag.
Whether she'll pass is the question.

Hij wist niet meer of hij dat werkelijk had meegemaakt of dat hij het gedroomd had.
He didn't know any more whether he had really experienced that or whether he had dreamt it.

(b) 'as if', in which case it replaces **alsof** (see above):

Of is often used superfluously after interrogative adverbs and pronouns in indirect questions (see 12.6) in much the same way as **dat** is sometimes used (see 12.2.1.1, 12.6). This practice should not be copied:

Ik weet niet wat of ze kan doen.
I don't know what she can do.

Note the following example which contains both a superfluous **of** and **dat**:

Ik weet niet wie of dat er zal komen.
I don't know who'll be coming.

For further uses of **of** as a coordinating conjunction see 12.1.1.3.

12.2.1.10   **Naar** is only found in higher style and usually in set expressions:

Naar ik meen is het Afrikaans een mengtaal.
Afrikaans is, I believe, a mixed language.

Naar men zegt . . .
It is said/one says . . .

Naar verluidt . . .
It is rumoured . . .

12.3   ADVERBIAL CONJUNCTIONS

Grammatically speaking these words are adverbs but they often function as conjunctions introducing clauses. Their adverbial qualities are, however, obvious from the word order which follows, i.e. inversion of subject and verb so that the verb remains the second idea, the adverb being the first idea in the clause. More adverbs than those listed below may function in this way:

alleen[1]	only
althans	at least
dus[1]	thus, hence, for that reason
daarom	thus, hence, for that reason
vandaar	thus, hence, for that reason
daarvandaan	thus, hence, for that reason
toch	nevertheless, but, however
al[2]	even if
ook al	even if
als[3]	as if
anders	otherwise
desondanks	in spite of it/that
intussen	in the meantime, meanwhile
inmiddels	in the meantime, meanwhile
integendeel	on the contrary
dan[4]	then

Al had hij het gedaan, ze hadden het me toch niet verteld (note the word order in the second clause – there is no inversion of subject and verb.).
Even if he had done it I would not have heard about it anyway.

Hij zag eruit als had hij dagenlang niet geslapen.
He looked as if he hadn't slept for days.

Mijn leerlingen zijn lui, toch zijn ze niet stom. (compare 12.1.1.4)
My students are lazy, nevertheless they are not stupid.

Hij is niet naar de vergadering gekomen, althans ik heb hem niet gezien.
He didn't come to the meeting, at least I didn't see him.

Voel je je ziek, dan moet je thuis blijven.
If you are feeling sick, (then) you should stay home.

Notes:

1 **Alleen** and **dus** can also be co-ordinating (see 12.1).
2 **Al** in this sense (see the first example above) is synonymous with **zelfs als**, which is subordinating.
3 **Als** in this sense (see the second example above) is the same as **alsof**, which is subordinating (see 12.2.1.8(f)).
4 This **dan** is used after a particular sort of 'if' clause, as in the last example above (see 12.2.1.5), but also after comparatives (see 9.2.6 and 12.2.1.8(e)).

12.4   CORRELATIVE CONJUNCTIONS

Correlative conjunctions are couplets of conjunctions that correlate two clauses of a sentence, i.e. each clause begins with a conjunction that forms a sense pair with the other. They can be classified as follows:

1 those that act as co-ordinating conjunctions in both parts of the sentence (see 12.4.1).
2 those that act as adverbial conjunctions in both parts of the sentence (see 12.4.2).
3 a few that don't fit into either groups 1 or 2 (see 12.4.3).

12.4.1   CO-ORDINATING CORRELATIVE CONJUNCTIONS

In the following cases the finite verb in each part of the sentence follows the subject (i.e. there is no inversion of subject and verb) and thus the conjunctions are behaving as co-ordinating conjunctions:

(of) ... of	either ... or (see also **ofwel**, 12.1.1.2)
hetzij ... of/hetzij (lit.)	either ... or
(noch) ... noch[1]	neither ... nor
zowel ... als (ook)[2]	both ... and
(en) ... en	both ... and (less common)
niet alleen ... (maar) ook	not only ... but also

(Óf) je doet het goed, óf je doet het helemaal niet.
Either you do it well or you don't do it at all.

Het verslag van de commissie bereikt de kamer hetzij aanstaande dinsdag, hetzij/of dinsdag over een week.
The lower house will receive the committee's report either next Tuesday or Tuesday week.

Zowel de leraar als de leerling hebben het boek gelezen.
Both the teacher and the student (have) read the book.

Hij is (én) voorzitter van de voetbalclub én van de tennisclub.
He is president of both the football club and the tennis club.

Niet alleen de jongens hebben gevoetbald maar ook de meisjes.[3]
Not only the boys played football but also the girls.

The accents on **of** and **en** above are in fact superfluous, but nevertheless commonly found. The new spelling rules do not permit the use of graves, only acutes, but **òf** and **èn** are nevertheless still commonly (even most usually) written with graves if they are written with accents at all, as a grave corresponds more closely to the way they are pronounced.

Notes:

1   There are a few things to watch out for when translating 'neither ... nor':

(Noch) mijn broer noch mijn vriend kon me helpen. (note the
   singular verb)
Neither my brother nor my friend could help me.

Ik heb gegeten noch gedronken.
I have neither eaten nor drunk anything.

When only one **noch** is used the verb is commonly in the plural because
it resembles **of ... of** in meaning, although the purist would insist on a
singular verb here too:

Mijn broer noch mijn vriend konden me helpen.
Neither my brother nor my friend could help me.

Ik heb gegeten noch gedronken only one **noch** is required as the sentence
does not begin with the conjunction.
   An English construction such as 'He may not stay here nor may he go
home' is simplified in Dutch to **Hij mag niet hier blijven en hij mag ook
niet naar huis** (**ook niet** = not either, see 16.1.4.7).
2   Inclusion of **ook** is considered rather archaic these days.
3   Compare the following, which is syntactically and thus semantically
   different:

**Niet alleen heeft hij het boek al gelezen (maar) hij heeft het ook al
   teruggebracht.**
Not only has he already read the book but he has also already
   returned it.

See 12.4.3.2.

12.4.2   ADVERBIAL CORRELATIVE CONJUNCTIONS

In the following cases the finite verb in each part of the sentence follows
the conjunction and thus the conjunctions behave as adverbs:

nu ... dan	one moment ... the next, now ... now
nu eens ... dan weer	one moment ... the next, now ... now
de ene keer ... de andere keer	one moment ... the next, now ... now
enerzijds ... anderzijds	on the one hand ... (but) on the other
aan de ene kant ... aan de andere kant	on the one hand ... (but) on the other
deels ... deels	partly ... partly
ten dele ... ten dele	partly ... partly
gedeeltelijk ... gedeeltelijk	partly ... partly

Nu zie je het wel, dan zie je het niet.
Now you see it, now you don't.

Enerzijds wil hij werken, anderzijds wil hij nog blijven studeren.
On the one hand he wants to work but on the other he wants to still
keep studying.

12.4.3   There are four correlative conjunctions that are at odds with the
patterns described in 12.4.1 and 12.4.2. They must be looked at one by
one:

12.4.3.1   **nauwelijks ... of**   scarcely/hardly ... when

The first half acts as an adverb, the second as a co-ordinating conjunction. This rather idiomatic use of co-ordinating **of** has other parallels (see
12.1.1.3):

Nauwelijks was ik thuis of mijn vader belde me op.
Scarcely/hardly had I got home when my father rang me.

or

I had scarcely/hardly got home when my father rang me.

12.4.3.2   **niet alleen ... (maar) ook**   not only ... but

As above, the first half acts as an adverb, the second as a co-ordinating
conjunction:

**Niet alleen heeft hij het boek verloren, (maar) hij heeft het me ook
niet vergoed.**
Not only did he lose the book but he didn't pay me for it either.

There is also a similar co-ordinating correlative conjunction (see the last
example under 12.4.1).

12.4.3.3

hoe ... des te   the ... the
hoe ... hoe

Although synonymous, these two correlative couplets require a different
word order:

hoe ... des te   (sub. conj. + adv. conj.)
hoe ... hoe   (sub. conj. + sub. conj.)

Hoe meer je studeert, des te meer zul je weten.
(but **des te meer je weten zult**, with subordinate word order, also
  occurs)

Hoe meer je studeert, hoe meer je weten zult.
The more you study, the more you'll know.

12.5   CONJUNCTIONS INTRODUCING INFINITIVE CLAUSES

Infinitive clauses contain no finite verb but rather an infinitive preceded
by **te**; at the beginning of the clause stands one of the conjunctions below.
Only **teneinde** is used exclusively as a conjunction in infinitive clauses.
All the other words have other functions as well:

om[1]	in order to (see 11.9.3.3)
	only to (much less common meaning)
teneinde (lit.)	in order to
alvorens[2] (lit.)	before
na[2]	after
door	by
met[3]	(see explanation below)
in plaats van[4]	instead of
zonder	without
van	from

Hij ging naar huis om zijn fiets te halen.
He went home (in order) to fetch his bike.

**De overlevenden kregen direct na de oorlog hun onroerend goed
  terug, om het na de machtsovername van de communisten
  opnieuw kwijt te raken.**
The survivors got their property back right after the war, only to
  lose it again after the communists took power. (see 11.9.3.3)

**Teneinde moeilijkheden te voorkomen wordt men vriendelijk
  verzocht dieren buiten te laten.**
(In order) to avoid difficulties, you are kindly requested to leave
  animals outside.

Door zo te doen, zul je niets bereiken.
By doing that, you will accomplish nothing.

Na urenlang gewerkt te hebben, is hij naar de bioscoop gegaan.
After having worked for hours he went to the movies.

Men wordt vriendelijk verzocht zijn sigaret te doven alvorens de bioscoop in te gaan.
You are kindly requested to extinguish your cigarette before entering the cinema.

12.5.1   Notes:

12.5.1.1   For use of **te** with or without **om** see 11.9.2 and 11.9.3.

12.5.1.2   **Alvorens**, which like **teneinde** is a very formal subordinating conjunction, and **na** + an infinitive clause can always be replaced by **voordat** and **nadat** + a subordinate clause:

Nadat hij urenlang gewerkt had, ging hij naar de bioscoop.
After he had worked for hours, he went to the movies.

12.5.1.3   A superfluous **met** functioning as a conjunction is often heard in the spoken language in progressive verbal constructions:

Je bent de hele dag bezig met dat kind te helpen.
You spend your whole day helping that child.

In spoken Dutch **met** can also sometimes replaces **door** in infintive clauses:

Met/door dat te doen, zul je niets bereiken.
You'll achieve nothing by doing that.

12.5.1.4   **In plaats van** and **zonder** differ in usage from **in plaats van dat** and **zonder dat** in the following way: when the subject of both clauses is the same, the infinitive clause construction can be used; but when the subjects are different, the appropriate subordinating conjunction must be used:

Zonder op te kijken liep hij door.

or

Hij liep door zonder dat hij opkeek.
He walked on without looking up. (same subject in both clauses)

but only

Hij kwam binnen zonder dat ik hem zag.
He came in without me seeing him. (different subjects)

Hij kwam bij me thuis in plaats van op mijn kantoor te komen.

or

Hij kwam bij me thuis in plaats van dat hij op mijn kantoor kwam.
He came to my home instead of coming to my office. (same subject
   in both clauses)

In plaats van dat ik haar naar huis bracht, deed hij het.
Instead of me taking her home, he did it. (different subjects)

Use of **zonder dat** and **in plaats van dat** when the subject of both clauses
is the same, occurs more in the spoken than the written language.

12.6 INTERROGATIVE ADVERBS AND PRONOUNS INTRODUCING INDIRECT QUESTIONS

Although these words are not strictly speaking conjunctions, they function
nevertheless as subordinating conjunctions when they introduce indirect
questions, i.e. answers to direct questions (see 8.6.5, 10.6):

wat	what
wanneer	when
waarom	why
wie	who
welk(e)	which, what
hoe	how
hoeveel	how much
in hoever(re)	to what extent
waar	where
waar ... heen	where ... to
waar ... vandaan	where ... from
waar + prep.	(see Relative pronouns, 8.5.3)

Direct question	**Wat heeft hij in zijn hand?**
	What has he got in his hand?
Indirect question	**Ik weet niet wat hij in zijn hand heeft.**
	I don't know what he has in his hand.
Direct question	**Waar komt ze vandaan?**
	Where does she come from?
Indirect question	**Ik weet niet waar ze vandaan komt.**
	I don't know where she comes from.
Direct question	**Welke boeken hebben ze gelezen?**
	What books have they read?
Indirect question	**Hij vroeg welke boeken ze gelezen hadden.**
	He asked which books they had read.

Direct question	**In hoeverre zal dat mogelijk zijn?**
	To what extent will that be possible?
Indirect question	**Ik weet niet in hoeverre dat mogelijk zal zijn.**
	I don't know to what extent that will be possible.

Note: Often a superfluous subordinating **of** or **dat** is used after these words in colloquial speech, but the practice should be avoided (see also 12.2.1.1, 12.2.1.9(b)):

Ik vroeg me af hoe of ze dat had kunnen doen.
I wondered how she had been able to do that.

Ik weet niet waar of ze de bruiloft willen houden.
I don't know where they want to hold the wedding.

Kun je me zeggen waar dat hij woont?
Can you tell me where he lives?

The same words are used as subordinating conjunctions in combination with **ook** to express 'whoever', 'wherever' etc. (see 8.6.5):

wat ... ook	whatever
wie ... ook	whoever
welk(e) ... ook	whichever
waar ... ook	wherever
hoe ... ook	however[1]

Wie het ook gedaan heeft, ik wens erbuiten te blijven.
Whoever did it, I wish to stay out of it.

(Note the word order in the second clause – there is no inversion of subject and verb.)

Waar hij ook woonde, zijn allergische klachten bleven bestaan.
Wherever he lived, his allergies remained.

Welke weg je ook neemt, je komt altijd bij de rivier.
Whichever road you take, you always get to the river.

The above can be replaced by **onverschillig wat/wie/welk(e)/waar/hoe** or **om het even wat/wie/welk(e)/waar/hoe** 'irrespective of what/who/which' followed by the same uninverted word order in the second clause as in the first example:

---

[1] Note that the English adverb 'however' is **echter**:

Hij heeft het echter niet kunnen doen.
He wasn't able to do it, however.

Onverschillig/om het even wie het gedaan heeft, ik wens erbuiten te blijven.
Whoever did it, I wish to stay out of it.

In addition to the above one will hear **wie dan ook**, **waar dan ook**, etc. Such expressions must not be confused with the interrogative conjunctions. They are used as follows:

Zoiets kan wie dan ook gedaan hebben.
Anybody might have done something like that.

Ik zal er hoe dan ook een vinden.
I'll find one somehow.

Kinderen van welke leeftijd dan ook werden toegelaten.
Children of whatever age were admitted.

Er is hier meer welvaart dan waar (dan) ook.
There is more prosperity here than anywhere.

13 PREPOSITIONS
(voorzetsels/preposities)

Because prepositions are the most idiomatic part of speech, each with a vast number of meanings in many cases, the following list can only serve as a guide to the usage of Dutch prepositions. To have listed English prepositions with their various translations into Dutch would have been unwieldy and the student would have been prevented from getting a feeling for the nuances of Dutch prepositions. By doing the reverse it is hoped a certain pattern in the usage of individual Dutch prepositions will emerge and facilitate the learning of them. It should be noted that they are often used as adverbs too, e.g. **De soep is op** 'The soup is finished', **Hij is boven** 'He is upstairs' (see 10.5). Only the most usual of meanings of each preposition in English are given next to the Dutch form at the beginning of each entry (e.g. **achter** 'behind, after') although in reality they may be rendered in a myriad of ways in English.

à   'to, at'

drie à vier weken (also **tot**)	three to four weeks
à vijf percent	at five percent
à f10,00 per stuk	at ten guilders each

aan   'on, at'

This preposition is often confused by English speakers with **op**. In as far as its meaning can be defined at all, one can say that a vertical 'on' is rendered by **aan** (but a horizontal 'on' is rendered by **op**) and 'on' or 'at' the edge of things is also **aan**:

het schilderij aan de muur	the picture on the wall
aan het plafond	on the ceiling
geen ster aan de hemel	no star in the sky
iemand aan de deur	somebody at the door
aan de kust	on the coast
aan zee (compare **op**)	at the seaside
aan het strand (compare **op**)	at the beach
aan land gaan	to go ashore
aan tafel (compare **op**)	at the table
aan de Rijn	on/along the Rhine

Mijn huis staat aan een gracht. (see **op**)	My house is on a canal.
aan de linkerkant/-hand	on the left-hand side
aan de telefoon	on the telephone
Jij bent aan de beurt.	It is your turn.
aan het begin/einde	at the beginning/end
Ik ben hard aan het werk.	I am hard at work.
aan de universiteit (compare **op**)	at the university (i.e. studying there)
Wat had zij voor kleren aan?	What sort of clothes did she have on?
Ik heb een gouden ring aan. (also **om**)	I have a gold ring on.
De lamp/het fornuis is aan.	The light/stove is on.
blind aan een oog	blind in one eye
doof aan een oor	deaf in one ear
een gebrek aan	a lack of
Er is (een grote) behoefte aan ...	There is a (great) need for ...
Ze weten niet wat ze aan je hebben.	They don't know what they have in you.
Wat heb je aan belasting betaald?	What did you pay in tax?
f2000 aan sieraden	f2000 in jewels
Ik herkende hem aan (door) zijn stem.	I recognized him by his voice.
verbeteringen aan het huis	improvements to the house
Ik kan er niets aan doen.	I can do nothing about it.
Ik heb er niets aan.	It's useless to me.
een bezoek aan Duitsland	a visit to Germany

achter   'behind, after'

achter het huis	behind the house
Hij zit de hele dag achter zijn bureau.	He sits at his desk all day.
Ik heb het volk achter me.	I have the people behind me.
de deur achter zich dichtdoen	to close the door behind one
Mijn horloge loopt achter.	My watch is slow.
Schrijf M.A. achter je naam.	Write M.A. after your name.
tien achter elkaar	ten in a row

afgezien van   'apart from, except for'

afgezien daarvan	apart from that
afgezien van mijn broer	apart from/except for my brother

aldus   'according to'

Found in formal style and journalese in particular, because of the frequency of quotes. It can only be followed by a noun or name; otherwise **volgens** is used (see **volgens**).

'...', aldus de minister-president	'...', according to the prime minister/the prime minister said

als   'as' (see Conjunctions, 12.2.1.8(g))

Note that the indefinite article is often not used after this **als**, depending on the idiom:

als kind	as a child
Ik wil het als asbak gebruiken.	I want to use it as an ashtray.
zich gedragen als een dame	to behave like a lady

behalve   'except (for), apart from'

'Except for' is of course always followed by an object pronoun in English but both subject and object pronouns are used after **behalve**, depending on the semantics of the statement:

Wie gaat behalve ik? (subj. pronoun)	Who is going apart from me?
Wie zag je behalve hem? (obj. pronoun)	Whom did you see apart from him?
behalve in de zomer	except (for) in summer
Behalve mijn moeder komt ook mijn oma.	As well as/apart from my mother my grandma is coming too.

beneden   'beneath, under'

Het is beneden zijn waardigheid.	It is beneath him.
beneden de Moerdijk	south of the Moerdijk[1]
beneden de veertig (also onder)	under forty
12 graden beneden nul	minus twelve degrees

---

[1] Synonymous with this expression is **beneden/ten zuiden van de grote rivieren**. Both expressions relate to the linguistic and cultural divide between the northern and the southern Netherlands, where the latter may or may not include Flanders depending on the context. These terms are also used when reporting on the weather in various parts of the country.

bij   'by, near, at'

Often preceded by **dicht/vlak** in the meaning of 'near':[2]

vlak bij het stadhuis	very near the town hall
bij het postkantoor	near the post-office
Ik woon bij (aan) het water.	I live near the water.
Hij heeft geen geld bij zich.	He has no money on him.
Ik woon bij mijn tante.	I live at my aunt's/with my aunt.
Ik kom zo bij u.	I'll be with you in a moment.
Wij horen bij elkaar.	We are/belong together (e.g. in a shop)
iemand bij zijn naam roepen	to call someone by name
iemand bij de hand nemen	to take someone by the hand
bij de tandarts/groenteman	at the dentist('s)/greengrocer('s)
Ik heb het bij V en D gekocht.	I bought it at V & D (a department store).
bij mooi weer	when the weather is nice
bij oostenwind	when an easterly is blowing
bij honderden	by the hundreds
twee bij drie meter	two by three metres
de slag bij Waterloo	the Battle of Waterloo
bij het ontbijt	at breakfast
Wil je een koekje bij de koffie?	Do you want a biscuit with your coffee?
Doe een kaartje bij de bloemen!	Put a card in with the flowers.
bij uitstek	par excellence
Ik heb het bij Dickens gelezen.	I read it in Dickens.
Ik ben bij Tiel-Utrecht verzekerd.	I'm insured with Tiel-Utrecht.
bij een firma werken	to work for a firm
bij een bezoek aan het museum	on a visit to the museum
bij nader inzien	on closer examination
bij zichzelf denken	to think to oneself
bij het raam/vuur zitten	to sit by the window/fire
bij de volgende halte uitstappen	to get out at the next stop
examen doen bij iemand	to do an exam for s.o. (i.e. a lecturer)

binnen   'within, in'

binnen een week	within a week
binnen het bestek van dit boek	within the scope of this book

---

[2] Note that the prepositions **dicht bij** and **vlak bij** are written as two words, whereas as adverbs they are written as one word **dichtbij/vlakbij** 'nearby'.

De bal lag binnen zijn bereik.	The ball was lying within his reach.
binnen de afrastering blijven	to stay within the cordoned-off area

boven   'above, over'

boven de waterspiegel	above water level
Je vliegt urenlang boven Australië.	You fly over Australia for hours.
Het ging boven zijn pet.	It went over his head/It was beyond him.
Zaandam ligt boven Amsterdam.	Zaandam is north of Amsterdam.
Hij is boven de vijftig. (see **over**)	He's over fifty.
twaalf graden boven nul	twelve degrees above zero
Ik geef de voorkeur aan een VW boven alle andere auto's.	I prefer a VW to all other cars.

buiten   'out of, outside, beyond'

buiten de stad	out of town, outside the town
buiten gevaar	out of danger
buiten beschouwing laten	to leave out of consideration
buiten mijn competentie	beyond my competence
Ik kan niet buiten hem. (see **zonder**)	I can't do without him.
Buiten haar bestond er niets voor hem. (see **behalve**)	Apart from her nothing existed for him.

dankzij   'thanks to'

dankzij jou	thanks to you
dankzij het mooie weer	thanks to the nice weather

door   'through, by' (see also 11.12)

door heel Nederland	throughout the Netherlands
Hij liep (dwars) door het bos.	He walked (right) through the forest.
door rood licht rijden	to drive through a red light
Het is door haar geschreven.	It was written by her.
Ik heb hem door Anneke leren kennen.	I got to know him through Anneke.
door en door stom	very stupid
door en door een dame	a real lady, a lady through and through

gedurende   'during' (see **tijdens**, a synonym)

gedurende het weekeinde	during the weekend
Hij was gedurende 3 weken ziek.	He was sick for 3 weeks.
(formal)	

in   'in, into'

Hij zit in de auto.	He is sitting in his car.
Ik zat in de spits.	I got caught in rush-hour traffic.
Ben je ooit in Engeland geweest?	Have you ever been to England?
in het Nederlands/Duits	in Dutch/German
Vertaal dit in het Frans!	Translate this into French.
in het algemeen (see **over**)	in general, generally
5 meter in de breedte	five metres wide/in width
in de bus/tram/trein (compare **met**)	on the bus/tram/train
Hij zit (in) een boek te lezen.	He's sitting reading a book.
Hij heeft zich in de vinger gesneden.	He's cut his finger. (see 11.21.2)
De slang heeft in zijn been gebeten.	The snake bit him on the leg.
in een boom klimmen	to climb a tree
in tweeën snijden	to cut in(to) two
Er gaan 16 ons in een Engels pond.	There are 16 ounces in/to an Eng. pound.
Hij is in de zestig.	He's in his sixties.
Er waren in de vijftig mensen.	There were fifty-odd people.
in het weekend	on/at the weekend
Dit was in de aanbieding.	This was on special.

jegens (lit.)   'to(wards)'

onze plicht jegens onze ouders	our duty to our parents
eerlijk zijn jegens mensen	to be honest with people

krachtens (lit.)   'by virtue of'

krachtens deze wet	under this law
krachtens zijn ambt	by virtue of his position/office

langs   'along, past'

langs het kanaal	along the canal
Ik reed langs jouw huis.	I drove past your house.
langs een andere route/weg (see **via**)	via another route/road
Kom een keer bij me langs!	Come and visit me some time.

met   'with'

When used with pronominal **er** (11.21.1, 15.3) or as a prefix with separable verbs (11.20.1) **met** becomes **mee**. In formal style it also occurs as **mede** in separable verbs, e.g. **mededelen = meedelen** 'to inform'.

We waren met z'n tweeën.	There were two of us.
met de post (also **per**)	by mail
met luchtpost	by airmail
met de auto/bus/tram/trein	by car/bus/tram/train
met dit weer	in this weather
met potlood schrijven	to write in pencil
met Pasen	at Easter
met Kerstmis/(de) Kerst	at Christmas time
Ik ben met vakantie. (see **op**)	I'm on vacation.
met of zonder (mayonaise)	with or without (mayonnaise) (i.e. when buying chips/fries)
De prijs steeg met 11%.	The price rose by 11%.

na   'after'

na het avondeten	after dinner
na achten	after eight
Melbourne is de grootste stad na Sydney.	After Sydney, Melbourne is the biggest city.
de op twee na grootste stad	the third largest city
na ontvangst van	on receipt of
de een na de ander	one after another
regel na regel	rule after rule

naar   'to' (places, see **aan** for people))

Ik ga naar Amsterdam.	I'm going to Amsterdam.
Ik ga naar huis.	I'm going home.
Ik ga naar boven/beneden/binnen/buiten.	I'm going upstairs/downstairs/inside/outside.
naar bed gaan	to go to bed
naar school gaan (see **op**)	to go to school
naar Parijs vertrekken	to leave for Paris
een steen naar iemand/iets gooien	to throw a stone at s.o./s.t.
naar iets grijpen	to grab at s.t.
Hij werd naar zijn vader vernoemd.	He was named after his father.
naar mijn mening	in my opinion
een film naar een roman van Dickens	a film of a novel by Dickens

naast   'next to'

Hij woont naast mij.	He lives next to me.
Naast tennis doet ze veel aan zwemmen.	Apart from tennis she also does a lot of swimming.

namens   'on behalf of'

Ik spreek namens alle aanwezigen.	I speak on behalf of all those present.

niettegenstaande   'in spite of' (see **ondanks**)

niettegenstaande het slechte weer	in spite of the bad weather

om   'around, for'

We zaten allemaal om de tafel.	We were all sitting around the table.
om de hoek	around the corner
Ik heb een gordel/stropdas/ halsketting om.	I have a belt/tie/necklace on. (see **aan** for ring)
De aarde draait om zijn as.	The earth turns on its axis.
Ik kan de kinderen niet om me heen hebben.	I can't have the kids around me.
om zich heen kijken	to look around
om tien uur	at ten o'clock
om die tijd van het jaar	at that time of (the) year
om de twee weken	every two weeks
om de andere week/boom	every other/second week/tree
De tijd is om.	(The) time is up.
oog om oog, tand om tand	an eye for an eye, a tooth for a tooth
om welke reden	for what reason
Ik heb het om jou gedaan.	I did it for your sake.
Ik ben om hem vroeg weggegaan.	I left early because of him.
Olifanten worden om hun ivoor gedood.	Elephants are killed for their ivory.
Hij deed het om de eer.	He did it for the honour.

ondanks   'in spite of, despite'

ondanks zijn ziekte	in spite of/despite his illness
desondanks	in spite of it/that

onder   'under, beneath'

onder het huis	under (neath) the house
bekend onder een andere naam	(well-)known under another name
onder Koning Willem I	under King William I
onder mijn voorganger	under my predecessor
onder de Duitse bezetting	during the German occupation
onder ons blijven	to remain between us (e.g. a secret)
Je bent onder vrienden.	You're among friends.
onder andere	among other things
onder het avondeten	during dinner
Onder het lezen ontdekte hij dat ...	While reading he discovered that ...
een dorpje onder Amsterdam	a village south of Amsterdam
Hij is onder de veertig.	He is under forty.
onder de vijftig minuten	under fifty minutes

ongeacht   'regardless of, irrespective of'

ongeacht het land van oorsprong	regardless of the/one's country of origin

op   'on'

In its basic meaning of 'on' Dutch **op** designates a horizontal 'on' (see **aan** for vertical 'on'). Otherwise its meanings are too diverse to define.

op (de) tafel	on the table
op school	at school
op (het) kantoor	at the office
op zee	at sea
op het platteland	in the country
op de hoek	on the corner
op de universiteit (see **aan**)	at the university (i.e. the campus)
op de gang (also **in**)	in the hall
op de bank/markt	at the bank/market
op het postkantoor/station	at the post-office/station
op het strand (see **aan**)	on the beach
op de voorgrond/achtergrond	in the foreground/background
het op een na grootste schip ter wereld	the second largest ship in the world (see 14.2.1.7)
op de foto	in the photo
Hij werkt op een fabriek.	He's working in a factory.

Ik woon op een gracht/de Prinsengracht.	I live on a canal/on the Prince's Canal.
op een feest	at a party
op een eiland	on an island
op Java/Kreta	in Java/Crete (i.e. islands that aren't countries)
op het tweede plaatje	in the second picture
iemand op de koffie uitnodigen	to invite s.o. for coffee
iemand op een bruiloft uitnodigen	to invite s.o. to a wedding
iemand op een diner trakteren	to treat s.o. to dinner
Hij had maar 5 cent op zak. (= **bij zich**)	He only had five cents on him.
in de nacht van vrijdag op zaterdag	during the night from Friday to Saturday
op vakantie (also **met**)	on holidays
op deze manier/wijze	in this way
op zoek naar	in search of
op afbetaling kopen	to hire-purchase
een aanval op	an attack on
een toast op de koningin	a toast to the queen
Hij ligt op sterven.	He is (in the process of) dying.
op z'n Frans/Nederlands etc.	à la française, the way the Dutch do etc.
op z'n vroegst/laatst	at the earliest/latest
op de maat van de muziek	in time to the music
Dat gebouw staat op instorten.	That building is about to collapse.
op dit uur	at this hour
de wet op het openbaar onderwijs	the public education bill/law
op een wenk van mij	at a sign from me
op (de) radio/(de) televisie.	on the radio/on television
op één voorwaarde	on one condition
Als kind heb ik altijd op klompen gelopen.	As a child I always used to wear clogs.
een klop op de deur	a knock at the door
Ze kookt op gas.	She cooks with gas.
op de fiets (also **met**)	by bike
op een hoogte van 2000 meter	at a height of 2,000 metres
een op de vijftig (mensen etc.)	one in every fifty (people etc.)
één telefoon op elke vijftig inwoners	one phone to every fifty inhabitants
Mijn auto rijdt een op tien.	My car does ten kilometres to the litre.
op twintigjarige leeftijd	at the age of twenty
(op) de drieëntwintigste	on the twenty-third

Al mijn geld is op.   All my money has gone (i.e. spent).
Er staat geen geld op de rekening.   There is no money in the account.

over   'over, via, about'

Het vliegtuig vliegt over de stad   The plane is flying above the city
  (heen).   (over).
Er liepen tranen over zijn wangen.   Tears were running down his
                                            cheeks.
Er waren over de honderd mensen.   There were over a hundred
                                            people.
overdag   during the day
Hij is over de zestig. (see **boven**) He's over sixty.
Het is al over achten.   It's already past eight o'clock.
vrijdag over een week   a week from Friday/Friday week
over vijftig jaar   in fifty years' time
over het algemeen (also **in**)   in general, generally
een boek/film over de oorlog   a book/film about the war
Dit boek gaat over de oorlog.   This book is about the war.
Je moet er niet over praten.   You mustn't talk about it.
Ik heb wat over.   I have something left.
De trein gaat over Leiden.   The train goes via Leiden.

per   'by, per'

per post/trein/tram (see **met**)   by mail/train/tram
5 keer per seconde/uur/jaar   five times a second/hour/year
Ze worden per dozijn verkocht.   They are sold by the dozen.

qua   'as far as . . . is concerned'

Hoe vind je dit boek qua presentatie? What do you think of this book as
                                            far as its presentation is
                                            concerned?

Qua aantal deelnemers was het een   As far as the number of
  succes.   participants is concerned, it
                                            was a success.

rond, rondom   'around'

Er staan mooie oude huizen rond   There are beautiful old houses
  het plein.   around the square.
Rond vijf uur beginnen we trek te   At about 5.00 we begin to get
  krijgen.   peckish.
rondom het vuur   around the fire
Rondom de stad loopt een singel.   A moat runs around the city.

sedert   'since, for' (see sinds[3])

sedert 12 mei	since the twelfth of May
sedert enige tijd	for some time

sinds   'since, for' (see sedert)

sinds de oorlog	since the war
sinds lange tijd	for a long time

te   'at, in'

This preposition, with the exception of the first example below, only occurs in standard expressions, in which case it is very frequently contracted with archaic case forms of the definite article (see **ten** or **ter**, 13.1). For the use of **te** with **om** before infinitives see 11.9.3.3.

te Amsterdam (lit.)	in Amsterdam
te paard	by horse/on horseback
te koop	for sale
Je bent f10 te goed.	You have ƒ10 to your credit.
en terecht	and rightly so
een schip te water laten	to launch a ship
te voorschijn komen	to appear
te binnen schieten	to occur (to s.o.)

tegen   'against'

Ajax speelt tegen Feyenoord.	A. is playing against F. (football clubs)
tegen de muur	against the wall
met mijn rug tegen de muur	with my back to the wall
Hij reed tegen een boom.	He drove into a tree.
tegen 8% rente	at 8% interest
tegen die prijs	at that price
Het is duizend tegen een.	It is a thousand to one (odds).
tegen acht uur	at about eight o'clock
Hij is tegen de vijtig.	He is about fifty.
Ik kan er niet tegen.	I can't stand it/It upsets me.
Ik heb er niets tegen.	I don't object (to it).
iets tegen iemand zeggen	to say s.t. to s.o.

---

[3] **Sinds** is more common than **sedert**.

tegenover   'opposite'

Hij woont tegenover een bank.	He lives opposite a bank.
recht/schuin tegenover	directly/diagonally opposite
Er zijn er 900 overleden in 1977 tegenover 1200 in 1978.	900 died in 1977 as against/ opposed to 1200 in 1978.
Hij is verlegen tegenover vrouwen.	He is shy with women.
Dat kun je niet doen tegenover je ouders.	You can't do that to your parents.

tijdens   'during' (see **gedurende**, a synonym)

tot   'until, till' (see 11.21.1)

When used with pronominal **er** (11.21.1, 15.3) or as a prefix with separable verbs (11.20.1) **tot** becomes **toe.**

Wij gaan alleen maar tot Amsterdam.	We are only going as far as Amsterdam.
tot nu toe, tot dusver	up till now
tot drie keer toe	up to three times
tot diep in de nacht	until late at night
Ze werden tot de laatste man gedood.	They were killed to the last man.
tot ziens	good-bye
tot en met (often written t/m)	up to and including
tot elke prijs	at any price
tot mijn verbazing/vreugde	to my amazement/joy
iemand overhalen tot stelen/meegaan	to talk s.o. into stealing/going along etc.

tussen   'between, among'

tussen de twee bomen	between the two trees
tussen deze mensen/bomen	among these people/trees
tussen 3 en 4 uur	between 3 and 4 o'clock
Dat moet tussen ons blijven.	That must stay between you and me.
Je moet kiezen tussen ...	You must choose between ...

uit   'out, out of, from'

uit een glas drinken	to drink from a glass
Hij komt uit Edam/België.	He comes from Edam/Belgium.

Hij is uit het dorp verdwenen.	He disappeared from the village.
een schilderij uit de 15e eeuw	a painting from the fifteenth century
Ik deed het uit liefdadigheid.	I did it out of charity.
uit wraak/jaloezie/vrees	out of revenge/jealousy/fear
iets uit eigen ervaring weten	to know s.t. from one's own experience
uit het Nederlands vertalen	to translate from Dutch
We gaan een dagje uit.	We are going out for a day.
De verloving is uit.	The engagement is off.
De kachel/het licht is uit.	The heater/light is off.
Heb je het boek al uit?	Have you finished the book?

van　　'of, from, off' (see also Possession 7.4)

Usually written with a small letter in people's names, e.g. **H. van den Berg.** (2.53)

Hij is net van Schiphol gekomen.	He has just come from Schiphol.[4]
de auto van mijn oom	my uncle's car
een tante van mij	an aunt of mine
een vriend van mijn moeder	a friend of my mother's
van het dak vallen	to fall off the roof
van 1990 tot 1997	from 1990 to 1997
negen van de tien mensen	nine out of every ten people
van plan zijn	to intend
van nut zijn	to be of use
Dit is van hout.	This is made of wood.
van brood leven	to live on bread
Hij is Nederlander van geboorte.	He is a Dutchman by birth.
iemand van naam kennen	to know somebody by name
Ik rammel/sterf van de honger.	I'm dying of hunger.
een schat van een meid	a really nice girl
een kast van een huis	an enormous house
van ja/nee zeggen	to say yes/no
Ik denk/meen van wel.	I think so.
Ik denk/meen van niet.	I don't think so.

---

[4] But **Hij is net uit Amsterdam gekomen** 'He has just come from Amsterdam' (see **uit**), Amsterdam is a city but Schiphol is an airport. If referring to where one comes 'from', i.e. in the sense of one's origins, **uit** is used (see **uit**), e.g. **Waar kom je vandaan? Ik kom uit Raalte/België.** 'Where do you come from? I come from Raalte/Belgium'. See **van . . . vandaan** under 13.2.3.

Note: The preposition **van** is often used colloquially before direct objects where it assumes a sort of partitive function (compare the use of French **de** in such cases):

Ik hoef niet meer van die lange omwegen te maken.
I no longer need to make long detours.

Ik heb van alles gezien.
I saw everything.

vanwege　'because of, on account of' (see **wegens**)

vanwege het weer	because of the weather
van overheidswege	on the part of the government

via　'via, from'

Hij gaat via Utrecht naar Amsterdam toe.	He is going to Amsterdam via Utrecht.
Ik heb het via mijn zuster gehoord.	I heard it indirectly from my sister.
Zij hoorde het via-via.	She heard it on the grapevine.

volgens　'according to, in . . . ('s) opinion'

volgens mij/hem	in my opinion/according to him
volgens de regels/wet	according to the rules/the law
Volgens mijn horloge is het vier uur.	By my watch it is four o'clock.
volgens artikel twee	in accordance with article two

voor　'for'

Ik heb iets voor je.	I have something for you.
voor de eerste keer	for the first time
voor alle zekerheid	for the sake of certainty
Hij is voor zijn leven geborgen.	He's fixed for life.
woord voor woord	word for word
stuk voor stuk	piece by piece
een voor een	one by one
Ik voor mij vond het lekker.	I personally found it delicious.
Ik heb het voor het avondeten gemaakt.	I made it for dinner.
iemand voor een diner uitnodigen	to invite s.o. to/for dinner
Ik heb het huis voor een jaar gehuurd.	I have rented the house for a year.
pal voor het postkantoor	right in front of the post-office

vóór   'before, in front of'

vóór het huis	in front of the house
Ik heb veel werk vóór me.	I have a lot of work ahead of me.
een eiland vóór de kust van ...	an island off the coast of ...
Het schip lag vóór Tokio.	The ship lay off Tokyo.
Ik heb het vóór het avondeten gemaakt.	I made it before dinner.

voorbij   'past, beyond'

Hij woont voorbij de kerk.	He lives past the church.

wegens   'because of, on account of' (see **vanwege**, which is more common is speech)

zonder   'without' (see 5.1.1(b))

een boek zonder kaft	a book without a cover
Hij was zonder hoed.	He didn't have a hat on.
Zonder u was het niet gelukt.	But for you it wouldn't have succeeded.
Ik kan niet zonder.	I can't do without it.

13.1   PREPOSITIONAL PHRASES

The following phrases made up of usually two prepositions and a noun are in common use, although several will be found predominantly in the written language. Those incorporating the preposition **te** usually have an enclitic form of **te** + **den** = **ten** or **te** + **der** = **ter**, these being the former definite articles in the dative case for masculine/neuter nouns and feminine nouns respectively (see chapter 4).[5] Sometimes the noun also takes a dative **-e**. Many of these expressions are commonly abbreviated, e.g. **i.p.v.** = **in plaats van** (see Appendix 3).

aan de hand van	on the basis of, judging from
aan de voet van	at the foot of
aan deze/die kant van	on this/that side of
aan weerskanten, -zijden van	on both sides of, on either side of
als gevolg van	as a result of
door gebrek aan	through lack of

---

[5] **Ter** as in **ter bevordering van** 'as a promotion of' and **ter verklaring van** 'as an explanation of' etc. is still productive with feminine abstracts ending in **-ing**.

door middel van	by means of
in het midden van	in the middle of
in naam van (or **namens**)	in the name of, on behalf of
in oorlog met	at war with
in plaats van	instead of
in ruil voor	in exchange for
in strijd met	contrary to, in defiance of
in tegenstelling tot	as opposed to, as distinct from
in vergelijking met	in comparison with/to
in weerwil van	in spite of
met behulp van	with the help of, by means of
met betrekking tot	with reference to
met ingang van	as from (dates)
met het oog op	in view/consideration of
met verwijzing naar	with reference to
naar aanleiding van	with reference to
onder auspiciën van	under the auspices of
onder invloed van	under the influence of
op grond van	on account of
op initiatief van	on the initiative of
op last van	by order of
uit hoofde van	on account of, owing to
te midden van	in the midst of
ter ere van	in honour of
ter gelegenheid van	on the occasion of
ter wille van	for the sake of
ten bate van	on behalf of, in aid of (charities)
ten bedrage van	to the amount of
ten behoeve van	on behalf of, in aid of
ten dienste van	for the use of
ten gevolge van	as a result of
ten gunste van	in favour of
ten huize van	at the home of
ten koste van	at the cost of
ten name van	in the name of
ten noorden van (or **benoorden**)	to the north of[6]
ten oosten van (or **beoosten**)	to the east of[6]
ten opzichte van	with regard to
ten tijde van	at the time of
ten voordele van	to the advantage of

---

[6] It is possible to use **benoorden, beoosten** etc., e.g. **benoorden de grote rivieren** = **ten noorden van de grote rivieren** 'north of the great rivers', but they are usually only found in the written language.

ten westen van (or **bewesten**)   to the west of[6]
ten zuiden van (or **bezuiden**)   to the south of[6]

13.2 NOTES ON PREPOSITIONS

13.2.1 PREPOSITIONS THAT FOLLOW NOUNS (POSTPOSITIONS)

A number of common prepositions can follow the nouns to which they refer in which case the direction of the action is emphasised rather than the place of the action. When followed immediately by the verb in subordinate clauses or by past participles or infinitives in main clauses, they can be confused with separable prefixes (see 11.20.1.1(d)):

Zij gaat de stad in.	She is going to town.
Hij ging de kamer uit.	He went out of the room.
Hij is het land uit gezet.	He was deported.
Hij kwam de kamer in/binnen.	He came into the room.
Roodkapje liep het bos helemaal door.	Little Red Riding Hood walked right through the forest.
De auto reed de hoek om.	The car drove around the corner.
Gaat u de eerste brug rechts over.	Cross the first bridge on the right.
We reden toen de hoofdweg op.	We then drove up onto the main road.
Ze voeren de zeeën over.	They sailed across the seas.
We fietsten het kanaal langs.	We cycled along the canal.
De jongens roeiden de rivier af.	The boys rowed down the river.
Hij gaat de berg op/af.	He is going up/down the mountain.
Je moet die kant op/uit.	You must go that way.

For prepositions following **ergens**, **nergens** and **overal** see 8.6.9.

13.2.2 USE OF **heen** WITH PREPOSITIONS

Several prepositions are used together with **heen** (which follows the noun) to indicate direction.[7] The meaning of a preposition + noun + **heen** is similar to that explained in 13.2.1 above but it may have a figurative meaning, as some of the following examples illustrate:

---

[7] **Heen** on its own, i.e. not used in combination with another preposition but as a separable prefix, is synonymous with **naartoe** (see 10.5) but is higher style:

We gaan er morgen heen/naartoe.
We are going there tomorrow.

Hij liep dwars door het perkje met bloemen heen.	He walked right through the flower bed.
door de eeuwen heen	over the centuries
langs elkaar heen praten	to talk at cross purposes
De kinderen renden om het park heen.	The kids ran around the park.
Hij keek om zich heen.	He looked around (him).
Het vliegtuig vloog over de stad heen.	The plane flew over the city.
Ik heb eroverheen gelezen.	It escaped me while reading.

13.2.3   DOUBLE PREPOSITIONS

Many of the prepositions given above can be used in combination with each other to further emphasize the position or direction of the action.

Hij is aan promotie toe.	He is due for a promotion.
Hij gaat naar huis toe.	He's going home. (see 10.5)
We gaan morgen naar Amsterdam toe.	We are going to Amsterdam tomorrow.
Ik ben net van Breda vandaan gekomen.	I've just come from Breda.
Het water stond tot aan zijn knieën.	The water was up to his knees.
achter in de tuin	at the bottom of the garden
Hij is achter in de twintig.	He is in his late twenties.
binnen in de schuur	inside the shed
boven op de kast	(up) on top of the cupboard
Dat gebeurde buiten mij om.	It happened without my knowledge.
midden in het bos	in the middle of the forest
Je gaat onder de brug door.	You go through under the bridge.
Hij kwam op me af.	He came up to me.
de op twee na grootste stad	the third largest city (see 14.2.1.7)
op Dolf na	except for Dolf
Hij is op winst uit.	He's out for a profit.
De klimop groeit tegen het huis op.	The ivy is growing up the house.
Hij reed tegen een muur aan.	He drove into a wall.
Het is net tegen blauw aan.	It is almost blue.
Hij reed tegen de wind in.	He was driving against the wind.
Dat was tegen alle verwachtingen in.	That was against all expectations.
Er lopen enkele drukke wegen tussen de woonwijken door.	A few busy roads run through the suburbs.
Ze begeleidden hem tot aan de grens.	They accompanied him up to the border.
tot nog toe, tot nu toe	up till now
nou, tot over drie weken	well, till three weeks from now

Tussen de huizen in staan bomen.	There are trees in between the houses.
vanaf volgende week	from next week
Ik kon het vanuit het raam zien.	I could see it from the window.
Ik kon het van het raam uit zien.	
tegen de stroom op zwemmen	to swim against the current
vóór in de auto	in the front of the car
Hij zat voor zich uit te kijken.	He was looking in front of him.
Ik heb iets voor bij de pudding.	I have s.t. to have with (the) dessert.
Het is voor na het scheren.	It is used after shaving.

Note: Sentences such as the following seem to be utilizing double prepositions as dealt with here but are in fact separable verbs (see 11.20.1) followed by a prepositional object (see 11.21) , i.e. **afvallen van**, **meegaan met**:

Hij viel van de ladder af.
He fell off the ladder.

Ze gingen met hem mee.
They went with him.

Many of the above prepositional pairs are written together, in which case they function as adverbs of both motion and place (see 10.5). The Dutch themselves are often confused here as to what is written together and what is written as two words:

Ik heb het achter in de auto gevonden.
I found it in the back of the car.

Ik heb het achterin gevonden.
I found it in the back.

achterin	in the back	**middenin**	in the middle
achterom	around the back	**onderaan**	at the bottom (of a
achteruit	backwards		page)
binnenin	inside	**onderin**	at the bottom (e.g.
bovenaan	at the top (of a		of a cupboard)
	page)	**tussenin**	in between
bovenop	on top	**voorin**	in the front

13.2.4 OMISSION OF ENGLISH 'OF'

It should be noted that the preposition 'of' is sometimes left untranslated in Dutch. This occurs in two cases:

1 with nouns indicating a quantity of the noun that follows which is consequently either in the plural or is an uncountable noun:

een fles bier	a bottle of beer
een doosje lucifers	a box of matches
een kist appels	a box of apples
een krat bier	a crate of beer
een lijst namen	a list of names
een groep mensen	a group of people

Note also:

een soort (van) vaas	a sort of vase
honderden/duizenden mensen	hundreds/thousands of people

2 with geographic names of the following kind:

het eiland Rhodos	the island of Rhodes
de provincie Utrecht	the province of Utrecht
de Republiek Suriname	the Republic of Surinam
het Koninkrijk België	the Kingdom of Belgium

14 NUMERALS (telwoorden)

14.1 CARDINAL NUMBERS (hoofdtelwoorden)

(on)even nummers '(un)even numbers'
(on)even getallen '(un) even numbers' (of houses, car registration
   plates etc.)
Drie is een oneven getal 'Three is an uneven number'.

0	**nul**	13	**dertien**
1	**een**[1]	14	**veertien**[3]
2	**twee**	15	**vijftien**
3	**drie**	16	**zestien**
4	**vier**	17	**zeventien**
5	**vijf**	18	**achttien**
6	**zes**	19	**negentien**
7	**zeven**[2]	20	**twintig**
8	**acht**	21	**eenentwintig**
9	**negen**	22	**tweeëntwintig**[4]
10	**tien**	23	**drieëntwintig**[4]
11	**elf**	24	**vierentwintig**
12	**twaalf**	25	**vijfentwintig**

[1] The numeral **een** is written **één** in contexts where it could be read as the indefinite article or simply to emphasise that it means 'one' and not 'a/an':

Ik heb maar één broertje en dat is meer dan genoeg.
I have only one younger brother and that is more than enough.

See 2.3.1, footnote 4.

[2] When pronouncing numbers deliberately as in giving telephone numbers, all derivatives of the word **zeven** are commonly pronounced **zeuven**, **zeuventien**, **zeuventig**, etc. to avoid confusion with **negen**. In The Netherlands, as in so many European countries, a seven is usually handwritten with a cross stroke, but is not printed that way, i.e. 7. This is to avoid possible confusion with 1, which is often written with a longer tail at the top than in English-speaking countries, but not as long as in Germany.

[3] Note that **veertien** and **veertig** deviate for historical reasons in spelling and pronunciation (see also footnote 5 below) from the basic cardinal numeral **vier**.

[4] In numerals combining **twee** and **drie** followed by **en**, a dieresis is required on the **en** to distinguish the separate syllable. The new spelling rules prescribe that a dieresis only be used in derived words, not compounds – these numerals are the only exception to that rule (see 2.3.2).

[5] The initial letters of the numerals 40, 50, 60 and 70 are unvoiced for historical reasons, i.e. one says **feertig**, **fijftig**, **sestig**, **seventig**. Combined with other numerals, the **v** in **veertig** and **vijftig** may be pronounced **v**, but in such cases the **s** in **zestig** and **zeventig** remains **s**.

[6] Note the initial **t** in **tachtig**. It has historical connections with footnote 5.

26	**zesentwintig**	101	**honderd één**[8, 9]
27	**zevenentwintig**[2]	153	**honderd drieënvijftig**[8, 9]
28	**achtentwintig**	266	**tweehonderd zesenzestig**[8, 9]
29	**negenentwintig**	1000	**duizend**[7]
30	**dertig**	1008	**duizend acht**[8, 9]
40	**veertig**[3, 5]	5010	**vijfduizend tien**[8]
50	**vijftig**[5]	6788	**zesduizend zevenhonderd achtentachtig**[8]
60	**zestig**[5]	200,000	**tweehonderdduizend**[8]
70	**zeventig**[5]	1,000,000	**één miljoen**
80	**tachtig**[6]	2,000,000	**twee miljoen**
90	**negentig**	one billion	**één miljard** (i.e. one thousand million)
100	**honderd**[7]		

14.1.1   NOTES ON CARDINALS

14.1.1.1   From 1,100 to 9,999 the Dutch commonly count in hundreds but may also use thousands as in English, e.g. 6,300 can be read **drieënzestighonderd** or **zesduizend driehonderd**, but even thousands are said in thousands, i.e. 2,000 is **tweeduizend** and not ***twintighonderd** (see 14.9 for hundreds in dates). For all numerals from 10,000 on, the same system as English is applied, e.g. 10,634 **tienduizend zeshonderd vierendertig**.

14.1.1.2   The Dutch use a full-stop when writing thousands, not a comma, but a comma may be used where we use a full-stop, i.e. instead of a decimal point: **10.000** and **28.000,00** (English 28,000.00) Thus a price is written like this: **ƒ25,95** (see 14.3).

---

[7] **Honderd** and **duizend** render 'a hundred' and 'a thousand'. **Éénhonderd** and **éénduizend** render 'one hundred' and 'one thousand', but are only used when an emphasis is required. But note that **een** 'a' or **één** 'one' are always used before **miljoen** and **miljard**.

[8] One will often find mistakes in Dutch texts with regard to the division of numerals over 100 if they are written out in full. The rule is that a space is left after the hundreds and/or thousands, but not between the multiples of the hundreds and/or thousands, e.g. **honderd twee** but **tweehonderd**. To write numerals together as in German is considered unwieldy, but such long numerals are as rarely written in Dutch as in English on the whole so one is seldom faced with the problem in practice.

[9] Note that no 'and' is inserted between **honderd/duizend** and the figure that follows. One does in fact hear **driehonderd en tien** or **duizend en zes** but this **en** is only found before the numerals 1 to 12 and is never necessary. But **en** *is* used in such cases in certain standard expressions:

Verhalen van duizend-en-een-nacht
Stories of 1001 nights

Ze praatten over honderd-en-een dingen.
They talked about a thousand and one things.

14.1.1.3

een goede veertig	a good forty, at least forty
een dikke honderd	a good hundred
een kleine zestig	no more than sixty
onder/over (boven) de zestig	under/over sixty
in de vijftig	about fifty
zo'n twintig jaar geleden	about twenty years ago
een jaar of twintig geleden	about twenty years ago

The last expression is very common in all sorts of contexts: **een man of tien** 'about ten people', **een stuk of zes** 'about ten books/trees/chairs etc.', **een boek of twaalf** 'about twelve books'.

14.1.1.4 Telephone numbers:
When reading a telephone number aloud it is common to divide the figure into couplets and read **tweeëndertig veertig eenenzestig** – 32 40 61, but it is also possible to read the numbers out individually. Nowadays Dutch phone numbers generally look as follows: 030-252 37 02: the first number is **het netnummer** or **het kengetal** of the town concerned and the second is **het abonneenummer**, many of which until recently consisted of the last six digits. Three quarters of all Dutch phone numbers were changed in 1995. All now consist of ten digits (**tien cijfers**), a **netnummer** of three digits and an **abonneenummer** of seven digits, or each number of four and six figures respectively. If an **abonneenummer** now contains seven digits and one does not read out the digits one by one, it is commonly read as follows as the first digit in many cases was added to the original number:

zeven zesenzeventig twaalf drieënvijftig   776 12 53

But geneally speaking whether one reads the numbers out as above or as **zeven zeven zes één twee vijf drie** seems to be a matter of personal preference.

14.1.1.5 'One in every ten (people)' etc. is said **een op de tien (mensen)**, but 'nine out of every ten (people)' etc. is **negen van de tien (mensen)**.

14.1.1.6 The English word 'number' can be rendered in several ways in Dutch:

het telwoord	is a numeral as in **hoofdtelwoorden** 'cardinals' and **rangtelwoorden** 'ordinals'.
het nummer	is a number allotted to a person, room, place etc. as in **telefoonnummer** or **Hij woont op nummer 5** 'He lives at number 5'.

het cijfer	is a figure, cipher (also a mark at school).
het getal	is an arithmetical number, **getallen optellen** 'to add up numbers'.
het aantal	refers to a quantity, i.e. **een aantal boeken** 'a number of books'.

Note: Strictly speaking **een aantal** 'a number of' + plural noun requires a singular verb, but it is commonly followed by a verb in the plural:

Een aantal mensen heeft /hebben het al gezien.
A number of people have already seen it.

Een aantal mensen is/zijn verdronken.
A number of people drowned.

14.1.2   DERIVATIVES OF CARDINALS

14.1.2.1   **Een** occurs as an inflected adjective, e.g. **van de ene dag op de andere** 'from one day to the next'.

14.1.2.2   **Honderd, duizend** and **miljoen** take an **-en** ending when they mean 'hundreds/thousands/millions of':

Duizenden mensen gingen naar het strand.
Thousands of people went to the beach.

14.1.2.3   **Met ons/z'n tweeën, drieën, vieren, vijven, zessen**, etc. Such expressions are very common and mean 'two of us/them' etc. Note that expressions with **ons**, which is less common than **z'n**, must have a **wij** as the subject of the sentence whereas those with **z'n** (never **zijn**) can have **wij** or **zij** as the subject:

We gingen met ons/z'n vieren naar de bioscoop.
Four of us went to the movies.

Zij hebben het met z'n tienen gedaan. (also **met hun tienen**)
Ten of them did it/There were ten of them who did it.

Theoretically any numeral can bear this ending (e.g. **met z'n vijfenvijftigen** 'fifty-five of them') but it is only common with lower numerals. It is in fact the only way the Dutch have of expressing 'There were five of us/them.'

14.1.2.4   A more intimate and colloquial form of the above is **met z'n tweetjes, drietjes**, etc. Note too **in z'n/d'r eentje** 'on his/her own'. The

-en ending is also found in expressions such as **een van ons tweeën** and in **in tweeën/drieën/vieren/vijven/zessen snijden** 'to cut in two/three' etc. These forms are also used in expressions of time (see 14.8).

14.1.2.5   Another derivative is **tweeling, drieling, vierling** etc. for 'twins', 'triplets', 'quadruplets' etc. These words take a singular verb:

Ze is in verwachting van een tweeling.
She is expecting twins.

Vandaag is er in Leiden een zesling geboren.
Sextuplets were born in Leiden today.

Note the following:

Ik ben er een van een tweeling.
I am a twin.

14.1.2.6   Note the use of the suffix **-tal** in the following expressions:

een dertigtal/veertigtal etc.
about 40 altogether

het elftal
the (football) team

Ik heb een vijftigtal leerlingen in de klas.
I have about fifty students in my class.

Note also **tientallen** + a plural noun meaning 'tens of': **tientallen mensen** 'tens of people', better expressed in English as 'dozens of people'.

14.1.2.7   **Enerlei**, **tweeërlei**, **drieërlei**, etc. mean 'of one/two/three kind(s)' but sound somewhat stilted whereas **allerlei** 'of all kinds/all kinds of' is commonly used.

14.1.2.8   **Het dubbele, driedubbele, vierdubbele**, etc. render 'twice/three/four times as much':

Ik heb het vijfdubbele betaald.
I paid five times as much.

Note the verbs **verdubbelen** 'to double', **verdrievoudigen/-dubbelen** 'to treble'.

14.2   ORDINAL NUMBERS (rangtelwoorden)

1st	**eerste**	22nd	**tweeëntwintigste**
2nd	**tweede**[10]	23rd	**drieëntwintigste**
3rd	**derde**	24th	**vierentwintigste**
4th	**vierde**	25th	**vijfentwintigste**
5th	**vijfde**[11]	26th	**zesentwintigste**
6th	**zesde**[11]	27th	**zevenentwintigste**
7th	**zevende**	28th	**achtentwintigste**
8th	**achtste**	29th	**negenentwintigste**
9th	**negende**	30th	**dertigste**
10th	**tiende**	40th	**veertigste**
11th	**elfde**[11]	50th	**vijftigste**
12th	**twaalfde**[11]	60th	**zestigste**
13th	**dertiende**	70th	**zeventigste**
14th	**veertiende**	80th	**tachtigste**
15th	**vijftiende**	90th	**negentigste**
16th	**zestiende**	100th	**honderdste**
17th	**zeventiende**	101st	**honderd eerste**[12]
18th	**achttiende**	121st	**honderd eenentwintigste**[12]
19th	**negentiende**	1000th	**duizendste**
20th	**twintigste**	8452nd	**achtduizend vierhonderd**
21st	**eenentwintigste**		**tweeënvijftigste**[12]
		1,000,000th	**miljoenste**

All ordinals from 'twentieth' on end in **-ste** in Dutch. Ordinals can be used as nouns or as adjectives and always preserve the final **-e**, i.e. they are invariable regardless of the number and gender of the noun that follows, e.g. **een tweede man** 'a second man', **een tweede huis** 'a second house' (compare **een grote man** and **een rood huis**).

14.2.1   NOTES ON ORDINALS

14.2.1.1   In certain standard expressions ordinals are found with the older case ending **-en**, e.g. **ten eersten male** 'for the first time', **ten tweeden male** 'for the second time'.

---

[10] **Tweede** actually contradicts the spelling rules of Dutch; in such an open syllable one would expect *twede. It is the only exception to the rule.

[11] In these ordinals the **f** or **s** preceding the **-de** ending is voiced under influence of the following voiced sound, i.e. pronounced **zezde**, **elvde** etc. (compare 11.1.2.1)

[12] Note the omission of 'and' from the Dutch translation of 'one hundred and twenty-first', but from 101st up to 112th (and all other hundreds and thousands) **en** can be inserted, although it is usually omitted, i.e. **honderd (en) eerste** '101st', **tweehonderd (en) zevende** '207th', **duizend (en) tiende** '1010th'.

14.2.1.2 The ordinals are often used as follows when listing points, i.e. firstly, secondly, thirdly, finally: **ten eerste**, **ten tweede**, **ten derde**, **ten laatste**.

14.2.1.3 Expressions such as 'every tenth tree/week' can be translated literally as **elke/iedere tiende boom/week** but are also commonly rendered as **Om de tiende boom is geveld** 'Every tenth tree has been felled'; **om de tien weken** 'every ten weeks', but note that in this expression 'second' is expressed by **andere** not **tweede**, e.g. **om de andere week** 'every second week' (= **om de week**).

14.2.1.4 **Hoeveel** and **zoveel** can also take the ordinal ending **-ste**.

De hoeveelste bezoeker is zij? (see. 14.9)
What number visitor is she?

Hij heeft me voor de zoveelste keer opgebeld.
He rang me up for the umpteenth time.

14.2.1.5 Foreign kings are always denoted by the ordinal as in English:

Karel de Vijfde, **Elisabeth de Tweede**

But the three Dutch kings (Willem I, II and III) are referred to by the cardinal numeral, i.e. **Koning Willem II** (pronounced **twee**).

14.2.1.6 The various English abbreviations 'st', 'nd' and 'th' can all be rendered in Dutch by **e**, e.g. **1e**, **2e**, **123e** etc., but one also finds **1ste**, **23ste**, and **2de.** There is little consistency here.

14.2.1.7 The Dutch express 'the second largest', 'the fourth most important' etc. by **de/het op** [cardinal numeral] **na** [superlative adjective], i.e. literally 'the with the exception of one/two/three etc. + superlative adjective':

Het op een na grootste schip
The second largest boat

De op drie na belangrijkste operazanger
The fourth most important opera singer

The following alternative word order is also possible:

Op een na het grootste schip
Op drie na de belangrijkste operazanger

14.2.1.8 **Andermaal** 'a second time' is used at auctions: **eenmaal, andermaal, verkocht** 'going, going, gone'.

14.3   FRACTIONS (**breukgetallen**)

1/4	**een kwart**[13]
1/2	**een half**[14]
1 1/2	**anderhalf (-ve)**[14]
2 1/2	**twee-en-een-half (-ve)**[14]
1/8	**een achtste (deel)**
2/3	**twee derde**[15] (**van de mensen etc.**)
3/8	**drie achtste**
1/16	**een zestiende (deel)**

0,5%	**nul komma vijf procent**[16]	('point five per cent')
1,8%	**een komma acht procent**	('one point eight percent')

---

[13] **een kwartier** (n)   1/4 of an hour (see 14.8)
een kwartaal (n)   a quarter (a period of three months)
een kwartje (n)   25 cents (Dutch currency only)

[14] The English word 'half' causes difficulties because the noun and the adjective in Dutch are different words unlike English, i.e. **de helft, half**. The way the two are used is best illustrated by examples:

de helft van de mensen	half the people
de helft van de fles	half the bottle
de halve fles	

Hij heeft de helft van de appel opgegeten.	He ate half the apple.
Hij heeft de halve appel opgegeten.	
Hij heeft de appel voor de helft opgegeten.	

Ik heb de helft van het boek al uit.	I have already read half the book.
Ik heb het halve boek al uit.	

voor de halve prijs	for half the price
voor de helft van de prijs	

'One and a half' is expressed by **anderhalf**, which behaves like a normal adjective taking **-e** in cases where the adjective is normally inflected:

anderhalf uur	one and a half hours
anderhalve meter	one and a half metres

Notice that **anderhalf, twee-en-een-half (-ve)** etc. are always followed by a singular noun: **drie-en-een-halve week** 'three and a half weeks'. In such expressions the **een** is usually swallowed in speech and hardly heard.

[15] 'One tenth of a pound' is **één tiende pond**. Note the use of the singular with fractions:

Twee derde van de bevolking is in de oorlog gestorven.
Two thirds of the population died in the war.

A plural of such fractions is possible if one refers to the parts as separate parts:

Twee derden van de taart zijn verkocht.
Two thirds of the cake have been sold.

Note also the use of a singular verb after a fraction or a percentage followed by a plural noun:

Ongeveer een derde/30% van de Nederlanders woont in een eigen huis.
About a third/30% of the Dutch live in a home of their own.

[16] One also hears **percent** and the noun is always **percentage** (n).

14.4 ARITHMETIC (**rekenen**)

optellen	to add	**4 plus/en 4 is 8**
aftrekken van	to subtract from	**4 min 2 is 2**
vermenigvuldigen met	to multiply by	**2 keer/maal 3 is 6**
delen door	to divide by	**10 gedeeld door 2 is 5**
tot 10 tellen	to count to 10	

'Ten squared' is **tien kwadraat** and 'ten to the power of seven' etc. is **tien tot de zevende macht**.

14.5 TEMPERATURE

1°   **één graad**
10°   **tien graden (Celsius)**
12°   **twaalf graden onder/boven nul**
Het heeft vannacht 12° (twaalf graden) gevroren or
We hebben vannacht 12° vorst gehad.
It was 12° below last night.

de maximum-, minimimtemperatuur	the maximum/minimum temperature
de gemiddelde temperatuur	the average temperature

14.6 AGE

Hoe oud ben je (bent u)?	How old are you?
Hij is pas tien (jaar oud).	Hij is only ten (years old).
Hij was nog maar tien (jaar oud).	He was only ten. (now dead)
Wat is je geboortedatum?	What is your date of birth?
Wanneer ben je (bent u) geboren?	When were you born?
Ik ben (op) tien maart geboren.	I was born on the tenth of March.
Ik ben (op) twaalf augustus jarig.	My birthday is on August the twelfth.
op veertienjarige (14-jarige) leeftijd	at the age of fourteen
op mijn/zijn etc. veertiende jaar	at the age of fourteen
tussen mijn/zijn etc. twaalfde en mijn/zijn etc. eenentwintigste	from the age of twelve to twenty-one
tussen (de) achttien en (de) twintig	between eighteen and twenty
Hij is in de zestig.	He is in his sixties.
een man van begin veertig	a man in his early forties
een man van ver in de zestig	a man in his late sixties
een man van achter in de zestig	a man in his late sixties
Hij is nog geen zestig.	He is not yet sixty.
een man van boven de vijftig	a man over fifty

een man van onder de vijftig	a man under fifty
Hij is over/onder de vijftig.	He's over/under fifty.
Hij is ruim veertig (jaar oud).	He is a good forty (years old).
Hij is een jaar of veertig (oud).	He is about forty.
Hij is midden veertig/rond de 45.	He is in his mid-forties.
de vijfenzestigplusser (65-plusser)	the pensioner
de tiener	the teenager
de eenendertigjarige etc.	the thirty-one-year-old etc.
de tachtigjarige.	the octogenarian
(de) minderjarig(e)	(the) minor
(de) volwassen(e)	(the) adult
een man van middelbare leeftijd	a middle-aged man

14.7 MONEY

een/één cent (c), **twee cent**, etc.	
een stuiver (c)	= **vijf cent**
een dubbeltje (n)	= **tien cent**
een kwartje (n)	= **vijfentwintig cent**
een/één gulden (c), **twee gulden,** etc.	
een rijksdaalder (c)	= **twee gulden vijftig**
een tientje (n)	= **tien gulden**

14.7.1 NOTES

***14.7.1.1* Cent/gulden** are always used in the singular when quoting prices. The plural **guldens** is used to refer to several one guilder coins whereas **centen**, one cent coins, no longer exist, e.g.

> **Geeft u mij alstublieft twee guldens en twee kwartjes voor deze rijksdaalder.**
> Please give me two guilders and two quarters for this rijksdaalder.

One cent coins were abolished in 1980, making **een stuiver** (five cents) the smallest available coin. Nevertheless Dutch prices still look as follows:

> **ƒ2,92** which is rounded off downwards (**afgerond naar beneden**).
> **ƒ5,93** which is rounded off upwards (**afgerond naar boven**).

Foreign currencies are also usually expressed in the singular when quoting prices: **tien pond, vijf frank, elf mark**, etc. Exceptions: **tien peseta's** 'ten pesetas', **vijf kronen** 'five crowns'.

14.7.1.2 The abbreviation for guilder is *f*, e.g. *f*10. It is derived from the word **florijn**, a currency unit used in the Netherlands in former times; compare the use of £ (derived from L for libra) for pounds in English.

14.7.1.3 Prices are written with commas, not decimal points: *f*12,50 (pronounced **twaalf [gulden] vijftig [cent]**), but the word **cent** is not necessary and not commonly expressed; compare $10.50, expressed as 'ten [dollars] fifty [cents]'. Note **5 gulden zoveel** '5 guilders odd'.

14.7.1.4 All the terms below occur in colloquial language. The word **piek** is used for guilder, (compare 'quid' and 'buck'), e.g. **Het kostte 10 piek**. In a similar way the word **ton** is used for 100,000 guilders, e.g. **Hij verdient een halve ton/vijf ton** 'He earns *f*50,000/*f*500,000. The word **mille** is used for thousands, e.g. **Het kostte twee mille** 'It cost *f*2,000'. The word **daalder** means *f*1.50, e.g. **Op de markt is je gulden een daalder waard** 'At the market your guilder is worth a guilder fifty.' And finally a **rijksdaalder** is referred to as **een riks** or **een knaak**.

14.7.1.5 Note the way the following is expressed:

Hij verdient *f*950 in de maand (per maand)/in de week (per week).
He earns *f*950 a month/a week.

14.8 TIME

Hoe laat is het?	What is the time?
Het is één uur.	It is one o'clock.
Het is vijf over een.[17]	It is five past one.
Het is kwart over één.	It is a quarter past one.
Het is tien voor half twee.[18]	It is twenty past one.
Het is vijf voor half twee.[17]	It is twenty-five past one.
Het is half twee.[19]	It is half past one.
Het is vijf over half twee.[17]	It is twenty-five to two.
Het is tien over half twee.[17]	It is twenty to two.
Het is kwart voor twee.	It is a quarter to two.
Het is tien voor twee.	It is ten to two.

---

[17] Regionally **na** is used instead of **over** in telling the time.
[18] It is also possible to say **twintig/vijfentwintig over één** and **twintig/vijfentwintig voor twee**, as in English.
[19] **Half twee, half drie** etc. are often also written as **halftwee, halfdrie**.

14.8.1   NOTES

14.8.1.1   Expressions of time

om acht uur	at eight o'clock
om acht uur precies	at exactly eight o'clock
stipt om acht uur	at exactly eight o'clock
klokslag acht uur	at exactly eight o'clock
om een uur of acht	at about eight
omstreeks acht uur	at about eight
rond acht uur	at about eight
tegen acht (uur)	at about eight
kort na acht (uur)	shortly after eight

14.8.1.2   There are also a number of expressions which add an **-en** ending to the numeral. They are frequently heard but can be avoided by using the alternatives given above:

Het is al na/over drieën, vijven etc.
It is already past three, five etc.

Het was intussen bij zessen.
It was six o'clock by then.

tegen achten
at about eight

kort na achten
just after eight

14.8.1.3   Remember that **een kwartier** in itself means 'a quarter of an hour':

Ik heb een kwartier gewacht.
I waited for a quarter of an hour.

drie kwartier
three quarters of an hour

vijf kwartier, but also **een uur en een kwartier**
one and a quarter hours

14.8.1.4   'A.m.' and 'p.m.' are rendered by **vm** and **nm**, abbreviations of **(des) voormiddags** and **(des) namiddags**. They are too formal for the spoken language, however. In natural speech one would say **om zes uur 's morgens/'s ochtends/'s avonds, om één uur 's nachts/in de nacht**, depending on the time of day.

14.8.1.5

Mijn horloge loopt voor/achter/goed.
My watch is fast/slow/right.

Ik heb het vier uur.
My watch says four o'clock/It's four by me.

14.8.1.6 Note that **keer, kwartier, jaar** and **uur** (all neuter nouns and perchance all ending in 'r') are not used in the plural after numerals or after **een paar** 'a few' and **hoeveel** 'how many', although **jaren** and **uren** can be used to emphasise duration:

Ik heb drie uur zitten lezen.
I sat reading for three hours.

Ik ben er een paar keer geweest.
I've been there a few times.

Hij heeft drie jaar in die fabriek gewerkt.
He worked in that factory for three years.

Hij heeft drie lange jaren in die fabriek gewerkt. (emphatic because of **lange**)
He worked in that factory for three long years.

But after indefinite pronouns used adjectivally like **enkele** and **enige**, **jaar** and **uur** are used in the plural:

Ze hebben enkele uren rondgewandeld.
They walked around for several hours.

Minuut and **seconde** (both common gender nouns) are always used in the plural after numerals, e.g. **vijf minuten geleden** 'five minutes ago', **drie seconden later** 'three seconds later'.

14.8.1.7

één keer in het uur/per uur; om het uur	once an hour
drie keer in de week/per week	three times a week
op het hele (halve) uur	on the hour (half hour)
tien over heel (half)	ten past the hour (the half hour)
tien over het hele/halve uur	ten past the hour (the half hour)

14.9 DATES

zondag (zo.)	**dinsdag (di.)**	**donderdag (do.)**	**zaterdag (za.)**
maandag (ma.)	**woensdag (wo.)**	**vrijdag (vr.)**	

januari (jan.)	mei	september (sept.)
februari (feb.)	juni[20]	oktober (okt.)
maart (mrt.)	juli[20]	november (nov.)
april (apr.)	augustus[21] (aug.)	december (dec.)

Days of the week and months of the year are nowadays written with small letters but are found in older texts with capital letters.

begin april	at the beginning of April
half/medio maart	halfway through March, mid-March
eind mei	at the end of May

It is important to note the following usage of cardinals and ordinals with regard to dates in Dutch. When the month is mentioned the cardinal is usually used, when not, then the ordinal, e.g. **Het is drie mei** 'It is the third of May', **Het is de derde** 'It is the third', but it is not incorrect to say **de derde mei**.

'On Friday the twenty-second of September' is **(op) vrijdag tweeëntwintig september**. The abbreviation at the top of a letter, for instance, is thus **vrijdag, 22 sept. 1997**; neither an **e/ste/de** nor a full-stop (as in German) follows the 22 as this is a cardinal, not an ordinal numeral. The complete abbreviation is written **22-9-97**, or because of computerisation these days also **22-09-97**.

Note the idioms **De hoeveelste is het vandaag?** 'What is the date today?'

The English word 'date' is rendered in two ways in Dutch: 22-9-97 is a **datum** (c) and 1997 is a **jaartal** (n) 'date'. As in English, when reading **jaartallen** aloud it is not usual to insert the word **honderd**: **negentien (honderd) zevenennegentig** 'nineteen (hundred and) ninety-seven'. If **honderd** is inserted, note that the 'and' in 'nineteen hundred and seventy-seven' remains untranslated.

in de zestiger jaren	in the sixties.
in de jaren zestig	in the sixties
in vijf jaar tijd	in five years' time. (i.e. in the course of five years)
over vijf jaar	in five years' time. (i.e. from now)
rond de eeuwwisseling	at the turn of the century.

14.10   WEIGHTS

het gram
het ons

---

[20] At times confusion arises in speech between **juni** and **juli** in which case they are pronounced slowly with the emphasis on the final syllable.

[21] The stress is on the penultimate syllable: **augústus**.

het pond (i.e. **een halve kilo** or **500 gram**; an English pound is only 454 grams)
de kilo

These weights are always used in the singular after numerals (as are **kwartier, uur, jaar** and **keer**), e.g. **vijf pond, twee ons** '200 grams'.
Fractions of these weights are expressed as follows:

één tiende gram	one tenth of a gram
anderhalf ons	150 grams
twee-en-een half ons, 250 gram, een half pond	250 grams
een halve kilo, een pond, 500 gram	500 grams
anderhalf pond, 750 gram	750 grams

Neither **pond** nor **ons** are official measures any more but are still very commonly used. It is very common for sliced meats, for example, to be sold by the 100 grams and a customer commonly asks for **één/twee/drie ons ham** '100/200/300 grams of ham'. Note also **een klein pondje**, a humorous alternative to **iets minder dan een pond** 'a bit less than a pound' and **ruim een pond** 'a good pound' (i.e. a little over a pound). One says *f*1,50 per pond/per kilo etc. or **een tientje het pond/de kilo**.

These days people usually refer to their own weight in kilos, e.g. **Ik weeg 70 kilo** 'I weigh seventy kilos'. Older people may still say their weight in pounds and it is still the norm to refer to a new-born baby's weight in pounds, although grams are used for tiny babies, e.g. **Het kind weegt zes pond/twaalfhonderd vijftig gram** 'The child weighs six pounds/1250 grams'. **Aankomen** 'to gain weight' and **afvallen** 'to lose weight' are both conjugated with **zijn** (see 11.7.2.1, footnote 18):

Ik ben 10 kilo aangekomen/afgevallen.
I have gained/lost 10 kilos.

Note the following alternative, impersonal way of expressing weight gain:

Er is tien kilo bijgekomen. (i.e. **bij mijn gewicht**)
I've put on ten kilos.

14.11 MEASUREMENTS

14.11.1 LENGTH, HEIGHT

de lengte	length (of objects), height (of people)
Hoe lang bent u?	How tall are you?
Ik ben 1,72 lang.	I am one one point seven two metres tall.
	(pronounced **één meter tweeënzeventig**)

The height of a tree, building etc. is **de hoogte**, e.g. **Hoe hoog is die boom?** 'How tall is that tree?'

If using imperial measurements, which the Dutch at home in Holland would never do (except in historical contexts), the words **voet** 'foot/feet' and **duim** 'inch/inches' are used.

Length up to one metre is usually expressed in centimetres.

Note: **de centimeter** 'the tape measure'.

de breedte	width
de grootte	size (i.e. largeness)
de maat	(shoe, shirt) size

14.11.2   SQUARE AND CUBIC MEASUREMENTS

vijf bij vijf (meter)	five by five (metres)
drie vierkante meter	three square metres
zes kubieke meter	six cubic metres

14.11.3   DISTANCE

Distances are measured in kilometres in Holland and the word **kilometer**, like **centimeter** and **meter**, is never used in the plural after numerals:

We hebben vandaag 20 kilometer gereden.
We drove 20 kilometres today.

But note **honderden/duizenden kilometers** 'hundreds/thousands of kilometres'.

Mijl (c) 'mile' can be used when talking of distances in English-speaking countries, e.g. **tien mijl** 'ten miles'.

Petrol consumption of a car is rendered as follows:

Mijn auto rijdt een op vijftien (i.e. **één liter op vijftien kilometer**).
My car does fifteen kilometres to the litre.

Speed is expressed as follows:

Hij reed tachtig (kilometer per uur).
He was driving (at) 80 kilometres an hour.

Compare:

Hij reed met tachtig (kilometer per uur) de rivier in.
He drove into the river at eighty kilometres an hour.

14.12 PLAYING CARDS

schoppen	spades
ruiten	diamonds
klaver	clubs
harten	hearts

de schoppenaas, **-heer**, **-vrouw**, **-boer**, **-negen** 'the ace, king, queen, jack, nine of spades'.

One can also say **twee harten**, **drie ruiten**, etc.

14.13 SCHOOL MARKS/GRADES

Marks (**cijfers**) at school and university in Holland are given out of ten, not as percentages. One expresses marks as follows:

Ik heb een zes voor wiskunde gekregen.
I got 60% for mathematics.

Marks are often expressed as follows instead of referring to the mathematical figure:

uitmuntend = 10, **zeer goed** = 9, **goed** = 8, **ruim voldoende** = 7,
   voldoende = 6, **bijna onvoldoende** = 5, **onvoldoende** = 4, **zeer**
   onvoldoende = 3, **slecht** = 2, **zeer slecht** = 1.

In a more general sense **een onvoldoende** is a fail (i.e. five or less):

Ik heb een onvoldoende voor geschiedenis gekregen.
I failed history.

15 Er

Er has four functions in Dutch: repletive, partitive, pronominal and locative. The four are dealt with separately below. It is possible to have various combinations of these in one clause; the complications arising from such combinations are dealt with in the notes following the description of the four functions, see 15.5.

15.1 REPLETIVE er

Indefinite subjects are very commonly placed after the verb in Dutch with **er** introducing the verb in much the same way as 'there' can be used in English, but the practice is much more common in Dutch and is often employed where a construction with 'there' would not be possible in English, as some of the examples below illustrate:

Er loopt een man op straat.
There is a man walking in the street/A man is walking in the street.

Er moeten nog veel meer mensen komen.
There should be a lot more people coming/A lot more people should be coming.

Er bracht een juffrouw koffie rond.
A young woman brought coffee around.

Toen kwam er een pastoor.
Then a priest arrived.

Wat is er gebeurd?
What happened?

Wie is er vandaag jarig?
Who has a birthday today?

On occasions, as in the last two examples, **er** can be omitted but the Dutch ear generally prefers a repletive **er** construction wherever possible.

To this category belong also **er is/zijn** 'there is/are'. It should be noted that **liggen**, **staan** and **zitten** (less commonly **hangen** and **lopen**) often replace 'to be' in Dutch and they then usually occur in **er** constructions:

Er zit een muis in de hoek.
There is a mouse in the corner.

Er staat een foto van haar in de krant.
There is a photo of her in the paper.

Er lagen vier boeken op tafel.
Four books were lying on the table.

Loopt er een gracht achter jullie huis?
Is there a canal behind your house?

Repletive **er** is frequently used in Dutch passive constructions (see 11.12.4.3) where there is no grammatical subject. There is a variety of ways to translate these constructions into English:

Er wordt (aan de deur) geklopt.
There's a knock at the door.

Er wordt te veel geroddeld.
There's too much gossiping going on/Too much gossiping is going on.

Er werd heel weinig gedanst.
There wasn't much dancing.

15.2 PARTITIVE **er**

This **er** is used with numerals and adverbs of quantity, often corresponding to French **en**. In English it means something like 'of them/it', but is usually not translated:

Hoeveel heb je er? Ik heb er drie.[1]
How many do you have? I have three (of them).

Hij heeft er genoeg.
He has enough (of them/it).

Het aantal is toegenomen. Vijftien jaar geleden waren het er honderd.
The number has increased. Fifteen years ago there were a hundred
  (of them).

Hoeveel bomen staan er (repletive) **in die straat? Er** (repletive)
staan er (partitive) **honderd.**
How many trees are there in that street? There are a hundred (of
  them).

15.3 PRONOMINAL **er**

This is the **er** which replaces the pronouns 'it' and 'them' (referring to things only) – after prepositions, i.e. *op het, *van het, etc. is an

---

[1] But **Hoeveel heb je?** 'How much have you got?' (i.e. money) does not require **er**.

impossible combination in Dutch; this must be rendered by **erop**, **ervan**, etc. **Op ze** 'on them', **van ze** 'from them' etc. can only refer to people, never things – the latter would also be expressed by **erop**, **ervan** etc. (see 8.1.2.4(d)):

De meeste (ervan) zijn te duur. (optional)
Most of them are too expensive.

Ik heb het brood ermee gesneden/Ik heb er het brood mee gesneden.
I cut the bread with it/them.

Ik kijk er vaak naar.
I often look at it/them.

Dat artikel stond in de Volkskrant. Dat artikel stond erin/er ook in.
That article was in the Volkskrant. That article was in it/in it too.

It is more usual in speech to place **er** immediately after the finite verb and the preposition at the end of the sentence, but before past participles and infinitives:

Ik heb er het brood toen mee gesneden.
I then cut the bread with it.

But note that pronominal objects go between the finite verb and **er** and that it is possible to put **er** after nominal objects (i.e. not immediately after the finite verb) if there is another word or expression which can be inserted between **er** and the preposition dependent on it:

Ik heb het/dat er toen mee gesneden.
Ik heb het brood er toen mee gesneden.

Without the adverb **toen** one has the choice here of either leaving **er** and the preposition together or else, as would be more usual in speech, putting the **er** after the finite verb:

Ik heb het brood ermee gesneden.
Ik heb er het brood mee gesneden.

Note however that with an indefinite direct object there is a distinct preference for separating **er** from its preposition:

Ik heb er brood mee gesneden.
I cut bread with it.

When the finite verb in a sentence with a pronominal **er** is a reflexive verb, **er** follows the reflexive pronoun:

Ik heb me er vreselijk aan geërgerd. (zich ergeren aan)
I was very irritated by it. (to be irritated by)

The above constructions must not be confused with **waar ... mee** etc. (see 8.5.3)

Note the following complicated usage of pronominal **er** where it is employed with verbs that are followed by a fixed preposition, i.e. verbs that take a prepositional object (e.g. **overtuigen van** 'to convince of', **denken aan** 'to think of' etc. – see 11.16.12 and 11.21). In all the following examples the object of the first clause containing a verb that takes a prepositional object is in fact the next clause and the **er** + preposition pre-empts that second clause, which can be an infinitive (as in examples one and two) or a subordinate clause (as in example three). Acquiring a feeling for the correct use of **er** in these constructions is one of the most difficult aspects of Dutch grammar:

Ik had er nooit aan gedacht het zo te doen.
I would never have thought of doing it like that.

Hij verdenkt er zijn vriend van een overval op een bank te hebben gepleegd.
He suspects his friend of having robbed a bank.

De administratie heeft erop gestaan dat ...
The administration insisted that ...

The same construction also commonly occurs with certain adjectives that take a prepositional object (see 9.5):

Ik ben ervan overtuigd dat ... (overtuigd van)
I am convinced that ... (convinced of)

Ben je er zeker van dat we op de goede weg zitten? (zeker van)
Are you sure that we are on the right road? (certain of)

Ik was er verbaasd over dat hij voor wiskunde slaagde. (verbaasd over)
I was surprised that he passed mathematics. (surprised at)

15.4 LOCATIVE er

This **er** replaces **daar** in unstressed position:

Ik ben er nooit geweest.
I have never been there.

Compare **Daar ben ik nooit geweest** which means essentially the same thing but where there is an emphasis on 'there'.

Zij heeft er tien jaar gewoond.
She lived there for ten years.

Je bent nog te jong om er in je eentje naartoe te gaan. (see
ernaartoe, 10.5)
You are still too young to go there on your own.

Locative **er** is usually used with the verb **aankomen** 'to arrive' when the
place is not otherwise mentioned:

Hoe laat ben je er aangekomen?
What time did you arrive?

15.5   NOTES

15.5.1   A repletive **er** and a pronominal **er** do not occur in the same
clause – the pronominal **er** is usually omitted:

Er keken veel mensen naar het programma.
There were a lot of people watching the programme.

Er keken veel mensen naar.
There were a lot of people watching it.

Daar keken veel mensen naar. (emphatic)
There were a lot of people watching that.

Er werd niet veel over gesproken.
It wasn't spoken about much.

Er staat erg weinig sportnieuws in de Volkskrant.
There is very little sports news in the Volkskrant.

Er staat erg weinig sportnieuws in.
There is very little sports news in it.

Er lag een laagje zand op.
There was a layer of sand (lying) on it.

Note the emphatic forms:

Daar moet melk bij.
Milk has to be added to that.

Hier staat geen prijs op.
There is no price on this.

15.2   When a clause begins with an adverbial expression of place, repletive **er** is usually dropped:

Er staan veel auto's op de parkeerplaats.

Op de parkeerplaats staan (er) veel auto's.
There are a lot of cars in the parking area.

15.5.3   More than two **er**'s in one clause is impossible. In a clause where the sense demands three, you either delete the prepositional **er** or rephrase using a relative clause:

Deletion:

Er keken drie mensen naar het programma.
There were three people watching the programme.

Er keken er drie naar het programma.
There were three watching the programme.

Er keken er drie naar.
There were three watching it.

Rephrasing:

Er keken drie mensen naar het programma.
There were three people watching the programme.

Er waren er drie die naar het programma keken.
There were three people who were watching the programme.

Er waren er drie die ernaar keken.
There were three who were watching it.

15.5.4   The verb **uitzien** always requires **er** and should be learnt as **eruitzien**. This is a very idiomatic usage of **er**.

Hij ziet er erg ziek uit.
He looks terribly ill.

Eruitzien translates 'to look' in the sense of 'to appear' as well as 'to look as if':

Hij ziet eruit alsof hij ziek gaat worden.
He looks as if he is falling ill.

In such a construction **er** and **uit** are usually written as one word but there is some inconsistency in this respect.

Note: **Naar** is used with this verb in impersonal constructions where the subject is **het**:

Het ziet ernaar uit dat het gaat regenen.
It looks as if it is going to rain/It seems that it is going to rain.

15.5.5   It is common when using a split pronominal **er** construction in a sentence in the perfect tense for the writer to join the preposition (which is actually dependent on the **er**) to the following past participle, treating the preposition and the past participle as if they belong to a separable verb:

Zie je die la? Ik heb er al je sokken in gedaan. (correct)
Zie je die la? Ik heb er al je sokken ingedaan. (incorrect)
Do you see that drawer? I've put all your socks in it.

(See also the last point in 11.20.1)

16 NEGATION (ontkenning)

16.1 POSITION OF niet/nooit

16.1.1 THE NEGATIVE FOLLOWS:

(a) *Adverbs of time*

Ik kom morgen niet.
I'm not coming tomorrow.

But for emphasis it can precede expressions of time, in which case an alternative time is either stated or implied:

We willen het dit jaar niet doen.
We don't want to do it this year.

But for emphasis:

We willen het niet dit jaar doen (maar volgend jaar).
We don't want to do it *this* year (but next).

Note: But **niet** always precedes **altijd**:

Zij verhalen worden niet altijd geloofd.
His tales are not always believed.

(b) *Definite direct objects*
The negative follows the direct object as long as it is definite, i.e. preceded by **de** or **het**, **deze** or **dit**, **die** or **dat**, a possessive or is a pronoun:

Hij heeft het/dit/dat/zijn boek nooit gelezen.   (definite)
He has never read the/this/that/his book.

Compare:

Hij heeft nooit een boek gelezen.   (indefinite)
He has never read a book.

Ik kan de schaar niet vinden.   (definite)
I can't find the scissors.

Compare:

Ik heb nooit een goede schaar kunnen vinden.   (indefinite)
I have never been able to find a good pair of scissors.

Hij leest het/dat boek niet.   (definite)
He isn't reading the/that book.

Leest hij het/dat boek niet?   (definite)
Isn't he reading the/that book?

Jij kent hem niet.   (def. pronominal
You don't know him.   object)

Ken je hem niet?   (def. pronominal
Don't you know him?   object)

The negative does of course always precede infinitives, past participles and separable prefixes in such sentences:

Ik wil het hem niet geven.
I don't want to give it to him.

but

Ik wil het niet aan hem geven. (see prepositional objects below)
I don't want to give it to him.

Heeft zij het boek nooit gelezen?
Has she never read the book?

Ik heb er mijn sokken niet in gedaan.
I didn't put my socks in it.

16.1.2   THE NEGATIVE EITHER PRECEDES OR FOLLOWS:

(a) *Complements of the verb zijn*

Dat is niet de bedoeling or **Dat is de bedoeling niet.**
That is not the intention.

Hij is niet mijn vader or **Hij is mijn vader niet.**
He is not my father.

(b) *Hier and daar* (see 16.1.3(c))

16.1.3   THE NEGATIVE PRECEDES:

(a) *Indefinite direct objects*
The negative precedes the direct object as long as it is indefinite, i.e. a noun preceded by **een**, **zo'n**, **veel** or indefinite pronouns like **iets**, **iemand** etc.:

Hij heeft nooit een auto gehad.
He's never had a car.

We zullen niet veel (dingen) kunnen kopen.
We won't be able to buy much (many things).

Heb je er nooit iets over gehoord?
Have you never heard anything about it?

For **niet een** see 16.1.4.1 below.

(b) *Expressions of manner*

Ik ga niet met de auto.
I'm not going by car.

Ik reis niet per vliegtuig.
I don't travel on planes.

De dokter zei dat mijn tante niet te hard mag werken.
The doctor said that my aunt should not work too hard.

(c) *Expressions of place*

Ik woon niet op de achtste etage.
I don't live on the eighth floor.

Zij is nooit in Engeland geweest.
She has never been to England.

Hij werkt niet in Amsterdam.
He doesn't work in Amsterdam.

Ik heb niet in de tuin gewerkt.
I didn't work in the garden.

In the previous sentence **niet** could also follow the expression of place but with a semantic difference:

Hij heeft in de tuin niet gewerkt (maar gespeeld).
He didn't *work* in the garden (but played).

The negative can either precede or follow the adverbs **daar** and **hier**, although they indicate place:

Hij is nooit daar geweest.
Hij is daar nooit geweest. (usually **Daar is hij nooit geweest**)
He has never been *there*.

but only:

Hij is er nooit geweest. (no emphasis on 'there')
He has never been there.

As **er** is an unemphatic **daar**, it can never be stressed by putting **niet** or **nooit** before it.

(d) *Prepositional objects*

Ik had nooit aan een dergelijke oplossing gedacht.
I would never have thought of such a solution.

Ze heeft niet naar zijn onzin geluisterd.
She didn't listen to his nonsense.

Ik heb het niet aan hem gegeven.
I didn't give it to him.

(e) *Predicative adjectives*

Het boek is niet groen.
The book isn't green.

Ik ben niet rijk.
I'm not rich.

16.1.4 NOTES

16.1.4.1 'Not ... a/any' or 'no + noun' are usually translated by **geen**:

Ik heb geen auto. (niet een is not possible here)
I don't have a car/I have no car.

Hij geeft geen geld uit.
He doesn't spend any money/He spends no money.

The combination **niet ... een** is possible when the noun it relates to is further expanded upon by means of a relative clause:

Ik wil geen medewerker uit Groningen.
I don't want an assistant from Groningen.

Ik wil geen/niet een medewerker die helemaal uit Groningen moet komen.
I don't want an assistant who has to come all the way from Groningen.

The combination **niet ... een** is also possible when a contrast is being made:

Ik heb niet in een jeugdherberg gelogeerd maar in een pension. (or **in geen**)
I didn't stay in a youth hostel but in a guest-house.

Note the following idiomatic use of **geen**:

Hij heet geen Marius.
His name isn't Marius.

Compare the following where a contrast is being made:

Hij heet niet Marius maar Hans.
His name isn't Marius, but Hans.

16.1.4.2 'Not one' is **niet een** or **geen een**. Accents are not needed on **een** here as there is no ambiguity possible:

Niet een van mijn vrienden kwam me bezoeken.
Geen een van mijn vrienden kwam me bezoeken.
Not one of my friends visited me.

Compare **geen van mijn vrienden** 'none of my friends'.

16.1.4.3 In substandard Dutch 'never ... a/any' is often expressed by **nooit ... geen**:

Zij hebben nooit geen auto gehad.
They have never had a car.

In standard Dutch this is said:

Zij hebben nooit een auto gehad.

16.1.4.4 Further uses of **geen**:

The following examples show how **geen** sometimes renders a simple English 'not':

Deze beesten eten geen gras.
These animals don't eat grass.

But this can also be expressed as follows:

Gras eten deze beesten niet.

Het waren geen gewone katten.
They were not/no ordinary cats.

Hij kende geen Nederlands.
He didn't know (any) Dutch.

The following expressions are all negated by **geen**, not **niet**: **dienst hebben** 'to be on duty', **dorst hebben** 'to be thirsty', **haast hebben** 'to be in a hurry', **honger hebben** 'to be hungry', **slaap hebben** 'to be sleepy' (see 11.6.2):

Hij had geen haast.
He wasn't in a hurry.

Ze heeft geen slaap.
She isn't sleepy.

16.1.4.5 'No(t) ... at all' is translated by **helemaal niet/geen**:

Ik heb er helemaal niet aan gedacht.
I didn't think of it at all.

Ik heb helemaal geen auto.
I haven't got a car at all.

Hij heeft helemaal geen geld.
He has no money at all.

Where 'all' is stressed here in English, Dutch stresses the last syllable of **helemaal**.

16.1.4.6 'Not ... until' is translated by **pas**[1] (never **niet ... tot**). In formal style **eerst** is found:

Hij komt pas morgen.
He's not coming until tomorrow.

Zij komen pas aanstaande maandag.
They are not coming till next Monday.

Eerst dan zal het geschieden.
Not till then will it happen.

16.1.4.7 'Not ... either' is translated simply by **ook niet/geen**.

Ik ga ook niet.
I'm not going either.

Zij heeft er ook geen.
She hasn't got one either.

16.1.4.8 'Not yet' is translated by **nog niet**:

Zij zijn nog niet thuis.
They aren't home yet.

---

[1] **Pas** here literally means 'only' and thus an alternative translation of **Hij komt pas morgen** is 'He's only coming tomorrow'. Compare the use of **pas** with age, 14.6.

16.1.4.9   Note the following affirmative/negative couplets:

iets	something[2]	**iemand**	someone, somebody
niets	nothing	**niemand**	no-one, nobody
ergens	somewhere	**ooit**[3]	ever
nergens	nowhere	**(nog) nooit**	never
wel	see 11.14		
niet			

Note: **nooit eerder** 'never before' (see 10.4.4).

16.1.4.10   In somewhat higher style the expression **al dan niet** is commonly heard. It is synonymous with **wel of niet**, thus with **mogelijk**, and is best rendered by 'possibly' in English:

Hij treedt binnenkort in het huwelijk, al dan niet gekleed in jacquet.
(formal)
He'll be getting married soon, possibly dressed in tails.

We gaan naar Berlijn, wel of niet (= al dan niet) met de trein.
(everyday)
We're going to Berlin, possibly by train.

16.1.4.11   'Even' is usually rendered by **zelfs**, while 'not even' is normally rendered by **niet eens**; nevertheless, **zelfs niet** does exist as an expression and is used after a list of negative things, e.g.

Hij kan niet eens lezen.
He can't even read.

Hij kan dit niet doen, hij kan dat niet doen en hij kan zelfs niet lezen.
He can't do this, he can't do that and he can't even read.

Zijn naam werd niet eens/zelfs niet genoemd.
His name wasn't even (= was not so much as) mentioned.

16.1.4.12   'Not very' is rendered by **niet erg**. The other words for 'very', **heel** and **zeer**, cannot be used in combination with **niet** (see 10.2.1):

Het huis is niet erg goed gebouwd.
The house is not very well built.

---

[2] For the relationship between 'something' and 'anything', 'someone' and 'anyone' etc. see 8.6.3 and 8.6.4.
[3] **Ooit** also frequently renders 'once': **Hier stond ooit een fabriek** 'A factory once stood here'.

APPENDIX 1: LETTER WRITING

THE ENVELOPE

THE TITLES

Dhr. L. Smit	Mr. L. Smit	**Prof. H. Segers**	Prof. H. Segers
Mevr. L. Smit	Mrs. L. Smit	**Dr. H. Segers**	Dr. H. Segers
Mej. L. Smit	Miss. L. Smit	**Drs. H. Segers**	(Dutch graduate title)[1]
Mw. L. Smit	Ms. L. Smit[1]	**Ds. H. Segers**	Rev. H. Segers[1]

Some people object to the abbreviation **Dhr.** and prefer to write **De heer** or **De Heer**.

Mej. is no longer current for a female of any age; all women are now addressed in correspondence as **mevrouw**. When addressing an envelope or letter to a little girl or boy, as is still sometimes done with English 'Miss' and 'Master', no title at all is used in Dutch.

The title **Mr.** before someone's name stands for **Meester (in de rechten)**, the title applicable to those with a degree in law and **Ir.** stands for **Ingenieur**, the title applicable to those with a degree in engineering. For other disciplines the title **Drs. (Doctorandus)** is used, the Flemish equivalent being **Lic. (Licentiaat)**. Other than on envelopes, these titles are nowadays most usually not capitalised, a practice which has been sanctioned by the most recent spelling reform.

The tradition of prefixing the names of those with one or other title with a rather long-winded form of address commensurate with the qualification of the person concerned, still lives on in some circles. Generally speaking these titles are used when the writer feels recipients might appreciate the recognition of their status. They are as follows:

Hooggeleerde Heer/Mevrouw Bots	a professor
Weledelzeergeleerde Heer/Mevrouw Bots	someone with a doctorate
Weledelgeleerde Heer/Mevrouw Bots	a doctorandus[2]
Weleerwaarde Heer/Mevrouw Bots	a dominee

---

[1] **Mw, Ds** and **Drs** are read **mevrouw, dominee** and **doctorandus** respectively.
[2] A medical doctor (a **dokter** or **arts**), as opposed to someone with a PhD (a **doctor**), is addressed with **weledelgeleerd**.

These titles may be preceded by **Aan de**.

THE ADDRESS

Bollenhofsestr. 20
3572 VN UTRECHT

Hauptstraße 26
Gerlingen 70839
DUITSLAND

Note that the number follows the name of the street. The town or city is often commonly written in upper case when typed or underlined when handwritten. If it is a letter for abroad this applies to the country, not the town. In 1978 postcodes were introduced in The Netherlands; they consist of four numbers followed by a space and then two capital letters and are placed before the name of the town, as illustrated above. They refer to the city block in which the house occurs and thus the Dutch postal code book is the size of a telephone book.

THE BACK OF THE ENVELOPE

afz. B. de Bruin
Hoogstraat 10
2509 BA 's-GRAVENHAGE

The Dutch always put the address of the sender on the back of the envelope. The abbreviation **afz.** stands for **afzender**. Note too that Dutch names in **de**, **den** or **van** are capitalized only when initials are not mentioned (see 2.5). In telephone books, library catalogues etc. such names are found under the noun, not the preposition or article, i.e. **Jan van der Linden** is listed as **Linden, J. van den**.

THE LETTER

ADDRESS AND DATE

The date is placed at the top right-hand corner under the sender's address, but the latter is not always included in less formal letters as it is always written on the back of the envelope:

10 september 1977

There is no dot after the numeral, nor is there a small **e** or **ste/de** (the abbreviations for ordinals) because in such expressions the cardinal numeral is used in Dutch (see 14.9). The months are always written with small letters nowadays.

MODES OF ADDRESS IN OPENING A LETTER

1 When writing to a firm use

Mijne Heren,
Geachte Heren,
Geachte Heer/Mevrouw, (the most recent, politically correct form)

2 When writing to an individual one doesn't know use

Zeer geachte heer De Bruijn,
Geachte mevrouw De Bruijn,
Geachte mejuffrouw De Bruijn,

The **zeer** need only be used when one is being hyperpolite or writing to people in high positions, i.e. professors, politicians etc. Alternatively the following titles are still sometimes used in the body of the letter, as they are on the envelope.

Hooggeleerde Heer/Mevrouw,	a professor
Weledelzeergeleerde Heer/Mevrouw,	someone with a doctorate
Weledelgeleerde Heer/Mevrouw,	a doctorandus, thus also a medical doctor
Weleerwaarde Heer/Mevrouw,	a dominee

3 When writing to acquaintances and friends use

Beste heer Meijer,
Beste mevrouw Meijer,
Beste mejuffrouw Meijer,
Beste Joop/Anneke,

Particularly close female friends, girl and boyfriends and relatives are addressed with **lieve**, but men (including relatives) address each other with **beste**:

Lieve Anneke,
Lieve tante Lien,
Lieve Hans, (a female writing to a male)

ENDINGS

1 When writing to a firm or stranger use

Met de meeste hoogachting, or
Hoogachtend,

If one has been in touch with the individual previously, one can replace the above with the following, which is not as distant and impersonal as the above:

Met vriendelijke groet(en),

2 To acquaintances and friends one writes

(Met) vriendelijke/hartelijke groeten,

This may be followed by, or simply replaced by

Je (or possibly under certain circumstances **Uw**)
Otto

In very informal letters one can end simply with

Groetjes, or **De groeten,**
Wim

(Veel) liefs, (= [lots of] love)
Paulien

EXPRESSIONS USED IN FORMAL LETTER WRITING

lectori salutem (l.s.)	to whom it may concern
uw kenmerk/referentie	your reference
ter kennisneming + name	cc + name (put at top of letter)
t.a.v. (ter attentie van)	att. (attention)
met verwijzing naar	with reference to
naar aanleiding van	with reference to
Met verwijzing naar uw brief van . . .	With reference to your letter of . . .
moge ik	I would like
Hartelijk (Vriendelijk) dank	Many thanks for
voor uw brief van 22 dezer	your letter of the 22nd inst.
op de 28ste dezer	on the 28th of this month
op 28 okt. j.l. (= jongstleden)	on the 28th October last
per 26 dec. a.s. (= aanstaande)	as from the 26th December next
uw brief d.d. 15 mei (= de dato)	your letter of the 15th of May
Wilt u zo vriendelijk zijn . . .	Please . . .
Gelieve mij . . . te sturen	Please send me . . .
Wilt u mij nadere gegevens/ inlichtingen verstrekken	Please supply further details
iets per omgaande sturen	to send something by return mail
het verschuldigde bedrag	the amount owed
Ik sluit . . . hierbij in	I hereby enclose . . .
Hierbij ingesloten vindt u . . .	Enclosed is . . .
ondergetekende	the undersigned
U bij voorbaat (voor uw moeite) dankend,	Thanking you in anticipation (for your trouble),

Uw spoedig antwoord tegemoetziende,	In anticipation of a prompt reply,
Met belangstelling zie ik uw antwoord tegemoet	I anxiously await your reply
Uw antwoord zie ik te zijner tijd gaarne tegemoet	Looking forward to hearing from you

It is no longer accepted practice to capitalize **u** and **uw** in letters, but one does still occasionally meet it.

Many married women in Holland sign and have letters addressed to them as follows: Mrs. A Smit, whose maiden name was Scherpenzeel, would be addressed in writing as **mevr. A. Smit-Scherpenzeel**. A married woman never adopts the first name or initial of her husband as is sometimes still done in Anglo-Saxon countries, i.e. Mrs. John Smith.

APPENDIX 2: PROPER NOUNS

1 COUNTRIES, INHABITANTS, NATIONALITIES, ADJECTIVES, LANGUAGES

The second column contains the name of the country, the third that of the male inhabitant (singular/plural), the fourth the name of the female inhabitant (usually the adjective plus **e**, see note (a) on p. 308, and the final column contains the adjective, which is usually also the name of the language and nationality.

	Country	Male (+ plural)	Female	Adjective (language)
Afghanistan	**Afghanistan**	**Afghaan, Afghanen**	**Afghaanse**	**Afghaans**
Africa	**Afrika**	**Afrikaan, Afrikanen**	**Afrikaanse**	**Afrikaans**
Albania	**Albanië**	**Albanees, Albanezen**	**Albanese**	**Albanees**
Algeria	**Algerije**	**Algerijn, Algerijnen**	**Algerijnse**	**Algerijns**
America	**Amerika**	**Amerikaan, Amerikanen**	**Amerikaanse**	**Amerikaans**
Angola	**Angola**	**Angolees, Angolezen**	**Angolese**	**Angolees**
Argentina	**Argentinië**	**Argentijn, Argentijnen**	**Argentijnse**	**Argentijns**
Armenia	**Armenië**	**Armeniër, Armeniërs**	**Armeense**	**Armeens**
Aruba	**Aruba**	**Arubaan, Arubanen**	**Arubaanse**	**Arubaans**
Asia	**Azië**	**Aziaat, Aziaten**	**Aziatische**	**Aziatisch**
Australia	**Australië**	**Australiër, Australiërs**	**Australische**	**Australisch**
Austria	**Oostenrijk**	**Oostenrijker, Oostenrijkers**	**Oostenrijkse**	**Oostenrijks**
Azerbaijan	**Azerbeidzjan**	**Azerbeidzjaan, Azerbeidzjanen**	**Azerbeidzjaanse**	**Azerbeidzjaans**
Belgium	**België**	**Belg, Belgen**	**Belgische**	**Belgisch**
Belorus	**Wit-Rusland**	**Wit-Rus, Wit-Russen**	**Wit-Russische Wit-Russin**	**Wit-Russisch**
Bhutan	**Boetan**	**Boetanees, Boetanezen**	**Boetanese**	**Boetanees**
Bolivia	**Bolivië**	**Boliviaan, Bolivianen**	**Boliviaanse**	**Boliviaans**
Bosnia	**Bosnië**	**Bosniër, Bosniërs**	**Bosnische**	**Bosnisch**
Botswana	**Botswana**	**Botswaan, Botswanen**	**Botswaanse**	**Botswaans**
Brazil	**Brazilië**	**Braziliaan, Brazilianen**	**Braziliaanse**	**Braziliaans**
Brunei	**Brunei**	**Bruneier, Bruneiers**	**Bruneise**	**Bruneis**
Bulgaria	**Bulgarije**	**Bulgaar, Bulgaren**	**Bulgaarse**	**Bulgaars**
Burma	**Birma/Burma**	**Birmaan, Birmanen Birmees, Birmezen**	**Birmaanse, Birmese**	**Birmaans/ Birmees**
Burundi	**Burundi**	**Burundiër, Burundiërs**	**Burundische**	**Burundisch**
Cambodia	**Cambodja**	**Cambodjaan, Cambodjanen**	**Cambodjaanse**	**Cambodjaans**

Country	Male (+ plural)	Female	Adjective (language)
Cameroons **Kameroen**	**Kameroener, Kameroeners**	**Kameroense**	**Kameroens**
Canada **Canada**	**Canadees, Canadezen**	**Canadese**	**Canadees**
Cape Verde Islands **de Kaapverdische Eilanden**			**Kaapverdisch**
Central African Republic **de Centraal-Afrikaanse Republiek**			
Chad **Tsjaad**	**Tsjadiër, Tsjadiërs**	**Tsjadische**	**Tsjadisch**
Chile **Chili**	**Chileen, Chilenen**	**Chileense**	**Chileens**
China People's Republic of China **China de Chinese Volksrepubliek**	**Chinees, Chinezen**	**Chinese**	**Chinees**
Columbia **Columbia**	**Columbiaan, Columbianen**	**Columbiaanse**	**Columbiaans**
Comores **de Comoren**	**Comorees, Comorezen**	**Comorese**	**Comorees**
Congo **Kongo**	**Kongolees, Kongolezen**	**Kongolese**	**Kongolees**
Croatia **Kroatië**	**Kroaat, Kroaten**	**Kroatische**	**Kroatisch**
Cuba **Cuba**	**Cubaans, Cubanen**	**Cubaanse**	**Cubaans**
Cyprus **Cyprus**	**Cyprioot, Cyprioten**	**Cypriotische**	**Cypriotisch**
Czech Republic **Tsjechië**	**Tsjech, Tsjechen**	**Tsjechische**	**Tsjechisch**
Denmark **Denemarken**	**Deen, Denen**	**Deense**	**Deens**
Dominican Republic **de Dominicaanse Republiek**	**Dominicaan/Dominicanen**	**Dominicaanse**	**Dominicaans**
Ecuador **Ecuador**	**Ecuadoriaan, Ecuadorianen**	**Ecuadoriaanse**	**Ecuadoriaans**
Egypt **Egypte**	**Egyptenaar, Egyptenaren**	**Egyptische**	**Egyptisch**
El Salvador **El Salvador**	**Salvador(i)aan, Salvador(i)anen**	**Salvador(i)aanse**	**Salvador(i)aans**
England **Engeland**	**Engelsman, Engelsen**	**Engelse**	**Engels**
Estonia **Estland**	**Estlander, Estlanders**	**Estlandse**	**Estlands**
Ethiopia **Ethiopië**	**Ethiopiër, Ethiopiërs**	**Ethiopische**	**Ethiopisch**
Europe **Europa**	**Europeaan, Europeanen**	**Europese**	**Europees**
Fiji **Fiji**	**Fijiër, Fijiërs**	**Fijische**	**Fijisch**
Finland **Finland**	**Fin, Finnen**	**Finse**	**Fins**
France **Frankrijk**	**Fransman, Fransen**	**Française**	**Frans**
Gabon **Gabon**	**Gabonees, Gabonezen**	**Gabonese**	**Gabonees**
Gambia **Gambia**	**Gambiaan, Gambianen**	**Gambiaanse**	**Gambiaans**
Georgia **Georgië**	**Georgiër, Georgiërs**	**Georgische**	**Georgisch**
Germany Federal Republic of Germany **Duitsland de Bondsrepubliek Duitsland (de BRD)**	**Duitser, Duitsers**	**Duitse**	**Duits**
Ghana **Ghana**	**Ghanees, Ghanezen**	**Ghanese**	**Ghanees**
Great Britain **Groot-Brittannië**	**Brit, Britten**	**Britse**	**Brits**
Greece **Griekenland**	**Griek, Grieken**	**Griekse**	**Grieks**

Country	Male (+ plural)	Female	Adjective (language)
Greenland	**Groenland**	**Groenlander, -landers**	**Groenlandse**	**Groenlands**
Guatemala	**Guatemala**	**Guatemalteek, Guatemalteken**	**Guatemalteekse**	**Guatemalteeks**
Guinea	**Guinea**	**Guinees, Guinezen**	**Guineese**	**Guinees**
Guyana	**Guyana**	**Guyaan, Guyanen**	**Guyaanse**	**Guyaans**
Holland	**Holland**	**Hollander, Hollanders**	**Hollandse**	**Hollands**
Honduras	**Honduras**	**Hondurees, Hondurezen**	**Hondurese**	**Hondurees**
Hungary	**Hongarije**	**Hongaar, Hongaren**	**Hongaarse**	**Hongaars**
Iceland	**IJsland**[1]	**IJslander, IJslanders**	**IJslandse**	**IJslands**
Ireland	**Ierland**	**Ier, Ieren**	**Ierse**	**Iers**
India	**India**	**Indiër, Indiërs**	**Indiase**	**Indiaas**[2]
Indonesia	**Indonesië**	**Indonesiër, Indonesiërs**	**Indonesische**	**Indonesisch**
Dutch East Indies	**Nederlands-Indië**			**Indisch**[2]
Iran	**Iran**	**Iraniër, Iraniërs**	**Iraanse**	**Iraans**
Iraq	**Irak**	**Irakees, Irakezen**	**Iraakse, Irakese**	**Iraaks/Irakees**
Israel	**Israël**	**Israëli, Israëli's Israëliër, Israëliërs**	**Israëlische**	**Israëlisch**
Italy	**Italië**	**Italiaan, Italianen**	**Italiaanse**	**Italiaans**
Ivory Coast	**Ivoorkust**	**Ivoorkuster, Ivoorkusters**	**Ivoorkustse**	**Ivoorkusts**
Jamaica	**Jamaica**	**Jamaicaan, Jamaicanen**	**Jamaicaanse**	**Jamaicaans**
Japan	**Japan**	**Japanner, Japanners**	**Japanse**	**Japans**
Jordan	**Jordanië**	**Jordaniër, Jordaniërs**	**Jordaanse**	**Jordaan**
Kazakhstan	**Kazachstan**	**Kazak, Kazakken**	**Kazakse**	**Kazaks**
Kenya	**Kenia**	**Keniër, Keniërs**	**Keniaa(n)se**	**Keniaa(n)s**
Kirgizia	**Kirgizië**	**Kirgies, Kirgiezen**	**Kirgizische**	**Kirgizisch**
Kiribati	**Kiribati**	**Kiribatiër, Kiribatiërs**	**Kiribatische**	**Kiribatisch**
Korea	**Korea**	**Koreaan, Koreanen**	**Koreaanse**	**Koreaans**
Kuwait	**Koeweit**	**Koeweiter, Koeweiters**	**Koeweitse**	**Koeweits**
Laos	**Laos**	**Laotiaan, Laotianen**	**Laotiaanse**	**Laotiaans**
Lappland	**Lapland**	**Lap, Lappen**	**Lapse**	**Laps**
Latvia	**Letland**	**Let, Letten Letlander/Letlanders**	**Letse Letlandse**	**Lets Letlands**
Lebanon	**Libanon**	**Libanees, Libanezen**	**Libanese**	**Libanees**
Lesotho	**Lesotho**	**Lesothaan, Lesothanen**	**Lesothaanse**	**Lesothaans**
Liberia	**Liberia**	**Liberiaan, Liberianen**	**Liberiaanse**	**Liberiaans**
Libya	**Libië**	**Libiër, Libiërs**	**Libische**	**Libisch**
Lithuania	**Litouwen**	**Litouwer, Litouwers**	**Litouwse**	**Litouws**
Macedonia	**Macedonië**	**Macedoniër, Macedoniërs**	**Macedonische**	**Macedonisch**
Madagascar	**Madagaskar**	**Madagask, Madagasken**	**Madagaskische**	**Madagaskisch**
Malawi	**Malawi**	**Malawiër, Malawiërs**	**Malawische**	**Malawisch**
Malaysia	**Maleisië**	**Maleisiër**	**Maleisische**	**Maleisisch**
Malaya	**Malaja**	**Maleiër**	**Maleise**	**Maleis**
Maldives	**de Malediven**	**Medediviër, Medediviërs**	**Maledivische**	**Maledivisch**
Mali	**Mali**	**Maliër, Maliër**	**Malische**	**Malisch**

[1] One says **op/in IJsland** and **op Malta** where in English we say 'in Iceland/Malta'.
[2] **Indiaan/Indiaans** = American Indian. **Indisch** = **Indonesisch** prior to 1948 and is still used in literature and when referring to colonial concepts, e.g. **een Indische rijsttafel**. **Indiaas** refers to the country of India, except that the Indian Ocean is **de Indische Oceaan**.

Country	Male (+ plural)	Female	Adjective (language)
Malta	**Malta**[1]	**Maltezer, Maltezers**	**Maltese**	**Maltees**
Mexico	**Mexico**	**Mexicaan, Mexicanen**	**Mexicaanse**	**Mexicaans**
Moldova	**Moldavië**	**Moldaviër, Moldaviërs**	**Moldavische**	**Moldavisch**
Monaco	**Monaco**	**Monegask, Monegasken**	**Monegaskische**	**Monegaskisch**
Mongolia	**Mongolië**	**Mongool, Mongolen**	**Mongoolse**	**Mongools**
Morocco	**Marokko**	**Marokkaan, Marokkanen**	**Marokkaanse**	**Marokkaans**
Mozambique	**Mozambique**	**Mozambikaan, Mozambikanen**	**Mozambikaanse**	**Mozambikaans**
Namibia	**Namibië**	**Namibiër, Namibiërs**	**Namibische**	**Namibisch**
Nepal	**Nepal**	**Nepalees, Nepalezen**	**Nepalese**	**Nepalees**
Netherlands	**Nederland**	**Nederlander, Nederlanders**	**Nederlandse**	**Nederlands**
Netherlands Antilles	**de Neder- landse Antillen**	**Antilliaan, -anen**	**Antilliaanse**	**Antilliaans**
New Zealand	**Nieuw- Zeeland**	**Nieuw-Zeelander, -Zeelanders**[3]	**Nieuw-Zeelandse**	**Nieuw-Zeelands**
Nicaragua	**Nicaragua**	**Nicaraguaan, Nicaraguanen**	**Nicaraguaanse**	**Nicaraguaans**
Niger	**Niger**	**Nigerees, Nigerezen**	**Nigerese**	**Nigerees**
Nigeria	**Nigeria**	**Nigeriaan, Nigerianen**	**Nigeriaanse**	**Nigeriaans**
Norway	**Noorwegen**	**Noor, Noren**[4]	**Noorse**	**Noors**
Pakistan	**Pakistan**	**Pakistaan, Pakistanen Pakistani, Pakistani's**	**Pakistaanse**	**Pakistaans**
Palestine	**Palestina**	**Palestijn, Palestijnen**	**Palestijnse**	**Palestijns**
Panama	**Panama**	**Panamees, Panamezen**	**Panamese**	**Panemees**
Papua New Guinea	**Papoea- Nieuw- Guinea**	**Nieuw-Guineër, Nieuw-Guineërs Papoea, Papoea's**		**Nieuw-Guinees Papoeaas**
Paraguay	**Paraguay**	**Paraguayaan, Paraguayanen**	**Paraguayaanse**	**Paraguayaans**
Persia	**Perzië**	**Pers, Perzen**	**Perzische**	**Perzisch**
Peru	**Peru**	**Peruaan, Peruanen**	**Peruaanse**	**Peruaans**
Philippines	**de Filippijnen**	**Filippijn, Filippijnen**	**Filippijnse**	**Filippijns**
Poland	**Polen**	**Pool, Polen**	**Poolse**	**Pools**
Portugal	**Portugal**	**Portugees, Portugezen**	**Portugese**	**Portugees**
Puerto Rico	**Porto-Rico**	**Portoricaan, Portoricanen**	**Portoricaanse**	**Portoricaans**
Qatar	**Katar**	**Katarees, Katarezen**	**Katarese**	**Katarees**
Romania	**Roemenië**	**Roemeen, Roemenen**	**Roemeense**	**Roemeens**[5]
Russia	**Rusland**	**Rus, Russen**	**Russische/Russin**	**Russisch**
Rwanda	**Rwanda**	**Rwandees, Rwandezen**	**Rwandese**	**Rwandees**
Samoa	**Samoa**	**Samoaan, Samoanen**	**Samoaanse**	**Samoaans**

[3] An inhabitant of the Dutch province of **Zeeland** is a **Zeeuw** (see Appendix 2, 2: Geographical Names).

[4] **Een Noor** = a Norwegian; **een Noorman/Noormannen** = Viking/Vikings; **een Normandiër/Normandisch** = Norman; **Oudnoors** = Old Norse.

[5] **Roemeens** = Romanian, **Romeins** = Roman, **Romaans** = Romance, **rooms-katholiek** = Roman Catholic.

Country	Male (+ plural)	Female	Adjective (language)
Saudi-Arabia	**Saoedi-Arabië**	**Saoedi-Arabiër, Saoedi-Arabiërs**	**Saoedi-Arabische**	**Saoedi-Arabisch**[6]
Scotland	**Schotland**	**Schot, Schotten**	**Schotse**	**Schots**
Senegal	**Senegal**	**Senegalees, Senegalezen**	**Senegalese**	**Senegalees**
Serbia	**Servië**	**Serviër, Serviërs**	**Servische**	**Servisch**
Seychelles	**de Seychellen**	**Seycheller, Seychellers**	**Seychelse**	**Seychels**
Sierra Leone	**Sierra Leone**	**Sierraleonees, Sierraleonezen**	**Sierraleonese**	**Sierraleonees**
Singapore	**Singapore**	**Singaporees, Singaporezen**	**Singaporese**	**Singaporees**
		Singaporaan, Singaporanen	**Singaporaanse**	**Singaporaans**
Slovakia	**Slowakije**	**Slowaak, Slowaken**	**Slowaakse**	**Slowaaks**
Slovenia	**Slovenië**	**Sloveen, Slovenen**	**Sloveense**	**Sloveens**
Solomon Islands	**de Salomons-eilanden**			
Somalia	**Somalië**	**Somaliër, Somaliërs**	**Somalische**	**Somalisch**
South Africa	**Zuid-Afrika**	**Zuid-Afrikaner, -Afrikaners**	**Zuid-Afrikaanse**	**Zuid-Afrikaans**[7]
Spain	**Spanje**	**Spanjaard, Spanjaarden**	**Spaanse**	**Spaans**
Sri Lanka[8]	**Sri Lanka**	**Srilankaan, Srilankanen**	**Srilankaanse**	**Srilankaans**
Sudan	**(de) Soedan**	**Soedanees, Soedanezen**	**Soedanese**	**Soedanees**
Surinam	**Suriname**	**Surinamer, Surinamers**	**Surinaamse**	**Surinaams**
Swaziland	**Swaziland**	**Swazi, Swazi's**	**Swazische**	**Swazisch**
Sweden	**Zweden**	**Zweed, Zweden**	**Zweedse**	**Zweeds**
Switzerland	**Zwitserland**	**Zwitser, Zwitsers**	**Zwitserse**	**Zwitsers**
Syria	**Syrië**	**Syriër, Syriërs**	**Syrische**	**Syrisch**
Taiwan	**Taiwan**	**Taiwanees, Taiwanezen**	**Taiwanese**	**Taiwanees**
Tajikistan	**Tadzjikistan**	**Tadzjiek, Tadzjieken**	**Tadzjiekse**	**Tadzjieks**
Tanzania	**Tanzanië**	**Tanzaniër, Tanzaniërs**	**Tanzaniaanse**	**Tanzaniaans**
Thailand	**Thailand**	**Thailander, Thailanders**	**Thailandse/Thaise**	**Thailands**
Tibet	**Tibet**	**Tibetaan, Tibetanen**	**Tibetaanse**	**Tibetaans**
Togo	**Togo**	**Togolees, Togolezen**	**Togolese**	**Togolees**
Tonga	**Tonga**	**Tongaan, Tonganen**	**Tongaanse**	**Tongaans**
Trinidad and Tobago	**Trinidad en Tobago**			
Tunisia	**Tunesië**	**Tunesiër, Tunesiërs**	**Tunesische**	**Tunesisch**
Turkey	**Turkije**	**Turk, Turken**	**Turkse**	**Turks**
Turkmenistan	**Turkmenistan**	**Turkmeen, Turkmenen**	**Turkmeense**	**Turkmeens**
Tuvalu	**Tuvalu**	**Tuvaluaan, Tuvaluanen**	**Tuvaluaanse**	**Tuvaluaans**
Uganda	**Oeganda**	**Oegandees, Oegandezen**	**Oegandese**	**Oegandees**
Ukraine	**(de) Oekraïne**	**Oekraïner, Oekraïners**	**Oekraïense**	**Oekraïens**
United Arab Emirates	**de Verenigde Arabische Emiraten**			

[6] Note that the word for an Arab in general is **Arabier** (pl. **Arabieren**) with the stress on the final syllable.

[7] The language Afrikaans is usually referred to as **Zuid-Afrikaans** in The Netherlands as **Afrikaans**, being the adjective derived from **Afrika**, can be ambiguous.

[8] Note the forms **Ceylonees** 'Ceylonese', **Singalees** 'Singhalese' and **Tamil** (pl. **-s**).

Country	Male (+ plural)	Female	Adjective (language)
United Kingdom	**het Verenigd Koninkrijk**		
United States	**de Verenigde Staten (de USA, de VS)**		
Uruguay	**Uruguay**	**Uruguayaan, Uruguayanen**	**Uruguayaanse**	**Uruguayaans**
Uzbekistan	**Oesbekistan**	**Oesbeek, Oesbeken**	**Oesbeekse**	**Oesbeeks**
Vanuatu	**Vanuatu**			**Vanuatus**
Venezuela	**Venezuela**	**Venezolaan, Venezolanen**	**Venezolaanse**	**Venezolaans**
Vietnam	**Viëtnam**	**Viëtnamees, Viëtnamezen**	**Viëtnamese**	**Viëtnamees**
Wales	**Wales**	**Welshman**		**Welsh**
Yemen	**Jemen**	**Jemeniet, Jemenieten**	**Jemenitische**	**Jemenitisch**
Yugoslavia	**Joegoslavië**	**Joegoslaaf, Joegoslaven**	**Joegoslavische**	**Joegoslavisch**
Zaire	**Zaïre**	**Zaïrees, Zaïrezen**	**Zaïrese**	**Zaïrees**
Zambia	**Zambia**	**Zambiaan, Zambianen**	**Zambiaanse**	**Zambiaans**
		Zambiër, Zambiërs	**Zambische**	**Zambisch**
Zimbabwe	**Zimbabwe**	**Zimbabweaan,-anen**	**Zimbabweaanse**	**Zimbabweaans**

NOTES ON NATIONALITIES

(a) The names of female inhabitants derived from adjectives are not used in the plural, but **Françaises, Friezinnen** and **Russinnen** are possible as they are not derived from adjectives; otherwise the plural is avoided by paraphrasing, e.g. **Die meisjes komen uit Australië** or **Die meisjes zijn Australisch.**

(b) When saying 'I am a Palestinian' etc. the indefinite article is often omitted in more formal style, i.e. **Ik ben Palestijn** (see 5.1.1(d)).

(c) Note that words ending in **-ees** go **-ese** in the feminine or when the adjective is inflected, but the plural of the masculine is always **-ezen**, e.g. **Albanese** 'Albanian', **Albanezen** 'Albanians'.

(d) Countries for which there is no special word for the inhabitant, or that have no particular adjectival form, or where this form is not generally known, usually paraphrase, i.e. **Hij komt uit Wales** 'He's a Welshman, **het oerwoud van Papoea-Nieuw-Guinea** 'the Papua New Guinean jungle'.

(e) Countries ending in **-ije** take the stress on the **-ij**, e.g. **Algerije, Hongarije, Bulgarije.**

(f) Under the 1954 spelling **Noord, Zuid, Oost** and **West** were hyphenated in the names of provinces, countries etc., but the corresponding adjectives and names of inhabitants were written as one word, e.g. **Zuid-Afrika, Zuidafrikaans, Zuidafrikaner.** Under the most recent reform, all are now written with hyphens, e.g. **Zuid-Afrikaans, Zuid-Afrikaner.**

(g) The latest spelling reform advocates continued use of capital letters for inhabitants and adjectives/languages although small letters in such cases are not infrequent in modern texts.

2   GEOGRAPHICAL NAMES

Dutch provinces	*Inhabitant (female)*	*Adjective*
Noord-Holland	**(Noord-)Hollander (-Hollandse)**	**Noord-Hollands**
Zuid-Holland	**(Zuid-)Hollander (-Hollandse)**	**Zuid-Hollands**
Zeeland	**Zeeuw (Zeeuwse)**	**Zeeuws**
Noord-Brabant	**(Noord-)Brabander (-Brabantse)**	**Brabants**
Limburg	**Limburger (Limburgse)**	**Limburgs**
Gelderland	**Gelderlander (Gelderse)**	**Gelders**
Utrecht	**Utrechtenaar[9] (Utrechtse)**	**Utrechts**
Overijssel	**Overijsselaar (Overijsselse)**	**Overijssels**
Drent(h)e	**Drent (Drentse)**	**Drents**
Groningen	**Groninger (Groningse)**	**Gronings**
Friesland	**Fries (Friezin)**	**Fries[10]**
Flevoland	**Flevolander (Flevolandse)**	**Flevolands**

Provincial capitals	*Inhabitant*	*Adjective*
Haarlem	**Haarlemmer**	**Haarlems[11]**
's-Gravenhage, Den Haag	**Hagenaar**	**Haags**
Middelburg	**Middelburger**	**Middelburgs**
's-Hertogenbosch, Den Bosch	**Bosschenaar**	**Bosch (Bossche)**
Maastricht	**Maastrichtenaar**	**Maastrichts**
Arnhem	**Arnhemmer**	**Arnhems**
Utrecht	**Utrechtenaar, Utrechter**	**Utrechts**
Zwolle	**Zwollenaar**	**Zwols**
Assen	**Assenaar**	**Assens**
Groningen	**Groninger**	**Gronings[11]**
Leeuwarden	**Leeuwarder**	**Leeuwardens**
Lelystad	**Lelystatter**	**Lelystads**

Note: The towns **Leiden** and **Gouda** and the region **Twente** have their own irregular adjectival forms: **Leids**, **Gouds**, **Twents**. Towns ending in

---

[9] The inhabitants of **Utrecht** are also known as **Utrechters**.
[10] **De Friese taal** but **de Friezen** (compare **Chinese**, **Portugees** etc.).
[11] In some standard contexts an adjectival form in **-er** is heard, e.g. **Groninger koek**, **Haarlemmer olie**.

-dam take the stress on **-dam**, e.g. **Amsterdam**, **Edam** etc. The inhabitant is an **Amsterdammer** etc.

Belgian provinces		*Inhabitant (female)*	*Adjective*
West-Vlaanderen	W. Flanders	**West-Vlaming** (**West-Vlaamse**)	**West-Vlaams**
Oost-Vlaanderen	E. Flanders	**Oost-Vlaming** (**Oost-Vlaamse**)	**Oost-Vlaams**
Antwerpen	Antwerp	**Antwerpenaar (Antwerpse)**	**Antwerps**
Brabant		**Brabander (Brabantse)**	**Brabants**
Limburg		**Limburger (Limburgse)**	**Limburgs**
Luik	Liège[12]	**Luikenaar (Luikse)**	**Luiks**
Namen	Namur[12]	**Namenaar (Naamse)**	**Naams**
Luxemburg[12]		**Luxemburger** (**Luxemburgse**)	**Luxemburgs**
Henegouwen	Hainaut[12]	**Henegouwer (Henegouwse)**	**Henegouws**
Vlaanderen	Flanders	**Vlaming, Vlamingen** (**Vlaamse**)	**Vlaams**
Wallonië	Wallonia	**Waal, Walen (Waalse)**	**Waals**

Provincial capitals[13]		*Inhabitant*	*Adjective*
Brugge	Bruges	**Bruggeling**	**Brugs**
Gent	Ghent	**Gentenaar**	**Gents**
Antwerpen	Antwerp	**Antwerpenaar**	**Antwerps**
Brussel	Brussels	**Brusselaar**	**Brussels**
Hasselt	Hasselt	**Hasselaar**	**Hasselts**
Luik	Liège	**Luikenaar**	**Luiks**
Namen	Namur	**Namenaar**	**Naams**
Aarlen	Arlon	**Arlenaar**	**Aarlens**
Bergen	Mons	**Bergenaar**	**Bergens/ Bergs**

Other important Belgian cities with two names (i.e. French and Dutch)

Tournai	**Doornik**	
Courtrai	**Kortrijk**	
Louvain	**Leuven**	
Malines	**Mechelen**	(stress on first syllable)
Ostend	**Oostende**	(stress on second syllable)

---

[12] All French-speaking provinces.
[13] In English we usually refer to these cities by their French names if there is not a specifically English form as in the case of Ghent and Brussels for example.

Other cities with different names in Dutch from English
(corresponding irregular adjectives given in brackets)

Aachen	**Aken**
Athens	**Athene**
Baghdad	**Bagdad**
Beirut	**Beiroet**
Belgrade	**Belgrado** (stress on first syllable)
Berlin	**Berlijn**
Bucharest	**Boekarest**
Budapest	**Boedapest**
Cairo	**Kaïro** (stress on the i)
Capetown	**Kaapstad**
Cologne	**Keulen (Keuls)**
Copenhagen	**Kopenhagen**
Dunkirk	**Duinkerken**
Florence	**Florence**[14] **(Florentijns)**
Frankfurt	**Frankfort**
Geneva	**Genève**[14] **(Geneefs)**
Gothenburg	**Gotenburg**
Hanover	**Hannover**
Jakarta	**Djakarta**
Leyden	**Leiden**
Lille	**Rijsel**
Lisbon	**Lissabon**
London	**Londen**
Milan	**Milaan (Milanees)**
Moscow	**Moskou**
Munich	**München**
Naples	**Napels (Napolitaans)**
Nuremberg	**Neurenberg**
Paris	**Parijs** (inh. **Parijzenaar**, fem. **Parisienne**)
Prague	**Praag**
Rome	**Rome (Romeins)**
Strasburg	**Straatsburg**
Tangier	**Tanger**
Tehran	**Teheran**
Tokyo	**Tokio**
Triest	**Triëst**
Turin	**Turijn (Turijns)** (stress on last syllable)
Venice	**Venetië (Venetiaans)**
Vienna	**Wenen (Weens)**

[14] Pronounced as in French.

Warsaw	**Warschau** (pronounced sh)
Ypres	**Ieper**

If there is not a specifically Dutch name for a town, the Dutch usually attempt to pronounce the name as in the language of the country concerned. In some cases they adapt the spelling to the sounds of Dutch; this is particularly the case with African and Asian names that are being transcribed from other than the Latin alphabet:

Beiroet, Kinsjasa, Loesaka, Mekka, Addis Abeba.

European rivers with different names in Dutch from English

Danube	**de Donau**
Meuse	**de Maas**
Moselle	**de Moezel**
Rhine	**de Rijn**
Ruhr	**de Roer**
Scheldt	**de Schelde**
Thames	**de Theems**

Provinces and regions of other European countries
(corresponding inhabitant and adjective given in brackets)

Alsace	**Elzas (Elzasser, Elzassisch)**
Balkans	**de Balkan, -staten**
Basque country	**(het) Baskenland (Bask, Baskisch)**
Bavaria	**Beieren (Beier, Beiers)**
Bohemia	**Bohemen (Bohemer, Boheems)**
Brittany	**Bretagne (Breton, Bretons)**
Burgundy	**Boergondië (Boergondiër, Boergondisch)**
Canary Islands	**de Canarische Eilanden**
Castile	**Castilië (Castiliaan, Castiliaans)**
Caucasus	**de Kaukasus (Kaukasiër, Kaukasisch)**
Channel Islands	**de Kanaaleilanden**
Chechnya	**Tsjetsjenië (Tsjetsjeen, Tsjetsjeens)**
Cornwall	**Cornwallis (Cornsman, Cornisch)**
Corsica	**Corsica (Corsicaaan, Corsicaaans)**
Crete	**Kreta (Kretenzer, Kretenzisch)**
Faeroes	**de Faeroër**
Gaul	**Gallië (Galliër, Gallisch)**
Hebrides	**de Hebriden**
Lombardy	**Lombardije (Lombardisch)**
Lorraine	**Lotharingen**
Normandy	**Normandië (Normandiër, Normandisch)**
Picardy	**Picardië** (stress on second syllable)
Pomerania	**Pommeren** (stress on first syllable)

Prussia	**Pruisen (Pruis, Pruisisch)**
Rhodes	**Rhodos**
Sardinia	**Sardinië (Sardiniër, Sardinisch)**
Saxony	**Saksen (Saks, Saksisch)**
Scandinavia	**Scandinavië (Scandinaviër, Scandinavisch)**
Schleswig	**Sleeswijk**
Siberia	**Siberië (Siberiër, Siberisch)**
Sicily	**Sicilië (Siciliaan, Siciliaans)**
Silesia	**Silezië (Sileziër, Silezisch)**
Styria	**Stiermarken**
Swabia	**Zwaben (Zwaab, Zwaabs)**
Tuscany	**Toscane (Toscaan, Toscaans)**
Tyrol	**Tirool (Tiroler, Tirools)**

Other geographical areas

Alps	**de Alpen**
Ambon	**Ambon (Ambonnees)**
Apennines	**de Apennijnen**
Ardennes	**de Ardennen**
Asia Minor	**Klein-Azië**
Atlantic Ocean	**de Atlantische Oceaan**[15]
Azores	**de Azoren**
Baltic Sea	**de Oostzee**
Bay of Bengal	**de Golf van Bengalen**
Bay of Biscay	**de Golf van Biskaje**
Bengal	**Bengalen**
Black Forest	**het Zwarte Woud**
Black Sea	**de Zwarte Zee**
Cape of Good Hope	**Kaap de Goede Hoop** (no article used before **Kaap**)
Caribbean Sea	**de Caribische Zee**
Caribbean	**het Caribische Gebied**
Caspian Sea	**de Kaspische Zee**
Catalonia	**Catalonië (Catalaan, Catalaans)**
Central Europe	**Midden-Europa**
Crimea	**de Krim**
Dolomites	**de Dolomieten**
Easter Island	**het Paaseiland**
English Channel	**het Kanaal**
Far East	**het Verre Oosten**
Indian Ocean	**de Indische Oceaan**[15]
Java	**Java (Javaan, Javaans)**

[15] Note the stress: **oceáán**.

Kurdistan	**Koerdistan (Koerd, Koerdisch)**
Lake Constance	**de Bodensee**
Latin America	**Latijns-Amerika**
Manchuria	**Mantsjoerije**
Mediterranean Sea	**de Middellandse Zee**
Middle East	**het Midden-Oosten**
Near East	**het Nabije Oosten**
North Pole	**de Noordpool**
North Sea	**de Noordzee**
Pacific Ocean	**de Stille/Grote Oceaan**[15]
Persian Gulf	**de Perzische Golf**
Polynesia	**Polynesië (Polynesiër, Polynesisch)**
Pyrenees	**de Pyreneeën (Pyrenees)**
Ruhr	**het Roergebied**
South Moluccas	**Zuid-Molukken (Zuid-Molukker, Zuid-Moluks)**
South Pole	**de Zuidpool**
South Seas	**de Zuidzee**
Tierra del Fuego	**Vuurland**
Urals	**de Oeral**
Vatican	**het Vaticaan** (stress on last syllable)
Virgin Islands	**de Maagdeneilanden**
Vosges	**de Vogezen**

3   HISTORICAL PERSONAGES

When referring to well-known people who have names normally written in an alphabet other than the Latin alphabet, the names are usually transcribed according to Dutch phonetics:

Chroetsjev, Jeltsin, Kaoenda, Tsjechow

This applies to other proper nouns as well, e.g. **de Likoed** 'Israeli conservative party' **Tsjernobyl**.

Kings of England, France, Germany etc. as well as popes are given Dutch names where such exist (see also 14.2.1.5):

Karel 'Charles', **Jacobus** 'James', **Lodewijk** 'Louis, Ludwig', **Boudewijn** 'Baudouin, Baldwin', **Hendrik** 'Henry, Heinrich', **Jan** 'John, Johann'.

Karel de Grote	Charlemagne
Lodewijk Napoleon	Louis Napoleon
Jacobus de Tweede	James II
Paus Johannes Paulus II	Pope John Paul II

Note: **Calvijn** 'Calvin', **Galilei** 'Galileo'. The names of many biblical personages are somewhat different in Dutch, e.g. **Noach** 'Noah', **Salomo** 'Solomon'. The stressed ending **-iaans** is added to surnames of certain figures of historical importance to create adjectives, e.g. **Breugeliaans**, **Freudiaans**.

APPENDIX 3: COMMON DUTCH ABBREVIATIONS (afkortingen)

Abbreviations can be of three kinds:

1 those that are simply a form of short-hand and which are read aloud as the words they represent, e.g. **f** = **gulden**, **bv** = **bijvoorbeeld**.
2 those that are regarded as words in themselves and may be (and usually are) pronounced using the letters, e.g. **KLM** pronounced KA-EL-EM. Such abbreviations are designated by an * in the list below.
3 a few abbreviations are read as words in themselves, not as letters. These acronyms are designated by + in the following list, e.g. **HAVO**.

Many abbreviations can take an article which agrees in gender with the final noun in the name, e.g. **het KNMI** because **instituut** is neuter. Sometimes other nouns are formed from these abbreviations, e.g. **de AOW** = **de Algemene Ouderdomswet**, hence **een AOW'er** 'a pensioner'; **de NSB** = **de Nationaal-Socialistische Beweging** hence **een NSB'er** 'a Dutch Nazi'. Where such derivatives of abbreviations in **-er** exist, the **Woordenlijst** permits both **AOW'er** and **AOWer**.

(de) aio+	**assistent in opleiding**	PhD student
(het) ABN*	**Algemeen Beschaafd Nederlands**	Standard Dutch
(de) ABN *	**Algemene Bank Nederland**	a Dutch bank
A'dam	**Amsterdam**	Amsterdam
(het) AN*	**Algemeen Nederlands**	Standard Dutch
(het) ANP*	**Algemeen Nederlands Persbureau**	Dutch News Agency
(de) ANS+	**Algemene Nederlandse Spraakkunst**	a Dutch grammar
(de) ANWB*	**Algemene Nederlandse Wielrijdersbond**	Dutch AA or RAC
(de) AOW('er)*	**Algemene Ouderdomswet**	pension(-er)
a.s.	**aanstaande**	next
a.u.b.	**alstublieft**	please
aug.	**augustus**	August
(de) AVRO+	**Algemene Vereniging Radio Omroep**	a broadcasting network
(de) AWW*	**Algemene Weduwen- en Wezenwet**	Widows' pension
bl., blz.	**bladzij(de)**	page
(de) BRD	**Bondsrepubliek Duitsland**	German Federal Republic
(de) BTW*	**Belasting Toegevoegde Waarde**	Value Added Tax
(de) BV*	**Besloten Vennootschap**	Pty. Ltd

bv	**bijvoorbeeld**	for example, e.g.
(het) CDA*	**Christen-Democratisch Appel**	a Dutch political party
Cie	**Compagnie**	company
(de) CP*	**Centrumpartij**	a Dutch political party
(de) CPN*	**Communistische Partij van Nederland**	Dutch communist party
(het) CS	**Centraal Station**	main station
dec.	**december**	December
derg., dgl.	**dergelijke**	and such, and the like
dhr.	**de heer**	Mr.
di.	**dinsdag**	Tuesday
d.i.	**dat is**	i.e.
d.m.v.	**door middel van**	by means of
do.	**donderdag**	Thursday
dr.	**dokter** (medical), **doctor** (PhD)	Doctor
Dr	**Drenthe**	Drenthe (province)
drs.	**doctorandus**	a Dutch academic title
ds.	**dominee**	Reverend
d.w.z.	**dat wil zeggen**	i.e.
e.d.	**en dergelijke**	and such, and the like
EHBO*	**Eerste Hulp bij Ongelukken**	First Aid
enz.	**enzovoort(s)**	etcetera
(de) EO*	**Evangelische Omroep**	a broadcasting network
(de) EU*	**Europese Unie**	European Union
excl.	**exclusief**	excluding
f.	**florijn** (= **gulden**)	guilder
febr.	**februari**	February
fl.	**florijnen** (= **gulden**)	guilders
fr.	**frank** (e.g. **50fr.**)	franc
Fr	**Friesland**	Friesland (province)
geb.	**geboren**	born, née
(de) gebrs.	**gebroeders**	brothers
Gel	**Gelderland**	Gelderland (province)
Gron	**Groningen**	Groningen (province)
(de) HAVO[+]	**Hoger Algemeen Voortgezet Onderwijs**	a secondary school
(de) HBS*	**Hogere Burgerschool**	a secondary school
Hfl.	**Hollandse florijnen** (= **gulden**)	guilders
HKH.	**Hare Koninklijke Hoogheid**	Her Royal Highness
HM	**Hare Majesteit**	Her Majesty
(het) HO	**Hoger Onderwijs**	tertiary education
(het) hs. (hss.)	**handschrift (handschriften)**	manuscript(s)
incl.	**inclusief**	including
i.p.v.	**in plaats van**	instead of

ir.	ingenieur	engineer (academic title)
i.v.m.	in verband met	in connection with
jan.	januari	January
jg.	jaargang	volume, series
Jhr.	Jonkheer	aristocratic title (Lord)
Jkvr.	Jonkvrouw	aristocratic title (Lady)
jl.	jongstleden	last, past
(de) KLM*	Koninklijke Luchtvaartmaatschappij	Royal Dutch Airlines
(het) KNMI*	Koninklijk Nederlands Meteorologisch Instituut	Dutch weather bureau
(de) KRO*	Katholieke Radio-Omroep	a broadcasting network
L	Limburg	Limburg (province)
l.g.	laatstgenoemde	the latter, last mentioned
lic.	licentiaat, licentie	Belgian uni. degree[1]
m.	mannelijk	masculine
ma.	maandag	Monday
(de) MAVO+	Middelbaar Algemeen Voortgezet Onderwijs	a secondary school
mej.	mejuffrouw	Miss
mevr.	mevrouw	Mrs.
m.i.	mijns inziens	in my opinion
Mij.	Maatschappij	company
(de) MO*	Middelbaar-Onderwijsakte	secondary teaching dip.
mr.	meester (in de rechten)	Dutch academic title
mrt.	maart	March
ms. (mss.)	manuscript(-en)	manuscript(-s)
(de) MULO+	Meer Uitgebreid Lager Onderwijs	a secondary school
mv.	meervoud	plural
mw.	mevrouw/mejuffirouw	Ms.
n.a.v.	naar aanleiding van	with reference to
(de) NAVO+	Noord-Atlantische Verdragsorganisatie	NATO
NB	Noord-Brabant	North Brabant (province)
n. C(hr.)	na Christus	A.D.
(de) NCRV*	Nederlandse Christelijke Radio-Vereniging	a broadcasting network
Ndl./Ned.	Nederlands	Dutch
NH	Noord-Holland	North Holland (province)
nl.	namelijk	namely

[1] This degree, and thus title, is the equivalent of the Dutch **drs**.

n.m.	namiddags	p.m.
(de) NOS*	Nederlandse Omroep Stichting	a broadcasting network
nov.	november	November
nr.	nummer	number
de NS*	Nederlandse Spoorwegen	Dutch Railways
(de) NSB('er)*	Nationaal-Socialistische Beweging	Dutch Nazi Party (Nazi)
(de) NV*	naamloze vennootschap	Pty. Ltd.
o., onz.	onzijdig	neuter
o.a.	onder andere(n)	among others/other things
OC en W	Onderwijs, Cultuur en Wetenschappen	Department of Education
o.i.	ons inziens	in our opinion
(de) oio⁺	onderzoeker in opleiding	PhD student
okt.	oktober	October
OLV	Onze-Lieve-Vrouwe	Our Lady
o.l.v.	onder leiding van	under direction of
o.m.	onder meer	among other things
Ov	Overijssel	Overijssel (province)
p., pag.	pagina	page
p.a.	per adres	c/o (on an envelope)
pct.	procent	percent
p.k.	paardenkracht	horse power
prk.	post(giro)rekening	postal account (giro)
(de) PTT('er)*	Posterijen, Telegrafie en Telefonie	PMG (PMG employee)
(de) PvdA *	Partij van de Arbeid	a Dutch political party
R'dam	Rotterdam	Rotterdam
resp.	respectievelijk	respectively, or
R-K, r-k	Rooms-Katholiek	Roman Catholic
sept.	september	September
(de) SNV*	Stichting Nederlandse Vrijwilligers	Volunteers Abroad
str.	straat	street
s.v.p.	s'il vous plaît (= a.u.b.)	please
t.a.v.	ten aanzien van	with regard to
	ter attentie van	att. (at top of letters)
t.b.c.*	tuberculose	t.b.
t.b.v.	ten bate van	in aid of
	ten behoeve van	on behalf of
(de) TEE*	Trans Europa Express	international express train
tel.	telefoonnummer	telephone number
(de) TH*	Technische Hogeschool	technical college

t/m	tot en met	up to and including
t.n.v.	ten name van	in the name of
t.o.v.	ten opzichte van	with relation to
(de) TROS⁺	Televisie- en Radio-Omroepstichting	a broadcasting network
Ts.	Tijdschrift	journal, magazine
t.u.	te uwent	at your place
t.w.	te weten (= nl., d.i., d.w.z.)	i.e., to wit
t.z.t.	te zijner tijd	in due course
u.	uur (e.g. om 5 u.)	o'clock
U	Utrecht	Utrecht (province)
(de) UB*	de Universiteitsbibliotheek	University Library
(de) u.d.*	de universitair docent	lecturer (university)
(de) u.h.d.*	de universitair docent	senior lecturer (university)
v.	van	of (also in surnames)
v., vr.	vrouwelijk	feminine
v.a.	vanaf	from
(de) VARA⁺	Vereniging Arbeiders-Radio-Amateurs	a broadcasting network
v. C(hr.)	vóór Christus	B.C.
v.d.	van de/den/der	of the (also in surnames)
vgl.	(men) vergelijk(e)	compare
vh.	voorheen	formerly
v.m.	voormiddags	a.m.
(de) VN*	Verenigde Naties	United Nations
(de) VOC*	Verenigde Oost-Indische Compagnie	Dutch East India Co.
(de) VPRO*	Vrijzinnig Protestantse Radio-Omroep	a broadcasting network
vr.	vrijdag	Friday
(de) VS *	Verenigde Staten	United States
(de) V.U.⁺	Vrije Universiteit te Amsterdam	Free Uni. of Amsterdam
(de) VUT⁺	Vervroegde Uittreding	early retirement
(de) VVD*	Volkspartij voor Vrijheid en Democratie	a Dutch political party
(de) VVV*	Vereniging voor Vreemdelingenverkeer	Dutch tourist bureau
(de) WW* [2]	Werkloosheidswet	unemployment benefits
(de) WA*	Wettelijke Aansprakelijkheid	third party insurance
(de) WAO*[2]	Wet op de Arbeidsongeschiktheids-verzekering	invalid pension
wo.	woensdag	Wednesday

[2] In **de WW zitten** 'to be on unemployment benefits/the dole', **in de WAO zitten** 'to be on an invalid pension'; the latter can also be expressed as **Hij loopt in de ziektewet**.

za.	zaterdag	Saturday
Zeel	Zeeland	Zeeland (province)
zg., zgn.	zogenaamd/zogenoemd	so-called
ZH	Zuid-Holland	South Holland (province)
z.i.	zijns inziens	in his opinion
ZKH	Zijne Koninklijke Hoogheid	His Royal Highness
ZM	Zijne Majesteit	His Majesty
zo.	zondag	Sunday
z.o.z.	zie ommezijde	p.t.o.

GLOSSARY OF GRAMMATICAL TERMS

abstract noun
: A noun having an abstract (i.e. non-concrete) meaning, commonly made with an abstract suffix, e.g. **gezelligheid** 'cosiness'.

active
: The active is the opposite of the passive. 'He is/was reading a book' is an example of a sentence in the active (i.e. the normal present/past tense) whereas the passive of this would be 'The book is/was being read by him'.

accusative (case)
: The case of the direct object in a sentence.

acute
: The name of the accent ´ placed on certain vowels in a few loanwords as well as for indicating stress in Dutch words.

adjective
: That part of speech which modifies or limits a noun, e.g. 'the *large* house'.

adverb
: That part of speech which modifies or limits a verb, an adjective or another adverb, e.g. 'He's driving *slowly,* a *very* large car, *terribly* slowly'.

adverb of manner
: An adverb or adverbial phrase that describes how the action of a clause is being performed, e.g. 'They go to school *by tram*'.

adverb of place
: An adverb or adverbial phrase that describes where the action of a clause is being performed, e.g. 'They are *at school*'.

adverb of time
: An adverb or adverbial phrase that describes when the action of a clause is being performed, e.g. 'They don't go to school *on Saturdays*'.

adverbial conjunction
: An adverb that is used as a conjunction, i.e. to join two clauses, but which also functions as an adverb is causing inversion of subject and verb in its clause as it functions as the

first idea in the clause, unlike coordinating and subordinating conjunctions.

adverbial prefix	An adverb that is functioning as a verbal prefix. (See 'separable verbs' and 'inseparable verbs'.)
agent	A person or a doer of the action of a verb in a clause.
antecedent	A word previously mentioned in the sentence which a later word refers back to.
article	See 'definite article' and 'indefinite article'.
aspiration	Some consonants, notably **p**, **t** and **k**, are pronounced in English allowing a puff of air to escape from the mouth. This is called aspiration. These consonants are unaspirated in Dutch.
attributive	An attributive adjective is one which stands in front of a noun and in Dutch may require an **e**-ending, e.g. **een oude man**. The opposite to this is a predicative adjective which does not stand in front of a noun and consequently does not ever take an ending, e.g. **De man is erg oud**.
auxiliary verb	A verb which is used in combination with the infinitive (see 'modal verb') or past participle of another verb.
bisyllabic	Consisting of two syllables. (See 'syllable'.)
cardinal number/ numeral clause	Basic numerals as in 'one', 'two', 'three', etc. A clause is that part of a sentence which contains its own subject and finite verb. A sentence may consist of either one or more clauses, e.g. 'I saw the man' (one clause), 'I saw the man who was stealing a car' (two clauses). (See 'main clause', 'coordinate clause', 'subordinate clause' and 'relative clause'.)
closed syllable	A closed syllable is one which ends in a consonant, e.g. **kat**, **kat-ten**; **man**, **man-nen**. (See open syllable.)
collective noun	A noun which in the singular form expresses a grouping of individual objects or persons, e.g. **volk** 'people'.
common gender noun	The term given to what were historically masculine or feminine nouns but which

have fallen together to form one gender in Dutch, i.e. **de** nouns.

comparative	The comparative of an adjective or adverb is that form which has '-er' added to it or is preceded by 'more', e.g. 'bigger', 'more interesting'.
complement	A word or words used to complete a grammatical construction, especially in the predicate, e.g. 'His name is *John*'.
compound noun	A compound noun is one that has been formed by putting two nouns together, e.g. **stadhuis** 'town hall'.
compound tense	A tense formed from an auxiliary verb plus the infinitive or past participle of another verb, e.g. **Het zal doodgaan** 'It will die', **Het is doodgegaan** 'It has died'.
conditional perfect tense	That tense which combines both a conditional 'would' and a perfect tense form consisting of have + a past participle, e.g. 'He would have done it' **Hij zou het gedaan hebben**.
conditional tense	The tense used in expressing conditions by means of 'would', often preceded or followed by a clause starting with 'if', e.g. If you did it, I *would be* very grateful'.
conjugate	Verbs are conjugated when they take endings corresponding with the first, second or third person. (See 'first person', 'second person', 'third person'.)
conjunction	A word which joins two clauses or phrases.
consonants	The non-vowel sounds of a language, e.g. b, c, d, f, g, h, j, k, etc. (See 'vowel'.)
continuous	The present or past continuous is another name for the present or past progressive. (See 'progressive'.)
coordinate clause	A coordinate clause is one which is introduced by a coordinating conjunction, i.e. one of the four joining words **en**, **maar**, **of** or **want** which coordinates its clause to the main clause (= makes it equal to), which is indicated by the finite verb in the coordinate clause not being relegated to the end of that clause, e.g. **Hij blijft vandaag thuis**

	want hij voelt zich niet lekker, where **want** is the coordinating conjunction and **want hij voelt zich niet lekker** the co-ordinate clause. (Compare 'subordinate clause'.)
coordinating conjunction	A conjunction such as 'and', but and 'or' which joins two coordinate clauses, i.e. clauses in which this equality is shown by the finite verb in both standing in second position.
correlative conjunction	Members of a pair of conjunctions the occurrence of which alerts the listener to the appearance of the other, e.g. the use of 'neither' alerts one to that of 'nor' to follow.
dative(case)	The case of the indirect object in a sentence.
decline	Synonymous with 'to inflect'.
definite direct objects	A direct object preceded by a definite determiner like 'the', 'that' or 'this' all of which designate a particular item, e.g. 'I don't know *that man*'.
definite article	'The' is referred to as the definite article, as it refers to a definite object, as opposed to 'a', the indefinite article. The definite article varies in Dutch according to gender and whether a noun is singular or plural.
demonstrative	A demonstrative, as the word implies, is a word that points out or distinguishes. 'This/these' and 'that/those' are examples of demonstratives.
dental ending	An ending that contains a **d** or a **t**, as the sounds are pronounced by letting the tongue touch the back of the top teeth, e.g. **-de**, **-te**, **-d** or **-t** as in **hoorde**, **blafte**, **gehoord**, **geblaft**.
derivative	A word that is derived from another, e.g. **gegeten** is derived from the verb **eten**.
descriptive grammar	See 'prescriptive grammar'.
dieresis	The accent written ¨ which is placed on a vowel to show that that vowel belongs to the next syllable, e.g. **reünie** 'reunion', where **eu** is not to be read as the sound in **deur** but the **e** and the **u** are to be read separate sounds.

diminutive	A diminutive in Dutch is a noun which has had the suffix **-(t)je** added to it to render it small, e.g. **een huis/een huisje** 'a house/a little house'.
diphthong	When two adjacent vowels are pronounced together in such a way that they produce a new vowel sound, the new sound is called a diphthong, e.g. **e** + **i** = **ei**.
direct object	The direct object in a sentence is the object of the verb, i.e. the person or thing that is having the action of the verb performed on it, e.g. 'I can see the man/the ball'.
double prepositions	Prepositions which are used in combination, e.g. **boven op de kast** 'on top of the cupboard'.
double infinitive	A double infinitive construction is one where a clause in the perfect tense has two infinitives at the end of it, rather than a past participle and an infinitive, e.g. **Ik heb hem zien komen** and not ***Ik heb hem gezien komen**.
dummy subject	This refers to one of the functions of **er** where **er** stands in first position in the clause in the position normally occupied by the subject, e.g. **Er ligt een boek op tafel**, which is a more usual way of expressing **Een boek ligt op tafel**.
emphatic imperfect tense	The form of the English imperfect that utilises the auxiliary verb 'did', e.g. 'She did have a child'.
emphatic present tense	The form of the English imperfect that utilises the auxiliary verb 'do', e.g. 'She does have a child'.
extended participial phrase	An adjectival phrase that contains a present or past participle which phrase is usually expressed in English by a relative clause, e.g. **De door hem gemaakte kast** = The cupboard which he made.
feminine noun	A noun which was considered feminine before masculine and feminine nouns fell together in Dutch to form the common gender, e.g. **de tafel** 'the table'. The concept lives on in those words which designate abstracts and usually, but not

necessarily end in certain still recognisable feminine endings, e.g. **de taal** 'the language', **de ziekte** 'the disease', **de gezelligheid** '(the) cosiness'.

finite verb
A finite verb is one which has a subject and takes an ending, e.g. **Hij schrijft een boek**. The opposite to this is an 'infinitive', which is the basic form of a verb that has not been defined as to who is performing it, i.e. it does not have an ending, e.g. **Hij gaat een brief schrijven**, where **gaat** is a finite verb and **schrijven** an infinitive.

first person
The pronoun 'I' is referred to as the first person singular and 'we' as the first person plural.

future perfect tense
The tense which is formed from 'will' + 'have' + a past participle (i.e. a future plus a perfect tense) which is expressed in Dutch by **zullen** + **hebben/zijn** + a past participle, e.g. **Hij zal het gedaan hebben** = He will have done it.

future tense
The tense which expresses events to occur in the future, expressed in English by either 'will', 'go' or the present tense and in Dutch by **zullen**, **gaan** or the present tense.

gender
Gender refers to whether a noun belongs to either of the two grammatical genders called common gender and neuter gender in Dutch, i.e. **de** and **het** nouns respectively.

genitive (case)
The genitive case in Dutch is a now archaic mechanism for showing either possession or rendering 'of' (**van**), e.g. **de heer des huizes** = **de heer van het huis** = the man of the house.

gerund
Used in English grammar to refer to a present participle (i.e. the '-ing' form of a verb) used as a noun, e.g. Reading is a worthwhile pastime.

grave
The name of the accent ` placed on certain vowels in a few loanwords.

half-long vowel
Dutch distinguishes between short and long vowels but has three vowels (i.e. **eu**, **ie**, **oe**) which are pronounced longer than

	short vowels but not as long as long vowels, except when followed by **r**, when they are too are pronounced long. (See 'short vowel'.)
imperative (mood)	That form of the verb that expresses an order, e.g. '*Put* it back in the drawer'.
imperfect tense	The imperfect tense, also called the simple past, is that tense of the verb expressed by a single word in Dutch, e.g. **schreef** 'wrote'. It contrasts with the 'perfect tense' or compound past which consists of two words, e.g. **Hij heeft geschreven** 'He has written'. (See 'perfect tense'.)
impersonal verb	A verb denoting action by an unspecified agent, normally used in the third person singular, commonly with 'it' as its subject, e.g. 'It is snowing'.
impersonal construction	A construction involving an impersonal verb, such as the previous example.
indefinite pronoun	A pronoun that stands in for any unspecified noun or nouns, e.g. 'all, some, many'.
indefinite article	See 'definite article'.
indefinite direct object	The opposite of a definite direct object, i.e. an object preceded by an indefinite determiner like 'a/an', 'every' or 'which' all of which designate any item, e.g. 'He ate *every biscuit*'.
independent pronoun	Used to refer to possessive when they are not followed by a noun and thus act as true pronouns and not as possessive adjectives, e.g. 'I returned *hers*'.
indirect object	The indirect object in a sentence is the person or object the action of the verb is applied 'to', e.g. He gave the book (direct object) to the girl (indirect object).
indirect question	A direct question reproduces a question verbatim, e.g. 'Where does he live?' The indirect question form of this is 'where he lives', e.g. 'I do(n't) know where he lives'.
infinitive	See 'finite verb'.
infinitive clause	An independent clause introduced by a conjunction which does not contain a finite verb but an infinitive, e.g. 'They did it *in order to help me*'.

inflect	To apply inflection to a word, i.e. a grammatical ending, e.g. 'the old*en* days'.
inflection	See 'inflect'.
inseparable verb	A verb that contains a prefix that is never separated from the verb, e.g. *be*loven 'to promise', *mi*slukken 'to fail'.
interrogative adverbs	Adverbs which ask questions, most of which begin with 'wh-' in English and **w-** in Dutch, e.g. 'what', 'where', 'when' **wat, waar, wanneer.**
interrogative	An interrogative is a question word, most of which start with 'wh' is English and **w** in Dutch, e.g. 'what', 'where', 'when', 'how'.
interrogative conjunction	When an interrogative adverb introduces an indirect question it functions as a subordinating conjunction and thus causes the finite verb in the sentence to be placed at the end in Dutch, e.g. **Ik weet niet waar hij op het ogenblik woont** 'I do not know where he is living at the moment'.
intervocalic	Standing between two vowels, e.g. **ro***de* 'red'.
intransitive verb	See 'transitive verb'.
inversion	Reversing position as in the subject following the verb when a clause begins with any other word but the subject, e.g. **Morgen komt hij terug < Hij komt morgen terug** 'He is returning tomorrow'.
locative	A locative **er** is one that that means 'there' with reference to place, e.g. **Ik heb er vroeger gewoond** 'I used to live there'. This is in contrast to other meanings of **er** which do not refer to place, e.g. **Er was eens een koning** 'Once upon a time there was a king'.
long vowel	See 'short vowel'.
main clause	A main clause, as opposed to a subordinate clause (see 'subordinate clause') is one which makes sense on its own, i.e. it has a subject and finite verb and is not introduced by a conjunction, e.g. **Hij blijft vandaag thuis omdat hij zich niet lekker voelt**, where **Hij blijft vandaag thuis** is the main clause in this compound sentence.

masculine noun	A noun which was considered masculine before masculine and feminine nouns fell together in Dutch to form the common gender, e.g. **de vloer** 'the floor'. The concept lives on in those words which designate masculine beings, e.g. **de jongen** 'the boy', **de Duitser** 'the German'.
mass noun	A noun not readily modified by a numeral or a noun denoting a homogeneous concept not subject to division, e.g. 'butter, bread, milk, music'.
mixed verb	A verb whose formation of its past tenses contains signs of both regular and irregular forms, e.g. **lachen/lachte/gelachen**.
modal (auxiliary) verb	A modal auxiliary verb is a verb which is always used in conjunction with an infinitive and which expresses the attitude of the subject of the action to be performed, i.e. volition (**willen** 'to want to'), obligation (**moeten** 'to have to/must'), permission (**mogen** 'to be allowed to/may'), ability (**kunnen** 'to be able to/can'). These verbs in both English and Dutch show many irregularities.
monosyllabic	Consisting of one syllable, e.g. **doen** 'to do'.
mood	A verbal inflection which reflects a speaker's attitude towards the action expressed by the verb, most commonly used in the context of the imperative (mood) and the subjunctive (mood).
negation	The act of putting into the negative commonly by means of the adverbs 'not' and 'never'.
neuter noun	A **het** noun, i.e. not a common gender noun. (See 'common gender'.)
nominal	Pertaining to nouns, e.g. in the following sentence **rode** is said to be used nominally, i.e. as a noun: **Ik heb een rode** 'I have a red one'.
nominative (case)	The case in which the subject of a clause stands.
noun	A word denoting a person, place or thing.
object	See 'direct object' and 'indirect object'.

open syllable	An open syllable is one that ends in a vowel, e.g. **maan** (closed) but **ma-nen** (first syllable open and second syllable closed). The **n** after **ma** is seen as belonging to the next syllable in Dutch. (See syllabification.)
ordinal number/numeral	Numerals that indicate order, e.g. 'first', 'second', 'third', etc.
partitive	This refers to one of the functions of **er**, i.e. that which is used in combination with numerals and quantities, e.g. **Ik heb er tien gezien** 'I saw ten of them', **Ik heb er maar een kwart gebruikt** 'I only used a quarter (of them/it)', where it refers to part of a greater whole.
parts of speech	The name given to the following grammatical concepts which together constitute the vocabulary of a language: noun, pronoun, verb, adverb, adjective, conjunction, preposition.
interjection	That part of speech which comprises words which constitute utterances or clauses in themselves, e.g. 'tut-tut', 'ouch'.
passive (voice)	See 'active'.
past participle	That part of a verb, derived from the infinitive, which is used to form the past (perfect) tense of that verb but which may also be used as an adjective, e.g. **Hij heeft het huis** *geverfd* 'He's *painted* the house', **het** *geverfde* **huis** 'the *painted* house'.
penultimate syllable	The second last syllable.
perfect tense	The perfect tense in Dutch is a compound tense, i.e. one formed from more than one word, where the finite verb is a form of the verb **zijn** or **hebben** plus a past participle, e.g. **Hij heeft een brief geschreven, Hij is naar huis gegaan.**
periphrastic form	Denoting a construction of two or more words which in other forms is expressed by inflectional modification of a single word, e.g. 'the son of Piet > Piet's son', **zou hebben > had**.
personal pronoun	Any one of the pronouns which indicate grammatical person, e.g. 'I, you, he, she, it, we they, me, him, her, us, them'.

phrase	A sequence of two or more words arranged in a grammatical construction and acting as a unit in a sentence, e.g. 'this morning', 'over there'.
plat	A label used in Dutch to refer to any linguistic phenomenon that is considered substandard, e.g. **Hij wast z'n eigen** for standard **Hij was zich**.
pluperfect tense	The pluperfect tense is that which consists of 'had' + a past participle in English and of **was/waren** or **had/hadden** + a past participle in Dutch. It expresses the past in the past in both languages.
polysyllabic	Consisting of more than one syllable, e.g. **belangrijk** 'important', which consists of three syllables.
possessive	Possessives are words like 'my/mine', 'your/yours' which indicate the possessor of a noun, e.g. 'This is my book/It is mine'.
postposition	A preposition which is placed after, rather than before a noun, e.g. **Hij ging de hoek om** 'He went around the corner'.
predicate	The finite verb in a clause together with all the words it governs and those which modify it, e.g. 'Jack *is here*'.
predicative	See 'attributive'.
prefix	An affix which is put before a word to add to or qualify its meaning, e.g. *her*halen 'to *re*peat'.
preposition	A word placed before a noun or pronoun to indicate its relation to other words or its function in the sentence, e.g. 'He lives *in* The Hague'.
prepositional phrase	A phrase in which the first word is a preposition, e.g. 'in town', 'after the war'.
prepositional object	The object of a verb which is preceded by a preposition, e.g. 'I was thinking *of you*'.
prepositional prefix	A prefix which as a separate word functions as a preposition, e.g. *aan*komen 'to arrive'.
prepositional adjunct	Synonymous with 'prepositional phrase'.
prescriptive grammar	That school of grammatical thought that prescribes what grammarians traditionally regard as correct, ignoring what is generally used in the spoken (and sometimes

written) language which may be at odds with such rules; the latter constitutes descriptive linguistics, i.e. describing what people actually say.

present participle
: The verbal participle which has present meaning (e.g. 'the *growing* plant') as opposed to the past participle which indicates completed action, e.g. 'The plant has *grown*'.

present tense
: That tense of the verb which describes the present, e.g. 'He *likes* children'.

progressive
: The present or past progressive is a variation of the present or past tenses that emphasises that an action is or was in the process of being performed, e.g. 'He is/ was reading' is the progressive form of 'He reads/read'.

pronominal
: Formed from a pronoun, e.g 'I like *him*', where 'him' is a pronominal object.

pronominal substitution
: Replacing a noun with a pronoun, e.g. 'The cow is calving > *It* is calving'.

pronoun
: That part of speech which is used as a substitute for a noun, e.g. 'That girl is very sweet > *She* is very sweet'.

proper noun
: The name of a specific person or place, usually capitalised, e.g. 'Bill', 'Edinburgh'.

reflexive
: Reflexive pronouns are used with reflexive verbs. They indicate that the action of the verb is being performed on the subject of the verb (i.e. the action reflects back), e.g. **Hij scheert zich elke ochtend** 'He shaves [himself] every day' where **zich** is the third person singular of the reflexive pronoun and **zich scheren** is said to be a reflexive verb.

relative clause/pronoun
: A relative pronoun connects a relative clause to a main clause, i.e. it relates back to a noun in the main clause, e.g. 'The man who gave me the money was very rich', where 'who' is a relative pronoun relating back to 'man' and 'who gave me the money' is the relative clause which in Dutch requires subordinate word order, i.e. the finite verb is sent to the end, e.g. **die mij het geld gegeven heeft**. (See 'subordinate clause'.)

schwa	This is the name given by linguists to that non-descript vowel sound that we hear in the first syllable of 'again' or in the second syllable of 'father'. Those speakers of English who pronounce 'film' as 'filem' are inserting a schwa between the 'l' and the 'm' to facilitate pronunciation of the cluster 'lm'.
second person	The pronoun 'you' is referred to as the second person. In Dutch there are two forms in the singular, **jij** and **u**, and two forms in the plural, **jullie** and **u** where English only has the one word for all functions.
semantics	The science of the meaning of words.
separable	A separable verb is one with a prefix (usually a preposition, e.g. **opbellen** 'to ring up') which separates from the verb and stands at the end of the clause in the present and imperfect tenses (e.g. **Hij belde mij op**) and which permits the **ge-** of the past participle to be inserted between it and the rest of the verb, e.g. **Hij heeft mij opgebeld**.
short vowel	A short vowel is one which is pronounced short and thus contrasts with the same vowel pronounced long, e.g. **lat** (short), **laat** (long). See half-long vowels.
stem	The stem is the root form of a verb once the **en** ending of the infinitive has been removed and the necessary spelling changes have been made, e.g. the stem of **lopen** is **loop** and of **schrijven** is **schrijf**.
stress	Refers to the syllable in a polysyllabic word which bears the main emphasis, e.g. **burgemeester**.
strong verb	Any verb which forms its past tenses by changing the stem vowel while retaining the same consonantal environment, e.g. **spreken – sprak, spraken, gesproken**.
subject	The subject of a clause is the noun or pronoun that is performing the action of the finite verb in that clause, e.g. 'The man/he is reading a book'. It determines what the ending of the finite verb will be, e.g. **De**

	man/hij leest een boek, but **Wij lezen een boek**.
subjunctive (mood)	A mood of the verb which pertains to an action being hypothetical.
subordinate clause	A subordinate clause is one which is introduced by a subordinating conjunction, i.e. a joining word which subordinates its clause to the main clause (= makes it secondary to) which is indicated by the finite verb in the subordinate clause being relegated to the end of that clause, e.g. **Hij blijft vandaag thuis omdat hij zich niet lekker voelt**, where **omdat** is the subordinating conjunction and **omdat hij zich niet lekker voelt** the subordinate clause. (See 'main clause' and 'coordinate clause'.)
subordinating conjunction	A conjunction which subordinates the information in the clause which it heads to the information in the main clause, indicated in Dutch by the placing of the finite verb in the subordinate clause at the end of that clause.
suffix	An affix which follows the element to which it is added, e.g. 'kind*ly*'.
superlative	The superlative of an adjective or adverb is that form which has 'st' added to it or is preceded by 'most', e.g. 'biggest', 'most interesting'.
syllabification	The rules for hyphenating words are different in Dutch from English where the derivation of the word is significant, e.g. 'be-long-ing', 'work-ed'. In Dutch words are always divided (syllabified) by starting each new syllable with a consonant, e.g. **kat-ten**, **ma-nen**, **be-doe-ling**, although **en** and **ing** are derivational endings that have been attached to these words.
syllable	A segment of speech uttered with a single impulse of air pressure and constituting the unit of word formation, e.g. 'lone-ly', consisting of two syllables.
syntactically	Relating to syntax, which refers to the patterns of formation of sentences and phrases.

tense	Verbal inflection that specifies the time and length of occurrence of the action or state expressed by the verb.
third person	The pronouns 'he', 'she' and 'it' are referred to as the third person singular and 'they' as the third person plural.
transitive	A transitive verb is one that can take an object, as opposed to an intransitive verb, which is one that cannot, e.g. He is reading a book ('read' is transitive because of 'book'), but 'He is going to Germany' ('go' is intransitive because 'to Germany' is not the object of the verb, merely an adverb of place telling you where the action of the verb is to take place.)
uncountable noun	See 'mass noun'.
unemphatic pronoun	The unstressed form of a pronoun, e.g. 'ya' for 'you', **je** for **jij**.
verb	That part of speech which expresses the action or state in a clause.
verbal noun	A verbal noun (i.e. an English gerund, see 'gerund') is rendered by an infinitive in Dutch, e.g. **het lezen van kookboeken** 'the reading of cookbooks'.
voiced	Pronounced with a vibration of the vocal cords, e.g. the sounds 'b' and 'd' differ from 'p' and 't' in that the vocal cords (i.e. the voice) are activated when pronouncing them, whereas 'p' and 't' are articulated in exactly the same way but with the omission of the voice; 'p' and 't' are thus termed voiceless.
voiceless	See 'voiced'.
vowel	A sound produced with vibration of the vocal cords by the unobstructed passage of air through the oral cavity.
weak verb	A verb that forms its past tenses by addition of the regular endings '-ed' in English or **-te/-ten** or **-de/-den** in the imperfect and -t or -d in the perfect in Dutch, e.g. 'I worked/I have worked' **Ik werkte/ik heb gewerkt.**

INDEX

The numbers given are paragraph numbers where the first number corresponds to the number of the chapter. In many instances relevant information is also to be found in paragraphs immediately following the paragraphs indicated here. The abbreviation 'n.' refers to a footnote in the relevant section.